Between Two Worlds

Film Europa: German Cinema in an International Context
Series Editors: **Hans-Michael Bock** (CineGraph Hamburg);
Tim Bergfelder (University of Southampton); **Sabine Hake**
(University of Texas, Austin)

German cinema is normally seen as a distinct form, but this new series emphasizes connections, influences, and exchanges of German cinema across national borders, as well as its links with other media and art forms. Individual titles present traditional historical research (archival work, industry studies) as well as new critical approaches in film and media studies (theories of the transnational), with a special emphasis on the continuities associated with popular traditions and local perspectives.

Concise Cinegraph: An Encyclopedia of German Cinema
General Editor: Hans-Michael Bock
Associate Editor: Tim Bergfelder

International Adventures: German Popular Cinema and European Co-Productions in the 1960s
Tim Bergfelder

Between Two Worlds: The Jewish Presence in German and Austrian Film, 1910–1933
S. S. Prawer

Framing the Fifties: Cinema in a Divided Germany
John E. Davidson and Sabine Hake

BETWEEN TWO WORLDS

The Jewish Presence in German and Austrian Film,
1910–1933

S. S. Prawer

Berghahn Books
New York • Oxford

First published in 2005 by
Berghahn Books
www.berghahnbooks.com

© 2005, 2007 S. S. Prawer
First paperback edition published in 2007

All rights reserved.
Except for the quotation of short passages
for the purposes of criticism and review, no part of this book
may be reproduced in any form or by any means, electronic or
mechanical, including photocopying, recording, or any information
storage and retrieval system now known or to be invented,
without written permission of Berghahn Books.

Library of Congress Cataloging-in-Publication Data

Prawer, Siegbert Salomon, 1925–
  Between two worlds : the Jewish presence in German and Austrian film, 1910–1933 / S.S. Prawer.
    p. cm.
  Includes bibliographical references and index.
  ISBN 1-84545-074-4 (hb.)
    1. Jews in motion pictures. 2. Motion pictures--Germany--History.
3. Motion pictures--Austria--History. 4. Jews in the motion picture
industry--Germany. 5. Jews in the motion picture industry--Austria.
I. Title.

PN1995.9.J46P73 2005

2005045719

British Library Cataloguing in Publication Data

A catalogue record for this book is available from
the British Library.

Printed in the United States on acid-free paper

ISBN 978-1-84545-074-8 hardback
ISBN 978-1-84545-303-9 paperback

To the memory

of

my father

Marcus Prawer

לזכר נשמת אבי

מרדכי בן שלמה פראור

Contents

Preface		vii
Acknowledgements		xii
1	Preparing the Ground	1
2	Dramas and Melodramas of the 'Silent' Period	16
3	Comedies of the 'Silent' Period	42
4	'Enlightenment' Films (*Sittenfilme*)	72
5	1929: A Year of Transition	82
6	Ironic Realism	115
7	Late Comedies	122
8	Confrontations and Enmities	141
9	A New Film Musical	160
Epilogue		197
Appendix		211
Bibliography		215
Index		219

Preface

When *Das Cabinet des Dr Caligari* (*The Cabinet of Dr Caligari*, 1919–20) directed international attention to the distinctive possibilities of German film soon after the First World War, four Jewish men could claim a share in its success: Erich Pommer, founder and guiding spirit of its production company; Carl Mayer and Hans Janowitz, who wrote its screenplay; and Robert Wiene, who directed it. The result depended crucially, however, on their cooperation with non-Jewish German colleagues: notably the designers Hermann Warm, Walter Reimann and Walter Röhrig, who drew on the example of Expressionist painters and graphic artists to fashion the look of the film, with its psychological and social implications; the cameraman Willy Hameister and his team of lighting experts; and a group of actors, notably Werner Krauss and Conrad Veidt, who fitted their appearance and movement to the non-naturalistic décor with a sure feeling for the expressive possibilities of the early cinema. Much of the inspiration of the screenplay derived from experience of the war with its senseless killings, and from sinister encounters with doctors, psychiatrists and arrogant authority figures. It also mirrored the psychological disorientation of a defeated nation deprived of many of its younger men, and faced with foreign occupation, loss of colonies, excessive demands by the victors, and internal struggles about the political reorganisation of the new state. At the same time, however, *Caligari*, like many other films of the period, drew on that fascination with the dark and uncanny which had been a feature of German cultural expression ever since the Romantic movement, where it had found its most influential but by no means sole exponent in the tales of E.T.A. Hoffmann. The malevolent hypnotist and his somnambulistic victim are distinctly Hoffmannesque figures. These were social and cultural experiences Jews and non-Jews could share; but Jews could also bring to the film cultural experiences of their own along with memories of persecution, discrimination, suspicious ostracism, and inter-Jewish divisions, over many centuries.

Caligari has been the subject of much debate, and many critics have pointed out how central its motif of the demonic fair is to the early German cinema. It reminds us, along with the associated motifs of magicians, hypnotists and *montreurs d'ombres*, of the fairground venues in which films were originally shown, of the fantastic magical tricks in movies made by

Méliès, and of the power exercised by those who could manipulate and control images. Here as elsewhere, German films are often self-reflexive. I have set out my own views on *Caligari* in two books named in the Bibliography of the present study, and won't reiterate them here. I would, however, like to restate my conviction that it is a mistake to interpret everything said or shown before 1933 in the light of Nazi racism and genocide. There is no straight line that leads from *Caligari* to Hitler. What matters in my present context is that despite anti–Semitic snipings, the young film industry in Germany and Austria saw harmonious cooperation between Jewish and non-Jewish men and women, born in the German and Austro-Hungarian Empires and beyond, who worked in the last days of those Empires and in the Republics that succeeded them. Such cooperation and interplay I take to have been an essential part of the creative force which produced the distinctive forms German and Austrian cinema took before it was deprived of its Jewish talents by the catastrophic advent of a Nazi government.

Within these parameters the present book seeks to concentrate attention on the involvement of men and women with Jewish ancestry in German and Austrian films before their expulsion. It will seek to show, with selected examples, some of the ways in which Jews participated in the manifold work needed to create a film: as producers, directors, writers, cinematographers, designers and actors – in harmony with non-Jewish colleagues amid a spattering of voices raised to discriminate between them, imputing commercially inspired sensationalism and alleged moral turpitude solely to Jewish influence. It will analyse films that treat problems of Jewish individuals and communities in different historic circumstances and in forms that range from satiric comedy to stark tragedy, while also showing gradations of Jewish attitudes and behaviour from religious orthodoxy and social separation to integration and acculturation in the social fabric of Berlin and Vienna. The play of inter-Jewish as well as Jewish–Gentile tensions and sympathies will come into view, alongside Jewish humour and self-irony; a Jewish sense of justice leading to battles against social and legal iniquities; and historical memories of persecution and discrimination resonating in later and apparently more enlightened days.

For understandable commercial reasons most of the films treated in this book were made in German studios, even where the directors and other members of the team hailed from Austrian dominions, or the films were set in Austrian lands. Something needs therefore to be said, by way of introduction, about the distinctive nature of a film industry that began in the last days of the Austro-Hungarian Empire and sent many of its finest artists to enrich the cinema of a wider world.

Historians of the cinema in Austria have documented how interest in the new art came to rival traditional interests in opera and operetta; its beginnings with Saturn and Sascha Films; and the way directors, actors and scriptwriters commuted between Austria and Germany, or moved to

Germany entirely, since Berlin in particular offered greater studio and capital resources, as well as distributors who supplied a wider market. In our special context it is noteworthy that the Austro-Hungarian dominions were the birthplace of many Jewish directors who later achieved German, or world-wide, fame; they included such figures as Alexander Korda, Billy Wilder, Michael Curtiz, Josef von Sternberg and Otto Preminger. The Austrian Emperor Franz Josef was among the early customers of the Cinematograph in Vienna's Kärtnerstrasse, and, like the German Emperor Wilhelm II (whose vacation journeys were captured in 'living photographs' by the Jewish entrepreneur Jules Greenbaum) he was glad to have himself and his entourage filmed by professional cinematographers. Count Alexander Kolowrat-Krokowski's Sascha was soon succeeded by Wiener Kunstfilm (which became Vita Film in 1918), Vindobona Film and others; and historians have counted some three hundred feature films produced in Austria by the end of the First World War. Production rose to a peak between 1918 and 1922, where it averaged about one hundred twenty films a year, and reduced to some twenty-four films a year once sound-films replaced the earlier 'silents'. Genres particularly favoured were biographies of musicians, plots constructed around popular singers like Richard Tauber, Martha Eggerth and Jan Kiepura, operettas and revue films, and erotic and slightly world-weary stories, often in opulent settings, directed by – and often starring – Willi Forst. Forst commuted between Vienna and Berlin, as did other actors and directors; and many Wienfilme were made in German studios. These were not always set in affluent contemporary circles, like *Fräulein Else*, directed by Paul Czinner in 1929, or a romanticised and sentimentalised Vienna of the past, like Friedrich Hollaender's *Ich und die Kaiserin* (1932–33) and Erik Charell's *Der Kongress tanzt* (*The Congress Dances*, 1931). G.W. Pabst's *Die freudlose Gasse* (*The Joyless Street*, 1925) was far from that sort of romanticisation: it showed a contemporary Austria in the grip of financial crisis and social deprivation, with panders and speculators profiting from widespread misery and impoverishment.

Besides the Hungarian-born Paul Czinner and Alexander Korda (né Sandor Kellner), ethnically Jewish directors who made films in Vienna included Robert Wiene (*Orlacs Hände/Hands of Orlac*, 1925) and H.K. Breslauer, whose *Die Stadt ohne Juden* (*The City without Jews*, 1924) will be considered in detail in a later chapter. One such director, Richard Oswald, paid musical tribute to his native Vienna in *Wien, du Stadt der Lieder* (*Vienna, City of Song*, 1930) and *Schuberts Frühlingstraum* (*Schubert's Dream of Spring*, 1930–31). Like Oswald, however, many other Jewish directors born in Austro-Hungary made films mainly in German studios: Joe May and Karl Grune, for instance; the same is true of Carl Mayer, whose importance for the diegeses of German art films during the 'silent' period can hardly be exaggerated; and such actors as Fritz Kortner, Elisabeth Bergner and Peter Lorre. The sharp-tongued, socially critical Viennese cabaret, like its German equivalent, had many Jewish performers, some of whom appeared in Austrian films: Gisela Werbezirk, for instance, and Armin Berg, who specialised in Jewish comedy, can be seen in *The City without Jews*. Fritz Grünbaum, a famous *conférencier* and writer of satirical comedy monologues, was featured in *Mädchen zum Heiraten* (*Girls Ripe for Marriage*, 1932), and alongside Max Pallenberg in a German film with an Austrian setting, *Der brave Sünder* (*The Virtuous Sinner*, 1931), directed by Kortner – a work that will also be considered in some detail later in this book.

After the Nazi takeover in Germany a handful of Jewish artists found limited scope for work in Viennese studios; but since Austrian films needed the German market to recoup their costs and make a profit, and Austrian production companies quietly adopted the rules and proscriptions of the controlling German film authority (Reichsfilmkammer), such opportunities soon dried up. It all ceased, in any case, when Austria became part of 'Greater Germany' after the *Anschluss* of 1938.

Some of the producers, directors, scriptwriters, actors, composers and designers to be encountered in the following pages will have come from an orthodox Jewish background. Some will have arrived in Vienna or Berlin from Eastern Europe, some (like the Nebenzahl family) via the USA and Britain – but all of them conformed in dress and manner to an emancipated European bourgeoisie and felt themselves part of the society and profession to which they made distinctive contributions alongside Gentile fellow citizens. When the films featured Jewish protagonists, whether in leading or subsidiary parts, these too, despite many differences and gradations, were usually German or Austrian in dress, manner and speech. But the films also showed orthodox Jews, in traditional garb, and with a distinctive culture, in medieval ghettos, and East European towns and villages, or as immigrants living in specific areas of Western cities; often along with characters driven, by love, ambition or desire for secular learning and culture, to leave such sheltering and confining enclosures for the wider vistas offered by Europe or the USA. Both groups are generally presented with sympathy, and Jewish religious ceremonial is depicted with respect; but not all Jews working in the German and Austrian film industry reacted favourably towards encounters with traditionally garbed. Yiddish-speaking East European coreligionists. Fritz Kortner, the son of an assimilated Viennese jeweller, looked with little sympathy on the Moldavian Jews he saw during his service with the Austro-Hungarian army in the First World War:

> I did not overflow with the sympathy and brotherly feeling I had expected and thought to be my duty. I shied away from these medieval figures in their long caftans, with side-locks on both sides of their face (which seemed grotesque to me) and long beards – and also from their women who wore wigs to cover their own hair. I felt terror before dead Jews killed in a pogrom, and failed to feel kinship with the living. ... Assimilation had distanced me

too far from them, made me feel a world away from the ghetto and its customs. I sought to further the beauty of the German language, shrank from its mutilation [in Yiddish], and felt frightened away from every absolute adherence to Judaism, including what was then its most modern form – the stirrings of Zionism ... (1969: 110–11)

Writing this in the 1950s, Kortner adds: 'I have learnt to think differently since' – as did many others after the shock of finding that Nazi racism made no distinction between the emancipated Jews of Berlin and Vienna, and their caftaned, bearded, side-locked and bewigged Eastern brothers and sisters.

The inner and outer separation described by Kortner, which I myself came to know all too well in my Cologne childhood – along with the disparagement of that wonderfully expressive medium, the Yiddish language – finds its equivalent in some the films discussed below, where we will also encounter Jewish 'dog eats dog' behaviour in the struggle to make a living, and self-aggrandising pretence for the sake of social advancement, among Western Jews. Yet most of the films show traditional Jewish societies and groups without rancour, even though some amusement creeps in occasionally; and Western assimilated Jews who behave in ways that are less than admirable tend to be exhibited in the tongue-in-cheek, self-mocking spirit familiar from Jewish jokes. None of this should be mistaken for the much-touted 'Jewish self-hatred'. The spirit of Lubitsch is worlds away from that of Otto Weininger.

Before their legally sanctioned exclusion from the *Volksgemeinschaft*, the community of the German nation, it would have been invidious to isolate a 'Jewish presence' from Gentile ones in the way I have tried to do in this book. After that injustice, however, and the slanderous denigration that prepared for genocide, the memory of an earlier, fruitful collaboration deserves to be remembered. The loss to the German and Austrian cinema entailed by Nazi racism is paralleled by losses in other fields of the artistic and scientific culture of these countries; a loss painfully felt by many who tried to rebuild German and Austrian cultural life after the Second World War.

Acknowledgements

I have been a dedicated cinema-goer all my life, and have been able to supplement what I saw in the cinema, and in film-society showings in Germany, England, the USA, Austrialia and New Zealand, through the kindness of the curators and staff of the Stiftung Deutsche Kinemathek, Berlin (now Filmmuseum Berlin); the National Center for Jewish Film, Brandeis University; Filmarchiv Austria, Vienna; and the British Film Institute. These allowed me to view their holdings, some of which have had to be reconstructed from a number of incomplete versions. Increasingly, too, 'silent' and early sound films have been shown in the best available versions on television, and have become purchasable on VHS and DVD. I have made liberal use of all such sources. While basing my argument, wherever possible, on the close analysis of representative films, I have included conspective surveys of various kinds to set these into their social and film-specific contexts. I hope, finally, that my programmatic avoidance of film-theoretical jargon will be understood, not as wilful ignorance, but as a desire to appeal to readers whose interest in Jewish, German and Austrian affairs is not confined to the cinema.

My book has profited most from the scrutiny and critiques of my friend and colleague Hans-Michael Bock. Beyond that I am deeply indebted to the writers of the books and essays listed in my Bibliography; to Kevin Brownlow, Horst Claus, Tom Kuhn and Margaret Dériaz; to Jill Hughes of the Taylorian Library; to the archives that provided illustrations and photocopies; and to the Provost and Fellows of The Queen's College, Oxford, who have constantly supported my work during the many years I have had the privilege of belonging to that distinguished and hospitable company of scholars. For my errors and conclusions, and for uncredited translations from German text, I am alone responsible.

Chapter 1

PREPARING THE GROUND

Davidson

My father's fiduciary office had many Jewish clients in the 1920s and 1930s, and from one of them I first heard an anecdote which seems to have lived a wandering life as part of the mythology of cinema entrepreneurship. It tells of the wife of a Jewish shopkeeper who had a toothache and found a dentist willing to give her emergency treatment in a district remote from her own. When she returned, relieved of her toothache, she had some exciting news for her husband: she had seen a queue waiting outside a storefront whose window advertised motion pictures; and those going in handed over money without, as yet, having seen the goods they were paying for. Whether the couple in question actually gave up their shop in order to deal in this unusual type of merchandise – entertainment, enjoyment, dream fulfilment, thrills, experiences transcending the everyday – the anecdote does not say; but many Jews did so, at first as travelling showmen, but very soon as owners or renters of permanent premises, occasionally arranged in the way of cabarets, with tables around which patrons sat eating and drinking while watching the show, but more often with rows of seats arranged in the manner of more prestigious forms of entertainment: the theatre and opera-house. The owners of such 'Kinematographen-Theater', (affectionately known as 'Kientopps') – Leo Leipziger in Berlin, Rudolf Mosse in Frankfurt, Leo Preiss in Breslau, Albert Lobenstein in Dresden – at first bought rather than hired the short films they showed; but even when hiring became more usual, it was up to the owners to arrange the programmes into a 'montage of attractions', hiring a commentator, or pianist, or small instrumental ensemble as the necessary complement of films as yet devoid of sound-tracks. Some films, indeed, particularly the *Tonbilder* of the Messter Company, came with phonograph records synchronised to accompany the filmed image of a famous singer or actor. Messter himself, one of the most important pioneers of the technical as well as the producing, distributing and exhibiting branches of the early German cinema, was not Jewish; but he had Jewish managers and associates, including Maxim Galitzenstein who became a director of the Messter Company shortly before the First World War.

Among Jewish businessmen fired with enthusiasm for the new opportunities opened up by the invention of the cinema was a traveller in curtain-materials, Paul Davidson, who began with a single shop-front cinema in Frankfurt am Main, but soon expanded his operations to include other German cities, founding a company to manage and control them: the Allgemeine Kinematographische Theatergesellschaft. It was this company which trumped the cinema Messter had built in Berlin in 1905 by opening the Prussian capital's first 'cinema-palace', the Union-Theater on the Alexander-Platz, in 1908. 'Union' was also the short name generally given to the company he founded a year later: the Projektions Aktien-Gesellschaft 'Union' or PAGU. The offices of this new company, dedicated to producing and distributing films as well as showing them in Davidson-owned and other cinemas, had its first offices in Frankfurt; but it soon became clear that the hub of activity in German cinema was Berlin, and Davidson therefore moved his headquarters there. He had built his first film-making studio on a Frankfurt roof-top; now, in Berlin-Tempelhof, he erected one of the 'glass-houses' that enabled early filmmakers to take advantage of natural light streaming in from the top and the sides.

The majority of films shown in Germany before the First World War came from abroad – from France, Italy, the USA, and Denmark. Davidson soon realised that in order to compete he had to think and act internationally. He therefore linked up with a star who had already proved her potential for popular appeal in a Danish film – Asta Nielsen – and signed her up along with her director-husband Urban Gad, forming a company called Internationale Vertriebs-Gesellschaft (International Film Sales). Peter Lähn has well described how Davidson attempted, through his two companies, Union (or PAGU) and IVG, to 'translate the quality formula of his film-theatres into the production sector'. Lähn quotes Davidson himself on the implications of this step, which marked the transition, once and for all, from the age of short films arranged into a 'montage of attractions' by individual cinema owners or mangers to that of the longer fiction film, often sold on star or genre value. As Davidson explained:

> I had not been thinking about film production. But then I saw the first Asta Nielsen film. I realised that the age of the short film was past. And above all I realised that his woman was the first artist in the medium of film. Asta Nielsen, I instantly felt could be a global success. It was 'International Film Sales' that provided 'Union' with eight Nielsen films per year. I built her a studio in Tempelhof, and set up a big production staff around her. This woman can carry it … . Let the films cost whatever they cost. I used every available means – and devised many new ones – in order to bring the Asta Nielsen films to the world. (Quoted in Elsaesser 1996: 84)

Lähn continues: 'PAGU developed into the most prestigious production company in Germany. The contract with Asta Nielsen involved twenty-four films, divided into annual series of eight. The first series met with huge acclaim and succeeded in setting the aesthetic standard that raised filmmaking to the status Davidson had aimed for' (ibid.)

Nielsen and Urban Gad made, in the end, some thirty films for PAGU and IVG between 1911 and 1915. Davidson saw to it that they had the service of fine cameramen (including Guido Seeber, Axel Graatkjaer and Karl Freund), excellent scene and costume designers, and the best possible studio conditions; he also left the choice of subjects largely to them, and gave the films wide and imaginative publicity – knowing that his star and her director had a sensitive feeling for the kind of plots, and the kind of central figures, that would appeal to contemporary audiences. Asta Nielsen's many and varied performances earned her the soubriquet 'the Duse of the Cinema'.

Having established himself as a supplier of films with stars and plots that held appeal for audiences in cinemas across the country, as well as limited sales abroad, Davidson consolidated his position by making each film a 'monopoly' of its production company – enabling that company to make the hiring of a potentially very popular film dependent on hiring a number of others with somewhat less appeal: a process that would later be called 'block booking'. The First World War helped to make this possible, for import restrictions dictated by the outbreak of hostilities made German exhibitors depend much more on native products and boosted the German film industry, particularly at the expense of the French. All these developments also lent force to 'star value': value attached particularly to the heroes and heroines appearing on the screen, but also to directors who consistently produced films that appealed to the increasing cinema-going public.

After Urban Gad and his Asta Nielsen films the director who did most to further the fortunes of Davidson's PAGU was Ernst Lubitsch, who not only starred in his own early works but also gathered together a repertory company that included the writer Hanns Kräly, the designer Kurt Richter, the cinematographer Theordor Sparkuhl, and the actress Ossi Oswalda. Lubitsch joined Davidson after a brief experiment with a company of his own, and eventually made thirty-nine films for PAGU – most of them before and some after it became one of four main units that merged into Ufa. Davidson enabled Lubitsch to assemble talented and congenial people around himself, and encouraged him, after the success of his early comedies, to try his hand at fantasy and history films. For Lubitsch's first step in this new direction, *Die Augen der Mumie Ma* (*The Eyes of the Mummy*, 1918), Davidson secured the services of Emil Jannings and Pola Negri, who both went on to become international stars with *Madame Dubarry* (*Passion*, 1919) and *Anna Boleyn* (*Deception*, 1920), both directed by Lubitsch. This, however, belongs to a later chapter in the fortunes of PAGU, after it had united its forces with the biggest of all German production and distribution companies, Ufa.

One of Davidson's less heralded but by no means unimportant achievements was to break the determination of a guild (Verband deutscher Bühnenschriftsteller) formed by German writers for the stage not to furnish materials for films. In 1912 he persuaded some important writers, including Gerhart Hauptmann in Germany and Arthur Schnitzler in Austria, to sign contracts with PAGU. Nothing ever came of this for Davidson; but such breaking of ranks did persuade the writers' guild to accept the inevitable and withdraw its resolution against collaboration with the emergent cinema. In 1913 even the most prestigious theatre director of his day, Max Reinhardt, signed a contract with PAGU and subsequently delivered two films, made in Italy as a kind of holiday amusement with members of his theatre company: *Eine Nacht in Venedig* (*A Night in Venice*) and *Die Insel der Seligen* (*The Isle of the Blest*). With the latter Davidson sought to lend cultural prestige to his newly opened Berlin picture palace, U.T. am Kurfürstendamm, in 1913. Neither of the Reinhardt films was a success with the public; but their very existence did help to increase the reputation and 'respectability' of the cinema in Germany.

By the time war broke out in 1914, Davidson had become a prestigious entrepreneur in the nascent German film industry, respected as a cinema owner, as a producer/distributor of films to be shown there, and as a man with an eye on the international market. He was therefore one of the first people approached by the General Command of the German Army when it decided, in 1916, to counter anti-German propaganda in French and American films with pro-German propaganda of its own. Davidson responded, in 1917, with *Das Tagebuch des Dr Hart* (*Dr Hart's Diary*), directed by Paul Leni – a film about the activities of a wartime medical unit, made under the auspices of a Photo and Film Agency (Bild und Film Amt, BUFA) set up by the army. Davidson's was in fact the only full-length feature film produced for BUFA, but encouraged by General Erich Ludenorff, a group of financiers, headed by Emil Georg von Stauss of the Deutsche Bank and including many Jewish members (Max von Wassermann, Paul Mamroth, Hermann Frenkel, Salomon Marx and others), formed a committee that consolidated Davidson's PAGU and others into a giant production, distribution and exhibiting syndicate named Universum Film Aktiengesellschaft (Ufa). Founded in December 1917, with help from the Deutsche Bank and other financial institutions represented on the committee, Ufa brought PAGU together with the pioneering Messter company, the German branch of the Danish Nordisk under its Jewish director David Oliver, the Vitascope company, as well as a number of smaller fry, leaving one of the larger companies, Deulig, controlled by Alfred Hugenberg, outside the new conglomerate. Davidson's PAGU or Union organisation continued to function as a division within Ufa, and he himself became a member of the central management committee and a salaried consultant on technical and organisational problems. PAGU brought to Ufa some of its most important assets: a good half of the studio complex at Berlin Tempelhof, including a glass-house for filming and a film-processing plant, a chain of fifty-six cinemas throughout Germany, and writers, directors and actors including Hanns Kräly, Lubitsch, Emil Jannings, Nielsen, Negri, Oswalda, Harry Liedtke and Erna Morena. One of the first films Pola Negri made for Davidson's unit within Ufa had as its theme Tsarist oppression of Jews: *Der gelbe Schein* (*The Yellow Passport*), directed by Victor Janson, first released in November 1918 – the same year as the two *Grossfilme* that were to establish Lubitsch and Negri as preeminent purveyors of prestigious films appealing to international as well as German audiences: *The Eyes of the Mummy* and *Carmen*. Like *The Yellow Passport* these too were made under the auspices of Davidson' unit within Ufa.

It cannot be denied, however, that despite the continued presence of PAGU as a production unit and his reputation as (to use a formulation by Stefan Grossmann) 'the Pied Piper' who lured the best talents of the German stage to seek their fortune in the motion picture industry, his importance within that industry declined after the foundation of Ufa. The fateful turning point came in 1922, when the great success of *Passion* and *Deception* (as *Madame Dubarry* and *Anna Boleyn* were retitled for English-speaking audiences) brought offers from the USA that neither Lubitsch nor Negri could refuse. *Die Bergkatze* (*The Mountain Cat*, 1921) was the last film these two made for Davidson; from 1923 onwards Lubitsch worked exclusively in America. When *Alles für Geld* (*Everything for Money*, retitled *Fortune's Fool* in the USA), directed by Reinhold Schünzel and starring Emil Jannings, appeared in 1923, Davidson's name appeared as director of production, but the production company was not PAGU or Union but Emil-Jannings-Film GmbH.

By then, however, Davidson had made his most serious error of judgement. Irked by his ever more subordinate position at Ufa he had resigned his position there and allowed himself to be appointed as one of the presidents of a new organisation, the European Film Alliance (EFA). This was a company set up by the Hamilton Theatrical Corporation, which was linked to Adolph Zukor's USA-based Famous Players. It was Zukor who had first suggested the founding of such a firm in order to penetrate European markets more effectively. The fortunes of EFA, however, were in the hands of the directors of the Hamilton Corporation, Samuel Rachman and Ben Blumenthal, with Rachman as the most disastrously active partner in Germany. Leopold Schwarzschild, the renowned German-Jewish editor of the journal *Das Tagebuch* (*Diary*), painted a vivid portrait of the personality and activities of a fellow-Jew whose family origins lay further east:

> Sami Rachman, who used to be an impressario of variety-shows somewhere in Galicia, arrives in Berlin alone but with self-glorifying letters of proxy, reserves a flight of rooms in the best hotel ... He concludes new contracts, buys manuscripts, forbids Davidson and Lubitsch to enter their own offices, insults, bribes, berates, distributes sweeteners, quarrels with everyone, soon keeps seven barristers out of breath with civil and criminal proceedings,

alleges slanders and libels, deliriously flings money around, breaks, finally, with his American colleagues, and is summoned back to the USA from the chaos he has created in Germany. Mr Blumenthal arrives in his place with his brother Ike, announcing that a period of sober activity is to begin. But by then little has been left to work on! (Quoted in Kreimeier 1992: 89)

Realising what was happening, Davidson and Lubitsch travelled to the USA to dissociate their production unit from Rachman, but the damage was done. Their last film together, *Das Weib des Pharao* (retitled *The Loves of Pharaoh* in English-speaking countries), made in 1921, appeared as a product of Ernst Lubitsch Film GmbH, and the sole achievement of EFA, the firm that was to have renewed Davidson's fortunes, was recutting and retitling a few previously made films for the American market. When Lubitsch, Negri and Jannings took themselves off to Hollywood, Davidson felt that there would be no place for him there. He tried to buy back his old firm, PAGU, from Ufa, but was rebutted – largely because it was thought that he was backed by American capital, and that selling out to him would give foreign producers a back-stairs way of penetrating the German film industry. Rejecting Davidson's offer and an even bigger one from Blumenthal, which would have reinstated Davidson as head of production, Ufa parcelled up its PAGU holdings in a way that virtually ended their existence as a separate unit. The name Projektions A–G "Union", PAGU, was now mainly used as that of a holding company to administer some real estate containing an Ufa picture-palace in Berlin, so that 'what had begun as a movie-house company ended as a movie-house company' (Bock and Töteberg 1992: 61). All this happened in 1922; two years later Davidson founded the Paul Davidson Aktiengesellschaft as an independent company to work in partnership with Ufa; but nothing came of that partnership, which was discontinued, by mutual agreement, in 1923.

Davidson had been one of the great enablers of the German film industry. He had seen the possibility of combining cinema ownership with film production and distribution, at first in Frankfurt, then in Berlin. He had furthered the move from one- or two- reelers to longer fiction films, with star power, backed by skilful propaganda, and had provided the directors and actors who worked for his outfit with the best technical support money could buy. He had realised that in order to flourish German films would need to acquire an international reputation and international distribution, and had been able to break into the international market – especially that of the all-important USA – with the help of Ernst Lubitsch and the team Davidson had enabled Lubitsch to assemble around himself. In 1923, deserted by that team, cold-shouldered by the now all-powerful Ufa he had helped to bring into being, superseded in all departments by younger men whose energies had not been used up, Davidson fell into a deep depression and took his own life.

The pioneering production firms founded, expanded and merged by Davidson were by no means the only ones started and run by Jewish entrepreneurs. Others in the same line, though never working on the same scale as Davidson, were Jules Greenbaum (born Julius Grünbaum, whose son Max became a distinguished cinematographer under his successive names of Mutz Greenbaum and Max Greene), Ludwig Gottschalk, Paul Oliver, Erich Morawsky, Siegmund Deutsch, H.R. Sokal (patron of the young Leni Riefenstahl), Julius Pinschewer (who pioneered animation and advertising shorts) and Romuel Rappaport. Heinrich Nebenzahl, who had moved from his native Kracow to New York, and thence to Berlin with his family, was one of the most successful of this group. After profitable ventures in the family-branch of the international egg-trade, he entered the German film industry in the second decade of the twentieth century. In 1917 he became business manager of Natur-Film Friedrich Müller; two years later he took over the Metro-Film GmbH, which issued films by the popular star of adventure and daring-do movies, Harry Piel, with whom he remained profitably allied through several other foundations. Among such foundations in which he had a hand was that of Nero-Film in 1925, in collaboration with the prolific and influential filmmaker Richard Oswald, and with a younger member of the Nebenzahl family. This was Heinrich's son Seymour, born in New York, who had turned from apprenticeship in the family egg-trade in the English port of Hull to lucrative banking and stockbroking, and settled in Berlin. Initially Harry Piel was once again a central and profit-generating presence in the new firm; but it soon became the most important independent company outside Ufa through Seymour's association with G.W. Pabst, whose *Die Büchse der Pandora* (*Pandora's Box*), *Westfront 1918*, *Kameradschaft* (*Comradeship*), and *Die 3-Groschen-Oper* (*The Threepenny Opera*), all appeared under the Nero emblem. Fritz Lang too, after his break with Ufa, joined the Nero team, which issued his first sound films *M* and *Das Testament des Dr Mabuse* (*The Testament of Dr Mabuse*). A later chapter will consider the work of Heinrich's nephews, Robert and Curt Siodmak.

The careers of Heinrich and Seymour Nebenzahl, and that of Seymour's son Harold, were celebrated in 2001 by a Congress and Retrospective in Hamburg, from which a richly informative publication resulted (*3 X Nebenzahl. Eine deutsch–amerikanische Produzentenfamilie zwischen Europa und Hollywood*, Hamburg, Cinegraph, 2001). We still await a similar congress celebrating and documenting the achievements of Paul Davidson.

Pommer

Like his father before him, and like many other Jewish pioneers of the film industry in Europe and the USA, Erich Pommer had an early taste of the textile and fashion business. The father, Gustav Pommer, gave up his draper's shop in provincial Hildesheim to lease a canning factory in Göttingen, before moving his business to Berlin in 1905 – the year in which his son, born in Hildesheim in 1889, concluded his secondary education and began an apprenticeship with a gentlemen's outfitters, the Jewish-owned Machol and Lewin. His sister, however, secured a secretarial post with the Berlin branch of the French film company Gaumont, and this family connection led to an interest in the international movie business which was henceforward to determine the trajectory of Pommer's career. In 1907 he was hired by the Berlin Gaumont first as a lowly 'messenger', then as an increasingly valued sales representative. Ursula Hardt, to whom we owe the most authoritative study of Pommer in English, quotes his own description of what happened to him in 1907:

> It was here that I first laid eyes on those boxes holding films of 300 meter length. They were then sold to fairground people who showed them while travelling from place to place. I believe I contracted a very special bug at the time, a bug I was never able to get out of my system. Even today, the smell of filmstrip draws me like a magnet when I find myself in editing rooms. That was the reason why medicine lost a candidate and Georges Grasset, director of the German branch of Gaumont, agreed to hire as a messenger the young boy I was at the time. (Hardt 1996: 16–17)

As a salesman for Gaumont Pommer began his inveterate habit of travelling in search of international contacts; here he met his future business partner Erich Morawsky, another Berlin Jew bitten by the film bug, and formed friendships with several of his later collaborators, including the great Jewish cameraman Karl Freund. Grasset soon promoted him to manage sales at the Vienna branch of Gaumont, from where he travelled throughout the Austro-Hungarian Empire and came to know the Balkans, which led to later association with Balkan-Orient-Film/Soarele. After brief service in the Prussian militia he was wooed away from Gaumont by another French firm, Eclair, and given responsibility for sales in Central and Eastern Europe and the Scandinavian countries. He soon set up a branch of Eclair based in Vienna, under a title which betrayed that his interest in film went beyond the merely selling part of the business: Wiener-Autoren-Film. Under this banner he began his career as a producer by sponsoring films of varying length with such alluring titles as *Mystery of the Air*, *Between Two Fires*, *Off the Straight and Narrow*. The outbreak of the First World War led to his conscription into the Prussian army; he served on the Western and Eastern Fronts, was wounded, and decorated after being mentioned in despatches, and became an army training officer before being assigned to the newly set up army film office, BUFA, in 1917.

While still in the army, Pommer had used some of Eclair's accumulated capital, frozen because Germany was at war with France, to found, in 1915, a Deutsche Eclair company, known as Decla, with a partner who soon sold out, giving way to Pommer's brother Albert and to his old friend Erich Morawsky, who looked after the firm's interests during Pommer's war service. Even at that time, however, Pommer kept himself informed, through daily letters exchanged with his wife, of what was going on at Decla, and took a hand in recruiting authors, directors and actors for a sequence of thrillers, comedies, and other entertainment features – a busy native programme which flourished while the war largely cut out the foreign competition that had dominated the market before 1914. The directors recruited by Decla included Otto Rippert, Alwin Neuss, and the young Fritz Lang (who wrote scripts before directing *Die Spinnen* (*Spiders*) for Decla in 1918/19), the cameramen Carl Hoffmann, and the actors Harry Lambert-Paulsen, Werner Krauss, Lupu Pick (a later director), Ressel Orla, and – under her married name Martha Daghofer – Lil Dagover. While keeping an eye on all this Pommer produced newsreels and documentaries for the army, and served for a while on the military censorship board.

Like many others in charge of the proliferating number of film-producing companies in Germany Pommer felt that while his firm was becoming a more and more significant player, the German film industry needed to consolidate if it wanted to prosper at home and abroad. He therefore initiated the first of several mergers in his career by fusing Decla with another film-production firm, the Rudolf-Meinert-Film-Gesellschaft, assigning Meinert the post of Chief of Production, while placing himself in charge of Export and Import. It was during this period that the newly merged company put itself – and Germany – on the international map with *The Cabinet of Dr Caligari* (1919/20), while Davidson's PAGU did the same thing with *Madame Dubarry*. Since nominally Meinert was in charge of production, Pommer's part in the inception of *Caligari* has been much disputed; there can be no doubt, however, that it was he who was first approached by the film's Jewish writers, Carl Mayer and Hans Janowitz, and that he encouraged the gifted team that came together to make the film along their own lines. It is certainly a key film in Pommer's career. A work of aesthetic merit, its style and story-line rooted in German Romanticism, Expressionism and *Jugendstil*, it proved to be his first international success; it fostered in him a belief that films of artistic quality with a distinctly German voice and style would appeal to discriminating audiences abroad and further the export chances of German films. It also brought him together with the greatest scriptwriter of the silent screen in Germany, Carl Mayer, and strengthened his belief in the importance of teamwork, such as that which had enabled the gifted designers, cameramen and actors to produce such a distinguished and distinctive film under Robert Wiene's direction. Whether he reflected that key elements in this success were provided by two Jewish writers, a Jewish film director and a Jewish director of Decla, we cannot know. He was proud of being a German who had served his country well in peace and war, and wanted to serve it further by making German themes, styles and production qualities renowned throughout the world, bringing profit as well as honour to a country shaken by a lost war, financial crises, and the travails of a republic born amid resentments and competing ideologies.

Seeking further alliances, Pommer concluded agreements with the publishing firm of Ullstein, which brought out novels that achieved wide popularity, often through serial prepublication in the firm's newspapers and journals before being filmed under Decla auspices. He also set up an organisation called 'Russo', dealing with Russian literary themes. April 1920, however, saw a much more important event in Pommer's career: the fusion of Decla with the rival firm Deutsche Bioscop to become Decla-Bioscop. Through this move Pommer's firm acquired – among other human and real-estate resources – a set of studios in Berlin-Neubabelsberg which were to become central to German film production in subsequent years.

The most fateful merger of all was in fact decided in a short period in which Pommer was ill and not in full control. Decla-Bioscop united its fortunes with Ufa, that *Universum Film Aktiengesellschaft* which was increasingly dominant in German film production, distribution and exhibition. This happened in 1921, without, however, sidelining Pommer in the way Davidson was increasingly sidelined. His company remained as a production unit, under his control, within Ufa; in the opening titles of the films that unit produced he was given full credit, as the unit was in many of the advertisements, on posters and in newspapers, which swallowed up a fair proportion of Ufa's budget. Ever since the successful prepublication advertisement campaign for *Caligari* Pommer had been as convinced of the importance of advertising as he was of product differentiation, artistic quality, and the necessity to export in order to recoup the costs of high-budget films. The latter were known as *Grossfilme*, as opposed to the more modestly budgeted films in popular genres intended for the German market only. He attracted to his unit many of the most talented directors of the silent cinema: Murnau, Lang, Ludwig Berger and others, who valued the excellent professional team with which he surrounded them, his involvement in initial stages of their project, his generous funding and respect for their independent decisions once he had given them the go-ahead. 'He proved himself,' said Ludwig Berger, 'an excellent teacher for me and others who directed films under his auspices. [He] knows and understands so much that even now ... I sometimes still see myself as his apprentice...' (Aurich and Jacobson 1998: 39–40).

In 1923 Pommer was voted onto one of the central control boards of Ufa, remaining in charge of the Decla-Bioscop unit and taking over directorships of the Davidson and Messter units. By taking control of Davidson's PAGU ('Union') company he effectively shut out Davidson himself, whose career never recovered its momentum after this. Pommer's niche-marketing strategies, supplying popular low-budget films for one set of the German public, and a series of more generously budgeted prestige films that would be recognisably German yet would also appeal to audiences for fresh filmic voices abroad, impressed the members of the professional organisation of the German film industry, SPIO, so much that they made him their chairman. But while the 1920s saw Pommer at the peak of his power, they also prepared the first downward slide of his career. His export strategies misfired; the all-important market for his expensive *Grossfilme*, the USA, never really fulfilled the hopes he had set on it. While American films were shown in important cinemas all over Germany, German ones failed to reach a wider public in the Americas. Even in relatively sophisticated New York German films tended to open not on Broadway and the streets leading off it in central Manhattan, but in Yorktown, a district inhabited by many people of German origin. An agreement with Paramount and Metro-Goldwyn-Mayer, named Parufamet and intended to benefit all three partners equally, proved far more advantageous to the Americans than to the Germans, and had to be abrogated by the disappointed party soon afterwards.

The soaring costs of Pommer's *Grossfilme*, particularly those directed by Fritz Lang, made Ufa slide more and more into the red and brought the firm to the very brink of bankruptcy. Pommer fell from grace; his contract was not renewed; and in 1926 Pommer took himself off to Hollywood, where he produced two films for Paramount (both starring Pola Negri), briefly worked for MGM, and produced one of Mauritz Stiller's least regarded films, *The Woman on Trial*. None of the films he oversaw under these auspices had anything like the popular and artistic success of those he had made in his German heyday: Berger's *Cinderella (Der verlorene Schuh)*, Lang's first two *Mabuse* films, Lang's *Destiny (Der müde Tod)*, Murnau's *Faust* and *The Last Laugh (Der letzte Mann)* and, especially, that tribute to quintessential German mythology, Lang's *Die Nibelungen*, scripted by Thea von Harbou and explicitly dedicated 'To the German People'. It was, however, the Lang–Harbou *Metropolis* which did most to overstretch Ufa's budget, and forced the departure of the producer who had sunk more and more of Ufa's capital in a project which, however prestigious and artistically valuable it seemed to many, had no chance of recouping its extravagant cost in the foreseeable future.

In the meantime, as Ufa slid deeper into bankruptcy, a rescuer appeared: the media-Tsar and right-wing politician Alfred Hugenberg. Hugenberg had always regarded Ufa as the most dangerous rival of his own film company, Deulig; he was now able to take it over, and put his own man, the efficient and sensible Ludwig Klitzsch, into overall control. One of Klitzsch's first acts was to recall Pommer, with a brief that included the adoption of production and budgeting methods he had had a chance to observe during his work in Hollywood studios. He made him chief of production of a central unit (Erich Pommer Produktion der Ufa), in which he was to exercise stringent financial control and employ directors like Joe May and Hanns Schwarz, who were not likely to indulge in *Metropolis*-like extravaganzas while making films the German public would like to see and might also prove exportable. Whereas before his departure for the USA it had been said of Pommer that his dogged pursuit of cinematic quality had 'snatched German films away from the perspective of housemaids', he now declared that ideally films should appeal to all classes, including 'Minna Schulze, the washerwoman' (*Das Ufa-Buch* p. 90ff).

The most urgent problem that faced Pommer after taking up his new duties at Ufa in 1928 was that of overseeing the costly and complicated transition from 'silent' to sound film within his production unit. He decided early on that the cost of this could only be recouped if films were released abroad in multilingual versions, usually made simultaneously with the German one. These would export the star value of actors like Lilian Harvey, Emil Jannings and Conrad Veidt, who could function in languages other than German, exchanging those who could not for accomplished local stars like Henri Garat and Laurence Olivier. After early experiments, including one in which the leading man, Willy Fritsch, was required to repeat the few German sentences the script required him to speak in English, French and Hungarian, Pommer embarked on a prestige project with which his name will always be as indelibly associated as it is with *Caligari*, *Die Nibelungen* and *Metropolis*: *Der Blaue Engel* (*The Blue Angel*), directed by an Austro-American director imported from Hollywood, Josef von Sternberg. This starred Germany's most internationally acclaimed actor, Emil Jannings, recently returned from his Oscar-winning career in Hollywood. Sternberg paired him with the hitherto only locally known Marlene Dietrich, whose international fame would soon eclipse that of Jannings himself. Sternberg directed both the German and the English version, though only the German one had the benefit of his final editorial supervision. Pommer gave him Ufa's best technical team, from cameramen to sound experts, prestigious script writers, excellent scene designers, tried and proved supporting actors – and a cabaret-honed composer who worked closely with Sternberg on the all-important music that held the film together: Friedrich Hollaender. Gramophone recordings of that music, in the form of songs sung by Marlene Dietrich, proved extremely popular and increased Ufa's profits considerably.

The team Pommer had assembled for *The Blue Angel*, which included Hollaender, the script writer Robert Liebmann, the cameraman Günther Rittau, the scene designers Otto Hunte and Emil Hasler, and the sound technician Fritz Thiery, was soon augmented by other composers (notably W.R. Heymann) and other cameramen and technicians, and assigned directors with a feeling for the new art form in which Pommer showed an overriding interest: films integrating songs and musical set-pieces in an amusing, affecting or thrilling plot. The best-known and most popular of these, including *Die Drei von der Tankstelle* (*Three Men from the Filling Station*, known in its French version as *Le Chemin du paradis*) and *Der Kongress tanzt* (*The Congress Dances*), will be considered in a later chapter. The stars at the centre of most of these films set up by Pommer for his production unit within Ufa were the immensely popular Lilian Harvey and (in the German versions only) Willy Fritsch, whom Pommer surrounded with able supporting casts. Harvey and Fritsch, the 'dream pair' of German film in the early 1930s, were not Jewish; the directors, writers and composers of many of the movies Pommer set up after his recall to Ufa, however, did have Jewish provenance – a fact that did not escape Josef Goebbels and the newspapers that supported the rising Nazi party, who forced Hugenberg and Klitzsch (right-wing nationalists, but not programmatically anti-semitic) into apologetic or face-saving statements.

In 1933 the atmosphere changed radically. While trying to keep some of their Jewish employees for a time, the Ufa management readily accommodated itself to the anti-Jewish orientation of the Hitler government and dismissed a large number of its Jewish staff. Pommer was one of the first to have his employment terminated by reason of the new national policy. For a man who had steadfastly fought for the 'Germanness' of his films, and had wanted to make other nations appreciate the specifically German quality of those he exported, who had served with distinction in the German army and held the Iron Cross, who was anything but religiously observant, it was a terrible blow to be suddenly proscribed as a Jew. He was better off than many, however, because of the international contacts he had made in his many export drives; and at forty-four years of age he still had sufficient energy to try and rebuild his career elsewhere. He already had a contract with Fox, and emigrated to Paris to produce a number of films under the Fox Europe banner, mostly with fellow exiles, including Ophüls and Lang; and then, after a brief and unsatisfactory stay in Hollywood, he joined Alexander Korda in London, where he founded the Mayflower Picture Corporation with Charles Laughton. For Mayflower, whose name indicated Pommer's ambition to appeal to American as well as British audiences, he made three films, one of which he directed himself after disagreements with the originally appointed director; all three starred Laughton, but none of them was commercially successful.

The outbreak of war in 1939 found Pommer back in Hollywood; but serious illness disrupted his capacity to work and diminished his energies. He managed to set up a couple of films, one of them teaming Laughton (unhappily) with Carole Lombard, the other directed by one of the few female directors in Hollywood, Dorothy Arzner. Neither of these impressed the Hollywood moguls or fired audiences with enthusiasm. No more work in American films came his way after 1941, though he did become a US citizen and was known, henceforth, as Eric (not Erich) Pommer.

Here the story might have ended – but Pommer's history, unlike Davidson's, did have a brief upturn. In 1946, a year after the end of the war, he returned to Germany, in American army uniform, and was given the task, by the occupying Western powers, of reorganising a film industry the Nazis had centralised, controlled and incorporated in their propaganda machine. Pommer's endeavour to rebuild the industry while purging it of its most committed Nazis and preventing the formation of vast cartels, raised many German hackles – he was accused of ruining German competitiveness on the international market. At the same time he incurred American suspicions that he was 'going native': that he was all-too-vigorously supporting German-made films at the expense of the imports with which the Hollywood studios were flooding a Germany starved, since the entry of America on the Allied side during the war, of popular American film-fare. Pommer endured this sniping from both sides for four years, returning to the USA a sadder and a wiser man. Though his health troubles increased, and despite his bad experiences as a control officer, Pommer was not yet ready to give up. He set up a company in Munich, significantly called Intercontinental Film GmbH, and shuttled between Germany and the USA as an independent producer, setting up a number of films, the most noteworthy of which was entitled *Children, Mother, and a General* (*Kinder, Mütter, und ein General*). This anti-war film, with memorable parts for Therese Giehse, Maximilian Schell and Klaus Kinski, was praised by critics but failed to arouse the enthusiasm of the German or the international public. Like many other exiles who chose to return after the war, Pommer had met much resentment and little willingness to help him achieve his previous eminence – handicapped as he was in any case, by increasing age and ever-increasing ill health. In 1956 he returned to California, disillusioned and sick. He died ten years later, at the age of seventy-seven, with many unrealised plans and no further effective input into the industry he had loved so much.

Erich, or Eric, Pommer never denied or abjured his Jewishness; but he thought of himself as a German patriot, whose international activities were devoted to making German films not only more profitable, but also more respected, in other countries. He cared passionately for German prestige. The films he sponsored were part of what he called his country's 'Niagara': just as the Niagara Falls were a feature specific to America, which other countries need not try to reproduce, so each nation had something specific to contribute to world cinema which other nations could and should admire and want to see, in order to supplement and widen their own experiences. He had great organisational skills and an imaginative approach to diversification and expansion. His support for large projects likely to result in internationally respected works of art got him into trouble at the peak of his career; but he recovered from that and balanced his *Grossfilme*, prestige products, with more modest and less expensive fare that could appeal to tastes throughout the classes and income groups that constituted his audiences. He had great empathetic understanding of the needs of the many and diverse directors he engaged, and made sure that they had the best casts, writers, designers, cameramen and technicians Ufa could muster; a sensitive feeling for plot-lines that would make a good film, and a sure instinctive understanding of when it was necessary to stop interfering and let the teams he had put together, and the director he had put in charge, go their only partially predetermined way. It was his tragedy that the unique talents he had dedicated to the service of German film were scorned and rejected at what should have been the mid-point of his career. He made what he could of what he was given elsewhere, but starting all over again was difficult even for a man who had the international contacts Pommer had built up over many years; and when he returned to Germany he had to fight his way in a chaotic situation against resentment on the German side and suspicion on the occupying American side. Aging and ill health did the rest, ending a broken career that never quite recovered its early momentum after its sudden, cruel disruption.

Thomas Elsaesser, in whose debt all serious students of German cinema necessarily find themselves, has admirably summed up Pommer's achievement:

> The close contacts of the German film industry with Paris, London and Los Angeles were finally, to a degree not always recognized, due to the constant journeyings and extensive network of connections of a single man: Erich Pommer … If competition, co-operation and commerce are spurred on on the one side by the logic of capital, it was Erich Pommer, on the other, who acted as the motor that kept the wheel of 'Filmbusiness' in Germany turning – and he intervened often enough to give that wheel a spin of its own. (Schöning 1993: 27)

What Elsaesser makes crystal clear is that, unlike Davidson, who had his sights firmly fixed on Germany, Pommer always saw German film in a wider, global, context. This did not mean, however, that he wanted to internationalise and homogenise the German and Austrian cinema. No one was more keenly aware than he that the cinema of every nation, with the aid of Jewish as well as non-Jewish contributors, added a distinctive voice to the great conversation of mankind.

Chapter 2

DRAMAS AND MELODRAMAS OF THE 'SILENT' PERIOD

Der Gelbe Schein (The Yellow Passport)

In 1918 Paul Davidson's PAGU, under the Ufa banner for the first time, brought out three films with Jewish themes. Two of these were comedies, directed by, and starring, Ernst Lubitsch: *Der Rodelkavalier* (*The Tobogganing Cavalier*), and *Meyer aus Berlin*. The third however, was a melodrama featuring a (non-Jewish) actress recently recruited from the Warsaw stage, Barbara Apolonia Chalupec, who had adopted the name Pola Negri in homage to an Italian actress whom she greatly admired. Pola Negri's speciality, in the German films she subsequently made, was playing fascinating foreign women and various species of vamp – often, like the Lorelei figure in the work of the great Romantic poet Clemens Brentano, victims of their own attractiveness to men. The title of this early Negri vehicle, *Der gelbe Schein*, looked back to the infamous Tsarist regulation, recently rescinded by the October Revolution, that the only Jewish women allowed residence in St Petersburg without exceptional government dispensation had to have the yellow identity papers issued to prostitutes. The screenplay was provided by Hanns Kräly, who worked closely with Lubitsch during most of the latter's career, and Hans Brennert; the film was directed by Victor Janson, one of the many actor-directors in the Weimar cinema, who also took one of the main parts, and Eugen Illés, who doubled as cinematographer. It starred Negri as Lea, whom we first meet as the ostensible daughter of an ailing Jewish shopkeeper and pawnbroker, Scholem Raab, played by Guido Herzfeld – the only Jewish member of the cast important enough to receive screen credit.

The kindly, widowed, decrepit Scholem, looked after by Lea and by a servant (who looks and acts as though she had been recruited from one of the Yiddish theatre troupes that occasionally performed in Berlin) lives in a Polish town inhabited by Jews and non-Jews alike – partly recreated in the Ufa-Union studios, with exteriors filmed in occupied Poland. The early *shtetl* scenes have an authentic look and feel, showing streets crowded with bearded men, women carrying babies, and people standing or sitting outside houses and shops, one of which is clearly selling old clothes. There is also a brief authentic-looking anteroom filled with a *minyan* of men praying in the house of a dying man. For much of this, and for some Hebrew/Yiddish shop-signs more convincing than the tombstone inscriptions in the film's studio-built cemetery set, the filmmakers went to a Jewish district in Warsaw, where they found the local colour they needed for their early scenes.

In between ministering to Scholem's needs and seeing to an occasional customer, Lea is shown poring over medical books, swaying like Bashevis Singer's Yentl over the Talmud, in order, as the title proclaims, to relieve Scholem's sufferings. She has a non-Jewish teacher, Ossip Storki, played by the film's director, Victor Janson; but she soon loses him, for he is summoned away to become tutor to the son of the governor of a remote district. Before leaving, Ossip visits the dying Scholem, who hands him a document containing a great secret; Scholem dies soon afterwards, and Lea, although she has been told of the infamous 'Yellow Passport' regulation, sets out to pursue her medical studies in St Petersburg. Stock shots of a train leaving, and one of a train reaching, anonymous-looking station platforms, eked out by a postcard shot of a square in St Petersburg, bridge the gap between the early Polish and the later Russian scenes staged in the Tempelhof studios and a nearby forest. Rejected by lodging-house keepers because she has no residence permit, Lea is forced to apply for the yellow identity papers at a police station where she is manhandled and treated with contempt by Tsarist officials, and has to wait in a room in which (as an impressive tracking shot of unhappy or resigned women reveals) she is thrust into a company whose way of making a living we can easily surmise. One woman, however, is treated by the police officials in a more cheerful, welcoming, bantering way: the happy-go-lucky, flirtatious Vera, played by Marga Lind. After a long wait, Lea is ushered into the inner office, where a surly official issues the yellow passport; and when tired and despondent after these discouraging experiences, she sinks down in the street, she is accosted by Vera, who offers to find her lodgings where no awkward questions would be asked, and where no immediate rent would be demanded. It is no surprise, after that, to find that the accommodating landlady, played by the excellent Margarete Kupfer, is the proprietress of what is euphemistically described as a 'dance palace' (*Ballhaus*). She looks Lea over, likes what she sees – as well she might, for the black-haired, fiery-eyed Pola Negri is a very attractive lady – and suggests that she might occasionally attend some 'parties' arranged at her establishment. Left alone in her room, Lea unpacks her few belongings and comes across a book Ossip had given her before going away; a book that had belonged to his dead sister. And lo and behold – inside the book Lea finds the identity papers issued to that sister, Sofia Storki. Under that name Lea registers at the university, assuming a non-Jewish identity as she registers to attend the classes of Professor Schukowski, played by Adolf Edgar Licho, who appears to be teaching medicine by writing things on a board that the students, sitting in tiered rows of a lecture theatre, write into notebooks that he afterwards inspects. At these classes she meets a fellow-student, Dmitri, who is soon smitten and induces her to relax occasionally at student parties in which Cossack dances seem to figure largely. Dmitri is played by Harry Liedtke, whom German audiences of the day found unaccountably attractive, and who here begins a career of playing the Weimar film's favourite *jeune premier* until Willy Fritsch supplanted him.

Our heroine now lives a double life: as Lea Raab with the yellow passport in thrall to a procuring landlady, and as the brilliant student Sofia Storki with papers that do not call either her religion or her virtue into question. Inevitably, the two identities clash: an arrogant student whose drunken advances she had rejected at one of her landlady's 'parties' drags Dmitri to one of these parties (which are, incidentally, very well staged, paced and photographed) where he sees her being forced to keep company with some coarse drunkards. He upbraids Lea as a hypocrite and deceiver, prompting her to attempt suicide.

In these St Peterburg portions of the film Lea is the only apparently Jewish character we meet. But halt! What about the paper the dying Scholem had given to Ossip Storki? What it contains is played out in the film's first crucial flashback. We see a Russian woman, dragging herself and a baby through the Polish streets and collapsing outside the house in which the childless Scholem and his wife live. They take her in, give her something to eat and put her and her baby to bed – only to find, the next morning, that the woman has disappeared, leaving a note to say that she is going to do away with herself and hopes they will look after her baby. They duly adopt the little girl and bring her up as their own, revealing the secret only to Ossip who, unaccountably, fails to pass it on to Lea. She is not Jewish at all, and need, by rights, never have had to have the yellow passport! But, I suppose, the paper handed over by a dying Jew would not have seemed sufficient proof of identity by the Russian authorities – so Kräly and Brennert have to pile up the coincidences to bring the film to its melodramatic conclusion.

As Sofia Storki, Lea is honoured at the university with a prestigious prize, handed her by Professor Schukowski. A newspaper account of this reaches Ossip, who knows his sister to have died many years ago, and who is given leave by his employer to investigate the matter by going to St Petersburg. There the university authorities direct him to Professor Schukowski, on whose desk he sees a photograph he takes to be of Lea, but which in reality is that of the Professor's long-lost sweetheart. A second flashback explains how that sweetheart, Lydia, became pregnant after a passionate encounter in the forest, how her lover promised to marry her but was summoned home, where his malevolent father detained him for a year after falsely writing to Lydia that his son had married someone else, and how, when he returned to claim her, he found only a note to say that she and the baby had left, destination unknown. All this leads to the soap-opera conclusion, heightened by colour-tinting in the copy I have seen: Lea has been found in the street after attempting suicide, and is taken to the hospital where Professor Schukowski is about to operate while a gallery of students look on. Lea's case is considered so urgent that he must take it at once: he operates in a tensely staged scene – he seems to be performing a tracheotomy – and thus saves the life of his own child. Great emotion all round, as the film ends with the Professor on the right and Dmitri (bearing flowers) on the left of Lea's bedside. The operation has been successful, and we surmise a wedding to come.

All this nonsense is efficiently directed and excellently photographed. A scene like that which shows Lea dealing with a customer who has brought items to pawn, in the foreground of a dimly lit shop where miscellaneous pledges and goods for sale can be discerned, while the bright back room containing Scholem and Ossip is well in focus, speaks volumes for the efficiency of the lenses and the sensitivity of the film-stock PAGU and Ufa could muster at this early period. The scene in the operation room at the end, with a hanging lamp uniting the patient in the front and the physicians in the middle distance without obscuring the further distance in which we can see a crowd of students looking down eagerly from the viewing gallery (though cinematic purists might find it too reminiscent of theatre staging) is, in its context, equally effective; and the atmosphere of the café and place of assignation, with dancing couples, amorous drunkards, conspiratorial waiters inviting gentlemen to a party with charming girls in a back room, could not have been better conveyed. Above all, the camera lens is in love with the young Pola Negri, who appears constantly in attractive close-ups and two-shots. One of these shots, indeed, is a classic of early German cinematography, enshrining a key moment of Weimar film. Tortured by the complications arising from her dual identity as Lea and Sofia, to which another identity, as Schukowski's daughter, will soon be added, our heroine contemplates suicide: a close-up shows her leaning against a mirror, in a two-shot with herself, which visualises that multiple identity in a striking, unforced, way. The *Doppelgänger* theme is compounded, in *The Yellow Passport*, by the fact that Pola Negri also plays Lydia, Lea's natural mother – ensuring that the mystery can be cleared up when a photo of the mother is initially mistaken for that of the daughter.

One aspect of the film makes it particularly valuable. Some of the opening sequences in Lea's home town were shot in the Nalewski section of Warsaw, which was then – during the First World War – occupied by German troops, whose commanders saw anti-Tsarist propaganda value in Janson's project. The Nalewski was a district almost entirely inhabited by Jews. Pola Negri, already a star of Polish films, was greatly moved by the experience of filming among a 'bearded and bewigged' population that could easily have 'stepped out of drawings of life made there two hundred years ago', and hoped that despite the prevailing anti-Jewish feelings of many of her fellow-Poles, the film she was making, on the eve of her departure for Germany and world stardom, would do something to spread tolerance and understanding. For us today these sequences have a documentary value that far transcends their narrative interest; for they allow us glimpses of the Warsaw Jewish quarter before its destruction in a later war, and of its inhabitants (some of whom seem to be curiously watching the filming going on their streets,) before they and their descendants were murdered during a later, far more malevolent, German occupation.

Pleasure in the message of tolerance and understanding Negri ascribed to the film cannot, however, be unalloyed, for it obviously fudges the issues it ostensibly deals with. What presents itself as a film about a Jewish problem turns out to have a heroine at the nub of that problem who is not Jewish at all. In fact, there need not have been a problem if only someone had spoken out! I am reminded of a quip attributed to Ring Lardner, Jr. (among others) about the 'moral' some people had drawn from *Gentleman's Agreement*, a Hollywood movie in which Gregory Peck, as a Gentile journalist, pretends to be Jewish in order to probe the extent of anti-Semitic prejudice and 'restriction' in the USA. What that film seems to teach, Lardner is reported to have said, is 'that you should never be mean to a Jew because he might turn out to be a Gentile'.

The plot device of an orphaned Gentile girl charitably adopted as his own by a Jew has, of course, a respectable ancestry in Lessing's great play about religious and ethnic interrelationship and mutual respect, *Nathan der Weise* (*Nathan the Wise*, first published in 1779). In that central work of the German Enlightenment, however, the girl becomes a bridge between the benevolent Jew and a Christian of good will, a Templar who is himself related to the wise Muslim ruler in the medieval Palestine in which the play is set. It is the Jew, beset as he is by Christian zealots less enlightened than he is, who proclaims the equality of the three great religions that meet and clash in the play, and who therefore becomes a commanding figure in the way the doddering Scholem, Lea's ostensible father, could never be.

In this context it is interesting to remember that in 1922, when a Jewish director and producer, Manfred Noa and Erich Wagowski, made a silent-film version of Lessing's play for the Bavarian Emelka company, their work was greeted with protests, especially in Munich, because it was deemed to be too pro-Jewish. *The Yellow Passport* avoided such criticism – not least because the prospect of marriage held out by the fade-out was not interracial after all. The clichéd Jews of the first reel (pawnbroking! old-clothes dealing!) make a pseudo-exotic background for a safe melodrama about the inhumanity of a régime that had been at war with Germany and had recently been overthrown. With its story of multiple identities, prostitution, threatened violations, illegitimate childbirths, successful or attempted suicides, secrets improbably kept, tyrannical real and benevolent adopted fathers, a daughter lost and found, drunken men and light women in a less than respectable establishment, and a climactic hospital scene in which a father manages to save the life of his long-lost child, *The Yellow Passport* is cobbled together to make a vehicle for the studio's latest asset, imported from Poland, who would soon go on to bigger things. Davidson paired her successfully with Lubitsch and co-starred her with Jannings in *Die Augen der Mumie Ma* (*The Eyes of the Mummy*), which played on superstitions about excavations and discoveries by contemporary Egyptologists in an uncanny tale that was forerunner of many 'Mummy' movies in other countries, with either supernatural or 'explained supernatural' elements. The same pairing ensured the success of *Madame Dubarry*, directed by Ernst Lubitsch, whose success in the USA, under the title *Passion*, sent Lubitsch, Jannings and Negri to Hollywood. Davidson remained behind, and his German career never recovered from the loss of his most important director and star.

While Pola Negri, who became one of the great icons of Weimar cinema, began her career with a film that showed her character as not born Jewish, but brought up and acculturated within orthodox Judaism, another of the most popular stars of the time, Lilian Harvey, made her first film for a Viennese company founded by her Jewish director, Robert Land, as a girl born Jewish but in disharmony with her orthodox patriarchal East European *shtetl* environment. The firm was called *Der Fluch* (*The Curse*, 1924–25), and it told the story of an unmarried mother who drowns herself because her daughter, played by Harvey, conscious of her mother's irregular status, leads an 'immoral' life and becomes subject of the 'curse' that forms the film's title. The screenplay was written by Ernst Weizmann and Walter Reisch, and thus had Westernised, assimilated Jews looking with compassion, but also with distance, at a kind of Jewish life they themselves had either never known or had left behind. Harvey, who appeared raven-haired in this film, was to become the Weimar public's blonde darling under the guidance of many other Jewish producers, directors, scriptwriters and musicians: notably, Erich Pommer, Wilhelm Thiele, Franz Schulz, Robert Liebmann, W.R. Heymann and Friedrich Hollaender. We will meet her again in a later chapter.

Das Alte Gesetz (The Ancient Law)

Ewald André Dupont wrote, and directed, films in many different genres before his German career was cut short by the Nazis; but he returned most often to the world of entertainment, theatre of various kinds, cabaret and variety – indeed, a film called *Varieté*, made in 1925 and starring Emil Jannings, Lya de Putti and Warwick Ward, is a classic for which he will always be remembered. One of his films is entitled *Zwei Welten* (*Two Worlds*): a programmatic title, for, himself of Jewish origin, he was perennially interested in the interplay of different worlds that obeyed strict, initially incompatible, rules.

The Ancient Law, first shown in 1923, takes its viewers into the world of orthodox Judaism in a Galician *shtetl*, where the ambition to become a professional actor is regarded as little less than apostasy. It then introduces them to three different kinds of theatre: one within the Jewish realm, confined to one special day of rejoicing, and two in the Gentile world without. Dupont made the film for one of the many smaller production firms in Berlin that had not yet been caught in the Ufa conglomerate; it was called Comedia Films, and did not long survive *The Ancient Law*. The screenplay was by Paul Reno, who cites as one of his sources the reminiscences of Heinrich Laube, who, at the peak of a chequered career, had become a director of plays at the prestigious Burgtheater of Vienna, still a court theatre between 1849 and 1867, and subject to overall control by a court-appointed *Intendant*. A look at the passage in question will help us place the plot-lines of Dupont's film. Laube is here talking about an actor called Bogumil Dawison, who had come to try his luck at the Burgtheater after experience with less prestigious theatre-troupes in Poland and Germany:

> I had just been appointed to my post at the Burgtheater when a young man appeared to give trial performances in character and juvenile parts. He was fairly successful with the public because of his lively, emotional acting, and his striving for effect at all costs, even if such effects were not always legitimate.
>
> The public urgently demanded to see new life in the Burgtheater; and though Bogumil Dawison, the actor in question, did not satisfy the more discriminating spectators, even these did not deny him a modest amount of applause.
>
> I now had to ask my chief [the *Intendant*, Count Lanckoronski] whether Dawison should be given a contract. I had the right to engage any actor for a year at a time, but did not think it proper to insist on this so soon after my appointment – especially in this case, since Dawison could give lively performances, but his lack of training ensured that he was incapable of conveying any kind of nobility.
>
> My chief did not like him at all. He called him coarse, graceless, and pushy. *Perhaps because Dawison was a Jew*? That may have played a small part. In essence, however, the *Intendant* rejected him because of his characteristic lack of corporeal grace, dignity, poise, and good manners ... When I came to cast tragedies I ruled Dawison out categorically. He could not play tragic parts. Even when he worked his feelings up to their highest pitch, the effect was sentimental. This made for theatrical excitement; in favourable cases it could even be moving – but he was incapable of portraying the profound agony of a noble soul. (Laube 1882: 175–6, my italics)

Dawison never did get a permanent engagement at the Burgtheater: his virtuoso performances – exciting, but often criticised for vulgar exaggeration – were mostly given at Hamburg and Dresden, and on a tour of the USA. Shylock was his most famous part; but he also played Franz Moor (the *evil* brother) in Schiller's *Die Räuber*, the no less unpleasant Moor Aaron in *Die Verschwörung des Fiesco zu Genua* (*The Conspiracy of Fiesco at Genoa*), as well as various parts in old and new comedies. Baruch Mayer, the central protagonist of *The Ancient Law*, is not identical with Dawison; but the mention of Laube's reminiscences in the credits, the mid-nineteenth century era in which the story is set, and various parallels with Dawison's origins and early adventures, suggest that Baruch is to some extent based on him. There are, however, important differences which will concern us later.

Baruch Mayer, played by Ernst Deutsch, is first seen in a Galician *shtetl*, in a Jewish community whose spiritual head, the rabbi, is Baruch's father. Rabbi Mayer, is played by the Polish-Jewish actor Avrom Morewski, who also acted as consultant for Jewish ritual, ensuring that the many scenes which featured Jewish worship and ceremony in the home and the synagogue have an authenticity that elsewhere is found mainly in the many Yiddish films in which such scenes were calculated to awaken warm memories of the Old Country even among those who had abandoned the piety of their East European home and were glad to live free from persecution and the constraints of strict orthodoxy. The rabbi is a figure of great dignity in this film, but he lives in a world so different from his wider surroundings that when he tries to fathom what kind of thing is weaning his son away from his religious studies and is given a copy of *Hamlet*, he tries to read it by opening it from the back – reminding us that Hebrew is not only read from right to left but that its pagination runs the opposite way from the pagination in books written in Western languages other than Yiddish. The *shtetl* types that surround the rabbi are portrayed with accuracy and sympathy: the man who wakes Jews for prayer in the morning, knocking at windows to make sure that the morning prayer is attended by at least ten adult men (a *minyan*); the *shammes* or beadle; a well-differentiated gathering of worshippers in the synagogue – and, above all, the all-important *shnorrer*, the beggar who enables better-off Jews, and poor ones as well, to practise the hospitality and the charity which is as much a religious duty as prayer, and who is also a welcome source of news as he goes from *shtetl* to *shtetl*, from large town to small town and village. In *The Ancient Law* he is brought vividly to life by the Jewish actor Robert Garrison. Garrison's Ruben Pick unites due deference with a dignity born of wider experience; understanding and love of the 'ancient law' with respect for inborn talents and urges that can find no adequate outlet within it. With a firm place in the traditional world of Judaism he can bring news of a wider world into it; and when Baruch has broken away, partly fired by Ruben's stories, the shnorrer's wanderings make him a mediator able to bridge the *geographi-*

cal distance between *shtetl* family and metropolitan son, and something of the *spiritual* distance as well.

Much of the appeal of this film resides in its recreations of Jewish ritual. It brings us glimpses of the inauguration of the Sabbath within the family, of Passover celebrations, the *Kol Nidre* service in the synagogue (with just a touch of exaggeration in the gestures of the congregants to remind us that for Dupont this is another type of theatre as well as a religious act). He also introduces a reading of the scroll of Esther at *Purim*, the Jewish Feast of Lots, with children making a licensed din with wooden rattles whenever the wicked Haman and his sons are mentioned – and focuses particularly on the *Purim* festivities outside the synagogue. These are the nearest traditional Judaism comes to the carnival atmosphere of the Christian world just before Ash Wednesday; they feature a jester who acts as master of ceremonies, and musicians, *klezmorim*, to heighten joy at the rescue of a Jewish community from threatened extermination in the days of Mordecai and Esther. These festivities traditionally include the performance of a *Purimshpil* in which amateur actors portray Esther, Mordecai, King Ahasuerus, and Haman, in home-made costumes, masks and false beards. The writer of this book has been both Ahasuerus and Haman in his time. In *The Ancient Law*, Baruch, impressive in robe and crown, has been cast as Ahasuerus; but his strict father thinks it beneath the dignity of a rabbi's son to take part even in such permitted representations. When the rabbi interrupts the proceedings by pulling his son away, Ruben Pick intervenes; trying to calm the atmosphere, he recounts what he has heard of the delights of the Vienna Burgtheater and unwittingly points Baruch in the direction he wants to go. Baruch feels sad at leaving not only his family but also Esther, the girl he loves – but when Ruben Pick continues his wanderings, Baruch follows him into a wider world.

There follows an encounter with a troupe of wandering players in comparison with whom the Vincent Crummles Company is the Old Vic. The director of this motley band, whose actresses increase the takings by being nice to gentlemen off the stage, is played by the portly Jakob Tiedtke as the very essence of sleaziness. The wealth of convincing detail of gesture, deportment and facial expression make his portrait of pomposity, greed, cringing deference, and willingness to pimp, as rounded and impressive as Robert Garrison's portrayal of an indigent Jew's decency, intelligence and helpfulness. The director – we never learn his name – sets Baruch to sweeping and shovelling horse-dung before letting him exchange the ghetto caftan for a motley costume in order to play Shakespeare's Romeo to a superannuated floozy impersonating Juliet. The performance is watched by a courtly group that had grown bored with its *partie de campagne* and found a welcome diversion in this primitive spectacle. The gentlemen look for sexual favours afterwards, which the Juliet is anything but unwilling to grant; but one of the ladies, an Archduchess, sees possibilities in Baruch and advises him to try his luck at the Vienna Burgtheater. At this point Baruch's Jewishness becomes an obstacle; a courtier ridicules the director for casting a young man with Jewish sidelocks as Romeo, whereupon the director shows Baruch the door. Encouraged by the Archduchess, however, Baruch makes for Vienna.

Germany's most popular female film star of the day, Henny Porten, has now come into view. The Austrian Archduchess, whom she plays, has, it appears, fallen in love with young Baruch, makes secret (chaste) assignations with him, but is in the end mindful of the obligations of class and court protocol. At a sad, last interview, she resigns herself to renouncing the man she loves. She does, however, actively engage herself in furthering Baruch's career, demanding, as her position at court allows her to do, that Laube auditions him. That leads to what became the most famous scene of the film when it was first shown. Known as 'Laube's breakfast scene', it shows the Burgtheater director summoning Baruch in the early morning, and eating and drinking his breakfast while Ernst Deutsch, as Baruch, declaims in the style that made Deutsch so acceptable to Reinhardt and his Berlin public. The camera focuses on the face of the actor who plays the heavily bearded Laube (a Jewish actor, incidentally, called Hermann Vallentin) as he becomes more and more impressed by the young man and determined to give him a try on the Burgtheater stage. In a symbolic scene before an ornate mirror we see Baruch, not without hesitation, cut off his Jewish sidelocks – and that, it seems, was all it took to make him acceptable to the Viennese public. When we next meet him, he is an elegant cavalier and (without having received any kind of training in acting styles except an abortive *Purim* play and a ridiculously inadequate production of *Romeo and Juliet* in some Austrian barn) an affluent member of the cast of one of the most famous theatres in Europe. Dawison never had it that easy! And the real Heinrich Laube must have turned in his grave over what happens next. To advance the career of the man she loves even further, the Archduchess detains a star actor, whom Laube had envisaged as his Hamlet, beyond the time appointed for the first read-through of Shakespeare's play; and Laube, annoyed at having been kept waiting, recasts the play and assigns the part of the Prince of Denmark to Baruch – who, of course, will be a complete success.

But wait! It's now *Jazz Singer* time. Baruch's father has not reconciled himself to his son's desertion, refuses to receive him when Ruben Pick persuades Baruch to visit his old home; his mother sadly follows suit, unlike Esther, who eventually follows him to Vienna and marries him. He has, we see, remained a good Jew at heart, and he has a great struggle within himself when the first night of the production of *Hamlet*, which will cement his reputation, is set (you guessed it) for the solemn eve of the Day of Atonement. No change is possible, Laube declares; and so we see Baruch sadly murmuring traditional prayers in his dressing-room before going out to give what we are meant to surmise will be the performance of his life.

If that, and the easy assumption of elegant Viennese life-style not only by Baruch but by Esther too, were not wish-dream enough, Ruben Pick, whom Baruch continues to receive as an honoured guest when he hits Vienna during his peregrinations, engineers a surprise visit of Baruch's parents to Vienna, where the old rabbi is so enthused by his son's assumption of the name part in Schiller's *Don Carlos* that he forgives the desertion. In a final scene we see Baruch and his mother beside the plainly dying rabbi, in happily restored family unity, while Esther, deeply moved, stands tearfully nearby.

It is astonishing to find the perpetrators of this exercise in having one's cake and eating it naming Laube's reminiscences as one of their sources. Once he has cut off his sidelocks, there are no anti-Semitic animadversions on the freshly baked gentleman-actor from Galicia, such as Dawison encountered throughout a career in which charges of vulgarity, milking of effects, and ungentlemanly conduct played a constant part until he died, from nervous exhaustion and with impaired wits, in 1872. What Laube really thought of the possibility of letting such a man play Hamlet we have already seen; his judgement was reiterated, some thirty years after his death, by the eminent historian of the nineteenth-century German and Austrian stage, Max Martersteig. Dawison's playing, Martersteig declares, had something 'inflated, affected, exaggerated; his nature lacked true artistry, and he substituted sensational effects for it ...' (1904: 453) Baruch has it far too easy: captivating Viennese theatre-goers, attracting the love of an Archduchess, fitting himself and his bride from deepest Galicia seamlessly into elegant society, and reconciling his orthodox father, for whom even taking part in a *Purim* play was anathema, to his son's *goyish* mode of existence based on the art of the theatre which so many Eastern European rabbis denounced as 'sitting in the seat of the scoffers'. Twentieth-century New York, the setting of *The Jazz Singer*, might offer such possibilities; but they were less easily resolved in the Austro-Hungarian Empire, with its East European outposts, in which Laube and Dawison lived out their lives.

It is right to be sceptical about these wish-dream transformations of Laube's account and what we know of the historical situation, but *The Ancient Law* offers its viewers many compensations. Chief among them are the reenactmants of Jewish ritual, overseen by Avrom Morewski, who played the rabbi; excellent performances by Deutsch, Garrison, Tiedtke and Vallentin; well-differentiated stagings in *shtetl* streets and rooms at *Purim* and among barnstormers in provincial Austria, as well as a recreation of the Burgtheater; and memorable set-pieces like Laube's breakfast scene. Lotte Eisner, the historian of the Weimar cinema, has spoken of the visual distinction Dupont and his cameraman, Theodor Sparkuhl, brought to their film, mentioning daguerreotypes that seem to come to life, crinolines sweeping across parquet floors or swishing over grass, light magically transfusing outdoor and indoor scenes. She praises particularly the subtle gradations of visual tones in a film that avoids the Scylla of 'Germanic immobility of ornamental form' and the Charybdis of 'decorative stylisation':

> Using here a checked jacket or a piece of striped trimming, there a vase of flowers or a strip of tapestry, [Dupont] seeks to capture the fleeting quality of the chiaroscuro. He makes the interiors vibrate with the atmosphere appropriate to each situation, marrying the velvet of the darks to the tender silk of the lights. Without taking the premeditation too far, he places his actors with infinite elegance and sensibility, as when, for example, the girl in love with Baruch hides her head in despair on her bed in an attitude which brings out her fragility beneath the heavy folds of her dress. Again, Dupont composes an authentic *Kammerspiel* scene between Henny Porten and Ernst Deutsch, with the dull glow of a taffeta gown blending into the half-light of the silent drawing-room reflected in the window behind them. The period costumes stop looking like fancy dress ... the richness of light in the blending impressions is magical.
>
> And even in the scenes of the dark-toned peasant ghetto, with what artistry he succeeds in avoiding brusque contrasts and forced highlights, maintaining, with the help of his cameraman, Theodor Sparkuhl, the vigour and *sfumato* of an etching of the school of Rembrandt! One need only compare these passages with scenes in Pabst's *Prozess*, a film which is also set in a Jewish orthodox milieu, in order to appreciate the full extent of Dupont's tact and extraordinary good taste. (Eisner 1973: 275–6)

Karl Prümm, in an essay about G.W. Pabst's post-Second World War film treating nineteenth-century accusations of ritual murder (*Der Prozess* [*The Trial*], 1948), has a welcome passage about the structural excellence of *The Ancient Law*, pointing out how the divided and distinctive worlds presented in the first part come together in a series of crosscuts towards the end: 'the glowing interior on the evening of Baruch's premiere in the role of Hamlet; the solemnly illuminated synagogue in faraway Galicia; the intense theatricality of the Yom Kippur prayer ritual and the festive atmosphere of the stage setting' (in Rentschler 1990: 203).

The Jazz Singer, the pioneering sound film of 1927, adapted from a play by Samson Raphaelson, directed by Alan Crosland and starring Al Jolson, has been called 'the stuff of American myth – a story that conflates charged issues of patriarchal order, family obligation, secular success, assimilation and racial identity' (Hoberman and Shandler 2003: 77). I am surprised that 'religion' does not figure in this list, given the prominence of Yom Kippur precepts in the story of a cantor's son; but with that addition, what Hoberman and Shandler here say of *The Jazz Singer's* 'conflation' applies to *The Ancient Law* as well. There are, however, significant differences between the problems and aspirations of Jolson's Jakie Rabinowitz, and those of Deutsch's Baruch. Jakie has only to move across from the Lower East side to another part of New York to reinvent himself as Jack Robin, the all-American vaudeville entertainer in black-face. Deutsch's Baruch, however, has to traverse countries and change languages, from Yiddish to High German; he has to change not only language, but hairstyle and dress in a Europe that does not have American melting-pot traditions; he has to find acceptance in Austrian court and professional circles when coming from a family whose head, learned in Jewish lore, is so unfamiliar with Western books that he tries to read them by opening them at the end and letting his eyes travel from right to left, as he would when reading the Hebrew scriptures and commentaries; and his aspiration is not to vaudeville culture, but to the highest pinnacles of European theatre, leading parts in plays by Shakespeare and Schiller. The Dupont of *The Ancient Law* shows a touching faith in the power of art to overcome profound differences, and uses it to project a common dream of German-Jewish and Austrian-Jewish symbiosis which was to be brutally shattered in the next decade. We shall see in a later chapter, however, that when he returned to an Austrian-Jewish theme in the programmatically titled *Zwei Welten* (*Two Worlds*, 1930) he saw reconciliation between traditional Judaism and Austrian social and cultural attitudes as more difficult, more accompanied by heartache and soul-searching, than the final scenes of *The Ancient Law* would seem to suggest.

Before he turned to scriptwriting and directing, Dupont had been a pioneering film critic, who sought to wean German film away from fantasy and the grotesque to greater realism; and like Erich Pommer at a later time, he made his mark on the English as well as the German cinema. *Atlantic* (1929), an early experiment in sound film based on the *Titanic* disaster, is difficult to sit through nowadays because so much of the dialogue proceeds at almost dictation speed. After all, Hitchcock showed, in the same year, how speech could be recorded at once naturalistically and, where appropriate, with psychologically meaningful variation of volume and emphasis. Of the other films Dupont made in England for British International Pictures (BIP), *Piccadilly*, also released in 1929, is the most relevant in the present context. It showed, as did *Atlantic*, his commitment to internationalising filmmaking: a German director, cameraman and designer working with actors from England and the USA to capture some of the feel of London in the late 1920s. It cast in the lead a Chinese-American actress, Anna May Wong, who found in Berlin the recognition that had been tardy in coming to her in Hollywood; Dupont's feeling for outsiders joined with his command of fluid cinematic form to bring to life Arnold Bennett's script which showed the rise of a Chinese scullery-maid to stardom as a dancer. The film dealt graphically with interethnic love and hate, showing not only the erotic involvement of a European man with a Chinese woman but also the indignation of an East London public at the spectacle of a black man daring to dance with a white woman. The interracial kiss, however, which some thought to have seen in the film and which would have made it difficult to sell in the USA, is a mirage: Dupont has the image fade before Jameson Thomas's lips actually meet the delectable mouth of Anna May Wong.

Die Gezeichneten (Marked Out)

This film about the aetiology of pogroms in Russia – based on what happened at Kishinev in 1903 and in other places during the aborted revolution of 1905 – is usually shown, in English-speaking countries, under the title *Love One Another*. The German title, however, which I translated 'Marked Out', describes more accurately what the film shows rather than what its makers hope it advocates. This includes the stigmatisation of Jews, the 'marking out' of all the characters by social position, nationality, ethnic origin, religious traditions and practices, gender – and the 'mark of Cain' (*das Kainszeichen*) on those who deliberately foment hatred and instigate murder. It can be called a *German* film only in a limited sense. Shot in and around Berlin in 1921, for Primus Film (another of the many small production companies that had sprung up during and just after the First World War, who provided the cameraman, Friedrich Weinmann, and used it to inaugurate its own cinema, the Primus Palast), the film nevertheless had its première not in Berlin but in Copenhagen. And that with good reason: its distinguished director, Carl Theodor Dreyer, was Danish, as were the author of the novel on which it was based, the designer, and some of the actors – notably one of the key players, Johannes Meyer. The other principal parts were taken by Russian actors, some of whom had come to Berlin from the Moscow Art Theatre – besides Wladimir Gajdarow and Polina Piekowska, who played the brother and sister at the centre of the story, they included Iwan Duwan-Torzow, who played the Jew-hater Suchowersky, and the Polish-born Boleslaw Riszart Srzednicki, who adopted the name Richard Boleslawski, found his way to Hollywood, and directed, in 1935, what still remains the best adaptation of *Les Misérables* ever committed to film. A few German players, including the (German-Jewish) Hugo Döblin, Adele Reuter-Eichberg and Friedrich Kühne (who played the police chief) figured low down on the cast list; but many of the extras were recruited in the Berlin district that housed recent immigrant Jews from Eastern Europe, and among the White Russian refugees who had fled the Bolshevik Revolution. The set designer, the Dane Jens Lind, had worked with Dreyer before (notably on *Blade af Satans Bog/Leaves from Satan's Book*), and the screenplay, adapted from a novel by Aage Madelung, was by Dreyer himself. An English version of that novel's title, *Love One Another*, was later used as the title of Dreyer's film in England and America. Written in 1912, the novel was based on conditions its Danish author had witnessed for herself: she had lived in Russia, married a Russian Jew, and had experienced a pogrom.

Primus Film had no studio of its own, and Dreyer had therefore to shoot most of the film on location: a necessity Dreyer complained about because of the constant removal of equipment from one place to another that might be quite a distance away. He made a virtue of this, however – location shooting gave his film the documentary look he was eager to preserve.

Keeping make-up to a bare minimum aided the documentary impulse; and Dreyer did his best to make his not over-imaginative cinematographer focus on telling gestures and facial expressions. Pogrom scenes gained a good deal of impact and immediacy by the employment of a large number of extras recruited from the Jewish immigrant population in and around Berlin, many of whom had personal experience of such atrocities. They lent realism to the East European village built in the Weissensee district of Berlin.

The trouble with the film, however, is that Dreyer had adapted a novel with a complicated and convoluted story-line, which even his simplifications – and a *deus ex machina* ending which hammers home the 'love one another' message – could not make easy to follow.

In bare outline the plot centres on Hanna-Libe, first seen as a little Jewish girl in a Russian village in which Jews and Christians live uneasily together. She is befriended by a little Russian boy, Fedya Sukowerski – but Fedya's father, an affluent merchant who resents Jewish competition, turns him against her, making him a Jew-hater who sees Jewish girls as potential subjects for rape rather than friends or marriage-partners. Hanna-Libe's parents enrol her at a Russian school, where she comes up immediately against religious intolerance: disdainful teachers force her to take part in Russian Orthodox prayer, and she is eventually expelled from the school when an innocent flirtation with Sasha, a friendly young Russian, is interpreted as a sign of ingrained Jewish immorality. Her erstwhile playfellow Fedya is one of the instigators of such slanders. Shamed and humiliated, Hanna-Libe flees to St Petersburg, where her brother, Jakow Segal, is allowed to live and earn his living as a lawyer – for Jakow has converted to Christianity. Although, as we know from *The Yellow Passport*, unconverted Jews had no right of domicile in Tsarist St Petersburg, no one at first questions Hanna-Libe's residence there when her brother finds her lodgings with a scientist friend's family. Here she meets her old acquaintance Sasha again – as Alexander Sokolow, now a member of a clandestine revolutionary group. This group has been infiltrated by an *agent provocateur*, employed by the Russian authorities to stimulate actions that will make it possible to arrest and punish the whole group and its leaders. This agent, a chameleon who appears under several names and in several guises (a wonderfully sinister performance by Johannes Meyer), calls himself Rylowitsch when we first meet him; he also has a brief to foment anti-Jewish feelings to distract the populace from the failings of the government and hold the Jews responsible for all its ills. Jakow Segal has had experience of such types in his legal practice, and lets Rylowitsch know that he sees through his game. Rylowitsch thereupon leaves St Petersburg and throws himself into his anti-Jewish mission: he disguises himself as a monk, a cowled figure that brings out Dreyer's special genius for staging the uncanny, and preaches anti-Jewish sermons all over the countryside. In Fedya and his father he finds ready seconders and accomplices. Hanna-

Libe, meanwhile, has been expelled from St Petersburg as a Jewess and has returned to her father's house in her home village, where Fedya's economically determined Jew-hatred is no impediment to his lusting after her. News that his mother is dying brings Jakow back to the village too. Jakow recognises Rylowitsch and threatens to expose him for what he is; but a pogrom incited by this *agent provocateur*, with the help of Fedya and his father, gives Rylowitsch the chance to shoot Jakow dead with impunity. In the course of the pogrom, the terrifying climax of the film, many Jews are killed; Fedya traps Hanna-Libe and prepares to rape her. She is rescued, in an ending contrived for the film, by the temporarily successful revolutionairies who (of course) include Sasha, imprisoned when his group had been denounced by Rylowitsch, but conveniently freed from prison by the insurrection of 1905.

The characters are all 'marked out' – *gezeichnet* – in their own eyes and those of others, by distinctions of social class, commercial interest, religious tradition and gender. Sexual desire plays across such divisions: either in friendship and love, as between Hanna-Libe and Sasha, or hatred that wants to overpower and possess the sexually desirable 'enemy'.

Dreyer is a master at orchestrating the glances between his characters to suggest their actual and desired relationships, and he knows how to convey the titillation of pogroms which open possibilities of rape alongside (and, of course, not excluding) murder. Rylowitsch, Fedya and the pillaging villagers not only rip up the bodies of their victims, but their possessions too. In one memorable scene pillows are torn open to make a shower of feathers fall like snow upon the street – a spectacle which cinéastes like to compare with a famous dormitory scene in *Zéro de Conduite*, but which recalls for me actual happenings I witnessed in my German home town during the 'Crystal Night' riots of November 1938. By converting to Christianity Jakow Segal had sought to erase the mark of Judaism that had stigmatised him in others' eyes – but it proves indelible, and in the end he shares the fate of the community he was born into. But *Die Gezeichneten* of the title are not only the victims but also the instigators and perpetrators of the pogrom; murdering their fellow-citizens they bear the Mark of Cain, the first murderer who killed his brother. There is the mark of business rivalry too, which exacerbates the anti-Jewish feeling already promoted by the official religion of the village community and stimulated by government machinations; or the mark of the female role which so delighted Tom Milne: 'a moment of pure Dreyer, when Hanna's brother quarrels bitterly with his father about his decision to leave home, his mother rushes forward to calm him, notices a button hanging loose on his coat, and is happily sidetracked into sewing it on again' (1971: 60). The motto 'Love One Another', proclaimed by the interracial and interreligious rescue at the end of the film, seeks to show that the marks can be, if not erased, at least disregarded or transcended – an optimism that may seem a little too easily won.

Dreyer was one of the masters of the cinema, and signs of that mastery show: lyrical forest scenes, memorable portrait studies, especially of bearded faces, impressive recreations of Russian village life, expertly marshalled crowd scenes, sinister apparitions of hooded figures, and the highlighting of features of the rural and urban worlds that characterise their inhabitants and speak of their inner life as well as their outward occupations. It would be hard to argue, however, that the overall effect of the film is as powerful as that left by *The Passion of Jeanne d'Arc*, *Day of Wrath*, *Michael*, *The Parson's Wife* or *Gertrud*. Some of the film's failings may be due to a cinematographer who could not always match Dreyer's vision; but ultimately the fault lies with the unwieldy source. 'Perhaps it was wrong,' Dreyer admitted, 'to condense this big work in order to make a film of it. It was necessary to cut, to prune, endlessly' (quoted by Milne 1971: 60). His art flourished in concentration rather than diffusion; despite his many tributes to Griffith, he did not command the epic sweep of *Intolerance*, whose St Bartholomew episode *Die Gezeichneten* echoes along with features of *Orphans of the Storm*. The conventionality of Dreyer's film, with its emulation of Griffith's 'nick of time' rescues, is shown up by comparison with his later, and greater, *Day of Wrath*:

> The final tragic point of *Day of Wrath* is that the coercions and repressions of social and dramatic discourse cannot be elided or avoided. Insofar as Herlofs Marte and Anne are indeed successfully turned into "witches," and are exterminated from their societies, Dreyer demonstrates that it is impossible to maintain the imaginative opening out of the repressive forms and structures of society that either one represents. (Even merely to name an individual as a witch or for her to accept the name is, of course, in and of itself a powerful strategy of control.) (Carney 1989: 169)

Carney also shows how the overall narrative progress of *Day of Wrath*, so characteristic of Dreyer at his most authentic, is repeated in *Gertrud* and *Ordet*:

> A character reaches outward at the beginning of the film, moving beyond social walls and imaginative boundaries, in a daring attempt at social connectedness and emotional relationship. Yet the effort is doomed. The possibilities of realizing one's ideals in the form of actual social relationships which are evoked early in the narratives are abandoned by their ends. The second halves of all three films reverse the direction of the narratives' and the characters' initial movements outward. Anne, Inger, and Gertrud are forced to withdraw from the actual societies of relationship they attempted to bring into existence. Spiritual or imaginative communities take the place of actual, worldly relationships. (Ibid.: 344)

The logic of *Die Gezeichneten* points the same way; in Dreyer's world the injunction 'love one another' is more than necessary, but all too difficult to follow.

It is greatly to Dreyer's credit, however, that despite its pasted-on 'happy end' his film avoids the evasions of *The Yellow Passport*, where the Jewish problem is 'resolved' when the heroine turns out not to be Jewish at all and thus avoids the frictions of an interethnic or interreligious marriage; or those of *The Ancient Law*, where the clash of world-views and principles between the rabbi of a Galician *shtetl*, on the one hand, and that of his newly urbanised and sophisticated son steeped in Shakespeare and Schiller, on the other, is as speciously resolved as the suspicion and even dislike that some of the aristocratic and middle-class Viennese theatre patrons felt when confronted with the raw talents of men from Eastern Europe: men like Bogumil Dawison, whose career in real life is acknowledged as the inspiration for that of the fictional Baruch in the imaginary world of an otherwise so well-made film.

Der Golem – wie er in die Welt kam
(The Golem – How He Came into the World)

In 1808 a German poet and collector of folksong, Achim von Arnim, collaborated with a philologist and collector of folktales and legends, Jakob Grimm, on a short-lived journal called *Zeitung für Einsiedler* (*Journal for Hermits*). He learnt from Grimm about Jewish legends that told of the making of *golems*, artificial beings moulded from clay and animated by mystical means; and when he came to write his most elaborate and covertly personal story, 'Isabella von Ägypten', he worked a golem into his plot. Cenrio, one of the characters of his tale, searching for means to placate a powerful Archduke,

> met again, at a peepshow, a learned Polish Jew, who had amused him, in earlier years, through his knowledge of the art of making golems. These are figures fashioned from clay in the shape of a human being, over which the mysterious and miracle-working Shemhamphorash [= *shem hamephorash*, 'the distinctive name', the name of God, the tetragrammaton] is spoken, on whose forehead the word Aemaeth [= *emeth*, truth] is written. This brings such golems to life and would make them useful for performing all sorts of tasks if they would not grow so quickly and thus become stronger than their creator. As long as one can reach their forehead, they can easily be annihilated – all one needs to do is wipe away the *Ae* from their forehead; this leaves *maeth*, which designates *death*. As soon as this is done, the golems crumble into a heap like dry clay. ... The old Jew was summoned, the Archduke asked him to make such a figure in the shape of the beautiful Isabella, and promised him royal rewards. The Jew warned him not to meddle with such images; in his native country, he said, they had caused many an unhappy accident ... (Schier (ed.), n.d.: 106)

It was through such Romantic writings that the notion of a golem entered German literature and culture. The strange spelling *Aemaet [h]* will be found to recur in the film to be discussed, though the process of making (and then disabling) the Golem is presented rather differently – for by then Jewish golem stories had been circulating freely in Germany and Austria. Many of these were collected and published by Chajim Bloch (*Oesterreichische Wochenschrift*, 1917), and subsequently, in augmented form, as a book; and they had found their way into several literary works in the German language, notably Gustav Meyrink's mystical thriller *Der Golem* of 1915.

Meyrink's novel is set in Prague; and while in earlier years stories about the making of golems had been attached to a variety of rabbis and cabbalists, by the time Bloch and Meyrink came to write, and Paul Wegener and Hendrik Galeen to make the first film on the subject (*Der Golem*, 1914), the tales had coalesced around one particular historical figure. This was Jehuda Loew ben Bezalel, who lived from 1512 to 1609 and was reverently known, among his flock in Prague, as the *Maharal* (= moreinu haRav Rabbi Loew – our teacher, the learned Rabbi Loew). It has been recorded that the Emperor Rudolph of Habsburg conferred with him in the Hradschin Palace on 16 February 1592; and while the Emperor's known interest in occult matters almost certainly led to their conversation (which seems to have been mostly carried on with a court official while the Emperor listened behind an arras), it was widely believed that the Maharal took the opportunity to plead the cause of the Jewish people subjected to discrimination and persecution in the Emperor's domains. Many stories were woven around this interview, some of them describing astonishing visions and entertainments conjured up by cabbalistic arts.

Like Meyrink's novel, the first film which the actor and director Paul Wegener and his Jewish scriptwriter Henrik Galeen based on such legends was set in *modern* Prague, not the Prague of the sixteenth century. In *Der Golem* of 1914 some workmen discover the abandoned clay figure of Rabbi Loew's Golem during renovation work at a synagogue. They sell it to a Jewish dealer in antiquities, played by Galeen himself, who has sufficient knowledge of the Cabbala and other mystical writings to be able to reanimate the figure and make it serve him in various menial ways. The animation has unexpected effects, however, for the Golem begins to covet the antique-dealer's wife, and runs amok when she rejects his advances. He eventually falls from a tower and is dashed to pieces. Wegener and his wife, Lyda Salmonova, shot another film variation of the Golem story, in 1917 (*Der Golem und die Tänzerin – The Golem and the Dancer*); but their most successful venture into this territory of Jewish legend was what would nowadays be called a 'prequel' to their first, recounting how Rabbi Loew came to make the creature in the first place. Hence the elaborate title *The Golem* (main title) *How he came into the World* (explanatory subtitle, relating it to the earlier film set in *modern* times).

This third Golem firm was made for Paul Davidson's PAGU unit and released in 1920, with Davidson himself figuring as producer. The screenplay was composed jointly by Wegener and Galeen; Wegener himself directed, with the help of Carl Boese; and Davidson saw to it that they had the very best his unit, and the Ufa studios, could provide. Karl Freund was the cameraman; Rochus Gliese designed the costumes; and the uniquely memorable sets were designed by one of the most celebrated architects of the day, Hans Poelzig, and built under the direction of another architect, Kurt Richter. The cast, too, was distinguished: Wegener himself played the Golem, Albert Steinrück Rabbi Loew, Ernst Deutsch (rapidly becoming a specialist in Jewish parts) the rabbi's assistant or *Famulus*, Lyda Salmonova (on Wegener's insistence) the rabbi's daughter Mirjam, Otto Gebühr (best known for his life-long impersonations of Frederick the Great) played the Emperor, and the winsome Loni Nest (the Shirley Temple of German silents) was the little blonde child who, playfully lifted up by the child-friendly Golem, innocently causes his destruction.

Little Loni's 'Aryan' blondeness is one of the many features of this film which recent commentators have adduced in support of their post-Shoa thesis that it is a document of German anti-Semitism. I disagree with this. Wegener was never anti-Semitic; Davidson, Galeen, Freund and Deutsch were themselves Jewish; and a little historical imagination should see the picturesque where post-Shoa critics see the degraded and oppressed, and the winsome where they see the aggressively 'Aryan'. The Jewish types the film introduces contain handsome and venerable people as well as others like the bribable guardian of the ghetto gate, whose acceptance of money to carry clandestine correspondence brings to mind the apothecary in *Romeo and Juliet*: 'My poverty, and not my will, consents'. Hans Poelzig, whose Expressionist designs dominate the film, was not conscious of making an anti-Semitic statement when he said that he wanted the very houses to 'speak with a Jewish accent' (*mauscheln*). Being shut into more and more overcrowded quarters (how full those narrow streets become!), forced to wear the stigmatising circular badges and pointed hats we see in the film, thrown into one panic after another (from the threat of merciless expulsion at the beginning of the film to the conflagration at the end), having to scratch a living in a sea of suspicion outside and lack of opportunity inside the ghetto, does not make for gracious living and courtly language. If a certain amount of cringing to less than admirable *goyim* is necessary, then that too is understandable. Worshipping God in the synagogue, supplicating or giving thanks to Him inside and outside the house of worship, is impressively presented by the film, as is the figure so important to Jews of earlier centuries: that of a learned and holy man who can win respect, through his learning and wisdom, outside the ghetto walls, and can communicate effectively with those who have control over his coreligionists. By virtue of the respect he commands, and by dint of the services he can perform for those in power (Rabbi Loew, we learn, has been able to avert danger from the Emperor by timely warnings, and even to save his life) such a man can bring about the annulment of 'evil decrees' that threaten ruin and death for the Jewish community. The *Maharal* is the community's mediator and intercessor before God and Emperor alike.

An 'evil decree' is precisely what sets in motion the action of *The Golem – How He Came into the World*. Rabbi Loew, played by Steinrück with dignity and authority, is discovered observing the starry heavens, with one constellation expressionistically highlighted, and reads there that another disaster is threatening his community: a disaster which becomes specific when a mailed first thrusts an Imperial decree onto the screen, reiterating accusations made against the Jews that begin by saddling them with guilt for the crucifixion of Christ and end by reproaching them for trying to make a living in a world that hedges them around with prohibitions and exclusions.

There follows a close-up of the Emperor, which shows him in ritual dignity, his crown on his head, applying the great seal to the decree of expulsion. A decree so solemnly ratified, we are to surmise, would be difficult to circumvent. The sealed scroll is then given to one of the young idlers standing around, a foppish figure of a knight who looks more like an Osric than a Galahad; his name, we learn, is Florian. Charged with delivering the decree to the Jews, Florian is ushered into the presence of the Chief Rabbi, played by Hans Sturm as a venerable elder with an impressive mass of white hair and beard that contrasts with the whispy growths of the *shammes* (beadle) who shows the knight in. The arrogant stance of the wretched Florian, who waves a long-stemmed rose about in these scenes, is met by the rabbi's deference to an emissary of the Emperor. Condescendingly Florian agrees to accompany the rabbi to the famous Rabbi Loew, to whom the community looks when danger threatens it and who must therefore take whatever actions the decree makes necessary. The parallel most viewers of the 1920s would see here is with the kind of Tsarist oppression and exclusion portrayed in *The Yellow Passport* and *Marked Out*. The sympathy of many cinema-goers would therefore be with the Jews rather than their persecutors; and what they are shown of the courtiers around the Emperor (beginning with the unattractively gap-toothed Florian, played by Lothar Müthel) is not likely to shift their sympathies another way.

Wegener and Boese intercut these scenes with others that show preparations for the making of a golem, who, the rabbi foresees, will help him avert the disaster threatening the Jews of Prague. Such preparations begin with books, huge learned tomes in which we see Rabbi Loew and Chief Rabbi Jehuda immersed. The latter, however, will be reading the Scriptures, Talmud and commentaries, while the former – as many a close-up shows – is studying something more esoteric, books of secret, mystical doctrines normally kept locked away in their own cupboard, but now taken out to show, with diagrams, how a golem can be fashioned and animated. Astrology, suggested by the opening reading of stars, plays an important part here, as some of the diagrams indicate.

We then have one of those images of descent which so often set symbolic bells ringing in the heads of seasoned film-goers. The rabbi goes down into the lowest recesses of his house – at the opposite extreme from the (equally symbolic) tower needed for observation of the stars which surmounts the house – and breaks the seal of a secret room, which he then enters. A drawing of a golem, surrounded and traversed by secret signs, is seen on the wall, echoing a similar diagram shown earlier in one of the rabbi's books; and in full view of this the rabbi now moulds a mass of clay into an image that gradually takes on human features. It is in one of these early scenes in the rabbi's house that we meet the rabbi's *Famulus*, played by Ernst Deutsch – pale, dressed in black, with huge expressive eyes that at intervals dwell with love on Mirjam, the rabbi's daughter – engaged at a furnace needed for alchemical experiments. Lyda Salmonova, who plays Mirjam, is the least satisfactory members of the cast; she seems rather too matronly for the girlish flirtatiousness she is asked to mime, and her later mimings of extreme physical passion employ a style one would have hoped the example of Asta Nielsen, who showed how real passions could be conveyed convincingly on the silent screen, had banished for ever.

Summoned from his subterranean task to meet the Emperor's emissary, Rabbi Loew sends a message in reply, reminding the sovereign of how horoscopes he had cast for him in the past had saved that sovereign's life, and asking for an audience. Mirjam brings a goblet to Florian from which she herself takes a sip, sidles up close to him, and receives the rose he has been playing with. Rabbi Jehuda and Rabbi Loew look apprehensively at these goings-on, fearing that Mirjam's sexual awakening would bring danger.

Back at his underground work Rabbi Loew tries to lift the heavy Golem statue but finds the strain too great; he is therefore forced to summon his *Famulus* for help, swearing him to secrecy about what will shortly transpire. Cut to Florian arriving at court with the Rabbi's request, back to the underground scene where the *Famulus* recoils with terror at the as yet lifeless Golem statue; then cut to Mirjam, left alone with Florian who has brought the Emperor's answer, and crosscutting between Loew and the *Famulus* dragging the statue upstairs, Mirjam and Florian in the throes of sexual desire, the *Famulus* unwrapping the statue while the Rabbi sees Florian's white horse in the street below and thus knows the messenger has arrived. Mirjam and Florian quickly draw apart when the Rabbi enters the room – but not soon enough to prevent the Rabbi's seeing what's been happening. The rabbi then reads the scroll Florian has brought in which the Emperor grants his request for an audience 'in memory of your services' and in the hope that he will entertain the court with his magic at a 'Rose Festival' (hence the rose Florian has been playing with). When the emissary has gone, the rabbi upbraids his daughter for her unseemly behaviour, even squeezes his hands around her throat, but then desists to say, ominously: 'You shame me, but I will soon have someone to guard you.' Another task, then, for the not yet animated Golem! A shot of Florian riding over a bridge contrasts strikingly with the crowded ghetto streets – there is so much more space outside – and introduces into the film one of those silhouette shots, often against a bright sky and dark foreground, which are as distinctive a feature of its style as the milling crowds in narrow streets amid bulging Expressionist houses, or the overfilled synagogue with agitated figures supplicating God, striking their breasts and lifting their hands.

Two large tomes dominate what follows: the first has a drawing of a golem interspersed with strange letters that resemble – but are not identical with – Hebrew ones, an astrological drawing, and a German text that tells how a golem 'was made long ago by a magician of Thessaly. Place the magic amulet on its breast, and it will live and breathe as long as it wears it'. But what is contained in the magic amulet? Watched with apprehension by his *Famulus*, Loew now brings a second, even more secret, tome, from which he learns that Ashtaroth guards the magic word which she can be forced to reveal by someone who possesses the key of Solomon and observes the right constellation of stars. Thessaly – Ashtaroth – Solomon: the Greek and the Hebrew, those ancient antagonists, are brought together with the Canaanite and Phoenician goddess of fertility mentioned in the Old Testament, by a wonder-working rabbi whose learning far transcends that of the coreligionists in whose service he uses whatever power his knowledge gives him. This power, as the Emperor acknowledges, has also done signal service to his Christian sovereign; and it is soon to be used to entertain the court.

We now approach the only conjuration scene in the German 'silent' cinema which can stand comparison with that in Murnau's *Faust*. In my view it is even better. The waving of a wand and an invocation to 'Astarte' brings a ring of fire – which involved building the whole set on a platform beneath which fire and smoke could be sent upwards. There follow electrically generated lightning flashes of an intensity never seen on screen before, and the gradual emergence of a terrifying head with smoke issuing from its lips. This smoke forms itself into the magic word AEMAET needed to animate the Golem. The *Famulus* faints in terror, as a corner of his garment that has strayed outside the magic circle catches fire; when the rabbi has resuscitated him, he tries in vain to keep his master from going further. Signalling the *Famulus* to bring the statue closer, Rabbi Loew prepares the amulet with the scroll containing the magic word inside it and places it into a hollow on the Golem's chest. By a substitution few cinemagoers will notice, Paul Wegener, made up exactly like the clay statue we have seen so far, has taken the place of that statue, opens his eyes, moves his head, and starts to walk unsteadily at the rabbi's command, knocking over the *Famulus* who happens to be in the way. This introduces a complicated relationship between the *Famulus* and the Golem which will be echoed in that between Frankenstein's assistant, played by Dwight Frye, and his creature, played by Boris Karloff, in the first of James Whale's

Frankenstein films that has – not by accident! – much in common with Wegener's.

I have introduced these early scenes in some detail in order to show that there is nothing intrinsically anti-Semitic in the narrative or the staging. The rabbi's magic is white rather than black, and employed less selfishly than Faust's. Mirjam is not, as some have claimed, a seductive Jewess out to snare a Gentile, but a silly sensual girl swept off her feet by a foppish courtier out for adventure and used to intrigue – a man she finds more attractive than the pale *Famulus* who has been her only young male companion so far. Rabbi Jehuda, like Rabbi Loew, is a venerable figure; and there are many attractive men, women and children among those who perforce crowd the ghetto to which they are confined by external decree, and from which another decree may summarily expel them. The Golem is created because Rabbi Loew feels he may help avert the misfortune that threatens the community. His obedience is tested by various domestic tasks imposed on him by his master (including shopping expeditions that accustom the ghetto population to seeing him among its midst and delight the ghetto children). The function for which he was given life is fulfilled when he is exhibited to the Emperor and his courtiers to relieve their boredom, and is able to use his superhuman strength to mitigate the disaster their stupidity and frivolity brought on them. He saves many lives, and gains the prize the rabbi had sought: the rescinding of the decree of expulsion with which the film opened.

The Golem himself is most impressively played by Wegener, who shows convincingly how consciousness dawns and grows in this creature – including a rudimentary aesthetic sense when he is delighted by a flower given to him by a young woman (played, incidentally, by Greta Schroeder, who would soon fascinate and ensnare a vampire in Murnau's *Nosferatu*). He also feels, as well he might, a special kinship with children, which leads to his destruction at the end of the film. More fateful, however, both to himself and other, is his increasing rage and resentment – at the rabbi, who threatens to take away the amulet that gives him life, at the *Famulus*, who tries to control him (vainly, as it turns out, like all sorcerers' apprentices), and at the knight who has invaded the house on an amorous quest. An arousal of tender feelings leads him to a clumsy investigation of Mirjam's prostrate body, to an attempt at abduction (dragging her by the hair), and then to saving her from the fire he had started by laying her gently on a ledge, well out of harm's way, where she can be found by her father and her fellow-Jews. We see him, in the end, break the heavy wooden bolt that secures the ghetto gates from the inside, and step outside onto a flowery meadow and into unwonted liberty. He is attracted by a group of playing children, who run away in fear – except for one fair-haired little girl who offers him an apple. He lifts her up tenderly, and when she playfully removes the amulet from his chest, he falls down lifeless. The other children return and play around him, covering him with flowers, but run away again as the ghetto folk, led by Rabbi Loew, approach and drag the Golem back into the ghetto whose gates close behind them. We know, however, that though the gates are closed, they are not locked – the bolt that secured them has been shattered. The film ends with a large version of the Star of David, of which we had seen other versions in various contexts earlier, to symbolise the eternal Jewish people from whom fourfold disaster has been averted: the decree of expulsion, now rescinded; a potentially calamitous fire, providentially put out; an inter-ethnic crisis averted by the death of the amorous knight while his intended plaything, Mirjam, survived; and the Golem, who had run amok after being created simply to serve, now made safe until his next revival: a revival anticipated by the first of the Golem films to which, as we have seen, *The Golem – How He Came into the World* was a 'prequel'.

My rejection of the newly fashionable reading of this film as anti-semitic is strengthened by what we see of the Emperor and his courtiers at the Feast of Roses to which Rabbi Loew has been summoned. The rabbi responds to the Emperor's request for magical entertainment with the earnest announcement that what he will be offering is no mindless pastime, but a vision of his people's patriarchal ancestry in the hope that it will arouse better knowledge of a community now crammed into ghettos, and greater respect for it. The magic must not be disturbed by frivolous talk and laughter, for this would turn the magical forces benevolently summoned up into dangerous ones threatening the assembled company. (It will be noticed that this theme of benevolent magic turning dangerous parallels the Golem story itself.) The scene that follows resembles an early version of the cinema, as a stage-like alcove lights up to show a patriarchal group traversing what resembles a screen, while behind them we see an endless procession of the Jewish people walking through desert sands (or a snowy landscape, as in *City without Jews*?) suggesting the plight of a people constantly forced into exile by decrees like that just promulgated by the Emperor – a suggestion strengthened by that Christian symbol of the Jewish plight, the Wandering (or Eternal) Jew, *der ewige Jude*. All the courtiers can do, however, at this solemn reminder, is roar with laughter at some quip by the court jester at the Wandering Jew's expense. This brings about the disaster the rabbi had warned about before acceding to the Emperor's request. It takes the form of the collapse of the hall in which the court is assembled, burying many under the rubble, forcing others to leap from high windows. The rabbi had, however, brought the Golem with him, to the great astonishment of the courtiers, some of whose overfamiliarity had angered the increasingly sensitised creature; but it is the Golem's strength which now saves the situation, as his master commands him to stop the roof from caving in completely by bracing its supports with his powerful arms and shoulders. He thus saves many lives, including that of the Emperor, who, in gratitude, rescinds the 'evil decree' which had caused Rabbi Loew to animate the creature in the hope of just such an outcome.

With its sets that have a strange organic quality, as if the ghetto houses were a body imprisoning – but also protecting – the smaller bodies huddled within them; its use of white rather than black magic, designed to help instead of harming anyone (though like all magic it is dangerous when tried by sorcerers' apprentices or when frivolous people disregard clearly issued warnings); its clear narrative line and smooth crosscuttings that establish relationships or simultaneities without confusion; its excellent performances by Steinrück, Wegener and Deutsch; its balance of silhouetted scenes before wide horizons and unencumbered landscapes against agitated scenes in crowded ghetto streets and festive crowds at the Rose Festival; its ability to use relatively simple cinematic resources to create cinematic magic that thrills through its transcendence of everyday experience; its depiction of a Jewish world ruled by all too justified fears, but also buoyed up by trust in the efficacy of prayer to God (to whom thanks must be given after averted disaster), and hope invested in sages that can mediate between the ghetto and the powers that have it at their mercy – with all this, and more, *The Golem – How He Came into the World* is one of the glories of the Weimar cinema. It tells a tale more fantastic than those underlying *The Yellow Passport, The Ancient Law* or *Marked Out*, based on themes that originated with Jewish mystics and cabbalists but also held appeal for German Romantics, later novelists and dramatists like Gustav Meyrink and H. Leyvick, and Hollywood filmmakers like James Whale. It deserves to be rescued from those read into it, under the impact of later events, anti-Semitic innuendoes that never entered the minds of its distinguished makers and participants.

Chapter 3

COMEDIES OF THE 'SILENT' PERIOD

Schuhpalast Pinkus (Shoe Salon Pinkus)

This film, made for Davidson's PAGU (Union) organisation, and first shown in the middle of the First World War, in 1916, was directed by Ernst Lubitsch, who also played the main part and had a hand in the screenplay credited to Hanns Kräly and Erich Schönfelder. *The Yellow Passport* had fulfilled the aims formulated by German generals keen to see entertainment value married to the kind of propaganda which put enemies – such as Tsarist Russia had been during the First World War – into a bad light, and Germans who could make so tolerant a film, into a good one. Lubitsch's comedies had nothing of this. They breathed a carnival spirit, animated by the irreverent temperament of the Jewish characters in which he had his first successes in the cinema, after comparatively minor parts on stages under Reinhardt's direction.

We first meet Sally Pinkus, the central figure of *Shoe Salon Pinkus*, as a schoolboy in Berlin, living with his portly, middle-class Jewish parents who are keen to see him do well at the *Gymnasium* he attends, but finding him more than reluctant to get up in the morning or to study for his exams. He is far more interested in flirting with the housemaid, squiring pretty schoolgirls around, chatting them up and buying them ice creams with the ample pocket-money his parents provide, between affectionate hugs from his mother and occasional slaps from his excitable but fundamentally equally affectionate father. At school, where he is always late ('Ich komme früh genug zu spät', he says as he turns over in bed – 'I'll be late soon enough'), he is clearly the class clown; the other boys watch with amusement how he again and again gets a rise out of his fiercely bearded martinet of a teacher with a mixture of impudence, apparent conformity and plain deceit. The teacher is played, with Prussian imperiousness and stiffness, by the scriptwriter Hanns Kräly; he and Lubitsch are clearly enjoying their double act, which ends when Sally, whom we have earlier seen persuading his father that he is hard at work studying for his exams while in reality he shuts his books to enjoy a forbidden cigarette, is caught cheating at these exams and is ejected from his school. The first of the three 'acts' into which the film is divided ends with his dejected appearance at the family meal, his father's rage, his mother's interposition of herself as he seeks to strike Sally (as we have seen him do earlier, when he breaks up a gaggle of girls assembled around his son), Sally's flight – and his glee as he sees through the keyhole that his father is now busy trying to pacify his mother. This is one of many 'outside the door' and 'through the keyhole' scenes, in this and many later films, which become an integral part of the elliptical 'Lubitsch touch'. We leave young Sally hugging and striking himself with glee.

Act two begins with an unsuccessful application to a prospective Gentile employer, who takes one look at Sally's damning school report and sends him away, refusing to listen to his pleas. Dejectedly Sally walks along a Berlin street and comes to a halt before a small, unfashionable shoemaker's shop. In front of the shop door he sees a delightful Gentile girl – played by an as yet uncredited Ossi Oswalda, who is destined to become one of the finest comedy actors of the German silent film. There seems to be immediate mutual attraction; and since the shop door bears a sign which signifies that Ossi's shoemaker-father seeks an apprentice, Sally applies, finds that the shoemaker attaches no importance to school reports, and is engaged as salesman and sweeper-up. He appears triumphantly at his parents' midday meal, and as he slurps his soup he tells them that his has secured a 'brilliant appointment' ('eine glänzende Stellung'): gleeful hugs and shoulder-clappings are his reward. He soon disappoints his employer, however, by lazing about, refusing to serve a customer who has a hole in his sock, altering the calendar to make it appear that the weekend has come a day early, snacking on an egg and strewing the shells all around the shop, and, when ordered to sweep up, preferring to take Ossi for a cuddle behind a pile of shoeboxes. His stormy love-making leads to a collapse of the sheltering boxes; the indignant father sees what has been going on and, taking his unsatisfactory apprentice by the scruff of the neck, literally throws him out into the street. Sally takes flight, not without a feeble shaking of his fist at his erstwhile employer.

We next see Sally at a newspaper office, where he puts in an advertisement extolling himself and asking for first-class firms to offer him suitable employment – not without being indignantly challenged by other customers whose queue he seeks to crash, and by a customer seeking to write out his advertising text only to find that Sally had appropriated the office pen. Sally leaves unrepentant and truculent. His advertisement pays off, however, and he is summoned for an interview to a more upmarket shoe emporium owned by a man called Meyersohn, played *con brio* by Guido Herzfeld. Unlike his previous employer, this one is clearly Jewish; and though he is at first disinclined to employ this brash young man, he soon sees something of himself in Sally when the latter's eloquence is given full rein. They shake hands, and Sally characteristically congratulates Meyersohn on having gained so valuable an addition to his staff. In the shop he is in his element among the female employees, to whom he tells jokes which one suspects to be off-colour, though his attempts to ingratiate himself with the manageress lead to a setback and subsequent ridicule. That is one mistake – but a worse one follows, when he is so taken with the pretty foot of a lady customer that he gives it an affectionate tickle. The customer leaves in high dudgeon, the manageress summons Meyerson who dismisses Sally – only to reinstate him when Sally proves more adept at persuading a wealthy dancer to buy a pair of shoes than the boss himself. Between this customer, called Melitta Hervé, and Sally an immediate spark of sympathy seems to fly, and Sally's offer to deliver the purchase personally to her home is graciously accepted. Meyersohn, however, is equally struck by this good-looking *shikse*, and seeks to deliver the shoes himself: a plan which miscarries when he arrives at Miss Hervé's house only to find that Sally has secretly repacked the parcel which now contains a dreadful broken-down old pair of men's boots. Going dejectedly down the stairs he meets Sally coming up with another parcel, containing the right shoes; his attempt to wrest it away and carry it up himself is frustrated when Sally enquires after Mrs Meyersohn – a veiled threat that he would tell the wife of her husband's amorous quest. This episode, by the way, parallels an earlier one, in which Sally's father chases him away from the housemaid only to flirt with her in the same way as his son had just done. Unlike Pinkus senior, however, Meyersohn has to retire in defeat, leaving the field open for Sally, who is graciously received ('I am the right one', he tells the dancer's puzzled maid), given a cup of tea, amuses his hostess by dunking some pastry into it, and is finally offered a generous loan to open a shop of his own with the dancer as silent partner. He accepts with alacrity, and bursts into Meyersohn's private office to abrogate his employment – keeping his hat on his head and smoking a big cigar whose smoke he blows into his former employer's face. This scene, introducing a self-confident Sally who no longer feels the need to kowtow to anyone, ends the second 'act' of this cinematic comedy.

Act three shows Sally as chief of the 'Shoe-Palace' that bears his name and gives the film its title. Sitting at his desk smoking his cigar and engaged in checking some papers with two deferential male clerks (a book-keeper and an accountant, perhaps?), he exudes a proprietary pride which appears even more clearly when he enters his emporium down an imposing staircase, sends his gossiping staff (we count six women and six men) sternly back to work, as Meyersohn had done when Sally was an employee, waking a slumbering messenger boy by slapping his head in the way he had once been slapped by his first employer. None of the employees appear to be Jewish – there is no equivalent of young Sally among them. He complains that he has a large staff, financed by the loan from Melitta Hervé, but as yet no customers. This is a challenge, however, which he is well prepared to meet. From a stage-side box at one of Melitta's dance recitals (the charming actress playing this part is an atrocious dancer) he advertises his wares and then distributes handbills announcing a show of fashionable footwear at his emporium the next day. The show is a success, the papers praise his ingenuity, his business thrives, and as he prepares to repay the loan he had from Melitta, he stops in the middle of writing a cheque to propose that they should marry and thus keep the money 'in the family'. Melitta agrees, and the film ends with an embrace.

The words 'Jude' or 'jüdisch' are never mentioned, yet there is no doubt that the central figure, his parents and his second employer are Jewish, while most of the other characters are not. The first clue is in the names. 'Sally' is a short form of 'Salomon' (Hebrew Shlomoh, Yiddish Shloyme); 'Pinkus' often served as a Latinisation/Germanisation of the Hebrew Pinhas, with welcome suggestions of the onomatopoeic German slang-term 'Pinke' or 'Pinke-Pinke' (= money). The actor Emil Jannings had a pet bird he called Pinkus, which he pretended to use as his financial adviser. Lubitsch often used names felt to be Jewish for the characters he played in his early films: Moritz Abramowsky (where 'Moritz' serves as a Germanisation of the Hebrew Moshe, Yiddish Moyshe), Moritz Rosenthal, Moritz Apfelreis, and Sally Meyer, where 'Meyer' is an equivalent of the Hebrew 'Me'ir', a name later adopted by an Israeli Prime Minister whose original American name had been Golda Meyerson. And a form of this last appellation 'Meyersohn', serves Lubitsch to indicate the Jewish provenance of Sally's second employer. But there are also physiognomic features which were felt to be particularly Jewish – those of Lubitsch himself recur with distressing frequency in the vicious caricatures with which the cartoonist 'Fips' whipped up anti-Jewish feeling in the scurrilous Nazi rag *Der Stürmer* – and a wealth of gestures, with hands, arms, the whole body, of which Lubitsch makes more than ample use. One particular movement of the right hand, lifting it shoulder-high and shaking the open palm vigorously backwards and forwards to indicate something dubious about a situation or an opponent, occurs with particular frequency, as does an expressive use of the tongue to suggest mockery or a gourmet's enjoyment of something seen, felt or imagined.

One of the intertitles of this silent film reads 'Sally schmust'. 'Schmusen' is a word that has come into the German language, via Yiddish and thieves' slang, from Hebrew *shemua*, meaning 'something heard', 'a rumour'; its basic meaning in German is 'ingratiating talk', 'spooning', 'soft-soaping', 'buttering up'. And that, precisely, is what we see Sally doing throughout this 'Comedy in Three Acts': with his parents, his teacher, potential and actual employers, fellow employees, customers, and a wider public in a theatre and at a fashion-show. We don't even have to read, in the intertitles, anything he actually says: we just watch how his torrent of speech is accompanied by constantly changing facial expressions and eye movements, a vast variety of hand movements and body positions which are so eloquent that we can mentally supply the unheard words that go with them. 'Schmusen' is not always successful: it does not prevent his being expelled from school or thrown out bodily by his first employer (the scriptwriter Erich Schönfelder, who plays that employer, must have enjoyed that!); but it gains him a lot of female attention – from his schooldays onwards he is shown to be adept at chatting up pretty girls and women – as well as material success.

'Schmusen' is central to the film in a wider sense. It is not only set in the milieu of the Berlin fashion industry, in which Jews were indeed prominent and with which Lubitsch had a strong family connection, but also in the world of advertising, in which once again many Jews had prominent positions. The inventive publicity director of Ufa, Rudi Feld, is a famous example. The very opening credits of *Shoe Salon Pinkus* illustrate the theme. They show a book opening at various pages to give us the names and photographs of the scriptwriters, and three of the principal players (including of course Lubitsch himself as actor *and* director); but they also tell us that the fashionable shoes featured in the film may be had in an actually existing emporium whose name and Berlin address are prominently displayed. The last page shown is given over to the word 'UNION', which designates the PAGU production unit controlled by Paul Davidson, and the Davidson-owned cinema at which the film was first shown. Within the film we are shown an advertisement Sally inserts in a newspaper after his first employer had thrown him out: in it he exaggerates the attractiveness of his own appearance, the nature of the shop in which he had gained his first experience of the footwear trade and of the position he had held there, and he ends with a coda that only leading firms in the trade need send in their offers of employment – others would be thrown into the waste-paper basket. This fantasy gets him an interview with Meyerson, who is at first inclined to dismiss him on sight, but is then won over by Sally's (eloquently mimed) 'Shmus' – and perhaps by a recollection of his own beginnings.

The very naming of his own firm, once Sally has become independent, is redolent of the connection between advertising and the cinema: he calls it a 'palace', Schuh*palast*, in emulation of large cinemas, picture palaces, like the later Ufa-Palast near Berlin's Zoo Station. And it is as the owner of this new 'palace' that Sally brings off his greatest advertising coup. At a dance recital of his business partner Melitta Hervé he appears in a stage box and enthuses the audience about the excellence of his wares in an eloquent speech accompanied by a flower-encompassed specimen of 1916 elegance brought onto the stage. After what we have just witnessed as an example of Melitta's terpsichorean incompetence this seems to come as a welcome relief to the audience, which shows itself eager to take one of the advertising flyers Sally hands out at the exit, and to turn up at the shoe-fashion show these promise. The staircase that leads from the shoe salon to the proprietor's private office has now been horizontally lengthened by a catwalk; a number of attractive ladies walk down the stairs and along the catwalk in Pinkus shoes, the virtue of each of which the proprietor demonstrates eloquently and gleefully; the models then pose on the stairs, with their skirts sufficiently raised to exhibit footwear and ankle to best advantage. The papers report the success of this, and Pinkus's business is lifted out of its initial doldrums into prosperity.

For its comic purposes *Shoe Salon Pinkus* uses a number of clichés of Jewish behaviour, most of which also feature in jokes circulating and eagerly retold in contemporary Jewish circles. Sally's disrespect for established hierarchies and authority – before he himself comes to *be* in authority – is disguised by apparent compliance, but ever and again suddenly revealed by a grin, a gesture, or an irrepressible quip. His characteristic way of deflecting possible aggression from non-Jewish fellow pupils is to make himself the class clown whom the others are only too glad to help in his various tricks. Urban Jews were often charged with physical awkwardness and ungainliness: Sally shows this by his inability to jump over a vaulting-horse in a physical training session; a failure he manages to disguise from the teacher but not from the boys in his class who watch him with glee. This trick, by the way, chimes in with, Sally's self-description in the advertisement he inserts in the job-seeker column of a newspaper: appearance is constantly substituted for reality, and Sally gains praise, or a job, as a reward for what he has not really accomplished. Sally's later trick of altering the size-number on a pair of shoes in order to flatter lady customers into believing that their feet are in fact smaller, and therefore more attractive, than they really are, is another instance of this. It also demonstrates a widespread feeling shared by many upwardly mobile Jews that role-playing is necessary for social advancement. This will figure again in a later chapter of this book, devoted to Carl Boese's *Keine Feier ohne Meyer* (*Without Meyer, No Celebration is Complete*, 1931), where role-playing does not obtain its object as easily as it tends to do in the garment industry films of the early Lubitsch.

As for Sally's gymnastic incompetence: when it is a matter of shinning up a climbing-rope that enables a view of a company of girls on the other side of the fence he has no difficulty at all, either in ascending or in rapidly slithering down when his teacher climbs up another rope to see what is happening. Sexuality is as potent a force in Lubitsch's films as the desire to get on; and these early works set in the Berlin garment industry exemplify one of the many themes of Jewish jokes to be taken up by this director: the attraction Jewish men feel towards Gentile girls when their families expect them not to 'marry out'. Sally is a master of charming girls and women individually and in groups – he squires them about, buys them ice cream, carries their parcels, tells them jokes, makes appreciative faces at them, and – above all – chats them up. 'Sally schmust!'. His joke telling in Meyersohn's emporium is a development of the class-clown idea: and here, as in the vaulting-horse scene, he collects unearned praise through a deft substitution of appearance for reality. As a boy he had assembled around him a circle of girls which is dispersed when his father pulls him away by the ear and slaps him for a previous misdemeanour; in Meyersohn's store his 'Ducdame' charm (as Jacques calls it in *As You Like It*) assembles shop-girls into a circle around him and has them shaking with laughter; but when Meyersohn appears to shoo them to work he holds Sally up as an example – for Sally has managed to slip up a ladder, unseen by his boss, and appear the very picture of diligence on the employer's behalf. Meyersohn and Pinkus senior share Sally's attraction to non-Jewish women: Pinkus *père* flirts with the servant-girl in exactly the same way as Sally had earlier, and Meyersohn tries to supplant Sally in Melitta's favour. Sally, at least, is in a position to offer an exogamous marriage, while the two elder men already have Jewish wives – a situation which, once again, is the subject of many a Jewish joke. Nor is *Shoe Salon Pinkus* innocent of the most unsavoury subject of such jokes (mainly those invented by fastidious German Jews about their East European coreligionists): what we see of Sally's morning ablutions does not inspire confidence in their efficacy. But then: he is a schoolboy at the time, one who prefers to stay in bed for that extra quarter of an hour before being shooed off to his unloved Latin lessons and regards washing as a luxury that can be dispensed with.

Lubitsch's father, a 'Mantelmann' or supplier of ladies' coats, and, briefly, Lubitsch himself, had been part of the Berlin clothing trade ('Konfektion'). Lubitsch senior had operated out of the Scheunenviertel, the Jewish district, which contained many jobbing tailors who supplied the goods he sold (as well, we should remember, as many early shop-front cinemas). Sally Pinkus's first employer has his shop in what is clearly an unfashionable district, and the wares displayed in this window are strictly utilitarian and out of tune with high fashion; Meyersohn's emporium is very much more up-market, and Sally's own 'palace' would seem to be located somewhere on or near the Kurfürstendamm. Lubitsch and his designers are adept at conveying such gradations to his audience through details of furnishing, décor and deployment of space, as Sally moves from his middle-class home, whose clumsy furniture and dingy wallpaper do not suggest fastidious taste, to the heights of the Berlin fashion industry. His way upwards is indicated by successive changes in dress: from the nightshirt which, to save time, he seems to be using as a daytime undergarment, and the knickerbocker suit with the incongruous approximation of an Eton collar he wears at school, he passes to a grey boy's suit he has outgrown, and then to a succession of ever smarter dark suits, culminating in the cutaway he sports as the proud proprietor of his 'palace'. His headgear keeps pace: we follow him from the school-cap of his early years' indicating the upward mobility his parents seek to ensure for him by enrolling him in a Gymnasium (a plan scuttled by his aversion to booklearning – he'll never become 'my son, the doctor'!) to the soft hat he wears as a humble job-seeker, to the bowler he dons when, sure of his own commercial flair, he persuades Meyersohn to employ him, to the top-hat of his shoe-palace apotheosis. The rise is accompanied by a change from the cigarettes he first smokes surreptitiously in his parents' house to the cigar that becomes as much successful Sally's trademark as it became Lubitsch's own.

The verbal wit that constantly appears in the intertitles with – one suspects – some input from Lubitsch himself, marries the German-Jewish with the Berlinese. 'Ihnen gesagt, Herr Lehrer', a phrase addressed to the teacher that veers between 'You should be so lucky', 'just listen to yourself', 'that applies to you as much as, or more than, to me', and 'I could wish it for *you*', is typically German-Jewish; but the answer, in this same exchange, to the teacher's 'I bet you overslept again!' – 'die Wette haben Sie gewonnen' ('that's a bet you've won') is Berlinese. The famous *Berliner Schnauze*, the ready tongue that has a quick and witty answer for everything, meets the wit that created the Jewish joke, whose mechanisms of condensation, indirect representation and displacement Freud analysed in a book that has found so many commentators and successors since its first publication in 1905.

Sabine Hake, to whom we owe the most incisive study of the early Lubitsch, has pertinently quoted Freud's reconstruction of the daydream of a poor boy on his way to a potential employer to whom he has an introduction: 'The content of his phantasy will perhaps be something like this: he is given a job, finds favour with his new employer, makes himself indispensable in the business, is taken into his employer's house, marries the charming young daughter of the house, and then himself becomes a director of the business, first as his employer's partner, and then as his successor' (*Standard edition of the Complete Psychological works of Sigmund Freud* ed. J. Strachey, London 1953–66, Vol. 9, p. 148 – quoted in 1992: 39). As Hake recognises, an early film like *Der Stolz der Firma* (*The Pride of the Firm*, 1914), directed by Carl Wilhelm and starring Lubitsch, follows this pattern very closely. Here a Jewish boy from the provinces loses his first job in the remote town of Rawitsch through an accident in which he clumsily smashes a shop window, but is given a recommendation to a Jewish employer in the Berlin clothing industry, where he is at first laughed at because of his provincial get-up and awkward speech and gestures, but soon learns to adapt himself and make himself indispensable, rises in the firm, and indeed, at the end, marries the boss's daughter, taking her on a honeymoon journey to Venice that takes a roundabout route via Rawitsch – the pride of his home town no less than that of the firm in which he is now a partner. Another film, however, *Der Blusenkönig* (*The Blouse King*, 1917), directed by Lubitsch, written by him with Erich Schönfelder, and starring him as another Sally, Sally Katz, proceeds rather differently. We find him once again employed in the rag trade and meeting the boss's daughter, who is anxious – indeed, over-anxious – to marry him. The daughter is played by the same actress whose character becomes the young man's bride in *The Pride of the Firm*; but this time, her Jewish features, mannerisms and matrimonial eagerness repel rather than attract young Katz. Nor is the lady's father at all eager for the match. He doesn't want another rag trade merchant in the family; he wants an academic, 'my son-in-law the lawyer', or 'my son-in-law the doctor'. Believing, however, that Sally is as eager to marry his daughter as the latter is to land him, he buys him off with an offer – eagerly accepted – of a partnership in his firm whose chief business is in fashionable ladies' blouses and similar garments. Well on his way to becoming the 'Blouse King' of Berlin, Sally goes off to woo the attractive non-Jewish manageress of the business of which he is now a partner. The fragment of the film which has been preserved shows him gleefully licking his finger (Lubitsch's use of the tongue in these films deserves a study in itself) as he presses the bell that gives access to his chosen lady's house. The intertitles of this fragment are full of recognisably German-Jewish turns of phrase – far more than *Shoe Salon Pinkus* which resembles it in other respects, and far more than *The Pride of the Firm*. In *Pinkus*, the young man is not an awkward provincial, but a true Berliner on the make – who, however, thwarts the ambition his parents share with the *Blouse King* boss (played by Guido Herzfeld, who plays Meyersohn, a very similar part, in *Pinkus*), the ambition to have an academic ('ein Doktor!') in the family, to pursue his upward climb in the fashionable footwear trade instead. He does not, however, become Meyersohn' partner or marry his daughter: he takes leave of his erstwhile boss, who had just tried to muscle in on Melitta Hervé, with characteristic insolence, by blowing cigar smoke in his face, and the marriage he contracts is once again a marriage outside the Jewish community.

A later stage of the 'Sally' character is suggested by a film made two years after *Shoe Salon Pinkus*, entitled *Meyer aus Berlin* (1918). Married to a devoted Gentile wife, affluent Sally Meyer (played, of course, by Lubitsch himself, who also directed the film scripted, once again, by Kräly and Schönfelder) has become tired of the business and matrimonial round and needs to get away for a while. He feigns an illness and persuades a friendly doctor to prescribe 'Tapetenwechsel' – a change of scene. After measuring some maps with a pair of compasses (getting all the distances wrong) he decides on the Tyrolese mountains as his holiday venue and buys what tourists consider a Tyrolese mountaineer's outfit. When he walks the Berlin streets in this garb he is asked where the masked ball is to which he is obviously going, and in which theatre or variety establishment he might be appearing in such a strange get-up; and when he arrives at his destination, we find that he has mistaken the Bavarian Alps near Berchtesgaden for the Austrian Tyrol. We know this because the mountain that dominates the scene is the Watzmann; Meyer remains blissfully ignorant of his geographical confusion, and asked whether he knows the Watzmann, he thinks 'der Watzmann' is a man he may have met sometime, who is married to … someone or other. The incongruousness of an obviously urban person with Jewish features appearing in German regional costume was a frequent subject of cartoonists in Wilhelminian and Weimar days – Karl Oberländer especially was an adept at not ill-natured cartoons on this theme which Lubitsch and his scriptwriters have adapted to their own comic purposes.

The plot, involving marital misunderstandings and reconciliations, does not here concern us. What is important is that Lubitsch's performance enables us to sympathise with a central protagonist who has nouveau riche characteristics, who is literally 'pushy' when faced with a queue or with a table-setting that does not provide him with a seat next to the lady of his choice, who fears physical exertion (there is a splendid dream sequence in which he reduces the height of the Watzmann he has been asked to climb by successive elimination of a nought from the number of metres that indicates its elevation); who gets up at a table d'hôte, at which everyone but he is dressed in sober evening clothes, interrupts all conversation by yelling for silence, and then introduces himself ('Sally Meyer aus Berlin'); who insults gentlemen who covet the acquaintance of a lady he has chosen to honour with his attentions; who refuses to fight a duel when challenged ('all right – if I'm late, start without me!'); who shows little interest in the glories of the Alpine landscape which he reluctantly ascends, and more in strong-smelling foods he carries in his luggage – Limburg cheese and a huge sausage one suspects of containing garlic. In spite of all this, his charming Gentile wife is patently enamoured of 'mein Sally'; and the most attractive lady in the fashionable Bavarian mountain hotel chooses him rather than any of her Gentile would-be suitors as her companion on the mountain-climb ('he is harmless', she writes to her husband, and she clearly finds him amusing). Just as he has succeeded in the Berlin business world, he succeeds, in the end, in reaching the top of the mountain whose ascent he had so dreaded. A mountain hut brings him together with the attractive lady he had accompanied, her husband, and his own wife – and there all discords are resolved and possible misunderstandings cleared up. And through it all, despite grumblings, complaints and solecisms, he remains what the title suggested: 'Meyer aus Berlin', a brash, self-made Jewish Berliner, whose ignorance of the sober habits of polite society in no way inhibit his self-confidence.

Much of Lubitsch's humour in these early films is a subtler version of that purveyed in the popular Jewish farces of the Berlin theatres owned by the Herrnfeld Brothers, some of which, like *Endlich Allein* (*Alone at Last*, 1913), also found their way onto celluloid.

The complete antithesis of Lubitsch's brash young go-getters, within the world of Jewish self-images, is of course that embodied, in one film after another, by Woody Allen. Allen's protagonists are insecure intellectuals, artists or pseudo-artists, alienated from Jewish households with oppressive, smothering mothers, wooing Gentile women and their world with fear of rejection and persecution never far from their minds, ambivalent about their sexuality and cultural identity, whose high anxieties and low self-esteem Allen transmutes into urban, sophisticated humour that has a wide appeal, well beyond the Jewish and Gentile middle-class intellectual circles of New York within which most of its story-lines are played out. Lubitsch is no less sophisticated: the famous 'Lubitsch touch' leaves the viewer completing a thought or guessing what might be going on behind the many doors that play such an important part in the settings and plots of his films. His own career shows him moving further and further away from the milieu he knew so well in his early years and transmuted into the Jewish comedy of his early films: from the clothing industry into the acting profession; from minor stage actors in companies directed by Reinhardt to more prestigious parts in humorous films; from film actor to film director and producer first in Germany and at last in Hollywood. None of the central protagonists of the early films have this striving away from the rag trade, despite their parents' ambitions for them; none aspire, like Lubitsch himself, from trade into art; but the art he practises has benefited enormously from his own experience of the milieu within which he grew up and which he came to regard with a humorous detachment not entirely unmixed with sympathy.

Perceptive critics have always felt that the brash self-assertiveness of Lubitsch's figures is a compensation phenomenon, making up for the fears of rejection and persecution that are never far from a Jewish consciousness. This feeling is strengthened if one looks at the final acting part that Lubitsch assigned himself in one of his self-directed films. In 1920 he assembled a distinguished cast (Paul Wegener, Pola Negri, Harry Liedtke, Aud Egede Nissen and Jenny Hasselquist among many others) for a film version of *Sumurun* – an Oriental pantomime devised many years ago for Max Reinhardt, from whose stage craft Lubitsch's films profited in so many ways. In it he played, as he had done for Reinhardt, a hunchbacked entertainer who knew his own appearance to be unattractive, whose beloved rejects him, who is slapped and pummelled by all and sundry and even bundled and thrown about in a sack, who is abjectly grateful for any kindness that comes his way, and who is left in the end in the characteristic Pagliacci stance of having to caper, sing, and make audiences laugh at his ungainliness, while his heart is breaking. Nothing could contrast more strikingly with the self-confidence with which his Pinkuses, Lachmanns and Meyers hurl themselves towards commercial and amorous success – but the two belong together, two sides of the same coin. And between them stands the figure Lubitsch assigns to Felix Bressart in *The Shop Around the Corner*, *Ninochka* and *To Be or Not to Be*: the timid Jew who would rather not be involved, who wants above all to avoid the trouble that is bound to come his way, who senses that his humanity is not being respected and asserts it, with trepidation but deep feeling, when he recites Shylock's 'Hath not a Jew eyes' speech while being cornered by Nazi enemies. He is no Shylock himself – his only revenge is a recitation of Shakespeare's words, a human dilemma transmuted into art. And above all the figures Lubitsch embodies in his Jewish comedies are placed into perspective by that which he assigned himself in what is my own favourite among all his early films: *Die Puppe* (*The Doll*) of 1919. There we see him introducing his delightful fantasy in the guise of a puppet master, who builds up a cardboard landscape and places stylised figures in its midst, which he then sets moving about in a self-created simulacrum of the world. Dilemmas, passions and fears are humorously distanced and transmuted, and at the end of the film we feel as we do at the end of Thackeray's *Vanity Fair*: 'Come, children, let us shut up the box and the puppets, for our play is played out.'

Die Stadt ohne Juden (The City without Jews)

The collapse of the Vienna stock market in 1873 inaugurated a period of anti-Jewish agitation in Austria, for which Wilhelm Marr found a new term in 1897: *Antisemitismus*. Anti-Semitism differed from hostility to Jews because of their religion – indeed, many Gentiles found Jewish religious customs and ceremonies exotic and picturesque; it attacked, instead, supposed 'racial' qualities Jews shared with one another, whether they were religious or not, acculturated or not, baptised or not. The new movement, spearheaded by ideologues like Georg von Schoenerer, did not at first impede a steady growth of Jewish representation in the arts, journalism, the legal profession and medicine, as well as in commerce; but anti-Semitic agitators found ready fuel in resentment at such successes and at the greatly increased immigration, during and just after the First World War, of traditionally garbed, bearded, Yiddish-speaking Jews fleeing such Austrian provinces as Galicia and Bukovina with their wives and children. Anti-Semitism was now accepted into the political programme of mainstream Austrian political parties; notably that of the Christian Socialists whose widely popular leader, Karl Lueger, was actually elected Mayor of Vienna in 1897 and held that post, despite opposition by the Emperor, until his death in 1910. Many student fraternities and other organisations began excluding Jews from membership; a still mostly unofficial *numerus clausus* was exercised by professional bodies; and anti-immigration policies directed mainly against Jews from Eastern Europe were constantly advocated throughout the postwar period and the 1920s, preparing the ground for the Austrian corporal who was to enact and implement far more lethal measures in the next decade.

It was this situation which led the Jewish journalist and novelist Hugo Bettauer, whose widely published views on sexual mores and public injustice made him a controversial (and in some quarters a violently hated) figure, to publish what he called 'playful thoughts on what Vienna would be like and how it would develop if the Jews actually followed the polite invitation [i.e. *Hinaus mit den Juden,* 'Jews Out!'] and left the city' (*Die Börse*, 13 July 1922, p. 16). The result was a novel called *Die Stadt ohne Juden*, first published in 1922, which its author described as 'an amusing book', 'a series of sketches held together in a harmless novelistic narrative' (loc. cit.). 'Harmless' was an exaggeration – its author never shunned controversy, and this was no exception. The satire was, admittedly, somewhat hit-and-miss, but some of it struck quite hard at actual political, social and cultural goings-on in the Vienna of its day.

When a young Viennese director, producer and film-company executive called Hans Karl Breslauer came to film the book a year and a half after its first publication, he deliberately toned down many of its controversial elements; and though he filmed not only in a Vienna studio but also in recognisable Viennese locations like the area behind the Burgtheater and in front of the Palais Liechtenstein, he moved the action from the Austrian capital to that of what the first intertitle calls *die sagenhafte Republik Utopia* ('the fabled Republic Utopia'). In concert with his scriptwriter Ida Jenbach he removed the more recognisable references to actual parties and politicians, ascribing the main anti-Jewish agitation not to the Christian Socialist party, but to a 'Pan-German' party operating in Utopia (of all places!). An anti-Semitic delegate of that party in the Utopian parliament, Councillor Bernart, is played by the great Viennese character-actor Hans Moser. This was the first of many film roles that made him so popular throughout Germany and Austria that even the Nazis dared not force him to abandon a principled stand which enabled him to keep his Jewish wife with him throughout the era of enforced divorces, deportations and murders that marked their nefarious rule. He never played an anti-Semite again: nor did he take part in any of the overtly anti-Semitic films with which the Nazis prepared the Gentile population for the mass murders and barefaced robberies to come. Their later, all too successful, policy of turning Vienna, along with much of Europe, into a 'City without Jews', has aroused new interest in Bettauer's novelistic sketches with their wish-dream of Jewish indispensability and power to retaliate.

This interest has extended to Breslauer's film too, despite the fact that it is clumsily directed. The director's handling of crowd scenes would have benefited from the lessons Lubitsch and other directors of the period learned from Max Reinhardt; and some of the actors are allowed exaggerated gesturings which one would have thought eliminated from films by the early 1920s. Such acting conventions were still, however, observed in some of the less sophisticated productions of the Yiddish theatre, from which many of the minor players in *City without Jews* had been recruited. The Vienna Jewish cabaret was also raided: two of its stars, Gisela Werbezirk and Armin Berg, are assigned crudely farcical business outdone by even cruder business from Gentile players who throw beer over one another or spit cherry-stones from the public gallery onto the heads of parliamentary delegates below. For all its faults and crudities, however, the film has considerable symptomatic interest in our present context, and we have every cause to be grateful to Filmarchiv Austria, who have lovingly restored what is left of it and made it widely available through a video that comes accompanied by a volume of excellently researched essays (to which the present chapter is inevitably indebted).

The copy so restored, based on one found in Dutch archives with Dutch intertitles that have been retranslated into German, is a fragment of that submitted to Austrian censorship in 1924: its 1,635 metres contrast with an original length of 2,400. The most painful gap comes at the end; we do not know what the final sequence would actually have looked like, though a synopsis issued at the time gives some idea of the frame which would have closed at the end and given the film a retrospective meaning not unlike that of Fritz Lang's infinitely superior *Woman in the Window*.

What we have now begins with agitated crowds demanding work and food, not without quarrelling within itself, followed by the spectacle of speculators rushing to telephones to buy dollars as the Utopian currency falls – supplemented later by a sequence in which *Schieber* (racketeers, profiteers) are seen enjoying themselves feasting and dancing in expensive nightclubs, and contrasting market scenes in which would-be purchasers complain at ever-rising prices and fight with market traders in a flurry of flying fruit and clouds of flour. In parliament the pliable Chancellor is persuaded to blame all ills on the Jews and propose their banishment from the state – a step against which the 'head of the State Church' warns him, calling it 'inhuman' and citing the biblical injunction to love one's neighbour as oneself. The delegates of the 'Pan-German' party led by Councillor Bernart and his colleague Councillor Volbert, however, call loudly for the implementation of a decree of expulsion. The Chancellor complies, arguing that despite long oppression Jews have used their sharp intellects to get to the top in the word: 'they sit in the greatest banks, they control industry, they write plays ...' 'We write plays too!', Gentile journalists object. 'Ah, but do you get them produced?', the Chancellor answers, with what is surely a dig at the dominance on Viennese stages of the works of Arthur Schnitzler and minor Jewish dramatists like Paul Lindau. Economically the expulsion will be underwritten by a promised credit of a hundred million dollars from an American millionaire called Huxtable. These arguments, and those of anti-Semitic councillors who maintain that the Jews 'plunder' Utopia and that they are 'responsible for all our misery', sway the assembly – and the decree is adopted and passed into law. It expels baptised Jews along with unbaptised ones, excepting only those whose parents had also been baptised. Children of mixed marriages have to go too. Jews are allowed to take their fortunes with them – or rather, that part of them which had been properly declared to the Utopian tax inspectorate.

The decree in this form hits not only the Liberal Councillor Linder, who had opposed its adoption and whose daughter Lotte is engaged to the Jewish painter Leo Strakosch, but also the anti-Semitic Councillor Volbert, whose daughter is married to a banker called Carroni who had earlier, however, horror of horrors, borne the name Cohn. That couple have a child, the apple of Volbert's eye, who must now accompany her father into banishment. This occasions violent and tearful domestic scenes in Volbert's house, where he is even beaten about the face by his formidable wife and upbraided by his cook.

We had first met Volbert and Bernart in a lively *Wirtshaus* scene in which the 'Jewish Question' is discussed and quarrelled about. Bernart is a drunkard who (as is confirmed later) habitually overindulges both at his *Stammtisch* – the table at the inn reserved for him and his cronies – and at home. He now falls asleep over his wine, with important consequences for what was to have been the film's conclusion.

The passing of the decree of expulsion leads to a series of intercut scenes of farewell. Carroni begins a journey that would eventually lead him to Zion (read: British-administered Palestine). His child would follow later; there is little time, for the Jews have only until Christmas to leave Utopia. Strakosch goes to Paris, where he continues what we are to take as a successful and lucrative career as a painter – it is all too characteristic of this film that we never actually see him paint or are shown any of his work. Isidor, Linder's Jewish man-of-all-work, takes leave of the Gentile cook who loves him and provides him with copious food for the journey in return for a promise that he will send her a picture postcard (*Ansichtskarte*, which she malapropistically calls 'Angesichtskarte', face-card: a nonsensical and unlikely malapropism which contemporary critics objected to, along with other crudities of these intertitles). Isidor too is going to Zion. We see these named characters, along with some journalists and other middle-class figures mount a train after taking leave of husbands, wives, finances, in-laws and friends not affected by the ethnic proscription. Their relatively comfortable journey is starkly counterpointed with the exodus of anonymous Ostjuden in traditional garb, who set out from wretched homes at the other end of town. One of the columns they form is preceded by rabbis carrying sacred scrolls, another is seen (on Christmas Eve!) trudging wearily through a cheerless snowy landscape.

The popular rejoicing which follows the departure of the Jews is short-lived. There are, it is true, now empty houses Gentiles can move into, and food prices have come down; but Jewish capital has been transferred abroad, the fashion houses and cafés have lost their best customers and trendsetters, Jewish-owned foreign banks give no further credit, the Utopian currency loses its value, Huxtable's promised millions evaporate after he becomes engaged to a millionaire heiress from the Chicago firm of Cohen and Cohn, Utopia is boycotted by travellers, hotels are empty and jobs are being lost, and the only way of carrying on any kind of public administration is by raising taxes. Now prices rise and rise, incomes vanish (memories of postwar inflation play a great part here) and the crowds of well-wishers greeting the Chancellor after the passing of the anti-Jewish decree now turn once again into crowds of protesters carrying placards demanding work and food, and displaying slogans of which only the words 'Down with ...' (*Nieder mit*) are readable on the screen.

In the meantime Carroni has written from Hamburg that he is taking his daughter with him (to 'Zion', presumably) and wants to divorce his Gentile wife. Isidor the man-of-all-work is actually seen in a fanciful Zion, having the time of his life joking with colonial soldiers, chewing on something as usual (can that be a Matzo one sees in his hand?), and playing cards, in the sunny open air, with some orthodox coreligionists. Leo Strakosch, however, sporting fashionably shaped whiskers, has returned to Utopia disguised as a wealthy Frenchman of the Catholic faith, revealed himself to his fiancée Lotte (but not to her father), and found an ally in a Gentile businessman hard hit by having to see the fashion-house and the restaurant associated with it (both of which he had taken over from their previous Jewish owners) go steeply downmarket. Leo takes a room in a leading hotel where he is received with copious bowings and scrapings as its only guest, and later rents an elegant villa where his fiancée Lotte Linder (played skittishly by Anny Milety, who appeared in most of Breslauer's films and later married him) can pay him affectionate visits. Leo's game, however, is not purely amorous. On a private press he prints posters he clandestinely pastes up all over the city, insinuating that the ousting of its Jews had brought the country to its present pass, and urging that Jews should be recalled to 'work honestly and faithfully' alongside their Gentile compatriots. Leo signs this appeal to an honest work-ethnic (which writers like Gustav Freytag had proclaimed as a bourgeois ideal proper to Germanic peoples not always lived up to by Jews and Poles) 'Bund der wahrhaften Christen' – 'League of True Christians'; and he suggests that the time has come to change the call 'Jews Out!' for a new one: 'Jews In!' or 'Jews Come Back!'.

This campaign has the desired result of strengthening the forces which are impelling the Chancellor and most of the Deputies in the same direction. But in order to rescind the decree of expulsion a two-thirds majority is required in parliament; and this cannot be attained if Councillor Bernart, whose anti-Semitism cannot be bribed away, casts his dissenting vote. Leo has a remedy for that too. He befriends the Councillor, sneaks into his house the night before the crucial vote and puts all the clocks back, plies him the next morning with French wines drugged with a sleeping potion, and then has him driven off by his, Leo's, chauffeur, into a remote part of the town and abandoned there. When he wakes up the chauffeur declares that the car has broken down, forcing him to make his way back on foot while he is being sought high and low by his parliamentary allies who, in the end, proceed to the vote without him. Leo is able to watch the consequent rescinding of the decree from the visitors' gallery. Cut to agitated street scenes in which newsboys sell extra editions with huge headlines announcing the repeal and the return of the first Jew, while Leo, who is that returnee, can now openly join his fiancée. He is at last able to convince her father that the 'Frenchman' who had been courting her is in fact her original betrothed, Leo Strakosch.

The most striking sequence of the whole film comes at the end as we now have it. So far we have seen a succession of street scenes straightforwardly photographed in and around Vienna by Hugo Eywo, and public and private interiors designed by Julius von Borsody to suggest classicising tastes (pillars and porticos) and bourgeois stuffiness – or, at the other end of the scale, ghetto poverty with dingy hangings and rickety furniture. One interior stands out because of its satiric detail: the living room of Councillor Bernart, symmetrically arranged and kept in bourgeois tidiness by his housekeeper, has two Chianti bottles strategically placed among his knick-knacks and ornaments, while in his bedroom swords and daggers are arranged in a sort of star-burst over his bed. In his drunken sleep he has a nightmare of Chassidically garbed angels swaying and bowing over his bed – and this prepares us for the scene in which a drugged Bernart awakes to find himself having to stagger back on foot and entering a house in high excitement in order to learn, on the telephone, what has been happening in parliament during his enforced absence. The house happens to be a psychiatric institution, where two doctors, mistaking his agitation for that of a madman, have him forcibly removed to a cell by the proverbial men in white coats. At this point the design of the film changes: we lurch into Caligari country. The cell in which Bernart finds himself incarcerated is composed of theatrical flats leaning inwards at crazy angles, dominated by a rhomboid window and an irregularly shaped chair with a cubist 'cushion', standing on a huge Star of David and surmounted by another smaller star of the same kind. Two doctors are seen observing the Councillor cowering inside and diagnosing his delusions: 'The man imagines he is a Zionist.' That is the last we see of Bernart in the extant fragment: but the contemporary synopsis issued by the Ideal Film Gesellschaft that distributed Breslauer's work tells us that at this point Bernart would have woken up, at a late hour, in the inn where we had earlier seen him fall into his drunken sleep. He then says to his Fellow-Councillor Volbert: 'Thank God this stupid dream is over – we are all human beings and don't want to hate – what we want is to live quietly alongside one another.'

The whole film, then, from the moment we saw Bernart fall asleep, has been a dream – and I suppose it would be charitable to say that its crudities, distortions and stereotypes were due to our inhabiting Bernart's consciousness. Whether this makes the unevenly directed film, which lurches between comedy, farce, romance, melodrama, and tearful presentations of the woes of Jews forced, once again, to wander, a better work of art, is (to say the least) doubtful. It does, however, place *The City without Jews* into a cinematic tradition of meaningful delusion that extends from *The Cabinet of Dr Caligari*, whose style is deliberately recalled, to *The Woman in the Win-*

dow and beyond; and it mirrors an instant conversion from rabid Judaeophobia to a humane recognition of common humanity whose credibility is hardly borne out by later events. What is certain is that the Gentile figures inhabiting Bernart's consciousness, headed by a weak and manipulative Chancellor, are for the most part no more admirable than the Jewish ones. 'Whether Jews or Christians,' the Chancellor sighs after bitter experiences, 'what they all have in common is Greed.' Among the principals only the Liberal Councillor Linder, and his daughter Lotte who forms the romantic centre of the film, seem untouched by the general corruption and corruptibility.

The Jewish figures that people the screen fall into four groups. The first of these is represented by two men who have either contracted or are about to contract, exogamous marriages: Alois Carroni (né Cohn), who has married the daughter of the anti-Semitic Councillor Volbert; and Leo Strakosch who is engaged to Lotte Linder. Both are fully acculturated in the 'Utopian' society which closely mirrors the Viennese society overtly portrayed in Bettauer's novel. Neither has any of the outward signs thought especially 'Jewish'; and to make sure of that the director/producer has chosen non-Jewish actors to embody them: Hans Effenberger plays Carroni, Johannes Riemann Strakosch. Their reactions to the events chronicled in the film, inaugurated by a Chancellor who begins his crucial speech by proclaiming himself a friend and admirer of Jews and ends by comparing them to aphids or rose-bugs that a wise gardener will eliminate, differ sharply. As we have seen, Carroni takes his child from a mixed marriage with him into exile, writing from Hamburg that he is divorcing his wife, before proceeding to 'Zion', while Leo Strakosch returns to Utopia in disguise, secures the cooperation of a Gentile financier, exploits public discontent by means of a poster campaign blaming present ills on the *absence* of Jews, and finds means of securing the crucial vote in the national assembly which rescinds the decree of expulsion.

Chief representative of a second group is Dr Jakob Krauss, editor of a journal called *Die Abwehr* (Resistance, Defence), who has physical characteristics centuries of caricatures and lampoons had labelled 'Jewish' in his nose, his posture, his gait, and his way of gesturing with his hands to emphasise his speech – but who happens to have had the good fortune of being the baptised son of baptised parents and therefore not liable to expulsion. This fact he proclaims with glee by climbing over the barrier that divides two sections of the journalists' gallery in parliament, thrusting out his pot-belly while placing his hands demonstratively on its two sides, breaking into a huge grin captured in close-up, and shouting: 'Ich bin ein waschechter Goi!' (I am a true-blue Gentile!). His use of the Yiddish-Hebrew term 'Goi' (usually spelt 'Goy' in English) is, of course, an additional marker of his Jewishness. In a later sequence he acknowledges that if one were to go by outward appearances, he too would have to go into exile: but 'appearances are deceptive'. It is this character – the baptised Jew officially defined as a non-Jew – who confronts Strakosch – the unbaptised

Jew passing as a French Catholic – with an appreciative chuckle at the success of his poster campaign credited to a (non-existent) 'League of True Christians'. 'A trick like that,' he says, 'could only have been thought up by one of 'Our People' – if you will pardon the expression.' 'Unsre Leut' is what German and Austrian Jews often called their coreligionists. In spite of his baptism, in spite of official declarations that classify him as a 'true-blue Gentile', Krauss has remained indelibly Jewish.

Krauss is not the only character whose Jewishness is confirmed by his use of language. Among the financiers we see rushing to the telephones at the beginning of the film in order to hedge themselves against the falling currency of their country by speculating in dollars, is a fat man whom we meet again after the passing of the decree of expulsion. He is in the process of transferring the bulk of his fortune to a Parisian firm marked as Jewish, like other firms and individuals in this film, by names: here the unlikely ones of Rosenblüh and Butterflock, elsewhere by more common ones like Cohen and Cohn. For this he needs the help of a Gentile colleague whom he pays two hundred million Utopian crowns commission. An intertitle gives us his thoughts: 'What a Ganef – he earns two hundred million in a flash!' The word 'Ganef' (often spelt 'goniff') is Hebrew-Yiddish for a thief. Into this second group we must also count the fat, hook-nosed London dealer, whom we see in an opulent interior lounging in an armchair smoking a fat cigar while he dictates to a (Gentile?) amanuensis standing deferentially by his side a message which will depress the value of the Utopian currency. Needless to say, this episode confirms the predictions of the Chancellor's more level-headed advisers that since Jews (as the Chancellor himself had said) control the big foreign banks, no help could be expected from that quarter; and it sets the stereotype of the Jew behind the scenes controlling the finances of the world beside that of a press controlled by men like Krauss who may be nominally Christian but have in fact remained Jewish in their hearts and loyalties. This makes sense, of course, as the dream of a confirmed anti-Semite; but it is hard to see why after such a dream he would have the complete change of heart that was (if we are to believe the contemporary synopsis) to occur at the end. Bettauer's novel has no such delusional framework: the happenings there take place in a real world, and the decision to recall the Jews is taken for material reasons that lead to a change of policy.

One component of this affluent middle-class group, which takes up several pages in Bettauer's novel, is introduced into the film by just one remark. Two ladies of the town are sitting in a café (that will itself soon go downmarket) and one of them laments: 'If my old Cohn has to leave, I'll go bankrupt.' Utopian Jews, it seems, are not only trendsetters in fashion and affluent customers of elegant establishments of various kinds, but also valued customers of non-Jewish women who peddle sexual favours. This stereotype, along with that of the sexual attraction that draws Gentile girls like Lotte Linder and Volbert's daughter to Jewish men, was to be exploited by fanatics who spoke of *Rassenschande*, defilement of the (Germanic or 'Aryan') race, well before this was declared culpable by Nazi laws.

The third group is represented by the low-comedy couple Kathy the cook and Isidor the man-of-all-work – both played by well-known Jewish cabaret artists, though only Isidor is marked as Jewish for the purposes of the plot. He is a fat man whose chief interest seems to be eating copiously and well, and finds what he needs in Linder's kitchen presided over by Kathy: another Gentile woman in love with a Jew. He is seen gorging himself in between hearty kisses; but when he decides to make his way to 'Zion' after the decree of expulsion, he rejects Kathy's offer to accompany him. After upbraiding Councillor Volbert, her employer, for being responsible for a decree that robs her of her lover and may drive her to suicide, she accompanies Isidor to the train, loads him with eatables, and settles for an occasional postcard from his new homeland. The film gives us a glimpse of a tourist 'Zion' in which Isidor seems to be perfectly at ease; he chats with a colonial soldier, glances at a passing Arab woman, and settles down at a table where he joins three traditionally garbed Jews in a cardgame. Excessive interest in food, along with in card-playing and other gambling activities, though universal, have often been seen as Jewish characteristics; one only has to read the biographies of Hollywood moguls to convince oneself of the reason for that.

The three groups mentioned so far do not interact with a fourth, which brings a quite different emotional atmosphere into the film: orthodox Jews in traditional grab that marks them as *Ostjuden*, immigrants from Eastern Europe. They are seen in poor, run-down, sparsely furnished rooms, in the synagogue, and excitedly gathering in the street, with all the stereotyped gestures, and excited rushings and swayings, that characterised stage-Jews in German-speaking lands. At the same time, however, the film seeks to give an ethnographically correct picture of Jewish ritual in the home and in the synagogue, with prayer-shawls, fringed undergarments, phylacteries and sacred books and scrolls. Much of the synagogue footage is missing in the film as we now have it – but a great deal of study and thought has clearly gone into the studio reconstruction of its architecture and furnishing, and many of the actors stem from a milieu in which familiarity with distinctive Jewish dress and orthodox ritual is taken for granted. At one point some attempt is made to lighten the atmosphere in keeping with the comic and farcical detail of the rest of the film: a group of bearded, gesticulating orthodox Jews is shown crowding around a newspaper one of them is holding (from which they learn that all Jews are to be expelled) while another one says: 'Couldn't they make an exception of *us*?' But this is an isolated instance. These scenes of expulsion watched over and enforced by the police are played almost entirely for pathos. We see sick and blind Jews, helpless women holding on to their children, first within the poor hovels they had made their home, praying to God to avert the evil, but then having to trudge on foot in long columns towards an uncertain goal – in part through a snowy landscape that makes their progress doubly difficult. Gestures of despair range from tearful cowering to hands uplifted towards a heaven that has not heeded their praying, and the one act of intended resistance – a Jew raising his fist towards a gendarme who is driving the Jewish family out of its house – is immediately subdued when the gendarme starts to draw his sword. These are mere victims, and it is significant that though the camera isolates suffering individuals as well as crowds, none of them is given a name.

The pathos of these scenes – particularly for modern audiences which have seen a far more lethal outcome of herding Jews out of their homes – overbalances the comedy and romance of the film, which is neither acted nor directed well enough to make such lurchings acceptable, and which in far too many places reinforces harmful stereotypes instead of combating them. It has, nevertheless, great symptomatic value, exhibiting the unwarranted optimism of those who believed that Jews would be felt indispensable in material as well as cultural ways once they had been removed from the scene – and that they were powerful enough to ensure a world-wide boycott which would force their readmission. It turned out far otherwise, and the myth of Jewish power (which lies behind such fantastic inventions as the conspiracies of imaginary 'Wise Men of Zion', concocted by Tsarist Judaeophobes and disseminated all over the world) was shown to be just that, at the cost of millions of Jewish lives. It is symptomatic too that the author of the novel on which the film was based, who had been subjected to many years of anti-Semitic vilification because of his advanced views on sexuality and his opposition to various forms of social discrimination, fell victim to a fanatic assassin's bullet soon after the film was first shown. He is best remembered now as the author of a novel on which G.W. Pabst based a far better film: *Die freudlose Gasse* (*The Joyless Street*), with its exposure of poverty in postwar Vienna in the grip of inflation, and of those who knew how to profit from the others' misery.

The Austrian Christian Socialist Joseph Schleicher, a friend of Mayor Lueger and a contemporary of Hugo Bettauer, confessed to a very different dream of a 'Vienna free of Jews'. His book *Das judenfreie Wien*, the Austrian historian Brigitte Hamann reports, advocated a 'moral rebirth' by driving Jews out of Austria to Budapest with the help of a total boycott of Jewish businesses and services, and then ending the 'Witches' Sabbath' of parliamentarianism. Oppositional demonstrations would be forbidden, large concerns would be taken into public ownership, and in a single day two hundred Jews would be hanged (alongside twenty delinquent 'Aryans'). In Poland and Ruthenia thousands would be hanged ... ('Einer von ganz Unten', *Der Spiegel*, No. 28, 2001 p. 137). It is, alas, easy to see which of the two 'dreams' came nearer to what actually happened after the *Anschluss* that annexed Austria to Hitler's Germany in March 1938.

Ost und West/Mizrekh un Mayrev (East and West)

In its fantasy-premise *City without Jews* addressed the uneasy relations between an increasingly upwardly mobile Jewish population, reinforced, but also feeling threatened by, immigration from further East, and their Gentile co-citizens at a time of growing, politically directed, anti-Semitism. Other films of the time address the problem in historical guise, focusing on sexual attraction between Jews and non-Jews. Otto Kreisler filmed an adaptation of Grillparzer's play *Die Jüdin von Toledo* (*The Jewess of Toledo*, 1919), which, like Henrik Galeen's take on Karl Emil Franzos's novel *Judith Trachtenberg* (1920), tells the story of a doomed love affair between an aristocrat (a king, in Grillparzer's case) and a *belle Juive*. In Jewish folklore that sort of tale is known as an 'Esterka' story, after the reputed infatuation of a king of Poland with a beautiful Jewish girl named after the heroine of the Book of Esther, whose biblical story has a happier outcome than those of the Spanish and Galician heroines at the centre of the two films just named. The sexes are reversed in Sidney Goldin's *Jiskor* (*Gedenket*, [*Remembrance*] 1924), starring Maurice Schwartz, Dagny Servaes and Oskar Beregi, in a dark tale of an aristocrat's daughter in love with a Jewish forester who repels her advances – a 'Joseph and Potiphar's wife' tale which, like the 'Esterka' stories, has an unhappier end than the its biblical prototype. The lady's father, a local count, has the young man arrested, humiliated by being made to dance in a bearskin before a jeering company, and then buried alive. This cruel affair is commemorated in later years by a Jewish community in a ceremony which gives the film its title while also forming its framework.

Another Austrian film, again directed by Otto Kreisler, takes its audience into Jewish history, highlighting the longing for a Jewish homeland so eloquently restated by the Viennese journalist, novelist and playwright Theodor Herzl in *Der Judenstaat* (*The Jewish State*, 1896), which is one of the founding documents of Zionism. The film was called *Theodor Herzl, Bannerträger des jüdischen Volkes* (*Th. H., Champion of the Jewish People*, 1919) and starred the actor Rudolf Schildkraut, a specialist in Jewish roles on stage and in film, as a Wandering Jew whose tribulations pointed to the necessity of acquiring the kind of homeland envisaged by the nascent Zionist movement. The *Wiener Morgenzeitung* of 29 February 1924 commented on the number of films released in recent years that showed traditional ceremonies and customs in Jewish communities, or had Judaeaphile tendencies, which took the non-Jewish population into unknown territories and enlightened them about conditions they had previously not known about, or had caused them to judge Judaism falsely. The paper hoped such pictorial representations would lead to more enlightened and tolerant views.

East and West, directed by the Jewish-American Sidney Goldin in 1923, does indeed show Jewish ceremonies in the Orthodox East European community: inaugurations of the Sabbath; synagogue services on the Eve and

Day of Atonement (including communal prayer, reading of the Law, all-night vigil, blowing of the *Shofar*); a wedding ceremony and attendant rejoicings; and customary celebrations in the house of an affluent Jewish merchant in Galicia. But this is not the exercise in Jewish nostalgia common in Yiddish films that habitually feature such scenes. Jeffrey Shandler, the author of a definitive study of *East and West*, has shown this in a characteristically well-chosen example: a tableau appearing about half-way through the film which depicts a pious East European family celebrating the beginning of the Sabbath.

> While the father recites the blessing over a glass of wine, the mother gazes on, embracing one of their three children; the other two stand with heads bowed reverently. The modest table, draped by a white cloth, is set with three symmetrically arranged candlesticks, a braided *challah* covered with a cloth, and a bottle of wine. The sanctity of the Sabbath is also signified by the father's fur-trimmed *shtraymel*, while his *kapote*, beard and *peyes*, the mother's lace-trimmed kerchief concealing her hair, the boys' *peyes*, *yarmulkes* and *arbe-kanfesn* symbolically extend the piety enacted by the father throughout the family (a thematic movement established visually by the tableau's classical triangular composition, with the father at the central apex, echoed in miniature by the configuration of the candlesticks).
>
> Viewed by Jewish audiences today, this tableau is likely to evoke a wealth of nostalgic, sentimental associations – the virtues of Old World piety and familial communion, the spiritual transformation that welcoming the Sabbath brings to the pious Jew, the integrity of East European Jewish faith in the face of poverty and oppression – in sum, much the same affective response engendered by the Barry Sisters' 1950s rendition of *Mayn mames shabes likht* (My Mother's Sabbath Candles) or the 'Sunrise, Sunset' sequence of the 1964 Broadway musical, *Fiddler on the Roof*. In fact, the scene's function within the film *Ost und West* is quite the opposite. Far from being a beatific vision of the virtues of piety, it is nothing less than a nightmare. Rather than presenting an idealised image of devotion to Jewish traditions, it is a young American Jewish woman's terrified vision of her future, trapped, by comic mishap, in marriage to a Polish *hasid*. (Shandler 1992: 69–70)

Nothing could differ more sharply than this from the reverent presentation of Jewish ritual in other German and Austrian films of the period – even in those which, like *City without Jews*, were little inclined to see the whole ethnic group through rose-tinted spectacles.

The culture clash involved here is central to Goldin's film, which shows how a resolutely modern New York flapper irrupts into the orthodox society of a Galician *shteltl*, in which her father, who has become rich in America, was born. The film's title, however, may mislead in two different ways. One is that it may suggest a dichotomy that can never be breached ('Oh East is East and West is West, and never the twain shall meet' – a sentence qualified in Kipling's poem, but not in the popular usage of that line). The film shows, in fact, that bridges can be built, and cross-overs effected, in a variety of ways. The other difficulty arises from the observation that the film presents not two worlds, but four, and the relations between them: that of the Jewish town (*shtetl*) or enclave in Galicia; that of the American self-made man who originated there and now visits his old home with his daughter, who is more completely Americanised that her father; that of the cultured Jewish family in Vienna that still has relatives in Eastern Europe which (unlike many others) it is glad to acknowledge, receive and further, enable a gifted young nephew to acquire and education that goes beyond the Torah-and-Talmud-centred learning he had been limited to in Galicia; and that of non-Jewish Orientalists, members of an 'Oriental Academy' based in Vienna, one of whom at first mocks the beard and sidelocks of the young students, only to be pulled up by another who is impressed by the sharp intellect and desire for knowledge hidden in that strange exterior. The young man soon wins general respect, is publicly honoured by the Academy which accepts him among its members, and writes the book *Ost und West* (foolishly retitled *Mazl Tov* in a rejigged American release), whose public presentation forms the climax of the movie and gives it the title it bore when it was released in 1923 as a co-production of Listo-Film, Vienna, and Picon Film, New York.

At the film's centre is a tiny bundle of energy, the Jewish-American flapper Molly, played by Molly Picon, who sets everyone by the ears when she visits her father's family in Galicia to attend her cousin's wedding. She brings her own punching-ball and boxing gloves, and actually knocks out a female servant who has displeased her, miming the sequence of a boxing match from initial feinting to knock-out blow, with water for reviving, fanning with a towel, counting out, and raising a boxing-gloved hand for victory. Dressed as an Orthodox boy (cross-dressing of this kind was Picon's trademark), she invades an all-male prenuptial ceremony, whose gestures she mocks by inviting her neighbour to 'shoot a quarter'. As a feminist protest this contrasts sharply with that of Bashevis Singer's Yentl, memorably embodied by Barbra Streisand, whose motives are a desire for the religious learning which Jewish traditions denied to women. Molly teaches the synagogue choir, made up of male religious students, to shimmy – and does it so effectively that even the servants, who are not too well disposed towards her, dance along to what one of them declares to be 'an American waltz'. The noise attracts Molly's uncle, the owner of the house, who sends the servants about their business, and the synagogue cantor and choir-master, who chases his charges away from Molly's dangerous influence. It is this same cantor, however, who laments the immigration quota that prevents him from following the example of Molly's father and emigrating to America in his turn.

Molly also secretes a novel inside the prayerbook she uses during the Day of Atonement service, cooped up in the segregated woman's gallery of the Orthodox synagogue, and reads that instead of the Hebrew prayers whose language she us unlikely to understand. Even her father, who presumably had the usual religious instruction in his Galician boyhood, seems unable to follow the services and is quizzically told by his brother that his acquaintance with prayerbooks seems to lag behind his familiarity with chequebooks. Worst of all: while other women are growing faint with hunger, Molly sneaks out of the synagogue on this solemn fast day and returns to her uncle's home where she gobbles up the food set aside for the family after their fast, hiding the remnants under the table to be finished off by the cat and the dog. 'That Amerikaner shikse,' the cook fulminates when she discovers this horror – no well-brought-up Jewish girl would or should behave in this way, even if she does have 'the appetite of an elephant'.

There are more tricks of this kind – but eventually one of these, in which she is abetted by the servants and her cousins, rebounds onto herself. On the eve of her cousin's wedding she dons that cousin's wedding-veil to play at marriage. A poor student whom her uncle is housing and feeding for charity's sake, is reluctantly dragged away from the kitchen corner in which he is studying his religious texts, and pressed to play the bridegroom in Molly's game. She discovers too late that by forcing the young man to place a ring onto her finger before witnesses, she has in fact contracted a marriage valid in Jewish law. The only way to annul such a marriage, which, as the tableau analysed by Jeffrey Shandler has shown, is a nightmare to her, is to induce her husband to give her a decree of annulment (*get*) approved by a rabbi. And so the initiative, the motor of the film, now passes to the poor student, played by Molly Picon's actual husband, Jacob Kalich.

Jacob (like his wife Kalich is allowed to keep his actual first name) is introduced into the affluent household of Molly's uncle *af kest* – to be housed and fed in accordance with the Jewish custom of supporting religious students and thus at once practising charity and ensuring the continuance of Jewish learning. His is a remarkable performance of a shambling, inhibited creature, always looking sideways instead of directly at a person, never standing up straight, hiding his nose in a book wherever possible, put upon by servants who see in him an idler not worth feeding and therefore fobbed off with scraps – with, of course, the traditional sidelocks (*peyes*) and a whispy beard, dressed in old-fashioned kneebreeches and caftan, with a round black hat on his head. This creature now sees himself married to Molly – and defies the rabbi, defies liberal offers of money from Molly's father, by refusing to give her up. Because of his defiance of the rabbi, who thinks it only right that Molly should be released from the serious consequences of her thoughtless prank, the whole community now turns against Jacob; he can no longer stay in the house of Molly's uncle, but is taken in by a poor couple who respect the stance he has adopted – out of genuine love for this strange girl from another world. In the end, however, he compromises. He and Molly will live apart; and if, after five years, she still refuses to marry him, she shall have her *get*. To that everyone reluctantly agrees.

Jacob now remembers that he has a wealthy uncle in Vienna, who has offered to take him into his house and his family. He travels to Vienna, finds his way across the city, arrives at the gates of his uncle's large garden in his Galician get-up. He deferentially approaches the gardener (who is unused to seeing such figures, except as unwelcome peddlars and beggars) and is unceremoniously bundled out. When the gardener, however, then describes the strange visitor to his employer, miming beard and sidelocks, he and another servant are despatched to bring Jacob back. He has, in fact, wearily collapsed at the gate; but seeing the two *goyim* approach, he takes to his heels and has to be caught and forcibly carried back into his uncle's house. He is received kindly, and directed to an 'Oriental Academy' where he would find materials facilitating the kind of research for which his thorough grounding in biblical and Talmudic Hebrew would be an excellent start.

His uncle then sets about Westernising him, pointing out, in the approved fashion of assimilated Austrian and German Jews, that a man's religion resides in his heart and not in his clothing. He points to a Star of David discreetly set into the wall of his house, indicating that one can be a good Jew at home while conforming in outward appearance and demeanour to the ways of the surrounding Gentile society. The lesson bears fruit: we see Jacob emerging from a barber-shop shorn of beard, moustache and sidelocks, and when we next meet him, studying in his uncle's house, he is wearing an elegant dressing gown and sporting a pair of spectacles to help an eyesight damaged by early poring over closely printed Hebrew books in inadequately lit surroundings. His whole demeanour changes – he stands up straight, looks directly at his interlocutors, sheds his hang-dog airs to assume a more and more self-confident manner. His studies at the Oriental Academy bear fruit; he becomes a respected scholar in the field, and after a public reading from his book he is formally received into the Academy Fellowship. Molly and her father have at this time been travelling in Europe to distract themselves from the awkward situation into which Molly's thoughtlessness has precipitated them; through machinations in which Jacob and his uncle are both involved, they receive an invitation to the reading, and to the elegant reception afterwards, where Jacob is mobbed for autographs by pretty women (we should all be so lucky!) and where the Uncle introduces them to 'his nephew, "Ben Ali"' – the suitably Oriental nom-de-plume Jacob has adopted as an author. He allows Molly to detach him from the company, she is clearly fascinated by him, begins to see him regularly, goes horse-riding with him (we never actually see them on horseback – the horses graze discreetly in the distance), and clearly falls in love. As a virtuous married woman, however, she reluctantly rejects his advances, sighing 'if only I were free'. Having thus passed every test of faithfulness and virtue, Molly is ready for the climactic revelation scene. She and her father are invited to the house of Jacob's uncle, and with the connivance of Jacob's aunt he dresses up in his former clothes, dons a wig with false side-whiskers, pastes on a beard, and presents himself to the company. Molly recoils at the sight, and the father, with threatening gestures, demands the *get* he has promised, now that five years have passed, so that the unfortunate marriage can be dissolved. He pretends to agree, and hands Molly the scroll which, she supposes, is her passport to freedom; only to find, when she unrolls it, the information that Jacob and Ben Ali are one and the same person. Whipping off wig and beard, he provides the ocular proof and asks whether she still desires the divorce. She doesn't, of course, and the film ends with a clinch (Goldin gives us a close-up of two eagerly whipping feet) while the rest of the company is bidden to look discreetly away.

The supporting cast is well chosen, presenting individuals who are also, recognisably, types. Molly's father, played with a good deal of mugging by Sidney Goldin himself, is a large, boisterous, clean-shaven man, who loves his Molly while also spanking her for yet another of her expected pranks, and has warm family feelings for the mother and brother he left behind to make his fortune in the new world. He has little polish, and even his Jewish education is rudimentary, leaving him unable to follow the Yom Kippur service. His family letters in German (or are they supposed to be in Yiddish?) have to be adapted from the formulae he uses in his business letters, forcing him to cross out 'Bestellung' (an order for goods to be supplied) and substitute 'Einladung' (invitation). After his European travels, however, he seems less uncouth, and in dress and manner fits in well when introduced to elegant company at the reception after Jacob' reading and at the no less elegant tea-table in the house of Jacob's uncle. Where Molly's father had Americanised his former name Braunstein to Brown, Jacob's uncle has Germanised whatever might have been his original family name, and is now called Alfred Fried (pronounced, as the American release of the film reminds us, 'Freed'). He is a large and dignified Austrian gentleman, played by Eugen Neufeld (the actor who was the Utopian Chancellor in *City without Jews*) in Burgtheater style. With his equally assimilated tall and handsome wife he moves as to the manner born through the spacious grounds and tastefully furnished villa with which the film has provided him. The couple seems to have no children of its own, and treats Jacob more like a son than a nephew from remote parts.

Where the air around Neufeld and the Fried household is redolent of Burgtheater, that around Saul Nathan and Laura Glucksmann, who play the Braunsteins, Mr Brown's Galician brother and mother, exudes the atmosphere of the Yiddish stage, as it took form in Poland, Galicia and Romania, and later migrated to the USA. Besides the irascible but fundamentally kindly patriarch Braunstein and his mother (who performs a charming, traditional solo dance to console Molly, but takes little other part in the action) the cast includes the local cantor and his choir, among them a huge fat young man whose circumference Molly characteristically measures against that of her father, but who shimmies along with the best of them; synagogue worshippers in full religious regalia; men keeping an all night vigil on Yom Kippur; assorted guests slurping soup at a festive banquet, performing traditional dances to the music of a Jewish band, and attending in various ways on Molly's newly married cousin and her husband. The couple is shut into a room away from the company, where husband and wife eat from the same plate to mark their new togetherness. An old woman listens at the door to make sure all is proceeding harmoniously. There is also a pair of comic servants: Mochle, the busy cook, much put upon by Molly (who even knocks her out with a boxer's punch at one point) and Shabse, the man-of-all-work – or rather, of as little work as possible – whose appetite for food matches that of Isidor in *The City without Jews*.

The non-Jewish characters in Vienna, seen in the library and assembly rooms of the Oriental Academy, are headed by a tall, kindly man in a clerical collar who helps the neophyte Jacob find the books he wants on the library shelves and who five years later welcomes the now Europeanised scholar as a full member of the Academy to whose field of study Jacob has made a much-appreciated contribution. Under the guidance of the uncle who has adopted the life-style of this cultured Viennese society without renouncing his Jewishness or denying his kinship with a young East European who seems at first his polar opposite, Jacob too becomes Austrianised. He now combines horse-riding skills with a kind of scholarship which goes beyond anything he could have acquired in his native town, and which makes him more acceptable to a circle that includes both Jews and non-Jews than exclusively Talmudic learning could have done. There was in fact a journal called *Ost und West*, to which Martin Buber contributed, which saw its main task as mediating between the culture of East European Jewry and a broader readership in the West.

J. Hoberman called Goldin's film 'a satisfying fantasy for Vienna's beleaguered Jewish community' – beleaguered, that is, by ever more vocal anti-Semitism – 'presenting a successfully Germanised Jew as a golden mean between the primitive *Ostjude* and the crass American'; and again: 'By arguing for adaptation as well as understanding, it suggests that beneath the *Ostjude*'s beard and *kapote* is a modern European waiting to be liberated' (Hoberman 1991: 68). That fantasy was to be perniciously reversed in *Der Ewige Jude* (*The Eternal Jew*), an anti-Semitic film with which Nazi propagandists prepared the population in Germany and beyond for the 'Final Solution' of 'the Jewish problem'. Eastern Jews were shown with beard and sidelocks, wearing the traditional caftan, and then shorn of facial hair and dressed in European clothes to suggest that these were the *real* Jews and their Europeanised ethnic relatives, baptised or not, were merely disguised for sinister purposes of exploitation and domination.

Sidney Goldin not only produced, directed, and acted in *East and West*, but co-wrote it with Eugen Preiss. There was also some input from Picon and Kalich, who had their own form of New York Jewish *shtik*. This took the movie out of the common pattern of filmed plays and novels, to which Yiddish and Jewish movies so often conformed. Shandler has rightly pointed to its use of universal folklore patterns – 'playing at marriage ceremony, test of constancy, woman persuaded (or wooed) by a trick, hero of unpromising appearance, marriage of poor boy and rich girl' (1992: 100) – which traverse its story of culture clashes and reconciliations in the Jewish world of the day. Goldin likes parallelisms that also present a contrast, as when a two-shot unites a *Shnorrer* (a Jewish beggar invited to partake of a rich man's meal in conformity with Jewish laws of charity) shovelling food into his mouth as fast as he can, with the needy student, another kind of charity case, sitting next to him and all but forgetting to eat while he watches his neighbour; he may, of course, already be yearning for the *Amerikaner shikse* that has so strangely swum into his ken. Parallelism and contrast extend over the whole film too, and govern its structure. When we first see Molly, she is carried into her father's presence on the linked arms of two young men; when Jacob first irrupts into Vienna, he is carried into the presence of his uncle in exactly the same way. Molly's horrified dream of what it would be like to become an Orthodox wife with a bearded and caftaned husband in a poor household full of children is paralleled by her later dream in which she sees a bearded Jacob on her left side – but then she turns to the right and sees Jacob's clean-shaven appearance in his guise as Ben Ali. Goldin and his cinematographer use simple superimposition to show the sleeping Molly and her nightmare/dream at the same time – paralleling an earlier use of the same device to indicate thoughts of Molly invading Jacob's studies by having her image appear on his forehead. In a similar way a Galician dance-scene at a Jewish wedding, becoming rather boisterous as the *klezmorim* strike up lively tunes, is paralleled and contrasted with a more stately dance at the Viennese reception in honour of 'Ben Ali'.

The superimposition device, as old as the cinema itself, is typical of the technical simplicity of the film, which proceeds linearly, without Griffithian intercutting; no scene outstays its welcome, the intertitles are often witty and far more sparing then those in *City without Jews*, with well-lit, well-photographed scenes telling its story simply and efficiently. Neither Molly Picon nor Jacob Kalich are conventionally good-looking, and Molly's looks are not improved by the bee-stung lips she paints over her own in emulation of some Hollywood star or starlet; but she carries it off by sheer energy, winsomeness, and feel for comic timing. Jacob's best features are his dark expressive eyes – and Goldin has wisely given them prominence through a number of extreme close-ups which allow us to observe the different ways he uses them in his two incarnations. The sideways glances of the shy Galician student contrast meaningfully with the confident gaze of the successful Oriental scholar.

Molly's disrespectful mockery of religious customs, and her sacrilegious behaviour on the most solemn feast of all, the Day of Atonement, have given offence, and even led to a call for the film's banning when it was first shown in the USA. But it all rebounds on Molly in the end – she goes too far for her own good, and is punished for it by the unhappy five years she spends between rejection of her involuntary marriage and acceptance of it when her husband has followed his uncle's precept, so often heard among German and Austrian Jews, that one can remain a good Jew in one's heart without looking like an East European Chassid. The presentation of religious ceremonies and Jewish customs in the Galician portions of the film is sometimes deliberately distanced (seen through a window, for instance); but what disrespect there is, is Molly's and not the film's. The solemnly binding nature of Jewish marriage 'before Moses and Israel' is recognised and accepted by everybody, East and West; and an intertitle reminds us, by using the traditional image of the 'golden chain' (*die goldene Kette, di goldene keyt*) of the bonds that tie a family together, however different their material circumstance, their surroundings, their educational attainments may be. Uncle Fried and his wife recognise their kinship with their as yet unemancipated nephew and receive him gladly; the Orthodox Braunsteins may disapprove of Molly's ways and ridicule her father's inability to find his way around a Hebrew prayerbook, but they never for a moment doubt that these strange visitors with the abbreviated name are members of their family whom – deep down – they love. With its often witty intertitles and its comedy spirit this film, produced for an Austrian company by an American director and American stars, and featuring a supporting cast made up of Gentile Austrians alongside Jewish actors originating in Eastern Europe, is not for people who lack a sense of humour. Those, however, who can appreciate its carnival spirit and more serious undertones will find it a richly rewarding work.

Chapter 4

'ENLIGHTENMENT' FILMS (*SITTENFILME*)

Anders als die Andern (Different from the Others) in its Context

It all started in the early days of cinema: because some entrepreneurs were Jewish, complaints about alleged moral delinquencies propagated and stimulated by films often had an anti-Semitic slant. As early as 1897, the *Linzer Morgenpost*, a local paper of Hitler's Austrian home town, complained about 'vulgar Jewish demoralising activities', ascribing to movies 'low, Judaising ways of thinking'; and in 1909, the *St Pöltener Zeitung* campaigned against cinematic 'smut' emanating from 'mostly Jewish entrepreneurs'. In fact, the films most often complained about, popular at *Herrenabende* (evening performances for adult men only) emanated from non-Jewish firms like the French Pathé Frères and the Austrian Saturn. The First World War largely silenced such voices, though the films continued to circulate; but they were heard again, after state censorship was briefly abolished in the young Weimar Republic, and a number of movies with titles like *Bridal Night in the Forest*, *Crying out for Women*, *Human Hyenas*, *The Hall of the Seven Sins*, *In the Claws of Sin* and so on promised more forbidden delights than most of the films actually provided. Others, like Robert Reinert's *Opium* (1918/19), introduced female nudity, hitherto proscribed in mainstream cinema, though liberally provided in privately shown movies like those by Saturn-Film, the first film company set up in Austria in the early years of the twentieth century. The Saturn offerings have been liberally documented in *Projektionen der Sehnsucht. Saturn: Die erotischen Anfänge de österreichischen Kinematographie* by Michael Achenbach and others (1999); and a more international selection may be viewed in the eight videos (so far) issued by VoltaMedia GmbH Paderborn, though unfortunately without details of date and national provenance.

Distinct from these, however, though particularly subject to anti-Semitically coloured attacks, was the new genre of *Aufklärungsfilme* or *Sittenfilme*, films of sexual documentation and enlightenment – sometimes described by their advocates and defenders on *Sozialhygienische Filmwerke*

(Films of Social Hygiene). The first and most prominent director of these, who also wrote or co-wrote the screenplays in collaboration with doctors, psychologists, and campaigners for legal reform, was Richard Oswald, born in Vienna as Richard W. Ornstein, the son of an affluent Jewish merchant.

The First World War had sharpened awareness of sexual needs and dangers that had long been the subject of literary works like Ibsen's *Ghosts* and Wedekind's *Spring's Awakening*, but had become the subject of wider scrutiny after the publication of Richard Krafft-Ebing's *Psychopathia Sexualis* in 1886, which had attributed to Jews 'abnormally intensified sensuality and sexual excitement'. This was noted particularly after the new subject of 'Sexualwissenschaft', sexology, attracted many Jewish practitioners – among them Magnus Hirschfeld, who founded a Yearbook of Sexology in 1899, Iwan Bloch, Max Marcuse, and (peripherally) Sigmund Freud. In this climate of opinion interested parties made the German army authorities aware of the propaganda and educative value of films that were not just demonstrations of medical facts, but combined these with some sort of exemplary story. Such films, it was hoped, might do much to alert men in the armed forces, and their dependants at home, to the dangers of the various types of disease that the promiscuous sexual contacts of wartime brought with them. Through the sponsoring agency of a German Society for Combating Venereal Diseases (*Deutsche Gesellschaft zur Bekämpfung der Geschlechtskrankheiten*) a hint was given to three Jewish filmmakers – Richard Oswald, Lupu Pick and Manfred Noa – that a film highlighting the dangers of venereal disease would be welcome. The resultant work, made in 1916–17, bore the biblical title: *Es werde Licht!* (*Let There be Light!*). It told of a young painter who contracted a venereal infection through a casual contact and went to some quack who pretended to have cured him; in this uncured state he won the affection of his brother's fiancée, married her, and in the course of time the infection spread to his wife and their daughter. He takes flight, leaving his daughter in his brother's care. The brother is in fact a fully qualified doctor, who specialises in syphilitic diseases of children, and manages to cure the girl, who – as a sign that she is indeed fully cured – is allowed to marry the doctor's son. The father returns, a physical and mental wreck, and in an affecting death scene dies in his daughter's arms. Oswald directed the film, crediting the central idea to Pick and acknowledging Noa's production design.

Oswald was anything but a novice in the film industry. The very title of the first movie in which he had appeared as an actor, *Halbwelt* (*Demimonde*, 1911), described as a 'theatre drama', was not a million miles away from those of his later 'enlightenment' or '*Sitten*' films, and had been followed, by 1917, by more than thirty other movies he had directed, or scripted, or both. He had tried many different genres before hitting on a recipe for films that would benefit as well as interest the paying public and would not be too expensive to produce. He took good care, however, to hire the best actors available, and to have his salons, drawing rooms, and places of public entertainment appropriately designed and furnished. It was hoped, moreover, that government-approved societies like that which sponsored the first *Let There be Light!* would continue to lend their approbation – especially because medical specialists were willing to cooperate. Since the latter were also social reformers, however, and were Jewish to boot, the opprobrium that many directed against Magnus Hirschfeld and Iwan Bloch hurt the films too. There were no nudities in these films – those were reserved to works lower down the line of respectability and to films that celebrated the healthy body, or purveyed medical instructions not designed for the general public; but commercial success was hoped for because of the curiosity value of subjects still regarded as taboo: homosexuality, abortion, satyriasis, sado-masochism – all in the ostensible service of 'enlightenment' and reform. With the help of designers like Noa and Josef Fenneker, Oswald and others who leapt onto the 'enlightenment' bandwagon, devised posters and advertising campaigns that promised rather more titillation than the films were able to deliver; for even in the short time during which mandatory state censorship remained in abeyance (it was reimposed in 1920), local police and civic authorities could shut a film show down if they thought it would give widespread offence, or attract the hostility of influential citizens. The films did, in fact, very soon bring out vigorous campaigners against them: religious groups, professional associations like those which united German jurists and high-school teachers, as well as individual self-appointed guardians of public morality and the sanctity of the criminal code.

It was soon noticed that Oswald and many of his collaborators were Jewish, and some of the other directors and authors of films in the 'enlightenment' mode were Jewish too. Among these the most notable were E.A. Dupont (*Alkohol*, 1919); Friedrich Zelnik (*Paradies der Dirnen/Leichtsinn und Lebewelt – Paradise of Prostitutes/Recklessness and Fast Living*, 1919) Max Mack (*Freie Liebe. Ein psychologischer Film/Free Love – A Psychological Film*, 1919); Lupu Pick (*Aus den Erinnerungen eines Frauenarztes: Lüge und Wahrheit*/Reminscences of a Gynaecologist: Lies and Truth, 1922); Kurt (later Curtis) Bernhardt (*Kinderseelen klagen euch an/The Souls of Children Accuse You*, 1927: a film *against* abortion, commissioned by the Catholic Church); and, belatedly, a version of Dr Friedrich Wolf's *Cyankali*, a controversial play about the iniquities of anti-abortion laws and backstreet practitioners, filmed in 1930.

Such works were soon lumped together with more sensationalist and pornographic movies under the rubric 'Schund- und Schmutzfilme', trashy and salacious films; and it is indicative of some of the inspiration behind such campaigns that at a meeting convened and chaired by Karl Brunner, one of the most prominent opponents of Oswald and the rest, almost all who contributed to the discussion began by declaring themselves anti-Semites. Needless to say, the burgeoning Nazi party found excellent ammunition here for their notorious accusation that Jews were out to corrupt and defile the 'Aryan' nations, and vigorously supported campaigns by Brunner and like-minded compatriots in Germany and Austria.

The first two sequels of *Let there be Light* (1917–18) carried on the theme of the original film by telling other stories exemplifying the dangers of venereal disease. The last sequel, however, entitled *Sündige Mütter (Strafgesetz 218) (Sinful Mothers: Criminal Code Section 218)*, joined another campaign, with collaboration from Magnus Hirschfeld: that against the harsh laws against abortion which penalised the poor, who, as the film shows, were forced to resort to the often fatal ministrations of backstreet abortionists, while wealthier women could ensure valid medical certificates that would procure them a safe abortion in some well-run hospital or clinic. This was followed by one of the best of Oswald's contributions to the genre, *Dida Ibsens Geschichte (Dida Ibsen's Story*, 1918) whose story-line excoriated forced marriages and depicted a clinical case of sadomasochism that elicited a quite frightening performance from Werner Krauss. Krauss's fellow-actors included Anita Berber, whose fascination on film was enhanced by her scandalous reputation as a nude dancer and drug addict, and a live python responsible for much sexual symbolism.

The year 1919 brought a film originally entitled *Prostitution*, which was also marketed, and either banned or mutilated by various censoring agencies, under the titles *Das gelbe Haus (The Yellow House)* and *Im Sumpfe der Grossstadt (In the Morass of Big Cities)*. In this film, one of several that Oswald called 'works of social hygiene' and on which Magnus Hirschfeld again acted as scientific adviser, 'Prostitution' appears in person before a world tribunal to defend her existence, and various cases are brought before this court which lead the judges to rule that they have no jurisdiction over an institution that has become an ineluctable necessity. Reform society first, they decree, and only after that can we sit in judgment on the oldest profession. After *Anders als die Andern (Different from the Others*, 1919), which will be considered in the concluding section of this chapter, Oswald interrupted the sequence of 'Enlightenment' films and turned to other genres. He did, however, occasionally return to related themes in later years: in *Halbseide (Not quite Silk*, 1925), for instance, the *Belle de Jour* of its day; in *Dürfen wir schweigen (Dare we keep Silent*, 1926), which tackled the question of medical confidentiality in cases where the patient is likely to spread the venereal disease he has contracted to partners ignorant of his condition; and in *Frühlings Erwachen (Spring's Awakening*, 1929), a version of Frank Wedekind's play about the agonies of adolescents in sexually repressive, and uninformative, societies.

A Closer Look at *Anders als die Andern*

Many will still remember how bold Basil Dearden, and his star Dirk Bogarde, appeared in 1961, when they dared to make a thriller called *Victim* that based its story-line on the problems faced by homosexuals under English law, and especially their vulnerability to blackmail. Well, Richard Oswald was there much earlier when he made *Anders als die Andern (Different from the Others)* more than forty years before. Written, produced and directed by Oswald in 1919, the film once again benefited from the collaboration of Magnus Hirschfeld, who also took the part of a doctor and lecturer in its story-line, to further his ongoing campaign for the reform of laws governing the behaviour of those whose sexual orientation differed from that of the majority. Confined by censorship, after 1920, to showings before medically qualified persons and in academic institutions, complete copies of Oswald's film have not, so far, been found. We do, however, have a re-edited version of its main plot, with changes to the order of scenes and the elimination of many subordinate parts and incidents. The names of two of the principal characters have also been changed. Many stills survive, however, along with a set of intertitles, which enable us to recognise what has been lost; and the re-edited version contains enough of the original to make an estimate of Oswald's aims and achievements meaningful. The existence of the re-edited version, entitled *Schuldlos geächtet (Guiltlessly Outlawed)*, which formed part of a film put together in 1927 by Magnus Hirschfeld under the title *Gesetze der Liebe. Aus der Mappe eines Sexualforschers (Laws of Love. From the Files of a Sexologist)*, gains significance as an indication that the problems Oswald's film raised in 1919 – the social and legal discrimination suffered by male homosexuals – were still acute eight years later.

Different from the Others tells the story of a homosexual violinist, Paul Körner, who speaks of his younger years to Else – a sympathetic listener, sister of his favourite pupil Kurt Sivers. The part of the listener has been eliminated in the later version, so that what was originally a flashback in the middle of the main action, now appears in chronological order at the film's beginning. It tells of an innocent friendship with a fellow schoolboy denounced as immoral by uncomprehending teachers – who have an ulterior motive in fastening the main blame on him rather than his friend, because the latter's parents are influential and could harm the school. They have, however, gauged young Körner's disposition correctly, even though he had committed no action that would have warranted the expulsion they decreed. This disposition appears more clearly in a later sequence, when his friends drag him away from his university studies to visit a brothel they have been frequenting. His disgusted resistance to the blandishments of some of the (remarkably attractive) ladies of the establishment is noted by the madam, whose expression clearly shows that she knows what is 'not in order' with this unwilling and unwelcome customer.

Abandoning his university studies for a musical career, he soon becomes a celebrated violinist. Recognising and accepting his proclivities, he visits a masked ball in an establishment favoured by homosexuals and there picks up a young man who agrees to accompany him home. That man, called Franz Bollek in the reedited version and Philipp Cisowsky in the original, turns out to be a blackmailer, who not only ruins him financially by increasing demands for money and by thefts from his home, but also destroys his (nonsexual but very close) relationship with his favourite pupil, Kurt Sivers. After vain attempts to 'cure' his homosexuality through hypnotic suggestion, he visits a doctor (played by Magnus Hirschfeld) who convinces him that no such 'cure' is possible, and that there is no reason why men programmed by nature in his way should not make valuable contributions to society. Encouraged by this, and goaded beyond endurance by the insolent blackmailer's escalating demands, he takes the risk of bringing charges of blackmail against him – a hardened criminal who does not hesitate to bring countercharges, incriminating himself as well as his victim, for offences against paragraph 175 of the German Criminal Code which made homosexual acts, even between consenting adults, subject to imprisonment. The court recognises the difference between the two men, but the judge has to uphold the law as it stands, and Körner receives a light prison sentence alongside Bollek's heavier one. Finding himself shunned by his acquaintances, forced to resign honourable offices at his clubs, his concerts cancelled and no new ones forthcoming, deserted even by his favourite pupil, Körner follows the course taken by many fellow-sufferers and commits suicide by taking poison.

The stars of the film are Conrad Veidt, in the year of his triumph as Cesare in *The Cabinet of Dr. Caligari*, as the blackmailed violinist, Reinhold Schünzel as the blackmailer, Fritz Schulz as the violinist's favourite pupil, and Anita Berber, cast against type, as Else, that pupil's sympathetic sister. The parts of the film in which Else and the rest of the pupil's family appear (Wilhelm Diegelmann as the father, Clementine Plessner as the mother) are now lost, as are those that featured Leo Connard as the violinist's father, troubled by his son's expulsion from his school, and Ilse von Tasso-Lind as his sister. Missing too are events in Kurt Sivers's home, and elaborately staged scenes in the foyer of a theatre or concert-hall, where the blackmailer confronts Körner and Else. Nor do we now have the funeral scene in which Kurt breaks down at his late master's coffin. We can still view stills of the lost portions, and I hope that the originals will one day be found – since even what we have now is only available because it turned up in a Ukrainian export-copy of Hirschfeld's *Laws of Love*.

Since he had at his disposal Veidt and Schünzel, two of the most eloquent faces in the early German cinema, Oswald worked throughout with big close-ups of faces and hands, showing subtle gradations of anguish, affection and cynicism. Veidt portrays a sensitive, gifted but fundamentally weak and neurotic type, given to physical collapse at crises but also roused to sudden rage that could easily collapse again, slipping at the end into an irresistibly suicidal frame of mind. Schünzel, a gifted director as well as actor, dominates the film in the way Iago usually dominates performances of *Othello*. He plays (horribly convincingly) an idler who hangs around cafés and bars favoured by homosexuals in order to batten on vulnerable creatures like Paul Körner. Fritz Schulz is not in the same league – but he mimes devotion and artistry prettily (eyes turning to heaven when he plays his violin) and has a fair shot at dawning realisation and disgust when the blackmailer takes him for a fellow-homosexual being paid for his services to Körner.

Schünzel's Bollek is cold, calculating, vulgar, coarse – but he also knows clearly what he is (homosexual like his victims) and accepts it with an irony that lends his performance an air of what later generations would learn to call 'camp'. It is worth remembering, in this connection, that the 'camp' phenomenon had been described over a decade before by the same Magnus Hirschfeld whose cooperation counted for so much in *Different from the Others*. In a volume Hirschfeld contributed to Hans Ostwald's *Grossstadt-Dokumente* (*Documents of Life in Big Cities*), entitled *Berlins Drittes Geschlecht* (*Berlin's Third Sex*, 1906) he itemised what he described as 'droll' (*drollig*) aspects of homosexual behaviour: self-irony, love of the grotesque, and a determination to convert 'life's tragedy' into 'life's comedy' (Hagener 2000: 88).

The passages showing the future violinist at school, in which Veidt's role is taken over by another actor, Kurt Giese, bring the film into proximity to a subgenre of the Enlightenment film: the dystopian school-story, designed to show the harm done to young minds by uncomprehending teachers and parents. The model here was the seminal play by Frank Wedekind already mentioned, *Spring's Awakening*, written in 1890–1, and subtitled *Eine Kindertragödie* (*A Children's Tragedy*). The subgenre is most famously represented by Sternberg's *The Blue Angel* of 1930, in which we see pupils take sadistic revenge on their pedantic teacher when the latter becomes vulnerable – a variant of the usual plot in which sympathies are wholly engaged on the side of the young.

'Silent' films were not usually seen in silence; but I have not encountered any of the music which must have accompanied *Different from the Other* and *Laws of Love* at showings not limited to the medical profession. Oswald develops his plot, however, in a variety of ways not dependent on music, whose interplay can still be studied even in the film's reedited form.

The most interesting of these, and the ones best calculated to concentrate attention on the faces Oswald and his cinematographer wanted to explore, are those in which brightly lit figures appear, either singly or in groups, within an otherwise complete darkness. The first of such scenes presents a teacher's tribunal before which the accused boy, played by Kurt Giese, has to appear after one of these teachers has accused him of homosexuality. Here we have Giese clearly visible in the foreground while a row of teachers, six well-assorted pedagogic types, sit at what we surmise to be a long table, their faces and hands clearly distinguishable, amid a darkness that is unrelieved by any sign of what kind of a room they are in. Veidt's expressive face and hands are equally isolated at various points; but what stays longest in the memory is the court hearing in which Körner and Bollek both have to answer to the law. All we see of the courtroom is a long horizontal wooden bar behind which the two defendants sit, apart from each other but on the same level, while they listen to the arguments of prosecutor and defender, and to the judge's verdict. The contrast between the deepening anguish of the one (culminating in physical collapse after the verdicts) and the cynical defiance, half-grins and folded arms of the other is all the more striking because there is nothing else to detract from our observation of their eloquent faces and hands.

Related to this most radical isolation of human beings from their physical environment is another mode of staging that appears at intervals from the school scenes onwards. Here an environment is suggested by a minimum of props – a papered wall, a table, two iron bedsteads, a cupboard or bookcase, student caps and crossed duelling sabres – that serve to indicate a study, or a dormitory, concentrating our attention on the facial expressions and body-stance of the actors. The brothel scene is a good example: it is crowded with happy couples, with their glasses and bottles before a vague background, against which two figures stand out: the uncooperative Körner, and the brothel madam, kiss-curled and gorgeously got up, who looks with unmistakable disgust at the customer who scorns her wares – for reasons long experience allows her to divine. She has, of course, a professional interest in disapproval of homosexuality.

There are, however, more elaborate studio sets, designed by Emil Linke, which reveal something of the nature of those who act within them, and the milieu in which such persons operate. Two of these are particularly important in the framework of the story as we now have it.

The first is Linke's construction and furnishing of the room in which the doomed violinist plays his piano, teaches his pupils and entertains his visitors. Its most striking (and symbolic) feature is its location below the level of the front door, ensuring that access means descent. It is richly furnished with beautiful carpets and rugs, a deep easy-chair, vases full of flowers, piano and music stand, pictures on the walls, cupboards with knick-knacks, mementoes and a clock, and dominated by a male statue on a plinth, wielding a long sword (Freudians beware!). Here the violinist, who is served by a valet, discards the sober garments he wears outside and in the concert-hall, and dons a loose dressing gown with an oriental pattern that transforms his appearance. Except at the masked ball all other characters in the extant portions wear dark formal clothes, though Sivers sports an open-neck shirt – as Körner does too, when at home, to give himself a Byronic look. Bollek's appearance grows more soigné as his blackmail and thieving allows him to buy more expensive clothes.

Another elaborate set represents what would nowadays be called a 'gay bar': the first, as far as I know, in the German cinema. This constitutes an ideal space in which the blackmailer can spread his nets in the foreground, while a platform at the rear is occupied by musicians. There are chairs at the sides, garlands slung from the ceiling, and the middle ground is left free for dancing couples in costume, male dancing with male. Here the violinist picks up his future blackmailer in the hope of a pleasant sexual encounter while the camera penetrates deep into the room, bringing the dancing couples (who at one time dance two by two in a ring), and the musicians at the back, into equal focus. There are other less elaborate but equally significant sets in the rest of the film which include, within the portions we have, a café and wine bar also frequented by homosexuals, a concert hall (in which we see ranks of applauding auditors at the front and sides, and a stage on which Körner performs at the rear), and a lecture hall (tiered benches in the middle ground, lecturer's platform at the front) in which Magnus Hirschfeld delivers a lecture about the nature of homosexuality and the invidiousness of paragraph 175, which receives the eager approbation of his young audience.

Everything described so far takes place amid studio sets and expert studio lighting. Oswald and his cinematographer, Max Fassbender, however, leave the studio behind on occasions, to film in the streets and parks of Berlin. One of these outside scenes has been preserved: a pleasant walk in the *Tiergarten* interrupted when Körner and Kurt, arm in arm and deeply engaged in conversation, encounter Bollek coming from another direction. Before they can draw away the blackmailer fastens on them, insinuating that their relation is anything but innocent, and malevolently hissing the words 'Hübscher Junge' ('Pretty boy') in the violinist's direction. Master and pupil pass on quickly, but the blackmailer has new ammunition now – and eventually a fight between Kurt and Bollek, when Kurt catches the blackmailer at attempted burglary, turns into a fierce fight between Körner and his tormentor. When the flustered and dishevelled Bollek taunts the relation between master and pupil by speaking to the latter as one homosexual paid by Körner to another, Körner feels forced, at last, to take Bollek to court – with consequences which the cynical blackmailer and would-be burglar can shrug off, but which prove fatal to his more sensitive and vulnerable accuser.

Oswald once described *Different from the Other* as a simple life-story ('eine schlichte Lebensgeschichte') wreathed around a lecture. That centrally important lecture, Dr Hirschfeld's disquisition on homosexuality and the need for legal reform, was reproduced in full in a series of intertitles of previously unmatched length – though only a few sentences from it survive in the re-edited copy. Here was another channel of information Oswald did not hesitate to use: one that conveyed the words the 'silent' cinema could not, as yet, reproduce in any other form. Such intertitles are supplemented by printed materials like the newspaper items which conjure up before Körner's eyes a long procession of fellow-sufferers driven to suicide; and by a final shot of the German Criminal Code, open at the invidious paragraph 175, which is boldly crossed through.

Different from the Others provided self-appointed guardians of public morality, whose demonstrations within and without German cinemas daring to show the film often took and explicitly anti-Semitic form, with some of their most effective ammunition. Was not this Jewish writer-director, seconded by a Jewish sex-therapist who actually played a part in the film, enlisting sympathy for a neurotic and (as the law then stood) criminal type, against teachers, lawyers and all those whose task it was to watch over the moral and physical health of the nation? Was he not making 'perversion' respectable by associating it with artistic achievement? Was he not infecting the vulnerable part of the nation, in particular its youth, by presenting transvestitism and men dancing with men in a way that might tempt them into similar practices, and worse? Did not the actor who portrayed a homosexual villain to the life, with a verve no other character possessed, have a Jewish mother, to match the Jewish parents of Oswald and other directors of 'Enlightenment' films? Do not these films question the very identity of postwar German men, after so many of the healthiest and most self-confident lost their lives on the battlefield? Are these Jewish filmmakers not attributing to 'Aryan' males the very 'abnormally intensified sensuality' and 'sexual excitement' with which Krafft-Ebing had credited their fellow Jews? Are not their depictions of 'drives' (*Triebe*) that cannot be resisted undermining the self-discipline, the inner strength, that was sorely needed when so many had perished in the war, and when Germany's enemies were weakening her with excessive demands for reparations alongside continuing occupation and blockade? All these questions, and the answers they all too readily suggested, were eagerly seized on by enemies of the Jews, who would soon rally around the National Socialist Worker's Party, and other groupings in Germany and Austria that openly inscribed anti-Semitism into their programmes. Their task was made easier by a proliferation of more meretricious filmmakers, who used the mantle of the *Sittenfilm* to lure audiences into the cinema with posters promising a degree of titillation the films themselves seldom matched in full. This need not, however, blind later audiences to the genuine nature of Oswald's social concerns, and the skilful way in which he embodied them in cinematic works of popular art.

What should never be discounted, when assessing the moral content and concern of films like *Different from the Others*, is a traditional Jewish sense of social justice, based on biblical and Talmudic traditions and strengthened by long experience of injustices in the Diaspora, as a factor impelling so many Jewish writers, directors, producers and reformers to cultivate and support type of film dedicated to the eradication of legal and moral inequities. Such traditions persisted even in families who were largely estranged from the Jewish religion, and found a response among the many non-Jewish colleagues who collaborated on 'Enlightenment' films. That such films also met hostility and incomprehension among upholders of traditional values and judicial attitudes should surprise no one who has observed the slow ways of social and legal reform.

Chapter 5

1929: A YEAR OF TRANSITION

The year 1929 was a fateful one for the German film industry. It was becoming increasingly obvious that the days of the 'silent' cinema were numbered. As the year sailed towards the Wall Street stock market crash and a world-wide financial crisis, patents for various modes of adding sound to film had to be sorted out, a particular system had to be decided on, spheres of interest and activity had to be negotiated (notably between Western Electric, Tobis and Klangfilm), studios had to be remodelled to allow sound-recording, cinema proprietors had to invest in new equipment, and the many musicians employed to provide accompaniments to the action on the screen saw the writing on the wall. Sound films were few, as yet, and technical difficulties abounded; but works like the Anglo-German *Atlantic* and the Ufa *Melodie des Herzens* (*Melody of the Heart*) whetted the appetite for better things to come. Gero Gandert, whose expert and authoritative compilation *Der Film der Weimarer Republik: 1929* forms the basis for this chapter (Gandert 1993), lists 219 full-length German fiction films (including some co-productions) of which nine have some music and sound effects, and seven include some speech. The industry employed many Jews as actors, directors, writers, cameramen, set-designers, musicians and publicity managers, and many production companies were owned or managed by Jewish entrepreneurs. There were no full-length feature films that year which had Jewish problems at their centre; but there was one short film, significantly entitled *Alte Kleider* (*Old Clothes*), directed by Johannes Guter, which played in a Jewish milieu and had a cast dominated by Jewish actors specialising in comic parts: Paul Morgan, Siegfried Arno and Felix Bressart – with Hugo Döblin added for good measure.

It would not, however, be true to say that characters identified as Jews did not figure in the plots of full-length feature films. Their names usually served as signals of recognition. In *Der Erzieher meiner Tochter* (*My Daughter's Tutor*) – a sadly witless clone of Lubitsch's *Die Austernprinzessin* (*The Oyster Princess*, 1913) – the fat Hungarian actor Huszar-Puffy played a character called Sami Goldstone, whose daughter has a hankering to marry into the aristocracy. In the same film A.E. Licho appeared as a rabbi. In *Madame im Strandbad* (*Lady in the Spa*), Robert Garrison has what is described as a 'Jargonrolle', a part that calls for 'Jewish' mannerisms, as the proprietor of a laundry who is persuaded to impersonate an American nabob in order to give the impression that the provincial spa in which he lives is a *Weltbad*, a spa that attracts visitors from all over the world. His name in this film is Jonathan Goldfisch. Garrison, whom we have already met as the itinerant beggar of *The Ancient Law*, was something of a specialist in Jewish roles, and was called on in this same year, 1929, to play a banker called Rothschild in a film based on the Kalman-Grünbaum operetta *Der Zigeunerprimas* (*The Gypsy Chief*); and when Garrison played an unnamed money-lender in another film that year, called *Achtung! Liebe! Lebensgefahr!* (*Take Care! Love! Danger to Life!*), no one could miss the implication that this character was meant to be Jewish. Huszar-Puffy was also pressed into a Jewish part again: in *Vater und Sohn* (*Father and Son*) he plays a partner in a law firm called Epstein.

Ever since Lubitsch's early films the name 'Pinkus' had been a favourite signal for Jewishness; it turns up again in a Harry Piel thriller, written by the prolific Robert Liebmann, called *Die Mitternachtstaxe* (*Taxi at Midnight*), in which Bruno Ziener plays S.W. Pinkus, the villain of the piece, who has swindled away millions, allowed others to take the blame and the punishment, and then tries to kill his accomplice when the latter, released from prison, claims his share of the loot. To cast actors in parts recognised as Jewish which involved cheating others out of large sums was a dangerous proceeding apt to recall a few trials of Jewish businessmen which made headlines more easily remembered than many others that involved non-Jews. The signal could be appearance and demeanour rather than a name: one need only recall how Hans Steinhoff had used, and directed, Kurt Gerron in the Anglo-German co-production of 1928-9 known as *Nachtgestalten* (*Creatures of the Night*) in Germany, and *The Alley Cat* in England. A 'Dr Pinkus' also figured in a film called *Was eine Frau im Frühling träumt* (*What a Woman dreams of in Springtime*): he plays a minor part as a solicitor and notary, and is acted by Ludwig Sachs. Such parts were usually assigned to Jewish actors; but even such well-known (and clearly Gentile) actors as Paul Hörbiger were occasionally pressed into Jewish roles, as when Hörbiger played the impresario Siegfried Nürnberger in Georg Jacoby's *Frauen am Abgrund* (*Women on the Edge of an Abyss*). It is salutary to remember that Veit Harlan, whose *Jud Süss* of 1940 paved the way for genocide, had thirteen years earlier played a Jewish barber in *Die Hose* (*Panties*) under a Jewish director, Hans Behrend, who was to perish in the Shoa.

One in-joke gleefully picked up by contemporary critics concerned an actor with features that many recognised as 'Jewish', called Siegfried Berisch. In *Fräulein Lausbub* (*Mischievous Miss*) Berisch was assigned the part of an equerry called *Arisch*: a pun on his actual name which played on the racist distinction, more and more common as Nazi propaganda took hold, between 'Aryans' and 'Semitic' Jews.

Two physically very disparate Jewish actors, the thin Siegfried Arno and the burly Kurt Gerron, combined to form a comic duo called 'Beef' and 'Steak', which, it was hoped, would give Germany a native equivalent of Hollywood's Laurel and Hardy and Denmark's Pat and Patachon, both very popular with German audiences. The films that featured Beef and Steak, however, including *Wir halten fest und treu zusammen* (*We Stick Together through Thick and Thin*) failed because of unsuitable scripts, poor direction, and insufficient character differentiation between the two principal comics.

In German films of the period Jews played most frequently roles which did not involve suggestions that the character they assumed was Jewish. They mostly appeared in supporting 'character parts'; but there were also star actors like Fritz Kortner, Elisabeth Bergner and Franz Lederer who were assigned leading roles. In 1929 Kortner was able for the first time to use not only his well-practised silent acting skills but also his stage-trained voice in the German exemplar of Dupont's *Atlantic*, filmed in an English- as well as a German-language version. For modern audiences the slow speed of utterance forced on the actors by the requirements of early sound recording makes his performance of the writer Heinrich Thomas less effective than it might have been. He had a very busy year: he could also be seen as a Scandinavian consul in Adolf Trotz's *Die Frau in Talar* (*The Woman in the Attorney's Gown*); as the demonic Dr Karoff in Kurt Bernhardt's *Die Frau, nach der man sich sehnt* (*The Woman One Longs For*), in which he effectively partnered Marlene Dietrich, in her best film before *The Blue Angel*; as President of an industrial concern manufacturing chemicals in *Giftgas* (*Poison Gas*), directed by Michael Dubson with some advice from Sergey Eisenstein; as a despotic sea-captain in Maurice Tourneur's disappointing adventure film *Das Schiff der verlorenen Menschen* (*The Ship of Lost Men*) – Dietrich again co-starred here, as a 'lost woman' among the male crew. A film like this makes one understand better than *The Woman One Longs For* Dietrich's later wish to forget all the films she appeared in before Sternberg took her in hand. Kortner also appeared as a tyrannical bourgeois father in Adolf Trotz's *Somnambul*; a Levantine convict just released from prison in Gustav Ucicky's *Der Sträfling aus Stambul* (*The Convict from Istanbul*); and Dr Schön, a newspaper tycoon in thrall to Louise Brooks's unforgettable Lulu in *Die Büchse der Pandora* (*Pandora's Box*). Is the director of that film, G.W. Pabst, hinting that he thinks of Kortner's character as Jewish when he has a ritual candelabrum, a *menorah*, appear in the background of the love-nest he has furnished for Lulu? Be that as it may, *Pandora's Box* features other Jewish actors in prominent character parts: Carl Goetz as Schigolsch, who might or might not be Lulu's father; Franz Lederer as the weak Alwa Schön, who follows his father as Lulu's lover and is driven to cheating at cards for her sake; and Siegfried Arno in a lively turn as a harried stage-manager.

Franz Lederer pops up again, in a well-acted but sadly novelettish film, *Die wunderbare Lüge der Nina Petrowna* (*The Wonderful Lie of Nina Petrowna*), the last of Ufa's lavishly mounted 'prestige' films of the silent era. He also played the part of a painter in a film directed by Georg Jacoby which highlighted the harshness of the German judicial system (*Meineid* [*Perjury*]), smaller parts in Dupont's *Atlantic* (where he was a doomed young husband caught in a disaster like that of the *Titanic*) and as a young French aristocrat in Julien Duvivier's *Maman Colibri*. Unlike these male actors Elisabeth Bergner appeared only once on German screens in this season. She played the title role in an adaptation of Arthur Schnitzler's *Fräulein Else*, directed by Paul Czinner and photographed to bring out Bergner's frail beauty by Karl Freund. This film will be briefly considered in the final chapter of this book. It joins an astonishing number of original scripts and adaptations from earlier sources filmed in the course of the Weimar Republic, which end with a suicide – a phenomenon not without social and psychological significance in the years after the First World War and before the advent of a hoped-for 'saviour' who would, as it turned out, lead Germany, and the Austria he incorporated into the Reich, into an even more cruel and disastrous war.

Nina Petrowna was one of three films produced by Erich Pommer, recently returned from Hollywood, some of whose studio-production methods he introduced to Ufa while also concerning himself with the negotiations that would inaugurate a new 'sound' era in the German cinema. His first venture into that territory was called *Melodie des Herzens* (*Melody of the Heart*), directed by a new protégé, Hanns Schwarz, who would become one of the important directors of German film musicals before the Nazi catastrophe drove him out just over three years later. *Melody of the Heart* had music by W.R. Heymann, Paul Abraham and the (non-Jewish) composer Robert Stolz, along with farmyard and other noises and sparse dialogue that required Willy Fritsch to repeat a few sentences in German, English, French and Hungarian for the four versions released for international distribution. It can't have come as a surprise to regular viewers of contemporary German films that the heroine of *Melody of the Heart*, played by Dita Parlo, ends by drowning herself. The most permanently valuable contribution to the German fiction film produced, in 1929, by a Jewish director working under Pommer's aegis, was Joe May's *Asphalt*, which will be considered later in some detail.

Asphalt was an expensive 'prestige film', premiered in Berlin at the renowned Ufa Palast am Zoo; but the majority of Jewish directors working in 1929 made less ambitious *Mittelfilme*, calculated to appeal to a wider, provincial audience in Germany and Austria, though it was hoped that metropolitan audiences would also respond positively to some of the themes and their cinematic realisations. Among the most successful Jewish purveyors of unsophisticated fare were Jakob and Luise Fleck, whose three films of 1929 catered for an appetite for operetta-like plots, love and intrigue in high places (*Der Leutnant seiner Majestät – His Majesty's Lieutenant*), stories of suffering, abuse and (of course) suicide in lower social regions (*Mädchen am Kreuz – Crucified Girl[s]*); and the problem so notably treated on the German stage in Ernst Toller's *Hinkemann*: the right of men made impotent by war-wounds to contract a marriage (*Das Recht auf Liebe*

– *The Right to Love*). This last was a 'problem film' that linked naturally to the 'Enlightenment' films discussed in the last chapter: a genre which, under the impact of two widely publicised court cases, involving juveniles that committed murder, veered into a subgenre, the 'Jugendfilm', treating the sexual, psychological and social problems of young people. Richard Oswald's adaptation of Wedekind's *Spring's Awakening*, belongs in this category, as does Conrad Wiene's Austrian *Eros in Ketten* (*Eros Enchained*), with its alternative titles *Sexualnot der Jugend* (*Sexual Distresses of the Young*) and *Halbe Kinder* (*Half a Child Still*). This, for once, had a happy ending, but not until poor Maly Delschaft had borne a child out of wedlock and suffered the hell of a correctional institution – just like Louise Brooks in *Tagebuch einer Verlorenen* (*Diary of a Lost Girl*), where the sadistic matron is memorably played by the eccentric Jewish dancer and character-actress Valeska Gert. Richard Loewenbein's *Verirrte Jugend* (*Youth Gone Astray*) combines the same subject with the colour-problem by featuring a star of African origin, El Dura, as one of its young people. Oswald also returned to his old territory by making yet another film about the problems of marriage: *Ehe in Not* (*Marriage in Trouble*), whose projected title *Ehe zu dritt* (*Three-cornered Marriage*) sufficiently indicates the kind of trouble the marriage is in. The film ends with the sobering recognition that even if the husband in question had ditched his wife and married the other woman, none of them would have been happy in the long run.

Oswald also filmed *Cagliostro*, which sought to rescue Giuseppe Balsamo from his sinister reputation as a rapacious charlatan and remake him into the sympathetic persona projected by the wholly undemonic German actor Hans Stüwe; and crowned an early success with a workmanlike remake of *The Hound of the Baskervilles*, with Carlyle Blackwell as a suitably Britannic Sherlock Holmes and Fritz Rasp (inevitably) as the villain Stapleton. The fastidious director Ludwig Berger did his reputation no favours with the Mady Christians/Gustav Fröhlich vehicle *Das brennende Herz* (*Heart Aflame*), and Paul Czinner's *Die Strasse der verlorenen Seelen* (*The Street of Lost Souls*) showed that Czinner was more in tune with the neurotically sensitive, androgynous Elisabeth Bergner than with the fiery diva Pola Negri around whose star image the film was built. Czinner was easily outshone by the young Kurt Bernhardt, whose already mentioned *The Woman One Longs For* conveyed something of the magnetism of Marlene Dietrich before Sternberg became her Svengali. She was effectively paired with Fritz Kortner at his most demonic and dangerous. Her partner in *Ich küsse Ihre Hand, Madame* (*I Kiss your Hand, Madam*), directed by another Jewish director, Robert Land, was Harry Liedtke; his rival for her affection was played by Karl Huszar-Puffy, and the title song was apparently performed by Liedtke: but the voice the audience heard was in fact that of Richard Tauber, synchronised by an early feat of cinematic technology. Robert Land employed Liedtke again, in a film that acknowledged by its very title that this actor occupied, in 1929, the place which would soon be held, in the early 1930s, by Willy Fritsch: *Der Held aller Mädchenträume* – the hero of every [German] maiden's dream.

How good such *Mittelfilme* could be is shown by a German-Hungarian co-production whose title, *Achtung! Kriminalpolizei!* (*Look out! Plain Clothes Police!*) puts it into the popular thriller category, but whose direction, by Paul Sugar and Lajos Lazar, and writing, by Lazar and Walter Reisch, places it far above the average. The pacing and editing of the opening scenes, showing a reporter shouldering his way through a crowd straining to get into a court room where a sensational trial is about to take place, would not have disgraced Fritz Lang; and the subsequent pacing and framing of shots, judicious choice of camera angles and close-ups (of feet as well as faces), perfectly conveys the nightmare of imprisonment, and the slow passing of time in solitary confinement, even when the prison staff is gentle and considerate.

Lazar and Sugar, who did not go on to have brilliant careers, are rewarded by some remarkably assured performances by the four principal women concerned (including a discreetly understated suggestion of a lesbian relationship), and an even more memorable performance, as a vain, vulgar and heartless seducer, by Hans Adalbert Schlettow, the stern Hagen of Lang's *Die Nibelungen* cast resolutely and successfully against type.

Achtung! Kriminalpolizei, with its subtitle *Gefangene Nr. 7* (*Prisoner Number Seven*) was calculated to appeal to the many fans of thriller and detective films, but offered something more than the common fare. Other genres given interesting turns by Jewish directors in this year 1929 included the historical epic: Lupu Pick directed, and Willy Haas wrote, *Napoleon auf Sankt Helena*, which limited itself to the captive Emperor's last sad years, eliciting an unusually quiet performance from Werner Krauss in the name part. Then there was the circus and variety film, *Katharina Knie*, directed by Karl Grune and adapted from Carl Zuckmayer's recently published play of the same name; and the domestic comedy, enriched by a film called *Ruhiges Heim mit Küchenbenutzung* (*Rooms to Let in a Quiet Home, with Use of Kitchen*), directed with a suitably light touch by Carl Wilhelm (who also had a hand in composing its screenplay). This was performed with quiet humour by an expert cast portraying landladies, henpecked husbands, domineering wives, tailors and dentists, and with welcome brio by the flamboyant actress Elisabeth Pinajeff as an opera star – ominously called Bella Donna – who is the cause of many complications. Wilhelm also directed another comedy in a petty-bourgeois milieu, *Teure Heimat* (*Dear Homeland*), which revolves around a young German mechanic persuaded to refrain from emigrating to the USA, who is involved in some thrilling episodes before landing the lady of his heart – played with great charm by the unforgettable non-Jewish actress Müller, whom we will meet again in a later chapter. Carl Wilhelm's *Zigeunerprimas* has already been mentioned: it is one of many attempts, by Lubitsch and others, to transfer to the silent screen the plot and characters of popular operettas – in this case the musical of the same name by Emmerich Kalman, with texts by Fritz Grünbaum and Julius Wilhelm. Ernst Verebes, a Jewish actor, had the important part of the gypsy chief's son.

Among Jewish directors kept busiest, in 1929, at supplying the market with acceptable films in popular genres, was Rudolf Meinert. *Das grüne Monokel* (*The Green Monocle*) is a detective yarn featuring one of the many detectives with English names created in the silent-film era as rivals to Sherlock Holmes. At least two of these were first performed by Jewish actors: Stuart Webbs (by Ernst Reicher) and Joe Deebs (by Max Landa). In *The Green Monocle*, the part of Stuart Webbs is assumed by Ralph Cancy; he has many adventures in his quest for the recovery of a stolen document, and at one point even impersonates the perpetrator he seeks to bring to justice. Meinert also adds to the proliferating adaptations of sentimental novels written by (preferably titled) ladies of a previous generation when he filmed *Die weissen Rosen von Ravensberg* (*The White Roses of Ravensberg*, written in 1887 by Countess Eufemia von Adlersfeld-Ballestrem. This has a plot of hair-raising nonsense about wrongful suspicions and accusations in high places, and ends with a clearing up of them all which paves the way for the marriage of one titled person to another. One shouldn't mock, I suppose, the need of people leading drab and poverty-stricken lives to live such wish-fulfilling daydream stuff vicariously in the darkness of the cinema; but for me it is a relief to turn from this to Meinert's second venture into Stuart Webbs territory, *Masken* (*Masks*), with its cast of bankers, gamblers and exotic criminals, its setting of banks, gambling hells, thieves' dens and harbour pubs with disreputable customers, and its exciting incidents of false imprisonment, muggings, and impersonations. But then: fans of Ballestrem, Hedwig Courts-Mahler and the like would no doubt have found my life-long addiction to detective novels and urban thrillers more unhealthy than theirs.

Another prolific provider of *Mittelfilme*, efficiently directed and acted films in popular genres, was Adolf Trotz. The very titles of his 1929 offerings constitute a programme. *Die Frau im Talar* (*The Woman in the Advocate's Gown*), has an eponymous heroine who commits suicide when she finds out that the forgery of which her lover has been accused, and in the prosecution of which she is involved in her official capacity, has in fact been committed by her own father. *Jugendtradödie* (*Tragedy of Youth*) features Rolant Varno, who would soon be the bane of Emil Jannings's amorous professor in *The Blue Angel*, but who is here the son of a washerwoman sent by the courts to a correctional facility for a minor misdemeanour, breaks out, is recaptured, and in the end commits a murder for which an even sterner imprisonment awaits him. If *Tragedy of Youth* swells the ranks of problem films highlighting society's failure to deal adequately with its adolescents, *Das Recht der Ungeborenen* (*The Right of the Unborn*), takes up the other side of the stance taken by most of the earlier films that had dealt with Section 178 of the Criminal Code. In a story involving a rich family and a poor one, Trotz's film stresses that the law is right in permitting abortion only when a doctor can certify that it is medically imperative, though still pleading for its relaxation in cases involving the overcrowded and overworked poor. *Somnambul*, yet another product of Trotz's industry released in 1929, cottons on to the perennial German interest in the paranormal, which had recently been stimulated by the activities of a Berlin clairvoyant, Elsbeth Günther-Geffers. Frau Günther-Geffers herself plays a clairvoyant in the film, which tells a story that once again, like so many German films of the time, ends with a suicide. Jewish actors of the calibre of Kortner, Jaro Fürth (prominent in Pabst's *Joyless Street*), Julius Falkenstein (unforgettable in Lubitsch's *Oyster Princess*), and Hugo Döblin, played in *Somnambul* roles which did not stretch them unduly or add to their reputation – though Falkenstein as a mesmerist is a collectable item for many fans. None of Trotz's films enthused the metropolitan critics; but they played well in outlying districts, recouped their costs, and disappeared from view when their director was forced to emigrate. He went to Spain, where he added four more films to the tally of those he had made in Germany, the last of them in 1936.

Some Jewish filmmakers of 1929 were able to make the transition from 'silent' to sound film with éclat before they too were driven into emigration. These included Wilhelm Thiele (né Wilhelm Isersohn), who forged his association with Lilian Harvey in *Adieu, Mascotte*, a story set in the Parisian *bohème*; it was made into a silent film and later given a synchronised soundtrack. Others who experimented with sound in the same year included Hanns Schwarz, Kurt Bernhardt and Reinhold Schünzel. We shall meet all these again in later chapters. The year 1929 was, in fact, Schünzel's most prolific year. He directed *Kolonne X. Ein Drama der Unterwelt* (*Column X: A Drama of the Underworld*), a forlorn attempt to make an American-style gangster film in a German setting; *Peter der Matrose* (*Peter the Mariner*), a sentimental story of a gentleman ruined by a woman who leaves everything behind to sail the seven seas, returns to find that the grounds of his action had been mistaken, but chooses to ship out again without renewing his former ties; and *Phantome des Glücks* (*Phantoms of Happiness*) which, unlike the other two, did not have Schünzel playing the lead as well as directing. The 'phantoms' of the title are chased by the director of an insurance company who ruins himself for the sake of a dancer, lands in prison, and there murders another inmate. The insurance company involved is called 'Prudence'; but the irony of that title is, alas, the only one in a film whose sticky sentiment holds little promise, either in its 'silent' form or when later given a synchronised sound-track, of the witty and stylish sound films with which Schünzel was to inscribe himself into the history of the German cinema.

Far more historically important, among the films of 1929, is Leo Mittler's *Jenseits der Strasse* (*Beyond the Street*), a serious and largely successful attempt to match the achievement of Soviet filmmakers with a story set in the lower depths of society. This carried on, as *Asphalt* did in its very different way, the traditions of the Weimar 'Street' film, pioneered by Karl Grune in 1923. It was not Mittler's first film, but it has become the one by which he is best remembered. It was, in fact, his only by accident: the director who had begun preparations fell ill and had to be replaced by Mittler, who acquitted himself well but was never given so challenging a task again in the German film industry, before being driven to emigrate. He went to Paris, where he filmed multilingual versions for Paramount in the Joinville studios. In 1936 he sailed for England and thence to the USA.

Many of the writers who provided original screenplays or adaptations of novels and theatre plays for the filmmakers of 1929 were also Jewish. They included Robert Liebmann, head of the dramaturgical department of Ufa, author of well over a hundred scenarios; Hermann Kosterlitz, who later metamorphosed into the Hollywood director Henry Koster; Willy Haas, Leo Lania, Walter Reisch, Kurt Siodmak (another Hollywood success, along with his brother, the director Robert Siodmak), and the young Billie (later Billy) Wilder. Among the Jewish cameramen of that year Karl Freund and Mutz Greenbaum stood out; set-designers and constructors included Edgar Ulmer, who later directed such Hollywood cult films as *The Black Cat* and *Detour*, as well as films in Yiddish and Ukrainian; Alfred Junge, who became one of the mainstays of British scenography, especially in the films of Powell and Pressburger; and Ernst Stern. Furnishings required by the set-designers were provided by the firms Beermann & Co. and Jonass & Co.; and costumes not already in the film companies' collections (Ufa had a huge store of them) could be obtained from 'Theaterkunst Hermann J. Kaufmann'. Rudi Feld revolutionised urban showmanship with his billboard designs and the cladding of cinema facades to reflect the themes of films being shown in such venues as the Berlin Ufa Palast am Zoo. He was a key contributor to the visual culture Janet Ward has analysed in a wide-ranging book entitled *Weimar Surfaces* (2001). Before his death in 1929, Artur Guttmann was, along with (the non-Jewish Giuseppe Becce), the most distinguished provider of the orchestral music which accompanied and illustrated prestigious films. Jewish medical reformers, headed by Dr Magnus Hirschfeld and Dr Levy-Lenz, once again advised on the content of 'Enlightenment' films or *Sittenfilme* likely to prove controversial and often to enrage the most conservative and traditionalist sections of German and Austrian society.

Ufa, with its important production unit headed by Erich Pommer, was flanked, in 1929, by a large number of smaller companies with Jewish directors. These included Greenbaum Film, Nero Film, Stein Film, H.R. Sokal Film and Deutsche Universal, controlled by the Hollywood Laemmle family. Among Jewish executive producers (*Produktionsleiter*) one could find, in 1929, Wilhelm von Kauffmann, the husband and impresario of Henny Porten, whose star would wane with the advent of sound films; Paul Kohner, who would later become and agent representing many of the German-Jewish emigré actors seeking work in the USA; Joe Pasternak, later producer of many a Hollywood musical; Arnold Pressburger and Gregor Rabinowitsch, with their internationally orientated Cine-Allianz. (The few names given here will be supplemented by an Appendix to this book.)

Despite their conspicuous presence in the film-industry, however, German and Austrian Jews never created, or aspired to, the 'empire of their own' through which the great studio moguls of Hollywood moulded the world-picture of their contemporaries. There were no Jewish studio tyrants, like Louis B. Mayer or Jack Cohn, no melting-pot audience of many nations that had to be provided with a unifying ideology presented as 'the American Way of Life'; and the concern which swallowed up a greater and greater number of its smaller rivals, Ufa, came under the control of right-wing nationalists like Alfred Hugenberg and Ludwig Klitzsch. A powerful figure like Erich Pommer, the nearest equivalent in the German film industry of Hollywood's Irving Thalberg, could be dismissed, reinstated and dismissed again, at a moment's notice; and it proved all too easy, after 1933, to bring Ufa, and eventually the whole of the German film establishment, under Nazi control. It was Goebbels, not Pommer, who created an ideological 'empire of his own'.

What is noticeable in 1929, however, is that although the management of the German film industry was not as widely under the control of Jewish entrepreneurs as that of Hollywood in the heyday of the studio system, Jews were a greater presence, proportionally, among the creative personnel at the sharp end of filmmaking. This did not mean ghettoisation: they worked, as I have stressed throughout this book, in harmony with non-Jewish colleagues in Germany and Austria. The loss of potential caused by their exclusion after the catastrophe of 1933 inevitably diminished the achievement, and the international importance, of the industry they had served so well. That industry, however, still had a considerable fund of talent left, and was able to build, even in Nazi times, on what had been so fruitfully pioneered by the earlier inter-ethnic collaboration that the Nazis tried, with cruel ingratitude, to write off.

There can be little doubt that the outstanding contributions to the art of the German cinema produced in 1929 were two films by a non-Jewish director with a star who was neither Jewish nor German: G.W. Pabst's *Die Büchse der Pandora* (*Pandora's Box*) and *Tagebuch einer Verlorenen* (*Diary of a Lost Girl*), both starring Louise Brooks. The first, as we have seen, had four Jewish actors in key parts; the second featured Kurt Gerron and Siegfried Arno in brief character roles – but its most memorable cameo came from the Jewish dancer and actress Valeska Gert. Her portrayal of a lesbian sadist in control of institutionalised girls has a disturbing quality unparalleled elsewhere among the films of that transitional year. *Asphalt*, however, deserves at least equal attention. Produced by Erich Pommer, it was directed by the prolific Joe May, among whose most popular previous productions had been the two parts of *Das indische Grabmal* (*The Indian Sepulchre*) of 1921, whose scenario had been written by Fritz Lang and Thea von Harbou, and whose thrilling story-line of peril and revenge earned it two later remakes – the last (and, alas, least adequate one) by Fritz Lang himself after his return to Germany in the 1950s.

A Closer Look at *Asphalt*

Subtitled *Der Polizeiwachtmeister and die Brilliantenelse* (*The Police-Constable and Diamond Elsa*), *Asphalt* belongs to a subgenre of German films that particularly attracted Jewish directors in the Weimar Republic: the 'Street Film' (*Strassenfilm*). Its most important example before *Asphalt* had been Karl Grune's programmatically entitled *Die Strasse* (*The Street*, 1923), whose stylised studio settings, co-designed by the Jewish Expressionist painter Ludwig Meidner, and wealth of symbolic detail, held the centre ground between the Expressionism of *The Cabinet of Dr Caligari* and the neorealism of Leo Mittler's *Beyond the Street*, subtitled *Eine Tragödie des Alltags* (*An Everyday Tragedy*). The directors of all these films were ethnically Jewish.

Joe May's *Asphalt*, co-scripted by Hans Szekely and Rolf E. Vanloo, begins with the hammering and streamrolling into place of an urban roadway by a row of navvies superintended by a black-clad inspector. Steam rises from the new surfaces around the letter ASPHALT, as the roadway in the making gives way to documentary shots of heavy traffic on roads well in place. This kaleidoscopic montage of Berlin streets and squares, photographed from a multiplicity of angles and superimposed one on the other, is succeeded by a contrasting shot of a caged canary – part of the furnishings of a bourgeois interior that the camera explores until it comes to rest on the old couple that has built this nest around itself. These sequences define the essential contrast of the 'street film': that between *Wohnstube* and *Strasse*, living room and street, the central paradigm of Grune's genre-defining work. In that work in 1923 the stiff bourgeois male had felt an irresistible urge to leave the safety of his sheltering and oppressive domestic interior for the enticing possibilities, and thrilling dangers, of the urban streets outside. Soon, however, he becomes involved in events so frightening to him that he is brought to the brink of suicide; and when, after brief incarceration on suspicion of robbery and murder, he is liberated, he is only too glad to return to the stuffy room he had deserted. He places his head on his wife's comforting bosom, and notes, as we do, that she has silently replaced on the table the soup he had earlier left uneaten.

The couple in the room shown in *Asphalt* show no such desire to escape – they seem content with their lot and their relationship, as the old man, played by Albert Steinrück, smoking a postprandial cigar, listens to his wife reading to him from a newspaper and expressing her wonder at all the strange things that seem to be going on in the world outside. We soon discover, however, that the old man and his son are police officers, and that the son, Albert Holk, is about to go out into the streets to regulate the traffic. The camera then focuses once more on the caged canary before giving way to another kaleidoscope of vehicles and pedestrians converging from all sides on the policeman standing in the midst of it all, pursuing his task of imposing order. Where there is a hold-up, because of a driver's error that nearly causes a collision, young Holk's good-natured and efficient interposition soon restores the orderly flow. The street in which all this takes place is one of Ufa's finest creations; designed by the experienced team of Erich Kettelhut, Robert Herlth and Walter Röhrig, it extended over three studios and their intervening spaces. The difficulties of controlling a vast number of cars, extras and principal actors, across such a set, and the superimpositions and montages produced by the camera team under the direction of Günther Rittau, have been admirably mastered by the Jewish director and his Gentile colleagues.

Movement stops for a moment as crowds, first seen from behind and then from the front, are arrested by a brightly lit shop window in which a mannequin is displaying attractive legs to advertise the stockings sold within. A team of thieves, led by a smartly dressed monocled man (played by Hans Albers in his preheroic days) is observed creating a diversion while its leader deftly relieves a woman's handbag of her purse – the camera then passes on over other shops to land, eventually, within a jeweller's establishment where Else, played by Betty Amann, is being shown diamonds by an elderly jeweller who is clearly fascinated by the play of her beautiful eyes. We watch as she deftly, unobserved, sweeps a diamond onto the floor and spears it with the tip of an umbrella that has had some sticky substance affixed to it. This introduces what will become the main plot of the film: the last-minute discovery of the loss, Else's arrest by the young policeman on his way home after traffic duty, and her slow expert seduction of him, after convincing her previous victim, the old jeweller, that he should drop charges because she had acted out of dire need – an intention foiled by the young policeman because as a dutiful servant of the state (*Beamter*) he is bound to pursue the matter. These scenes, which also include a confrontation between the old jeweller and a son less susceptible to female charm, are remarkable because they proceed largely through a series of close-ups and individual reaction shots that effectively contrast with the crowd scenes within which they are embedded. The scenes set in a studio-constructed Berlin are later supplemented by nocturnal scenes in an equally studio-bound Paris, where Else's lover and patron, played once again by the actor who had exerted his menace in *Look Out! Plain Clothes Police!* (Hans Adalbert Schlettow), is masterminding the break-in into a bank through a tunnel dug underneath the asphalt of the city's streets. This robbery subplot fits into the main scheme because it combines its realistic delving with a symbolic one. It suggests how much more is hidden beneath the surface of the city than meets the inquisitive eye, and it parallels Else's burrowing into depths of the young policeman's psyche that are concealed under his bourgeois propriety and professional conscience. It also carries on the theme of urban crime begun with pickpocketing among crowds and sophisticated robbery in a jewellery store.

The seduction scenes in which Else begins her undermining of the young constable's conscience take place in the back of a taxi called to convey her and her escort to the police station. These broach one of the central themes of the 'street' film and one that would be of particular concern to many members of the original audience. Else explains that the crime she had tried to commit was motivated by direst need – she claims to have been unable to pay her rent and to have faced eviction, from the flat which was her sheltered place, onto the street. 'And I am so terrified of the street!', she exclaims. The obvious implication is that she was in danger of becoming a 'street-walker' or prostitute. She then cleverly lures the young man into her flat by appealing to his professional training: would she not need her identity papers to face charges at the police station? She lives close by, and the constable could come up with her to ensure she didn't attempt to escape. Once inside the surprisingly spacious flat the young man's resistance is skilfully undermined, ending with her twining herself about his body – at which point the camera moves downwards to show her bare feet hooked around his policeman's boots. This proves a potent symbol for the enchantment that struggles against duty – more particularly against Prussian *Beamtenplicht*, the duty of state officials.

Succeeding scenes, which show Else, in her turn, succumbing to her young victim's attractions, work out the consequences. We see her affectionately contemplating his photo on an identification card he had left behind – after which the camera moves across the room to another photo, framed on a table: that of Else's lover, a sinister-looking personage who calls himself 'Consul Langen', and who is even then proceeding from his Parisian hotel towards his Berlin *pied-à-terre*. The news of his approach is conveyed to Else by a letter sent for her to a fashionable Berlin bar, whose manager is played by the great Jewish actress and cabaret performer Rosa Valetti. This brings into the film a scene of action familiar in the Berlin of the 1920s, and allows us to see Else in jewelled finery and amid scenes of conspicuous consumption that disabuse the audience of belief in the truthfulness of her earlier professions of direst poverty. She sends young Holk his policeman's identity papers back and accompanies it with the gift of a box of expensive cigars. Furious at what he conceives to be an attempt to 'pay' him for the dereliction of his duty, he storms out of his parents' house and up the stairs that lead to her flat – only to succumb again to her physical magnetism, even more powerful now because it is reinforced by her own attraction to him. This time, however, his earlier belief, partially shared by the audience, that she was driven to crime by utmost need is deliberately shattered by her violent reaction to his proposal of marriage: she flings jewels, banknotes, and sumptuous furs onto her bed, challenging him: if the officer still wants to marry her – there she is! As he sadly prepares to leave, she runs after him, seizing his in her arms with the cry: 'Don't let me go under!' He relents, they kiss, and are interrupted by the appearance of the 'consul', who has let himself into the flat with his key and has observed them, unnoticed, for some time. A fight ensues when the 'consul' violently assaults his rival, and in its heat the 'consul' is killed.

This leads to a restatement of the theme that sets *Beamtenpflicht* against passion and sentiment, as we return to the flat in which the young man lives with his parents. The mother reacts to her son's confession ('I have killed a man'!) with horror but also with a close, comforting embrace; the father, however, whom we have hitherto only seen in civilian clothes, now dons his police uniform and in rigid stance confronts the son who is hanging his head with guilt and shame before him. He willingly follows his father to the station, where we see his statement being taken – a scene interrupted by the frantic entrance of the mother, ushering in Else who has told Frau Holk exactly what has happened and now attests that her young lover had acted purely in self-defence. She then relates the whole story, beginning with her attempted theft. The Holk family is now free to go, pending further investigation, while Else is arrested. The film ends with Else being led down a corridor towards the cells, stopped for a moment by the young constable she had seduced but had come to love. He now assures her – within sight of his parents, who are not likely to be delighted by this turn of events – that he loves her and will wait for her. She lays her hand gently on his cheek and walks firmly on, towards the cells in the background, as the film fades out.

This story of seduction, crime and atonement is conventional enough: but its treatment, and the themes it adumbrates, are timely and brilliant. The use of uniforms and identity papers to drive home the theme of officialdom and its prescribed duties undermined by human passion, strikes at German (especially Prussian) traditions whose confirmations and underminings pervade many other films of the period, from those extolling Frederick the Great to very different treatments of the role and status conferred by uniforms in *The Captain of Köpenick* and *The Last Laugh*. The mastery of Joe May and his team at conveying vivid impressions of the urban scene, with its serried crowds, vehicles, stores, brightly attractive shop windows, cinemas and advertising signs, transcends previous attempts of the same kind. These passages throw into relief the film's imaginative use of close-ups, single figures or duos, which explore that landscape of the human face and the emotions it registers in ways the 'silent' cinema had made possible in a wholly new way.

Incidental felicities abound – like the moment in which we watch young Holk, dishevelled after the unquiet, conscience-burdened night that follows the scene of passion and first dereliction of duty, open the door to a young messenger in impeccable Sunday attire, who delivers a package from Else. The appearance of this messenger, like that of Osric in *Hamlet*, contrasts so strongly with that of the dishevelled constable that he is etched for ever into the spectators' consciousness – even though he leaves immediately afterwards, never to return. The beauty of Else, enhanced by the finery we have a first chance to observe during her visit to the Eden Bar, is similarly set off by the physical plainness of the Bar's manageress who hands her the ominous letter announcing the approach of the 'consul' after his Parisian exploits.

Realism and symbolism unobtrusively combine as Joe May's film explores the possibilities of cinematic language opened up by earlier pioneers but here used again to excellent purpose. These include a use of different-sized lettering, and unusual arrangement, in the intertitles, to denote changes of tonal volume and emphasis:

('Ist

das

Not?').

('Does *that* suggest desperate need?'). Photographic superimpositions, combining as many as five different images in a single frame, suggest the urban chaos to be mastered, or tie together the domestic interior and the asphalted streets outside when traffic images converge from all sides onto a birdcage and its cherished pet before giving way to the small figure of the young constable in the midst of the traffic he has to regulate. Underground burrowing for nefarious purposes has a realistic and narrational basis, but also suggests descents into such psychological undergrounds as are explored in Pabst's Freudian *Geheimnisse einer Seele* (*Secrets of a Soul*). Additional devices familiar from other films of the period, which May uses to take his audiences with him, are ominous stairways ascended by a man going to meet his fate; a huge shadow suggesting approaching danger; mirror images at moments of crisis, indicating divided consciousness and externalising the *Doppelgänger* within; silks, furs and costly jewels enhancing a beautiful woman and the temptations of sex and wealth; and the contrast, endemic in the subgenre of the 'street film', between the protective but stuffy bourgeois interior and the lures and threats of the urban jungle outside.

The film's title, designed to indicate the city streets over which its young protagonist has to exercise state-sanctioned control, acquired ominous overtones when it was incorporated in the insulting compound *Asphaltliteraten*: urban writers and intellectuals thought rootless, lacking in Germanic feeling for blood and soil. Jews became favourite targets for this particular insult flung at them by their German enemies.

By 1929 many Jewish critics and sociologists had entered the relatively new field of film reviewing – not the kind of 'field' that would prevent their becoming targets of the *Asphaltliteraten* slur. There was, in addition, a noticeable increase in anti-Semitic comment on films and their Jewish personnel in right-wing and (of course) in Nazi-controlled journals. This could be insinuating rather than direct, as when a performance by Fritz Kortner, in a non-Jewish role, is described as that of a slavering Shylock ('ein geifernder Shylock') by the *Deutsche Allgemeine Zeitung*. It could also be entirely misdirected, as when a work by the (impeccably Gentile) Erich Waschneck is branded 'echt jüdische Frechheit' ('typical Jewish impertinence') by the Nazi *Völkischer Beobachter*. The *Deutsche Zeitung* assures a film of which it disapproves of 'Beifall des Bayrischen Platzes' – applause from an audience drawn from a district inhabited by many Jews. The same journal has another go at Jewish spectators when it notes that after a showing of *Ums tägliche Brot. Hunger in Waldenburg* (*For Daily Bread. Hunger in Waldenburg*), a documentary exposure of intolerable conditions in a German mining district by Leo Lania and Phil Jutzi, 'the members of an alien race who were present applauded and then drove home in their elegant cars'. The film was shown in Britain, in this same year of 1929, under the title *Shadow of a Mine*. The *Völkischer Beobachter* declared itself particularly outraged by *Ludwig der Zweite, König von Bayern* (*Ludwig II, King of Bavaria*), released by the German branch of Carl Laemmle's Universal Corporation, whose executive producer was Joe Pasternak. It called Laemmle, who had made anti-German films in the First World War, 'a Jewish film-king, enemy of Germany', and capped this later by castigating Prince Louis Ferdinand of Prussia for attending a reception in Hollywood given in his honour by 'the Film-Jew Carl Laemmle', who had insulted his grandfather, Emperor Wilhelm II, in a movie called *The Kaiser, Beast of Berlin*.

The *Deutsche Zeitung*, whom we have already met attacking Jewish spectators, went a step further when it took the opportunity of a showing of a film about the 'White Slave' trade, scripted by Robert Liebmann, to assure one of its *bêtes noires*, Deputy Chief Constable Dr Bernhard Weiss of the Berlin police, that despite his denials Jews (wearers of 'caftans') were centrally concerned in cases of *Mädchenhandel*, traffic in girls. Even the *B.Z. am Mittag*, which could hardly be accused of anti-Semitic tendencies, could not resist an occasional dig, such as ironically bestowing the title 'Dichterfürsten' (princes of poetry), traditionally reserved for Goethe and Schiller, on a quartet of scriptwriters bearing such suspiciously Jewish names as Katscher, Seidenstein, Siodmak and Ehrlich – authors of a film that could only appeal to the many who did not make great demands on the art of the cinema: ('die grosse Menge der nicht allzu Anspruchsvollen'). The film in question, *Mascottchen*, was directed by Felix Basch and produced by Greenbaum-Film GmbH.

The *Deutsche Zeitung*, once again, took the occasion of an 'Enlightenment' film by the Jewish director James Bauer, starring Walter Rilla, which questioned the workings of German law in a case of incest, to thunder against 'a clique that deliberately attacks German feelings of morality and justice', reserving a special degree of ire for a Jewish lawyer, Dr Wertheimer, who had defended the film's thesis. The paper reminded its readers that the same lawyer had recently acted as defending counsel in criminal cases brought against the Jewish businessmen I.B. Kutisker and the brothers J. and H. Barmat, accused of deception and bribery. It was the same paper which termed Dyk Rudensky, who had just directed a harmless film called *Die Ehe der Maria Lavalle* (*The Marriage of Maria Lavalle*), in which had had also acted a minor part, 'the Soviet Jew Rudensky', who had surely been 'sent by Moscow to work for the Bolshevist cause'.

The Nazi journal *Der Angriff* specialised in attacks like that on handsome Franz Lederer, who had recently portrayed a young Russian officer in *The Wonderful Lie of Nina Petrowna*. He was being foisted on the public, the journal alleged, by a 'Jewish clique'; it added that as a young lover he looked 'damnably Jewish' – *geradezu verboten jüdisch*. On 14 November 1929, however, *Der Angriff* really went for the jugular. Under the heading 'How come, Mr Hugenberg?' it told this president of the German National People's Party, media-tsar and majority shareholder in Ufa:

> Make an end of this management by Jews, employment of foreigners and nepotism at Ufa; transform it into a German enterprise in which German people find work and earn their honest crust ...

and on 1 December the same paper protested against the showing of *The Jazz Singer*, accusing Hugenberg of sanctioning the importation of 'Pan-Jewish' propaganda into the Ufa-owned Gloria Palast cinema:

> If Mr Hugenberg fails to force his business-Jews into sparing the German public such disgusting Pan-Jewish propaganda, the public will have to help itself. The National Socialists will not hesitate to conduct a political campaign against Ufa, after proof that Hugenberg's influence counts for almost nothing there, and that forces are there at work whose deliberate plan is the decomposition of the national culture towards whose realisation the German people is striving.

What Hugenberg heard here was the authentic voice of Josef Goebbels, who went on to back up with threats his call for the withdrawal of *The Jazz Singer* from German cinemas within three days. Hugenberg's organisation found it expedient to discuss this demand with officials of the NSDAP (*National Socialist Workers' Party*), and *Der Angriff* reported the outcome with some satisfaction on 12 December. Ufa, it reported, was bound by contracts and therefore found itself unable to withdraw *The Jazz Singer* at this time. Hugenberg's people, however, had given the party to understand that the organisation stood ready, within the framework of political neutrality which was its general principle, to take account in future of the feelings of those who supported the world-view of National Socialism that was finding millions of adherents in Germany.

In the course of this campaign, *Der Angriff* had specifically named Noé Bloch, Gregor Rabinowitsch and Erich Pommer as executives of which the German film industry should rid itself. One wonders whether these three, and the hundreds of others who would soon be driven into exile or murdered by a Nazi regime, heard the wake-up call when Hugenberg capitulated so easily in 1929. (See Gandert 1993: 159, 227, 273, 299, 385–86, 412–15, 427–28, 513–18, 569, 736, 849, 864, 866, 869, 870 *et passim*.)

Figure 1. Paul Davidson (1867–1927). (Deutsches Filminstitut).

Figure 2. Erich Pommer (1889–1966). (Deutsches Filminstitut).

Figure 3. E. A. Dupont (1891–1956). (Deutsches Filminstitut).

Figure 4. Ernst Lubitsch (1892–1947). (Deutsches Filminstitut).

Figure 5. Richard Oswald (1880–1963). (Deutsches Filminstitut).

Figure 6. Fritz Kortner (1892–1970). (Deutsches Filminstitut).

Figure 7. Kurt Gerron (1897–1944). (Deutsches Filminstitut).

Figure 8. Elisabeth Bergner (1897–1986). (Deutsches Filminstitut).

Figure 9. Young man on the make: Ernst Lubitsch, *Schuhpalast Pinkus* (1916). (Deutsches Filminstitut).

Figure 10. Yearning aspirations: Pola Negri and Guido Herzfeld in *Der gelbe Schein* (1918). (Deutsches Filminstitut).

Figure 11. Love and blackmail: Reinhold Schünzel (left) and Conrad Veidt in *Anders als die Andern* (1918–19). (Filmarchiv Austria).

Figure 12. Uncanny world: Werner Krauss (left), Conrad Veidt in *Das Cabinet des Dr. Caligari* (1919–20). (Deutsches Filminstitut).

Figure 13. Dangerous magic: Ernst Deutsch (left), Albert Steinrück, and Paul Wegener (right) in *Der Golem, wie er in die Welt kam* (1920). (Deutsches Filminstitut).

Figure 14. Austrian aristocrat, Jewish actor from the East: Henny Porten and Ernst Deutsch in *Das alte Gesetz* (1923). (Deutsches Filminstitut).

Figure 15. An American girl amidst Galician admirers: Molly Picon and extras in *Ost und West – Mizrekh un Mayrev* (1923) (National Center for Jewish Film, Brandeis University).

Figure 16. Driven out: a sad procession in *Die Stadt ohne Juden* (1924). (Filmarchiv Austria).

Figure 17. An antisemite's nightmare: Hans Moser in *Die Stadt ohne Juden* (1924). (Filmarchiv Austria).

Figure 18. Innocent seductress, weak victim: Louise Brooks and Franz Lederer in *Die Büchse der Pandora* (1928–29). (Deutsches Filminstitut).

Figure 19. Urban Passions: Gustav Fröhlich and Betty Amann in *Asphalt* (1928–29). (Deutsches Filminstitut).

Figure 20. Distorted visions from below: Heinrich Gotho and Sybille Schmitz in *Überfall* (1929). (Deutsches Filminstitut).

Figure 21. Love amid water and sunshine: Brigitte Borchert and Wolfgang von Waltershausen in *Menschen am Sonntag* (1929–30). (Deutsches Filminstitut).

Figure 22. Organizing space around a star: von Sternberg's way with Marlene Dietrich in *Der Blaue Engel* (1929–30). (Deutsches Filminstitut).

Figure 23. Ritual degradation: the innocently accused Jewish officer stripped of his insignia – Fritz Kortner in *Dreyfus* (1930). (Deutsches Filminstitut).

Figure 24. The unsuccessful suitor: Oskar Karlweis and Lilian Harvey in *Die Drei von der Tankstelle* (1930). (CineGraph – Hamburgisches Centrum für Filmforschung).

Figure 25. Grotesque authority: Felix Bressart in *Der Herr Bürovorsteher* (1931). (Deutsches Filminstitut).

Figure 26. Puzzled bureaucrat meets stuffed monkey: Max Pallenberg in *Der brave Sünder* (1931). (Deutsches Filminstitut).

Figure 27. A comedy of errors resolved at last: Käthe von Nagy as the manicurist meets Willy Fritsch as the waiter in the room they have unwillingly shared turn-and-turn-about, in *Ich bei Tag und du bei Nacht* (1932). (Deutsches Filminstitut).

Figure 28. Man to "man": Renate Müller in drag and Adolf Wohlbrück as "his" suitor, in *Viktor und Viktoria* (1933). (Deutsches Filminstitut).

Figure 29. A brief idyllic moment in a tragic life: Joseph Schmidt as Riccardo and Charlotte Ander as Nina in *Ein Lied geht um die Welt* (1933). (Deutsches Filminstitut).

Figure 30. Siegfried Arno (1895–1975). (Deutsches Filminstitut).

Figure 31. Friedrich Hollaender (left) and Siegfried Arno: composer and actor/singer, prominent in the Weimar cinema, reunited in Hamburg (1955). (CineGraph – Hamburgisches Centrum für Filmforschung).

Chapter 6

IRONIC REALISM

Menschen am Sonntag (People on Sunday)

As a reaction against 'Expressionist' and fantasy films, historical spectaculars and popular melodramas, many filmmakers began to feel, towards the end of the 'silent' period, that something nearer to life as actually lived, especially in cities, a 'new sobriety', or new realism, was becoming necessary for the health of the German film industry. This feeling found memorable expression in *Menschen am Sonntag (People on Sunday)*, released in 1930. Exactly who did what in this shoe-string production is difficult to determine, in face of conflicting testimony. Robert Siodmak seems to have done most of the directing, assisted for a few days by Edgar G. Ulmer; it was written by Billie Wilder from an idea by Kurt Siodmak; and producer credit went to 'Filmstudio 1929 Moriz Seeler', set up by the poet and head of an experimental theatre group whose name appears in this title. Small occasional subventions came from the Siodmaks' uncle, Heinrich Nebenzahl. All those named were of Jewish ancestry, and one of them, Seeler, disappeared in Riga in 1942, presumed murdered by Nazis or Nazi sympathisers, while the Siodmaks, Wilder and Ulmer found different degrees of fame in Hollywood. The work they produced, a take on a Sunday outing in the Berlin of the summer of 1929, is a classic that convincingly married documentary and narrative elements and gave new life to the German 'street' film by taking it out of the studio and the realm of melodrama – whether bourgeois, as in Grune's *The Street*, or proletarian, as in Mittler's *Beyond the Street*.

At the centre of *People on Sunday* are five young Berliners who are not professional actors, wear no make-up they would not use in everyday life, and keep in the film the names, and jobs, they occupy in reality. They are: Erwin, a taxi-driver, who lives in a bed-sitting room with a salesgirl, Annie; Walter, a commercial traveller for a firm of wine-merchants; Christel, a professional model; and Brigitte, an employee of an Electrola record and gramophone shop. None of these continued as film actors; when shooting came to an end, they all returned to their previous avocations.

The story enacted by these five protagonists is embedded in carefully chosen documentations of Berlin life on Saturday evening, Sunday, and Monday morning. We see crowds streaming home after business hours on Saturday – in cars, lorries, trams, buses; on motorbikes, on bicycles on foot; in workmen's clothes and cloth caps, smart business suits, summery dresses; in crowded streets, among business premises with name-plates, advertisements, and carefully arranged window displays. Policemen regulate the traffic, street-cleaners are getting busy. In the midst of all this we see Erwin picking up the last fare of the day (the opening close-up of the number plate of his taxi, IA-10088, helps to tell us that we are in Berlin); Brigitte, assisting a colleague in setting up the record-shop's new window display; Wolfgang – always familarly, and significantly, called Wolf – making notes of sales and orders outside the premises of his wholesale wine firm; and Christel, entering a building which has the name of a small film company among other signs to the right of its door. The central narrative then gets going when Erwin, underneath a jacked-up car working on its wheel, is called out by a colleague saying that Annie is on the phone asking whether he'll take her to the pictures that night. He somewhat grudgingly agrees: 'She only wants to see Willy Fritsch – never mind, it's Garbo next week.' Christel, meanwhile, is standing at the busy junction of Hardenbergstrasse and Joachimsthalerstrasse, near the 'Zoo' Railway Station, waiting for someone who has agreed to meet her, while the camera, high over their heads, shows us Wolf circling her more and more obviously, clearly hoping for a pick-up. He is in luck; Christel has been stood up, and after chatting her up, he guides her across the busy traffic to a restaurant terrace. Over coffee and a milk-shake he amuses her by dropping water on a caterpillar, and having lightened the atmosphere, is able to persuade her to join him on a land and water excursion to Nikolassee on the following day. They shake hands on this in comradely fashion – but we know, from their previous conversation, that she is wary, convinced that 'all men are egoists'.

The plot develops further as we see Annie, sloppily dressed and doing her nails, on a sofa-bed in the bed-sitting room she shares with Erwin. When Erwin enters, he doesn't even look her way; she makes no move to get up as he settles down to a bottle of beer and what looks like some semolina or rice-pudding dish. He takes out a newspaper, throws the *feuilleton* section over to Annie, and props the paper up against a bottle to read while he eats. A dripping tap by a primitive washstand makes him turn round; Annie looks at him, but neither makes any move to try and stop the persistent drip. After his frugal meal Erwin starts to shave, and gets a rise out of Annie by taking a photo of Willy Fritsch from a whole array of film-star postcards pinned to a wall, dropping a large dollop of shaving soap onto it. That gets Annie going – she takes down another photo, of a dark-haired actress for whom, we presume, Erwin has expressed a liking, and crimps it up by using the curling-irons with which she has been working on her hair in preparation for the promised visit to the cinema. That visit, however, is thwarted when Erwin disagrees with Annie about the way she proposes to wear her hat. Wolf bursts in on them during the ensuing quarrel, which results in a mutual tearing up of film-star photos; he is not surprised, takes Erwin's part, and the two of them settle down to cards and beer, leaving Annie quietly fuming on a chair. The beginning relationship of Wolf and Christel is thus overshadowed by the dysfunctional relationship of Erwin and Annie and the male bonding that effectively shuts her out – observed by an ironically registering camera. They all agree, however, to go to the Niklassee on the following day.

The room shared by Erwin and Annie is the only domestic interior explored in the film, and significant details are as carefully picked out by Eugen Schüfftan's ever-moving camera as those of Berlin streets, parks, and green environs. They include such features as an incongruous Victorian bust on an improvised pedestal, and a recalcitrant wardrobe whose door reopens by itself every time Erwin or Annie try to close it. The house-proudness suggested by the 'artistic' bust has long vanished by the time we see the room, along with the once affectionate relationship of those who cohabit there.

The film now shifts to Sunday morning, with Berlin waking up gradually – just single figures in quiet streets and on green patches, including two tramps sleeping on benches in the *Tiergarten*. A small cluster of people waits for transport out of the city in the morning light. An ominously foreshortened overhead shot of three forbidding facades joined around a dark inner court prepares us for a return to Erwin and Annie's room. He is just getting out of bed to make himself ready for their excursion – but efforts to rouse Annie are of no avail. The camera shows us that no one has made any effort to clear up after last night's card game. Cards and empty bottles litter the table on which Erwin now writes a note telling Annie to meet him at Nikolassee at 10 a.m. that morning. At the door he turns back to leave the sleeping girl three cigarettes.

Now the camera takes us among crowds of people, streaming out of the Berlin centre and suburbs in search of green surroundings. Speedy cross-cutting shows all manner of vehicles carrying people to where they want to go, until the most rapid travelling-shot so far accompanies a train along its outward route. That leads us to Nikolassee station, where among the crowds coming down the station steps we recognise dark-haired Christel, who has brought along her best friend, the fair-haired, rather shy, very feminine, Brigitte. Both are wearing attractive, sleeveless, summer dresses, contrasting with the Sunday suits worn by the two men already waiting below. Christel introduces Brigitte, Wolf introduces Erwin; and while the last-named goes off to phone a neighbour to find out whether Annie is up yet, the three others proceed to the lake-shore, where they get into their bathing-suits. Erwin, having found out that Annie has not yet roused herself, joins them, and they all follow Christel into the water. Telling details picked out by the camera exploring the relations establishing themselves between the bathers are counterpointed by equally well-chosen details of

Berlin at its Sunday rest, and of other excursionists enjoying the sunny weather at Wannsee, along with those who cater for their pleasure. These last include a beach photographer, a man hiring out pedal boats, and a uniformed brass band entertaining a crowded restaurant garden.

The film's story of changing relationships, partly improvised with the help of the lay cast, is held together by deliberate parallelisms, visual hooks and eyes, implied contrasts, and a frame that takes us back to Erwin and Annie's apartment before returning to Berlin on a weekday 'like any other': Monday morning crowds balancing the Saturday afternoon crowds at the beginning. What happens in between is, in brief, that Wolf finds no chemistry in his relations with Christel, while that of Wolf and Brigitte leads to full erotic satisfaction; that Christel turns jealously away from her 'best friend' until, during a ride on a pedal boat, the men start flirting with two good-looking young women in a rowing boat who have lost one of their oars. Erwin, practical as ever, sees the oar floating away, retrieves it and returns it to the young woman. Their common jealousy and resentment now brings Christel and Brigitte closer together again. When they all return to the city in the evening, Brigitte, now clearly in love with the smooth operator Wolf, asks whether they will meet again next Sunday; Wolf agrees, before walking on with Erwin, who shares his last cigarette with him. Erwin returns home, to find, with eloquently mimed amazement, that the room has remained in precisely the untidy state in which he had left it, and that Annie has managed to sleep the whole day away, only now drowsily rousing herself from her bed.

Among the significant parallels, embodying no less significant contrasts, which hold the film structurally together, is that between a race in the water between Christel and Wolf, and a race through the woods between Wolf and Brigitte. In the former instance Wolf's playful ducking of Christel, ending with an attempted kiss, is indignantly answered by a slap in his face. He thereupon turns away from her, and finding that Brigitte does not know how to swim, begins to teach her by supporting her in the water. Brigitte had earlier asked Erwin to help her do up a strap on her bathing costume, but had bridled at his attempts at a mild flirtation by blowing down her back. Now, however, she surrenders willingly to Wolf's arms, as they buoy her up at the shallow end of the lake. In the later sequence it is Brigitte who initiates the race. First she playfully seizes Wolf's hat and throws it into the air. It lands in a tree, and Wolf has to help her climb to retrieve it; and then she runs ahead, away from the others, with Wolf close on her heels. As he catches up with her, flirtation becomes something more serious. The camera tactfully recedes, upward and along the adjacent trees, descending on a place where some rusty tin cans and other detritus have been left, before retracing its path to find Brigitte lying back in postcoital lassitude, and Wolf up on his feet, adjusting his clothes and ready to go. From now on it is Brigitte who focuses affectionately on Wolf. Wolf remains his cool self, though he is clearly ready to continue the adventure, and agrees to meet her again next Sunday.

The ironic camera-eye which had picked out a rusty tin can while a love-affair is being consummated comes into play again a little later, during the quartet's excursion on a pedal boat. A torn sleeve on Wolf's previously immaculate shirt, and two small rents on its back, suggest that for all her initial shyness, Brigitte's love-making has been vigorously enthusiastic. We are led to reflect, however, that Erwin and Annie may have been similarly involved at the beginning of a relationship whose decay we observe at the start of the film as well its end; and that Wolf's opportunities as a commercial traveller, his pick-up techniques demonstrated in his initial targeting of the wary Christel, and the easy way in which he prepared the initially shy Brigitte for more serious attentions, are danger signals impartially registered by the camera eye. But we never feel that the film invites us to take an unsympathetic attitude to the different temperaments depicted; even Annie's Sunday lassitude may have its explanation in her weekday work as a sales-girl who has to stand on her feet for hours on end while dealing with a stream of customers.

A particularly telling example of the film's avoidance of crude sardonic effects begins when Erwin picks out two comic postcards depicting grossly fat women disporting themselves in the sea – images he sees displayed on a rack outside the kiosk from which he makes his phone-call about Annie. The film cuts from this to a group of plump elderly ladies bathing in the waters of the lake; but there is nothing at all gross or grotesque about their innocent fun. On the contrary: we come to rest on the charming spectacle of a smiling grandmother helping a little naked grandson enjoy himself in the shallow part of the water. She is only one of the incidental characters that come momentarily, but unforgettably, into view. The most varied group of these, plucked from the crowd, is formed by a beach photographer and members of the public who have their snaps taken. The poses they adopt, ranging from a parody of a glamour shot by the actress and dancer Valeska Gert to the grimacing and giggling of assorted children, make for a gallery that would not disgrace an album by Helmar Lerski or any of the other talented portrait photographers of the Weimar Republic. At the same time their self-consciousness before the camera helps to throw into relief the remarkable naturalness of the five people at the centre of the film, who seem to be living out their Sunday adventure unconscious of the observing lens. We have to remind ourselves that these are not professional actors, and that only Christel will have had earlier experience of prolonged exposure to the camera eye.

The beach-photographer incident performs another important function in the structure of the film. In a work in which we are conscious of time moving relentlessly on towards the next working day it introduces a moment of stasis as the holiday-makers get themselves ready to be photographed and we are shown what the camera has captured – in an early example of the freeze-frame, which had not, in 1929, become the cliché it became after Truffaut demonstrated what wonderful things could be done with it.

Between the central incidents of the story, and the camera's excursions away from them to the Sunday quiet of the Berlin streets which the holiday-makers have left behind for the day, there are subtle visual links. An obvious example is the shot of Christel's hands, as she sleeps after her swim, and the subsequent cut to Berlin on the same Sunday, which opens on a shot of a hairdresser's window advertising manicures at a special price. When the camera returns to the people on the beach, it moves from sleepy Christel's hands across Wolf's body to show that his face is turned towards Brigitte, who is nestling on his arm – a series of shots that economically register the changing relationships. There are tiny touches, too, which point to possible developments: as Brigitte gazes lovingly at Wolf during their pedal-boat excursion, a barge passes on which a heavily pregnant woman looks benevolently across at them. Other such touches highlight character along with financial constraints: Wolf joins the girls after the pedal ride, and when Erwin, left to pay the boatman, finds he has run out of cash, Wolf stands aside and lets Christel find the necessary money. Tiny incidents can change mood: Erwin's dropping of his own sausages into the sand after he has been showing off by tossing up those intended for the others and catching them on a plate, causes general laughter that eases the tension caused by Christel's resentment of Wolf's attentions to her friend. Realistic observation and ironic touches do not preclude sympathy. We come to care for these people, share their concerns over a broken gramophone record or a failing relationship, speculate on signs that point to their past or their future as part of the Berlin crowds we see in imaginatively selected and tellingly combined documentary shots.

As the crowds stream into Berlin's business districts, and children go back to school, on Monday morning, intertitles tell us that 'this is a day like any other', when 'Sun, Forest, and Love' are just memories, and Berliners 'yearn for the next Sunday'. We see two of them back at work: Wolf charms an elderly lady customer who has placed an order with him, and Brigitte, looking and moving quite differently, in her sober saleswoman's outfit, from the shy and amorous girl on her Sunday adventure. A final ironic touch shows her bringing out a forgotten package to a customer and passing a huge poster showing a grinning, clownish face with its forefinger in the air. What the poster advertises, in fact, is 'the latest hit song', *der neueste Schlager*, which turns out to be an English comic song by Leslie Sarony: 'I Lift Up my Finger, and I say "Tweet Tweet"'. Besides its suggestions for the mood of the film, the poster takes us into the realm of popular international entertainment, which is as much part of contemporary Berlin as its imported Garbo films, traffic, street cleaners, policemen and photographers; its impressive and its more sordid buildings; and the multitude of big or small firms whose advertisements, shop signs, shop windows and delivery lorries the film has shown us in the course of telling its central story, behind which we discern the presence of another pupular song of the time: "Wochenend und Sonnenschein" ("Weekend and Sunshine"), a great favourite in the repertoire of The Comedian Harmonists.

The image of the man with the monitory finger also has, however, immediate relevance to Brigitte's involvement with Wolf. Sarony's song, written in 1929, talks from the man's point of view about all manner of domestic perturbation. It talks of people shouting and 'cussing', of making a fuss when things don't go right, of wives telling their husbands 'where [they] ought to be' (try that on Wolf!), of babies screaming and shattering a couple's dreams – for all of which the singer has a mantra: 'I lift up my finger and I say: Tweet, tweet/Shush shush, now now, come come'. This might annoy his female partner even more than shouting might have done. The warning, what marriage or cohabitation might do, reinforces that presented by the spectacle of the decayed relationships of Erwin and Annie. But here, once again, it won't do to overlook the subtleties and complexities of the film, which takes care to introduce a moment of unobtrusive tenderness and consideration into Erwin's behaviour towards Annie. Ready to leave for his Sunday outing, he turns back at the door to place three cigarettes for her on the table – and, of course, he does expect her to follow when she wakes up.

On screen, the only Jewish presences in *People on Sunday* are a few actors and casual models in the beach-photographer scene, along with a few Jewish names on business signs seen in the documentary footage of Berlin streets. But when the director originally envisaged for the film, Rochus Gliese, left after a few test-shots at the Wannsee and in the streets of Berlin, its creative impulses and their translation into celluloid came from a group of Jewish middle-class enthusiasts sensitive to the 'New Sobriety' movement in German cultural life. They brought to their cinematic vision of five Gentile workers, their city, and its recreational environs, an unsentimental distance that governed their ironic, realistic, yet never unsympathetic depiction, along with a sure feeling for cinematic form.

When, after some reluctance on the part of distributors and cinema managers, the film was shown in Berlin in February 1930, its quality was recognised by critics and public. Its distribution was limited, however; not least because the rapid change-over to sound film pushed 'silents' to the margin. It came to an end altogether when racist decrees made its Jewish production team – some of whom had already left Germany – unwelcome, along with their work. The members of that team were, however, young and adaptable enough to refashion their careers abroad; and the later fame of Wilder, Zinnemann, the Siodmaks and Schüfftan has encouraged dedicated restorers to reconstitute the film from copies in a variety of locations,* and attracted to its artistry the admiring attention it so richly deserves.

---

* The process of reconstituting *People on Sunday* is described in exemplary fashion by Martin Koerber in Meyer and Read (2000). A video of the film as reconstructed in the Nederlands Filmmuseum has been issued by the British Film Institute (BFIV 086) in 2001.

Chapter 7

LATE COMEDIES

Keine Feier ohne Meyer
(Without Meyer, No Celebration is Complete)

Among the many Jewish performers who enriched German and Austrian film comedy before 1933, three deserve special mention. One of these is Curt Bois: a slim, volatile, infectiously energetic player who is unforgettable even in brief appearances such as that in Lubitsch's *Oyster Princess*, where he plays an astonishingly youthful orchestra conductor whose jerky rhythmic movements set everybody dancing. As the star of such films as *Der Jüngling aus der Konfektion* (*The Young Man from the Ragtrade*), directed by Richard Löwenbein in 1926, and *Der Fürst von Pappenheim* (*The Prince of Pappenheim*), directed by Richard Eichberg in 1927, he rivalled Lubitsch's performances as a young man on the make. He emulated the feats of Lubitsch's characters in getting round the boss, but not his amorous successes. It was no accident that the first of his sound films, directed by Max Nossek in 1931, should be called *Der Schlemihl* – someone who is maladroit and accident-prone. Famous for his scat-singing turns in German cabaret, and his drag-part in *Charley's Aunt*, he rivalled Chaplin's *A Woman* in his elegant facility for dressing up in women's clothes. This last talent, brilliantly exhibited in the otherwise not very distinguished *Prince of Pappenheim*, was used by the Nazis in two viciously anti-Semitic films, released in 1937 and 1940 respectively, to insinuate Jewish degeneracy. He was in good company there: Peter Lorre's celebrated performance as a murderer in Fritz Lang's *M* (1931) was used in the same way by Nazi propagandists. Bois also had a distinguished career as a character-actor on the German stage. His memorable cameos in Hollywood films, and his performances in Swiss and German films after his return from forced emigration, do not fall within the purview of the present study. Since he first faced the movie camera as a seven-year-old stage performer in 1908, and made his last film in 1987, he held what was the record for the longest-lasting film career when he died in 1991.

The career of Max Pallenberg, a Jewish actor from Vienna who achieved fame on musical and dramatic stages before dying in a car crash in 1934 at the age of forty-seven, was necessarily much shorter. He appeared in a number of short farcical films in the 'silent' era, often as a clownish figure called Pampulik: *Pampulik als Affe* (*P. as a Monkey*, 1912); *Pampulik kriegt ein Kind* (*P. gets a child*, 1912); *Pampulik hat Hunger* (*P. is Hungry*, 1913). He made just one sound film, however, which now preserves his memory: *Der brave Sünder* (*The Virtuous Sinner*, 1931) which will be described later in this chapter.

A much more prolific career than Pallenberg's was that of the long-nosed, rubber-faced, lanky, flexible-bodied Siegfried Arno. Like other comedians easily identified as Jewish, Arno often played non-Jewish parts in his many films. He appeared, for instance, as Manon's manipulative brother in Arthur Robison's *Manon Lescaut* (1925–26); as a village lad in Carl Lamac's *Die Kaviarprinzessin* (*The Caviar Princess*, 1929); as the flute-playing uncle who transforms an all-too-staid bourgeois girl into a swinger in Lamac's *Das Mädel mit der Peitsche* (*the Girl with the Whip*, 1929) – co-starring, in the two last-named, with the attractive Czech comedienne Anny Ondra. He even got to play an Austrian Emperor, Francis II, in Richard Oswald's *Lützows wilde verwegene Jagd* (*Lützow's Wild Hunt*, 1926–27). At other times, however, his character is explicitly shown to be Jewish, as in *Moritz macht sein Glück* (*Moritz makes his Fortune*, 1930) and *Familientag im Hause Prellstein* (*Family Gathering in the House of Prellstein*, 1927); or recognised as Jewish even when not specifically named as such. This is true, for instance, of his harried stage-manager in *Pandora's Box* trying to make what is intended to be Lulu's first stage appearance run smoothly in the face or ever greater obstacles. He is the very incarnation of what was known in contemporary Berlin as 'the Jewish rush', *die jüdische Hast* – the feverish activity of people having to make their way against impediments. A famous poem by Walter Mehring, in the repertoire of the Jewish cabaret artist Paul Graetz, identified this rush as specifically Berlinese ('Berliner Temp'):

Mit der Uhr in der Hand, mit'm Hut auf'm Kopp
Keine Zeit! Keine Zeit! Keine Zeit!

(With watch in hand, with hat on head –
No time! No time! No time!
(Heimat Berlin)

Arno's Sigi Meyer, in *Keine Feier ohne Meyer* of 1931, one of a series of short and full-length comedies the same actor made in that year, translated Mehring's lines into a physical picture: we see him constantly running from one appointment to another, across the whole of Berlin, wearing a succession of hats and looking openly or surreptitiously at a watch he takes out of his pocket.

Scripted by Fritz Falkenstein and Curt J. Braun, the film is directed by the non-Jewish Carl Boese, who had co-directed *The Golem – How He Came into the World*, and had since shown a particular predilection for working with Jewish comedians, whom he put into unlikely situations – especially military farces starring such less than martial types as Arno and Bressart. *Drei Tage Mittelarrest* (*Three Days Confined to Barracks*, 1930), starring Bressart, is the best known of these.

In *No Celebration* (as I will call *Keine Feier ohne Meyer* from now on), Arno plays his individual variation on two characters well known in traditional Jewish life and in Jewish literature from Sholem Aleicham to Israel Zangwill: the *Shadchen* or marriage-broker, and the *Luftmensch*, who has to conjure some sort of living for himself out of thin air. He is also – and this is where, in the end, he defeats himself – in a hurry to move socially upward. When we first see him, he has just moved from central Berlin to one of the suburbs, and from there he conducts a campaign to marry into the family of a Stadrat, a respected member of the local council, who is taken in by Meyer's self-aggrandising fantasies – he pretends to be the *Generaldirektor* of a huge concern with wide international connections and a turnover of millions. The town councillor's daughter, however, whom he has in his sights, wants none of him, for she already has a sweetheart of modest means who is not acceptable to her father; he wants his daughter to make a wealthy marriage, and "Generaldirektor' Meyer seems to meet the bill. She has her grandmother on her side, a very commanding old lady with a healthier dose of scepticism than her gullible son.

Meyer's chief weapon, in his struggle to get on, is *Schmus* – a constant stream of words, adjusted in tone and vocabulary to the class and type of individual he happens to be talking to, accompanied by a rich repertoire of facial expression, body stance, body movements and gesturing. This proves equally effective when he persuades two people who at first want none of each other that they are really perfectly suited and ready for love and marriage, or when he makes his prospective father-in-law believe, with a few throwaway remarks during a card game, that he has enormous business connections at home and abroad. The film makes us conscious that Meyer is in fact operating in a world of huge uncertainty: one of his flannellings mentions bank failures in the USA, with their repercussions in the Weimar Republic. There is also a pathetic stenographer who seeks employment in his office, who sighs how difficult it is to find a job in a world controlled by male bosses with wayward ideas. It's all played for comedy – indeed for farce at times, especially in a Feydeau-like climactic episode of mistaken identities and purposes in a hotel; but as we will find again when considering a musical comedy like *Die Drei von der Tankstelle* (*Three Men from the Filling Station*), the hard times from which such entertainments offer escape have a way of shining through. Even the eagerness of a reasonably affluent, upper-middle-class public official to marry off his daughter to a (surely Jewish!) businessman with international connections indicates the uncertainty of professional men who have had experience of inflation and devaluation and who now pin their hopes on financial speculators operating on a global scale.

Meyer feeds this hunger for escape from the narrow bounds of a dodgy national economy by casual mentions of multi-million business dealings with New York, Chicago, London, and even China. The film shows clearly, however, that Meyer deceives himself more than others when he thinks that the airy verbal edifice he builds up will not, in the end, collapse. This is, in fact, the common fate of the *Luftmensch*; and the way he responds to the collapse is a test of his resilience and his resolve to build henceforth on more solid ground.

The producer, Gustav Althoff, and the director, Carl Boese, have done their star proud by surrounding him with a sterling cast of character actors peopling the largely non-Jewish world in which Meyer operates. Chief among them is Ralph Arthur Roberts, whose Councillor Goebel, with his high stiff collar, formal black clothes, authoritarian bluster hiding inner uncertainties, and a face permanently skewed to hold a monocle in place, is the perfect foil to the volatile and flexible Arno. The Councillor's mother is played by the great Adele Sandrock, who had bravely and successfully made the transition from tragic heroine on the Wilhelminian stage to *komische Alte* – a comedienne specialising in peremptory old ladies. Her deep-voiced growls subdue the Prussian peremptoriness of her son, for she knows the weakness and uncertainty that it covers, and her scepticism relativises her son's credulity and gullibility. Goebel's daughter is played, with the right degree of perkiness, by Dina Galla, who witnesses for us that Anglicisation – or, rather, Americanisation – had made some progress in the Weimar Republic: for although the credits inform us that she has been christened 'Else', she is always called 'Mary' by all the other characters. She is, however, out-acted by two other favourites of Weimar film. The first of these is Maly Delschaft, as Meyer's capable secretary, who has obviously had closer relations with her boss that the latter tries, unsuccessfully, to keep out of the office ('Don't call me Sigi!' 'Don't address me with *Du*!'). To him she is always 'Fräulein Kruse' until, in the final moments of the film, when his hopes of marrying into the Goebel family have collapsed, she becomes 'Kruselein' and is asked to marry him – which offer she accepts with alacrity, for there is love and respect between them despite all the sparring that had led her to leave his employ and go into the marriage-brokering business on her own account. She thus becomes his business as well as his marriage partner, and their Jewish–Gentile alliance will tether the *Luftmensch* to reality. He can now devote his verbal talents to building up a useful introduction agency with someone at his side who is likely to deflate any further attempts at building fantastic castles of international finance in the Weimar air.

The second, and to me most memorable, of these actresses is Lucie Englisch, in a performance at once hilarious and pathetic as the slow-witted stenographer Marie, whose given name resembles that of 'Mary' and furthers the flurry of mistaken indentities and cross-purposes in the film's final sequences. Her slowness of utterance and understanding is perfectly set off by Meyer's nervous rapidity – which defeats itself because he won't let Marie get a word in edgeways and thus prevent him from making at least one of the mistakes that lead to his discomfiture. The presence of Marie in the later parts of the film introduces a serious note into the farcical goings-on: she is a fatherless girl, whose fiancé has taken himself off to the USA and who is constantly forced into wrong positions when all she is trying to do earn a living. In a way she 'explains' Meyer – for what else is *he* trying to do but use his wits to make his way in a world that has no traditional place for him? He is, of course, more fortunate than poor Marie (who ends up with a belly-ache and no job) in being quick-witted; but in the end his quickness, his *jüdische Hast*, leads to schemes of social advancement that are bound to collapse. How could he possibly have fitted into the Goebel family once his deception had been discovered – as it was bound to be once he was married? It's just as well that the break happened before that event. He is far better off with his ex-secretary, who known who and what he is, accepts him on his own terms, and will help him with his *Shadchones*, his marriage-brokering, after brokering her own with her saddened and sobered Sigi.

Meyer's speech contains no Yiddish or Hebrew words, no specifically Jewish turns of phrase. He is a verbal chameleon, dropping as easily into flowery speeches about 'storms of life' and 'rustling of silk robes' as into curt Berlinese like 'Schnauze, Liebling' ('shut up, sweetie' – said to an underling hired to act as witness to a marriage contract); yet the very rapidity of his utterance, along with his appearance, manner, and the conjunction 'Sigi Meyer', marks him as Jewish. There is one other character – a huge woman from whom a small man, one Naftali Nussbaum, played by the tiny Jewish actor Siegfried Berisch, is seeking a divorce – who can match Meyer in volubility; but her's is all on one note, with none of the variability of tone and speech-register characteristic of Arno's Meyer. The script allows him to test that power in a well-chosen variety of settings: his office, with its two separate little waiting rooms, in each of which a potential client has to be persuaded that his or her happiness is waiting in the other room, and during a rapid tour by taxi. This takes him first to a registry office, witnessing two clients' marriage vows; then to a divorce court, where he finds means to distract a voluble termagant's outpourings sufficiently to enable the judges to pronounce the divorce decree in her little husband's favour. He takes advantage of this outcome by charming the newly divorced woman into becoming his client in her search for a more suitable partner. From the court he rushes to a wedding reception that has degenerated into chaos after the new husband is discovered making up to another woman. There, at least, Meyer is able to restore order and harmony.

The role-playing of his voluble speech is matched by a variety of costumes, contrasting with the unvarying costumes of Goebel and his mother. We see him in the Berlin streets giving out flyers advertising his services, dressed in cloth cap and plus-fours; in his office, wearing a dark suit with a white stripe just a tinge too wide and too loud; at the registry office, the divorce court and the wedding reception in full formal gear, morning-suit, top hat and all; and as guest in a hotel in a sober grey suit, which prepares us for his deflation at the end. He is also in formal dress when calling at Goebel's house to propose marriage to Mary – but there he is clearly ill at ease, and is terrified by a dog that attacks him while Mary is making her escape through a window in order to join Walter, the man she really loves. Walter is in fact a friend of Meyer, who does not know that the 'Mary' Walter seeks to marry is identical with his own Mary; when he therefore advises Walter to elope with his beloved and be found together with her in a hotel room, thus compromising her and forcing her father to consent to their permanent union, he is thwarting his own marriage plans. The stratagem succeeds, and Meyer has to console himself by contracting a more suitable marriage with the young woman who had been his secretary and now becomes his business partner.

The film's most striking episode, which elicits the most virtuoso performance from Arno, occurs when Councillor Goebel surprises Meyer outside the door of the latter's modest office, and has to be persuaded that his prospective son-in-law is a director of Rheinische Stahlwerke, the most prestigious firm in the building. He therefore steers Goebel away from his own door to that leading to the Stahlwerke's suite of offices. Opening that door he takes the deeply impressed Goebel through the whole suite, peering nervously around each room while counting on Prussian respect for what is conceived as authority by barking peremptory orders at one astonished employee after another, finding imaginary faults and omissions or commending someone's work, giving others no chance to reply or object as he hurries his visitor on. They land, in the end, in a hospitality room, fortunately empty, where Meyer locks the door, illuminates a sign outside saying 'Conference in Progress. Do not Disturb', and brings chaos into the Stahlwerke's affairs by answering a telephone call with bogus and damaging information. He also helps Goebel and himself to the firm's cigars and brandy, spilling half a bottle of the latter onto the floor in his nervous haste. He presents a cross between the Captain of Köpenick and Gogol's Government Inspector, leaving the *Stahlwerke*'s office staff congregating outside the door he has locked, asking themselves: Who *was* that? Could he be a new inspector, a member of the *Aufsichtsrat*? By the time the top man arrives and uses his key to unlock the door, Meyer has already ushered his guest out by another door that leads into the corridor and thence to the exit stairway.

Boese's direction is unobtrusive, allowing his competent cinematographers to photograph settings (including some fascinating views of the streets of Berlin and a nearby bathing and sailing lake) and actors without flashbacks or tricky angles, and dosing establishing shots and close-ups judiciously to give full scope to his talented cast. He does, however, show his understanding of the possibilities of the sound film in an early sequence in which sound and image are deliberately contrasted in order to confront illusion with reality. We see Goebel, his mother and his daughter breakfasting in their garden, where the town councillor is extolling the virtues he perceives in his prospective son-in-law. He is not the handsomest of men, he concedes, but he is well turned-out and looks good. Then, as the voice blusters on, the image changes. He is enormously industrious, Goebel's voice maintains, hard at work every morning from 9 o'clock onwards – what we see is Meyer asleep in his bed when his bedside alarm shows 9.10. He 'takes his car to his office' – and we see him rushing for the local train to take him into central Berlin. He is '*Generaldirektor* of what must be an enormous concern' – and we see the name 'Meyer' at the very bottom of a list of firms occupying a multistory office building, and watch his rush into his very modest office on the top floor, with a tiny waiting room on each side. It is hard to think of a more economic and effective way to expose the nature of the *Luftmensch* and the hollowness of his pretensions.

It will be clear, by now, that *No Celebration* is in the tradition of Lubitsch's early Jewish comedies. In fact, however, Arno's persona is less confident, more nervous, than Lubitsch's, and more easily discomfited. And as anti-Semitic attacks proliferated and became more voluble in the Weimar Republic, spilling over into the cinemas and the streets, German film companies and exhibitors became more wary of making films whose humorous intentions could be misunderstood and could be presented as casting general aspersions on Jewish business integrity. After 1931 Boese and his Jewish star comedians made no more films of this kind in Germany, and after 1933 Boese had no difficulty in adapting his skills to the requirements of the Nazi entertainment industry. It was left to Lubitsch himself to find new ways of developing the tradition in the USA, especially through his use of Felix Bressart, veiling his Jewishness in *The Shop around the Corner* and *Ninotchka*, but making it explicit in the ever astonishing *To be or not to Be*.

In 1940, the same year as *The Shop around the Corner*, Edgar J. Ulmer, who had served his cinematic apprenticeship in Weimar Germany before emigrating to the USA, took up the theme of the marriage-broker whose own matrimonial plans go awry until good woman takes him in hand. The dialogue is in the American variety of Yiddish; its Yiddish title is *Amerikaner Shadchen*, but it is also known by its English title *American Matchmaker*. The working out of the story, and its whole atmosphere, is very different from that of *No Celebration*, for Meyer's American counterpart, Nathan Gold, operates solely with a community of Jewish immigrants from Eastern Europe and their assimilated children, while as far as we can see, the only fellow-Jew Meyer meets in his business or his private life is the henpecked Naftali Nussbaum whom he helps to a welcome divorce. Unlike Gold, Meyer presents himself as counsellor in all departments of life, acting as an enquiry agent helping to separate unhappy marriages as well as arranging what he hopes will be happy ones. Both films have a scene in which friends grow merrier and merrier as they drink together. In *American Matchmaker* this results in the singing of a *nign*, a Jewish tune, with appreciative swaying that leads into a *redl*, a Jewish circle dance performed by men. In *No Celebration*, on the other hand the friends' drinking session results in a virtuoso exercise in extemporary nonsense rhyming, in the German language of course, that culminates in a repetition of Meyer's internally rhyming motto, which is also the title of the film:

> ....
> Keine Henne ohne Eier,
> Keine Feier ohne Meyer.

> ....
> No hen without eggs
> No celebration without Meyer.

The cultural differences are profound, as are the performances, for Leo Fuchs, a pleasing performer very popular with the Yiddish-speaking public of the day, lacks the comic verve and variety of Siegfried Arno; but *No Celebration* also has its *nign*. This is a song arranged by the film's musical director, Artur Guttmann, with lyrics by Karl Wilczynski and the film's producer Gustav Althoff. It is heard throughout the film, as solo, duet, chorus or plain orchestral piece, and it enunciates the theme of the companionate marriage which Meyer and his 'Kruselein' contract at the end; and it has just the right touch of melancholy to temper the sweetness.

> Nur wenn Du willst werd ich dich küssen,
> Nur wenn Du willst, bleib ich bei Dir.
> Du wirst bestimmt dran denken müssen,
> Drum sage heimlich Ja zu mir.

> Denkst Du dann oft, in späten Jahren
> An unsre Liebe, unser Glück:
> Nur wenn Du willst werd ich Dich küssen
> Der erste Kuss kehrt nie zurück.

> I'll kiss you only if you want it,
> I'll stay with you only if you want.
> You will, I'm sure, remember this:
> So, secretly, say 'Yes'.

> When, in later years, you often think back
> On our love, our happiness:
> I'll kiss you only if you're willing
> The first kiss never returns.

That is the masculine version: female singers reserve space for themselves: 'Nur wenn ich will, *darfst* Du mich küssen' 'You're only *allowed* to kiss me if I am willing'.

The problem of Meyer's obvious Jewishness never comes up in this film; even those opposed to his marriage with 'Mary' Goebel never mention it; yet his name and demeanour would leave few people in doubt. As in several of Lubitsch's early comedies, what is contracted at the end is marriage between an assimilated Jew and a Gentile woman. It would not be very long before overweening and murderous racial fanatics would officially brand that *Rassenschande*, a disgrace for the (supposedly superior) 'Aryan' race, of which the Germans were proclaimed the primary representatives and champions on earth. Unlike such fellow-artists as Kurt Gerron, Paul Morgan, Fritz Grünbaum, John Gottowt and Hans Behrendt, Arno escaped their killing machines and lived on to give distinctive performances in Hollywood films, returning to the German stage after the war to find new admirers of his comic talents to swell the ranks of the surviving old. But that is another story, and a subject for a different book.

Der brave Sünder (The Virtuous Sinner)

Actors, it used to be said, can expect no laurels from posterity. The invention of the cinema has happily altered that situation; and one of the merits of *Der brave Sünder* (*The Virtuous Sinner*, 1931) is that it has preserved for us one performance of the multifaceted actor Max Pallenberg. He was famous for theatrical improvisations and recitations; performances in operettas, especially Offenbach's *La Belle Hélène* (Menelaus) and the same composer's *Orphée aux Enfers* (Jupiter); as Rappelkopf, at once comic and terrifying, in Nestroy's *Der Alpenkönig und der Menschenfeind* (*The Elfin King of the Alps and the Misanthropist*); as a Figaro darkly rebellious against a master who claimed for himself the *ius primae noctis*, in Beaumarchais's play; as a hysterically clamorous *Malade imaginaire* in Reinhardt's production of Molière; and finally, a year before his death in 1934, Mephisto in Goethe's *Faust*: an earthy folk-tale devil quite unlike the suavely terrifying figure of Gustav Gründgens which defined the part for my generation. He had held out against the cinema after his early farces; but disenchanted, while living in Berlin, with what he saw as deteriorating conditions in the German theatre, he yielded, in 1931, to the persuasions of Arnold Pressburger to commit one of his by then legendary performances to film.

Pressburger, like Pallenberg, was Austrian and Jewish. He had been president of the Austrian Alliance of Cinema Industrialists in the early 1920s; had held a leading position in the Viennese Sascha production company under Count Kolowrat; had migrated to Berlin, where he had allied a branch of Sascha with various German production companies (Kiba, Phoenix), and found the Allianz Tonfilm GmbH, which had links with London's Associated Film Industries; and he had cut a distribution deal with Ufa. He strongly believed in the importance of making sound films as internationally distributable as possible, either through simultaneously shot versions in other languages or as remakes. Early production of the Allianz included a German version of Carmine Gallone's *City of Song* (*Die singende Stadt*, 1930), starring the Polish tenor Jan Kiepura; *Danton* (1930–31), starring Kortner, Gründgens, Granach and Lucie Mannheim; and a military farce which had proved a runaway success when it was first released in the Germany of 1930, *3 Tage Mittelarrest* (*Three Days Confined to*

Barracks), starring Felix Bressart, Lucie Englisch, Max Adalbert and Fritz Schulz.

In setting up his new project, Pressburger brought Pallenberg together with three other Jewish artists who had found fame in Germany as well as their native Austria. The first of these was Alfred Polgar, a humorist, satirist, critic and *feuilletoniste*, who had adapted Valentin Kataev's Soviet play *Rastratchiky* for the German-speaking stage under the title *Die Defraudanten* (*The Embezzlers*); he was now invited to collaborate on the fashioning of a screenplay of this work that would be tailored to be requirements of Max Pallenberg's art. The second was Fritz Kortner, who had wanted, for some time, to move away from his place in front of the camera into a director's chair. He now worked alongside Polgar on the screenplay of *The Virtuous Sinner* and directed the result – his first and only such commission before his forced emigration in 1933, The third was one of the great *conférenciers* of the Austrian and German cabaret, a witty satirist of social conditions with a fine line in gentle Jewish self-mockery: Fritz Grünbaum. The resulting film was mostly shot in the Ufa studios at Babelsberg, and distributed in France in a synchronised version under the title *Pichler, Banquier*.

The adjective in the film's German title, which I have translated as 'virtuous', requires a brief comment. 'Brav' is commonly used in admonitions to children to be well-behaved and obedient ('sei schön brav!'); from there it has acquired a somewhat pejorative flavour when applied to adults: honest, but over-deferential, conformist, unadventurous. It has an ironic flavour in the film's title which is absent from its earlier use by Schiller, who makes his Wilhelm Tell declare that a good and decent man thinks of others first and himself last ('Ein braver Mann denkt an sich selbst zuletzt'), or by Heine when he says of himself that he has been 'ein braver Soldat im Befreiungskriege der Menschheit' – 'a good soldier in mankind's War of Liberation'. Its conjunction with 'sinner', in 'Der brave Sünder', is, of course, a deliberate paradox or oxymoron. It is *not* equivalent to its English cognate 'brave'.

Though made in Berlin, and though featuring the Essen-born Heinz Rühmann as Wittek, the cashier subordinate to Pallenberg's 'Herr Oberkassierer Pichler' in a provincial branch of the international finance and trading company INTRAG, *The Virtuous Sinner* has a distinctly Austrian atmosphere. Most of the actors speak with Austrian accents, and the setting is the Austria of which it has been said that it is an experimental station for apocalypses ('Versuchsstation für Weltuntergänge') where conditions may be 'desperate but not serious'. The two characters at the centre of the story, head-cashier Pichler, played by Pallenberg, and cashier Wittek, played by Rühmann, move from their provincial office to the capital, Vienna, where their firm has its head offices, and back again after three days and two nights of shocks, exaltations and adventures quite outside their normal experience.

The film's episodic structure leads its viewers from the living room of a dysfunctional family to a conscientiously but inefficiently run office about to be defrauded by its director; to a provincial bank; into rainy and windswept streets where a horse crushes the head cashier's bowler hat; to a metropolitan hotel (seen against a panorama of Vienna, with St Stephen's cathedral looming overall) and a fashionable restaurant with dancing, singing and variety turns; and a quiet *Heurigen* garden with soft music and a violinist going from table to table. The two provincial adventurers at the centre of the story then find themselves waking from a drunken sleep in a black dancer's flat and in a gambling den where they hope to recoup money they had had to pay out the night before when their defaulting chief had not turned up to foot the bill for their entertainment. There follow brief scenes in the hotel room where the director is preparing to leave the country with his loot, accompanied by a blonde mistress; and a police station, where he finds that he is not to be arrested as a thief, but respectfully handed back the money recovered from the confidence tricksters who had got it away from his subordinates.

In an open field Pichler has a memorable encounter with a cow, whom he finds the soulful and patient companion he had not found in his wife. He considers suicide, and leaves a last 100 schilling note for a tramp – 'when he wakes up he will think the hand of a fairy ...' But the hand to which the film cuts here is that of a rural gendarme, who arrests the tramp on suspicion of stealing the money. At a table outside a rural inn Pichler is summoned, along with Wittek, to a police station – he already has a length of rope in his pocket with which to end his life, and has composed a letter to the 'Honoured Herr Direktor' exonerating Wittek from any wrong doing. But instead of being arrested and imprisoned for misappropriating the firm's money he is merely asked to confirm the tramp's claim that he had given him the banknote; and he finds a 'Wanted' poster on the police noticeboard which indicts the director and – by obvious implication – exonerates Wittek and himself. The last scenes take us back to the provincial office, and thence to a restaurant where a party is in progress to celebrate the marriage of Wittek to Pichler's daughter Hedwig.

Far from decrying this structure we should recognise how well it suits a road movie that takes its protagonists on adventures in places and situations outside their previous experience, subjecting them to shocks, exaltations and depressions to which they have to react as well as their natures will allow. The film is, moreover, held together by a number of strong recurrent themes. The first of these is the response to the fickle nature of money: money lacked, money paid out, money transported on behalf of others, money lost, found again, lost again, money gambled, money stolen ... Innocent men are forced to part with funds not their own in circumstances not of their making, small-time crooks steal from them but are caught, a big-time crook – the Director, no less – gets away with more cash even than he expected, though he too is robbed by a mistress who spirits some of it away in her brassière. The second main theme is social hierarchy and hegemony. We see a father trying to establish his authority over a family that thinks he does not earn enough; a head cashier trying to preserve his authority by keeping private affairs and thoughts out of his professional life without ever succeeding. The pecking order of Director, head cashier, cashier and porter is strictly observed, and social hierarchies kept well in view in office, hotel, restaurant and open spaces where gendarme encounters tramp. Defence of territory is part of this, whether in actual space, like the office from which Pichler, ejects his daughter ('Hier ist *kein* Papa!') and which is guarded by a sign that forbids entry without previous appointment; or an ideal space, as that mentally erected in a dancer's bedroom by the head cashier who orders his less grandiloquently titled companion to make coffee: 'What, here?', Wittek asks. 'Of course, here', his superior replies. 'We are in our office. Office is not a place but a state of mind. Where we are, there is the office, from eight to one, and from two to seven.' Other places are mentally remodelled into offices: directed to the Engel Bar by a hotel porter, Pichler politely enquires what office hours are kept there. Told that they are open till three in the morning, he is deeply impressed: 'They work hard in Vienna!' And an evening angelus bell heard in the open fields is greeted with the word 'Büroschluss' – the office is closing.

Another important theme is the difficulty of gauging a person's nature, calling and intention from his outward appearance, body language and speech. One salient instance of this occurs in a restaurant scene in which a Peter Lorre look-alike is declared by Klapka, the pessimistic office porter played by Fritz Grünbaum, to have a criminal face ('Verbrechervisage'), and suspected by Pichler of having dark designs on the firm's money in Pichler's briefcase. When this man politely asks if any of the gentlemen could name a robber and murderer in seven letters – clearly a crossword clue – their darkest suspicions seem confirmed. Yet when Pichler, rushing to catch a train to Vienna, leaves the precious briefcase behind, it is the man with the 'criminal face' who runs all the way to the station to restore it to its owner. In the same way a confidence trickster is mistaken for a policeman; real policemen who are thought to be about to arrest the 'virtuous sinners' (or the real embezzler) are found to have a quite different intention; and a series of misapprehensions, provoked by Chinese whispers, transform Pichler and Wittek into millionnaire landowners ('alter Landadel ... Millionäre') and Pichler himself into Direktor von Härtl. What is broached here is the age-old theme, so prominent in Austrian literature, of the deceptive nature of reality, the world as illusion, which merges with the 'fickle money' theme when a large win in a gambling joint turns out to be a win in gambling chips only: the money into which the chips should have been converted has vanished, abstracted by crooks.

Pichler and Wittek try, all the time, to make sense of their experiences, with metaphysical assumptions repeatedly brought down to earth. Looking up to heaven, to the skies in which we have just seen the defaulting Director, Max von Härtl, make his escape in a monoplane, Wittek's glance encounters some telegraph wires and induces, wrongly as it turns out, that they are bearing the news of their apparently so culpable loss of the firm's money to a wider world. He now feels himself ruled by the eternal laws of Fate: 'Ein ewiges Gesetz waltet über uns'. Pichler's reply brings us down to earth: 'Das Strafgesetz': Austria's criminal laws. These are, clearly, the 'eternal laws' by which Pichler believes himself ruled.

An equally revealing exchange takes place when the two adventurers find that they are safe because the Director's embezzlement will account for the missing money without involving them in any apparent wrongdoing. Pichler declares, with apparent piety: 'A Higher Being has taken our guilt upon Himself.' Wittek takes this in a religious sense ('Man könnte fromm werden') – but Pichler's hierarchies are of this earth. 'Why go to extremes?', he asks. 'I mean the Director.' Even in front of a 'Wanted' poster declaring von Härtl to be a criminal, for Pichler he is still a 'Higher Being' – 'ein Höherer'.

And through it all, from the very beginning, there resounds the great theme of identity and self-image. Ludmilla, Pichler's unloved wife, asks scornfully, when she sees him handling the knife he has taken up after reading the news of a demented official slaughtering his family (Why 'demented', he keeps on asking himself, in the midst of family pandemonium): 'Do you know what you are?' The answer she has in mind is doubtless unflattering; but he answers, in words that make her tearful: 'Married to you for thirty years. Sad enough!' It is, however, a question that rankles in his mind, and comes to the surface again when a dancer sings, at his restaurant table, about 'Vulcan eyes'. 'I don't understand, what does she mean?' he asks; and Wittek glosses: 'She says that in the Herr Oberkassierer's eyes there is a volcano.' Yes, he muses, as a different Pichler begins to appear, under the influence of alcohol and music, 'once upon a time, I was just that – an eagle – a Double Eagle – a Stromboli. Women ... Gambling ... Now I am just a hillock.' But then he finds himself happily dancing with the graceful black singer, delighted by the (not ill-natured) laughter of other guests ('freundliche Leute', he murmurs); and after scrabbling on the floor to retrieve the precious briefcase he had dropped and extricating it from a circle of knives a Cossack variety act had cast around it, he forms a bond with these dancing knife-throwers and is carried by them, shoulder-high, to his table. When they are kissed by a Russian bass he scrambles up to collect a kiss for himself, and he gabbles in imitation of Cossack speech when one of them excitedly confronts the restaurant manger in a variety of Russian.

His adventures in Vienna bring the little man to the brink of suicide; and when Wittek asks him how far he thinks they are from home, he replies: 'About – an eternity.' When the timely discovery of von Härtl's theft has exonerated him, however, and he arrives home the next day to find himself appointed 'provisional director', he draws himself up with a new self-confidence – 'Why provisional?' – and it is an authoritative Director who accepts Wittek's congratulations and marches at the head of Wittek and Klapka to effect his transmigration to his new office. For a moment he seems to relapse into his old deferential self, wiping his feet and preparing to knock at the Director's door. He soon recovers himself, however; and having been shown by Wittek, in a wordless pantomime involving Hedwig's picture, that Wittek and Pichler's daughter are in love and want to marry, he phones a curt message to Klapka which he is to pass on to Wittek: 'Tochter bewilligt' – 'daughter granted'.

Pichler's newly confident persona blossoms in the final scene which discovers him delivering a postprandial address at the wedding banquet for Hedwig and Wittek. The speech is a Polgar–Pallenberg masterpiece of platitudes gone awry and sheer gobbledegook, delivered while the audience follows the newly-weds in drifting away to the dance-floor, from where we can still see the orator, through a glass partition, holding forth to no one but his wife and a deaf old man. The dance music, however, is relayed from the Engel Bar, where Pichler had his memorable encounter with a black dancer and a troupe of Cossack knife-throwers; and as the knife-throwers' martial tune comes over the air-waves, Pichler suddenly moves his arms in abrupt jerky rhythms, seizes a sharp knife and plunges it into the table in front of him with a fierce glare like that of Dr Caligari. His wife is unimpressed: '*You* – and escapades?'. Sadly deflated, he finds himself talking to the deaf of man, the last audience that remains to him, brooding, as he had done before, on the meaning of all that has happened to him. 'What is Man?', he asks; and when he repeats this question by shouting it in the old man's ear, the latter has his answer pat: 'Ein armes Luder' – ' a poor wretch'. Yes, Pichler agrees, in words that have all the witty Austrian-Jewish melancholy and love of paradox in them: 'Man *is* a poor wretch, but he doesn't know it. If he *did* know it – what a poor wretch he would be!'

This downbeat conclusion did not help the film, and it never became the popular success it should have been. My cinema-going aunts, who had driven my five-year-old self round the bend with sobbing renditions of 'Sonny Boy', dubbed into German from Al Jolson's American in *The Singing Fool* ('Strahlende Sterne / Leuchten von ferne / Leuchten für Dich, Sonny BOY!'), now laughed themselves even sillier over *Three Days Confined to Barracks* and lovingly reminded each other of episodes and songs from *Three Men from the Filling Station*; but they never so much as *mentioned The Virtuous Sinner*. By the time I could go to the cinema by myself the film had disappeared from accessible screens. Some discerning critics had praised it – but though its French version recouped some its cost, its producer and star lost heart, and Pallenberg never got to play the Good Soldier Schweik in the film he had hoped to make next. Nor did Kortner direct another film before his enforced emigration. By moving behind the camera he had hoped to mitigate the hostility increasingly directed at the too-frequent appearance, on screen, of his 'alien' face – his 'rassefremdes Gesicht', as he himself characterised anti-Semitic views of it in his autobiography. There too his hopes had been dashed; nor did he find in the USA the opportunities his talents warranted. After an unhappy time in Hollywood he returned to Germany after the war to become a distinguished, very demanding, and not uncontroversial, theatre director before he died, in Berlin, in 1970. Pallenberg had died much earlier, in 1934; but he did have the satisfaction of playing the part he had so wanted to play, Goethe's Mephisto, under Reinhardt's direction, in the fateful year 1933, and of seeing at least one of his performances preserved for posterity in *The Virtuous Sinner*.

And what a performance it is! Juggling sentences and syllables, stumbling over his words, grasping an opponent's lapels or shoulders, now shouting, now muttering, Pallenberg brings out facet after facet of this little man, with his ridiculous moustache and crooked pince-nez, whose very nonsense yields unexpected insights, exposing his weaknesses, hang-ups, dignities, delusions, depressions, shocks and exaltations. One cannot imagine that anyone scripted the many repetitions and half-completed sentences into which Pichler's speeches dissolve – they smack of the improvisations for which Pallenberg was famous. One aspect of this torrent of words must, however have been fully planned: the insight into his mental processes yielded by the constant intrusions, at inappropriate moments, of words and events that rankle painfully inside him. Thoughts of the 'demented' man who slaughtered his family (could not a *sane* man be driven to the same deed?); money flung literally, and not just metaphorically, 'out of the window'; the sandwich his wife had forgotten to put into his pocket, for the first time in thirty years ('Neglect of marital duties!'); the coughing of a customer who had been kept waiting a long time only to find he had come to the wrong firm – 'Coughs around here at the INTRAG – let him go and do his coughing at the RUBAG!'

The words of his boss rankle particularly. Though he seems deferentially to agree to everything, he is outraged by a line in the song the Director half-sings to himself as he haughtily gives instructions to his head cashier: 'Ganz ohne Weiber geht die Chose nicht ...' – 'The whole thing can't go right *quite* without women ...' 'Libertine', Pichler mutters to himself when he is out of earshot, before confronting the nonplussed Wittek with the question: 'Why can't the whole thing go right without women?' He then supplies his own emphatic answer: 'Ganz ohne Weiber geht die Chose *ja!*' What most riles him, however, and goes round and round in his head, is his boss's off-hand remark that there is no relying on anyone nowadays – not even on Pichler. He refers back to this throughout the next scenes, and his subsequent actions are designed to show that he *can* be relied on to do the right thing even in unexpected circumstances. An actor of great intelligence, sophistication and quick wit has here slipped into the skin of a much more limited, less intelligent, Austrian citizen and convincingly portrays the reactions of such a man during three days and two nights of unprecedented experience. We smile at his gaffes and *faux pas*, sympathise with predicaments that bring out unexpected facets of his personality, and are constantly pulled up by reminders of how much of him there is in all of us.

Pallenberg is well served by his supporting cast. Heinz Rühmann is Wittek, modest, respectful, diffident – a song he sings in his cups, a German equivalent of 'I'm shy, Mary Ellen, I'm shy', defines much of his nature; but after many false starts, he does manage in the end to convey to his 'Herr Oberkassierer' that he wants to marry his daughter, and gets his wish. That daughter, played by Dolly Haas, is looked on by her father as a 'tender lamb' that has to be sheltered from office wolves: 'My daughter is *not* going into any office' are the film's opening words. What we see, however, is an attractive little termagant, who fights fiercely with her older brother, slams doors, and takes the initiative by setting her cap at Wittek. To see the newly-weds dancing together is to realise that the sexual initiative is hers too. Josefine Dora, as Pichler's wife in a marriage that has gone stale, Peter Wolff, as his son whose chief interest seems to be flirting with waitresses, Ekkehard Arendt, as the suave Director von Härtl, haughty with subordinates, womanising and seeking an unencumbered life of pleasure by embezzling the office funds, Louis Ralph, as the plausible confidence trickster 'Kommissar' Krull, and a large cast of accomplished actors in small but important parts – all give vital support without obscuring the central performance.

Two of them, however, deserve special notice. The first is the most beautiful, graceful and sexually alluring presence in the film: Rose Pointexter, as a sinuous young black dancer with an enchanting smile and wonderfully flashing eyes, whose endearing personality enchants even Pichler after she has plied him with champagne and dragged him off into a dance. When he wakes up in her bed the next morning, fully dressed and clutching his briefcase, he thinks he must be in Africa ('ich sehe schwarz', he says, in an unexpectedly literal use of the idiom that describes someone who habitually looks on the dark side of things); and after she has dragged him into her bathroom and settled him in the bath, she tells Krull, who has come to enquire, that nothing happened – 'not even a kiss'. Another facet of Pichler's character, one might think.

The second of these highly memorable supporting actors is Fritz Grünbaum – the great cabaret artist who was to fall victim to the Nazis after their seizure of power, and die in a concentration camp. As Klapka, the porter lowest in the office pecking order, he is of small stature, respectful, slow of speech, pessimistic about anyone's chances in a world beset by robbers, murderers and 'Individuums' that are not to be trusted. His drooping moustache is constantly straining a beerglass, and his little beerbelly is incongruously swathed in a flowered waistcoat. He is as adept at significant wrenchings of the Austrian language into unexpected contortions as Pallenberg himself. Where Pichler conveys what his marriage has come to mean to him by addressing his wife as 'Du lebenslängliches Weib' – using the adjective that normally describes the sentence of life imprisonment passed on a criminal by a judge – Klapka answers the telephone after the Director's defalcation has been discovered: 'Hier INTRAG – Beschränkte Gesellschaft mit Verhaftung'. This wrenches the usual description of a Limited Liability Company into a statement that says the company is now inhibited in its operations (for the police have temporarily closed it down) and it has suffered an arrest ('Verhaftung'), the common term for the arrest of a criminal. One of the many pleasures of this film is to see Pallenberg and Grünbaum interacting – either in exchanges where one of them shouts and splutters while the other drags his words evenly along, or with heads on each other's shoulder as Pichler tries to make Klapka understand that he wants his purposes and destination kept secret from the suspicious crossword-puzzler at the next table.

Kortner's direction, aided by the imaginative black-and-white effects conjured up by Günther Krampf and the designs of Julius von Borsody, brings out his performers' qualities in a series of efficiently staged set pieces. These range from the turbulence at a breakfast table, suggestively seen, at one stage, through the bars of a parrot's cage, to a chase after a bowler hat through traffic, wind and rain, to a gambling scene that has an unforgettable extreme close-up shot of Pallenberg's eyes, hugely magnified by the lenses of his pince-nez, rolling in a frantic effort to follow the course of the ball on which his fate by then depends.

Into the midst of all the realistic staging, however, Kortner injects one of the finest surrealist sequences in the early German film. It begins with the drunken Pichler's focusing on one of the plaster putti that decorate the Engel Bar as they had another, more downmarket, 'Angel' establishment in Sternberg's *The Blue Angel* the year before. The putto turns his head, smiles and salutes Pichler who has just emptied another bottle; it suddenly takes wing, along with a whole crowd of putti from all quarters of the restaurant. This begins a nightmare sequence that weaves together what is happening here and now – the ever more urgent presentation of a huge bill for the evening's entertainment – with memories, distorted and magnified, of earlier experiences, irradiated with soul-stuff. Some of these memories are of music: the song-fragment about the necessity of women sung by the Director; tunes accompanying the various turns in the Engel Bar; and recollected folksongs like 'Ein Jäger aus Kurpfalz'.

Pichler finds himself transported to a nightmare version of his office, beset by clamouring customers, with a piratical Klapka throwing a huge knife in his direction. This is, however, intercepted by a determined looking Frau Pichler, in whose hands it seems to exude even greater menace. But now an image from the real world intrudes into the vision, as the restaurant bill had earlier, to mark the real moment of crisis which will transform the head cashier seeking to show his utter reliability into the 'sinner' of the film's title. We see his hand move into the briefcase he had so jealously guarded to extract the firm's money to pay the bill he and Wittek had run up in the mistaken belief that their Director would meet it. The danger this poses takes on the face of a fiery-eyed monster, like the vision of Moloch in Lang's *Metropolis*, bringing recollections of the recent journey to Vienna when the vision resolves itself into a railway engine pulling a train through a landscape. Pichler and Wittek are perched on its top, facing the wind and the rain with an umbrella blown inside out – as it had been when they were vainly chasing through the driving rain to save Pichler's bowler hat from disaster. The top hat he is wearing in the vision recalls the one he had had to don, incongruously, when his normal headgear had been lost – just like the professor in Sternberg's *The Blue Angel*. The Pichler of this nightmare vision is then carried upwards by the winds, like 'Flying Robert' in *Struwwelpeter*, to land on top of a steeple, like Münchhausen. As tower bells begin to play, we are reminded of *The Blue Angel* once again – for one of the tunes we now hear is that which had constantly reminded that film's professor, as they now do the *Herr Oberkassierer*, of the code by which a good citizen, *ein braver Mann*, must live: 'Üb immer Treu und Redlichkeit/Bis an dein kühles Grab ...' 'Be ever faithful, ever honest, until you reach your cool grave', and do not stray even a finger's breadth from the path of righteousness. This warning invocation brings tower and steeple, with the man clinging to it, crashing to the ground, onto a railway line. An approaching train then runs over the Pichler of this vision; and as it departs into the distance, the prone man – presumed dead, though miraculously undamaged – sits up for a moment, makes a final pronouncement: 'Schade um mich' ('Pity about me!') and lies back with finality.

The film now returns to its previous more realistic mode, which has some of the grace and lightness of René Clair. Pichler prone on the railway line merges into the actual Pichler waking, strangely enough, in a female dancer's bed, with her sleeping face next to his. He is, however, fully dressed, overcoat and all, and holds the fatal briefcase close to his chest. Wittek, arising drowsily from a nearby couch, asks where they are: Pichler shows him the sleeping black dancer and opines that they must be in Africa. He is highly indignant, however, at what he thinks Wittek is insinuating when the latter shakes his head at learning where Pichler had spent the night. The head cashier has some memorable encounters in this unfamiliar apartment: with 'Africa', with his own double reflection in a pair of adjacent mirrors, and with objects that include a large cloth dog, a stuffed monkey mounted on a tree branch (whom he informs, along with Wittek, that 'office' is not a place but a state of mind), and a huge rubber swan, nodding at Pichler's head after the dancer has packed him off into the bath. Kortner also ensures that we are made aware, through an open door behind Wittek's back, that the bathroom contains a bidet – an object neither of its visitors is likely to have encountered before. I will refrain from Freudian analysis of the surrealist sequence which ends in this return to the realistic mode; but it does seem to me to reproduce a dream-experience more plausibly than those rather obviously concocted for psychoanalytic dissection in Pabst's *Geheimnisse einer Seele* (*Secrets of a Soul*, 1926).

The film's music, by Nikolaus Brodszkey, with song-lyrics by Fritz Rotter, and orchestrations by Artur Guttmann, fits the milieu in which it is performed: the Engel Bar, and a garden establishment among trees in an outlying district – Grinzing perhaps. It is performed by the small orchestra of the Engel Bar, which accompanies the guests' dancing and various turns: the female dancer with her male backing group, the Cossack knife-throwers, a Russian bass, and a crooner whose open mouth is startlingly isolated in a huge close-up as he sings: 'Nur wer Dich heimlich kennt/Und Dich sein eigen nennt/Der kennt des Lebens Licht ...' 'Only he who knows you, secretly, and calls you his own, knows the light of life ...' Rühmann renders Wittek's song about shyness and Dutch courage very touchingly: 'Heute hätt ich Mut, Dir viel zu sagen,/Aber gerade heute bist Du fern von mir' 'I'd have the courage to tell you much today, but just today you are far away from me.' And as the camera moves away from central Vienna, past a another view of St Stephen's Cathedral over some trees to a restaurant garden, we hear a gentle song in praise of the city: 'O Wien, Du mein Anfang und Ende ...) ('Vienna, my beginning and my end ...'). None of this, not even Rühmann's song, ever achieved anything like the popularity reached by the film, cabaret and revue compositions of Friedrich Hollaender, Werner Richard Heymann or Mischa Spoliansky in the early 1930s; but it helps to frame and support a virtuoso performance by one of the great Jewish stage-personalities whose name has now paled besides that of Heinz Rühmann, whose career extended unbroken over a multitude of films (and all changes of régime) from *Das deutsche Mutterherz* (*The Heart of a German Mother*) in 1926, to his last television appearance in 1994, the year of his death. It is only because of Rühmann's appearance in *The Virtuous Sinner* that TaunusVideo rereleased the film on a VHS cassette. I fervently hope, however, that this will enable Pallenberg to gather his well-deserved laurels from posterity.

Chapter 8

CONFRONTATIONS AND ENMITIES

Two Worlds (Zwei Welten)

E.A. Dupont's *The Ancient Law*, discussed in an earlier chapter, had topical interest when it was released in 1923 because of the recent influx of Eastern European Jews into Germany and Austria, and anti-Jewish measures in the Ruhr district. It had been preceded in 1918 by Dupont's *Ferdinand Lassalle. Des Volks-Tribuns Glück und Ende* (*F.L. The Prosperity and the End of a People's Tribune*), which chronicled the love of a Jewish political thinker for a titled German lady as well as his diverse relations with Bismarck and the most famous of all German Jewish poets, Heinrich Heine. By alluding, in its title, to Grillparzer's classic play about the life and death of the Austrian king Ottokar II of Bohemia (*König Ottokars Glück and Ende*), *Ferdinand Lassalle* gives its Jewish 'People's Tribune' Fallhöhe, a height that makes his fall more tragic. In his thriller of 1920, set in London's East End, *Whitechapel. Eine Kette von Perlen und Abenteuern* (*Whitechapel. A String of Pearls and Adventures*), Dupont introduces a Fagin-like figure, Feibel, played by Guido Herzfeld more in the spirit of Ron Moody than Alex Guiness, but balances it by two sympathetic Jewish protagonists who cross Feibel's designs: the flower-seller Rahel, played by Grit Hegesa, and the toy-seller David, played by Fritz Schulz.

These 'silent' films were followed up, 1930, by Dupont's sound film made at the Elstree studios of British International Pictures, in association with Greenbaum-Film GmbH, and shot in three languages, English, German, and French, with different casts and modified dialogue. There was also a 'silent' version for the benefit of cinemas that had not yet installed sound-reproduction equipment. It was entitled *Two Worlds* (*Zwei Welten, Les deux mondes*); its German shooting script was by Franz Schulz and Dupont himself; and the dialogues of the English version were adapted, under Dupont's supervision, by Miles Malleson.

Two Worlds returns to the *milieu* within which *The Ancient Law* has opened: a small Galician town, with a separate quarter occupied by a religiously observant Jewish community. This time, however, we see it in wartime, during the Russian campaign of 1917, when the territory changed its occupation repeatedly between the Austro-Hungarian and Russian armies. The principal personages who dramatise the clash of the 'two worlds' of the title are the Austrian colonel in charge of the detachment occupying the little town at the beginning; his son, who is a lieutenant under his command; a Jewish clockmaker; his daughter Esther; and a cobbler named Mendel. The colonel and the lieutenant bear the aristocratic prefix 'von' in their family name (von Kaminsky); the clockmaker and his daughter bear the less prestigious name Goldscheider – a name not untypical of the secular names borne, in addition to their Hebrew ones, by Jews in the Austro-Hungarian and German empires.

The film begins with a time of the year in which tensions between Christians and Jews in Eastern Europe often broke into violence: that in which Easter and Passover coincide. It takes its audience into a church in which a priest reminds his hearers of the command to love one's neighbour as oneself, and into a synagogue in which a rabbi recalls the same maxim in the Jewish scriptures. In what follows, however, the festive celebrations of the Austrian officers are interrupted by news of 'trouble in the Jewish quarter'. This 'trouble' turns out to be a pogrom, unleashed by Christian townsfolk who chase and beat worshippers emerging from the synagogue, break into their houses, throw out and burn their furniture, smash their crockery, and try to rape their women. The Austrian colonel, whose duties include the protection of local citizens, orders his reluctant son, Lieutenant Stanislas von Kaminsky, to put himself at the head of a small detachment and see to the restoration of peaceful coexistence. The Austrian troops arrive on horseback, and a gunfight ensues between them and the pogromists in which a stray bullet from an Austrian rifle kills Goldscheider's young son. The clockmaker and his daughter have sought protection in their own house; but a fiercely bearded pogromist breaks in, locks the father into a room, and prepares to rape the daughter. He is foiled, however, by Lieutenant Stanislas, who throws him down the stairs before he can carry out his fell intention. He also frees Goldscheider; but at that moment a solemn procession of bearded Jews brings in the body of the latter's only son. The distraught father bitterly confronts the Lieutenant with the charge that the troops he commanded had failed in their duty to protect the inhabitants of the occupied territory, but had instead ended a promising young life. In his grief he attacks the Lieutenant physically, but is easily shaken off. As the Lieutenant prepares to leave, he passes Esther lying distraught over the body of her brother; he gives a military salute, and goes out.

This has been the first of a number of confrontation scenes around which the film is built. Here Dupont indulges his delight in close-ups, semi-close-ups and shot-reverse-shots of strongly marked features, well lit and photographed in often dark surroundings. The bearded faces of Goldscheider and his friend Mendel fare especially well under the cameras of Griffith's favourite photographer, Charles Rosher, and Mutz Greenbaum, and so does the deliberate contrast between them and the smooth-faced

Austrian officers. Greenbaum is here at the start of a long and distinguished career as cinematographer and director, much of it in Great Britain under the name Max Greene.

As has already been seen, directors of films with a Jewish theme or background liked to take the opportunity of showing something of Jewish religious ritual. *Two Worlds* had introduced a brief scene of synagogue worship and established the consonance of the Christian injunction to love one's neighbour as oneself with similar rabbinic precepts – an important factor in our appreciation of the social and moral conflicts at the heart of the film. We now watch Goldscheider and his daughter sadly obeying the religious command to celebrate Israel's liberation from Egypt at a Passover ceremony known as the *Seder*. With the body of their son and brother still in the house, remembrance of the slaying of the Egyptian firstborn while those of the Israelites were spared has a bitterly ironic ring – and so has the traditional praise of a Creator 'Whose mercy endureth for ever'. At the same time, however, by highlighting precisely these sections of the Seder celebrations Dupont also suggests an unshakable faith in the God of Israel in the face of evils unleashed by men to whom He has accorded free will.

From these sad celebrations the film now cuts to the merry ones of Austrian soldiers singing to a guitar played by one of them, and thence back to Goldscheider's house in the Jewish quarter, where the father is keeping a vigil by his son's body. Two soldiers arrive at the door demanding his attendance at Austrian headquarters. When he arrives there, he is made to stand by the door while being accused of attacking an Austrian officer by the seated Lieutenant, who does not trouble to interrupt a card game he is playing with a similarly uniformed friend. Here Dupont makes the most of a second confrontation of his 'two worlds', with alternate views of the two officers playing their game in a relaxed posture and a well-lit portion of the room, while the black-clad, beetle-browed Godscheider stands glowering in a darker part. Told that his attack merited a court martial that would impose at least three *years* in prison, the clockmaker is informed by the Lieutenant, who has just won his card game, that he will be merciful and only impose three *days* arrest – insisting, however, that he should be thanked for his leniency. This satisfaction Goldscheider refuses to give to the man he regards as responsible for the death of his son. 'I have nothing to say.' 'Right, then – *four* days. *Now* will you thank me?' Stubborn silence. '*Five* days, then – orderly, march the prisoner out.' But the Lieutenant good-naturedly calls the orderly back: 'See that he is not treated too badly – he's a poor devil.'

We now cut to the Austrian colonel, summoned to a meeting of superior officers to discuss a Russian offensive that has just begun in Lithuania. He telephones his son, the Lieutenant, telling him to be ready to receive messages announcing further developments, adding 'Don't get into any scrapes!' 'Fat chance! Who is there here to get into scrapes with?' The answer to that question arrives immediately when an orderly announces that the Lieutenant as a visitor. That turns out to be a soubrette, Mizzi

Staudinger, with whom the Lieutenant once had a liaison in Vienna which she seems now eager to resume. The two of them perform a merry variation of military drill which ends in a kiss, just before the film cuts to the darkness of a prison in which Goldscheider has to sit while outside the funeral procession of his son passes by. We cannot make out his face clearly, but have to imagine what his feelings must be at being prevented from saying the prescribed funeral prayer, the Mourner's *Kaddish*, at his son's graveside. The contrast between the two worlds, and their power relation, is at its starkest when the sound-track breaks into a jaunty tune which accompanies a performance by Mizzi and a chorus of six leggy showgirls, dancing and singing before a company of delighted Austrian soldiers full-throatedly joining into the refrain. The introduction of this scene is essential for Dupont, whose fascination with theatrical showbusiness of all kinds pervades his films – most conspicuously in *Der weisse Pfau. Tragödie einer Tänzerin* (*The White Peacock. A dancer's Tragedy*, 1920); *Varieté* (1925); *Moulin Rouge* (1927–28); and *Piccadilly* (1928). The German version of *Two Worlds* is particularly full of music; Dupont introduces Austrian and Russian marching songs, Lieder that had become folksongs ('Ich hatt einen Kameraden' – 'I once had a comrade'), and specially composed items by composers who include Friedrich Hollaender, and Otto Stransky. Some of these songs have a Jewish tinge: 'Rosa, wir fahren nach Lodz' ('Rosa, we're travelling to Lodz') and 'Ich hab ka Geld in meinem Kasten' ('I have no money in my coffer'). There are also brief snatches of traditional Jewish liturgy.

From the well-lit, tatty, but enthusiastically received front-theatre production, *Two Worlds* cuts to a darkened room where the Lieutenant is sleeping by the telephone while his orderly keeps watch in an outer chamber. Mizzi enters and wakes the Lieutenant, eager for a night of love. He is all too easily persuaded to leave his orderly in charge, with two bottles of wine to cheer the latter's vigil, and to desert his post with Mizzi on his arm. We accompany the pair through a darkened street to a primitive hostelry, whose proprietor shows them into a sparsely furnished candle-lit room containing a bed as its most necessary amenity. Cut to the orderly, receiving a telephone message which we do not hear, and then settling himself comfortably back to savour more of his wine. We have to surmise that this is one of those important instructions the Colonel had ordered his son to listen out for, but for which the orderly has had none of the specific commands to which he is accustomed. Cut back to the Lieutenant's lovenest, where he is now awakened by an alarm clock set by Mizzi for 9.30 a.m. She herself had moved out with her troupe in the early hours, leaving an affectionate note. Marching music sounds from outside, and a cut to the column of soldiers it accompanies gives us another chance to see the beautiful onion-domed set Alfred Junge had designed for the Christian part of the town. The soldiers marching in are *Russian*, the Austrians having strategically withdrawn. It is now dangerous to harbour an Austrian officer, and the landlord shoos the Lieutenant out of his house as quickly as possible.

Fleeing on a rapidly commandeered horse the Lieutenant is pursued by Russian soldiers; in an exchange of fire he kills one of their officers but is himself wounded. He collapses in front of Goldscheider's house, where Esther rescues him, dragging him into a room where he sinks into unconsciousness. This triggers the third of the film's confrontation scenes. This time the two worlds are those of age and youth – of Jewish father and Jewish daughter. Goldscheider is ready to hand over the Lieutenant, whom he holds responsible for the death of his son, to his Russian enemies. He is, however, prevented from putting this into effect by his daughter's threat: she too, she declares, will be arrested by the Russians on a charge of aiding the fugitive they are combing the houses for. Threatened with losing his daughter, after he had just lost his son, Goldscheider has to give in. He admits the Russian soldiers pounding on his door with a cajoling, ingratiating manner quite different from any we have seen him adopt before – recalling similar conciliatory mannerisms Jews felt driven to assume in the face of powerful secular authorities in *The Golem – How He Came into the World*. Little seems to have changed in the intervening centuries. The altered manner is particularly marked in Goldscheider, who had earlier even attacked the Lieutenant physically. He now plies the Russians with drink, and falls in with Esther's suggestion that he declare the wounded man in his house to be his own son. The suspicious Russians force him to *swear* to the truth of this statement; and as he swears 'by God', Dupont's actors (Randle Ayrton in the English, Hermann Vallentin in the German version) register unmistakably how difficult it is for him to load the heavy sin of false swearing onto his soul. Nothing but solicitude for his child's life and safety could have him do so.

From the Jewish father attempting to save his daughter by harbouring a man he considers his enemy, the film cuts to the Austrian colonel, in a ruined house, worrying about the fate of his son. A time-gap of some two months now ensues, showing us that son, the Lieutenant, dishevelled and unshaven, fretting at his involuntary imprisonment where the earlier power relations have been dramatically reversed. Esther seeks to comfort him while her father, whose protection is all that stands between the Austrian and his death at Russian hands, refuses to speak to him or acknowledge his presence. Clearly falling in love with the Jewish girl who has nursed him back to health, he complains that her father refuses to acknowledge his confession that he had not behaved very nobly before, and to respond to the Austrian's desire 'to bridge the chasm between You and Me'. Could he and Esther not become friends? 'No', she replies, suppressing her real feelings in recognition of the divided worlds in which they live: 'You are my prisoner, and I am your gaoler. But your people will return, and you'll be free again. Colonel von Kaminsky's son – and I, the daughter of a Jewish clockmaker. What will become of our friendship then?' But when Russian soldiers are heard singing outside, she admits her fear for him, whose longing to be with his fighting comrades has driven him again and again to look out of the window and will soon induce him to venture into the street muffled in a civilian greatcoat, his face hidden by a scarf. In staging the conversation in which Esther denies 'friendship' while the two participants are clearly falling in love, Dupont shows characteristic reticence. He hides both their faces at the moment of greatest emotion; the Lieutenant has his arms on the table and rests his face on them, while Esther is seen only from the rear as she gazes out of the window. We have to guess at the emotions which Goldscheider suspiciously surmises when he appears at the door to summon his daughter to the Eve of Sabbath celebrations: a chance, for Dupont, to show the ritual lighting and blessing of the Sabbath candles, matching the Seder celebrations in an earlier sequence.

Goldscheider's worries lead him to a consultation with his old friend Mendel the cobbler (played by Donald Calthrop in the English and Paul Graetz in the German version). This takes place in the clockmaker's workshop, in which the clocks are now ticking again after Goldscheider had ritually stopped them at his son's death. What is he to do in face of the love growing between his daughter and the aristocratic Gentile in her care? The 'Two Worlds' theme rings out loud and clear now. 'He is an officer and an aristocrat. Among his own people such a man is half a god. The Emperor himself protects him. Do you think such a man would sit at table with us?' 'And yet he does!' 'Ah – but he has to. He is cut off from his own people – but instead of being just grateful that I am putting myself and Esther at risk for him, he is making eyes at my daughter. But I'll protect her'. Goldscheider now asks Mendel to advise him on the form such protection might effectively take. Mendel, a more devious character, obliquely suggests amid pinches of snuff that one could – 'I say, one *could*, not that one *should*' – write an anonymous letter to the Russian commandant, offering to give the Austrian up in return for a promise of immunity to those who had sheltered him. But Goldscheider recoils from this: though the man's people had killed his son and, by imprisoning him, prevented him from ritual leave-taking, he could not act in such a treacherous way if any other way of protecting his daughter could be found.

The way he finds, the next scene shows us, is that of another direct confrontation. The Lieutenant has returned from a dangerous venture outdoors, and the worry Esther had felt about his safety moves both young people so much that their love breaks out more clearly than before and culminates in a kiss. Goldscheider has observed this, and after Esther has left he at last challenges the Lieutenant directly. 'I have lost my son. I beg you: do not take my daughter from me as well.' 'I don't understand.' 'Not understand? A father asks you for his only child…I am old, but can read in the eyes of the young. And what I see now, in your eyes and those of my daughter, tells me that there will be a tragedy.' 'Like a thief?' the Lieutenant asks, stung by the suggestion of underhandedness. 'Yes – but you shall not accuse me of being underhand. That is why I have come to you.' 'I am not afraid of your threats. But', The Lieutenant replies, in words which seem to bridge worlds whose irreconcilability Goldscheider continues to assert, 'I am sorry to find in you prejudices I have overcome in myself.' He little knows, as yet, that Goldscheider's fears will prove to be only too well founded when his own aristocratic father, who is also his superior officer, confronts him over an infatuation incompatible with his provenance and station in life.

After another shot of Esther gazing out of her window, again seen from the rear so that we have to guess at her emotions, we are shown Goldscheider leaving his workshop and entering that of the cobbler whom we have come to know as his best friend and confidant. Cross-cutting shows us Esther, listening to a song of love and loss performed by a street-singer in the lane below, and the Lieutenant, who enters to embrace Esther of whose love he is now sure, as Goldscheider confronts his friend with his decision. 'Mendel – write the letter!' There follows a comic sequence – the only one in what is on the whole a sombre film – in which we see Mendel trying to make a Russian orderly understand that he has an important personal letter to deliver to the commanding officer. Yiddish is close enough to German to render communication with Austrian occupiers easier than with monolingual Russians. After a good deal of comic pantomime, with the letter handed backwards and forwards, it is at last taken by a Russian NCO and brought to his commander, who puts it on the table without opening it – for the fortunes of war have once again favoured the Austrians, and the Russians are packing up to leave. Exhausted by his efforts Mendel has fallen asleep in a corner of the anteroom guarded by the Russian orderly.

Dupont now cuts to a shot of the Russian flag being lowered, to the sound of the Tsarist anthem ('God the All-Terrible …'), and the Austrian flag being raised, to the sound of the national anthem of Imperial Austria ('Gott erhalte Franz den Kaiser …'). Mendel wakes from his slumbers to find that instead of a Russian an Austrian soldier now shares the room with him. His comic confusion is signalled by rapid alternations of the Russian sentry (seen only in Mendel's memory) and the Austrian one (who is actually before him). But the comedy ends here, when Mendel realises that it may have been the Austrians and not the Russians who have found his letter, and that this bodes ill for himself and (especially) for Goldscheider.

Mendel's agonized question, 'Where is my letter?', will receive its answer in the penultimate example of the great confrontation scenes which are the film's most memorable feature. This one takes place between Colonel von Kaminsky, sitting at a desk in his office, and his son, Lieutenant Stanislas, standing by his side. The Colonel does not come the heavy father, or the heavy superior officer. His son is of age, a human being responsible for his own actions; but he endeavours to make him see the consequences of his vowed determination to marry a Jewish clockmaker's daughter. Is the Lieutenant serious about that? 'Yes, perfectly serious'. 'Right then: you'll have to leave the army; and I can't ever recognise such a girl as my daughter-in-law. You'll have to find some civilian profession; and when children arrive, as they will, you'll have to adopt the motto: 'a poor house, but a happy one'. When the Lieutenant declares, with a depressed look which shows his distaste for the prospect his father had opened before him, that he is still willing to marry Esther Goldscheider – across the vast gulf of nationality, religion and class – the father says curtly, 'Then everything is perfectly satisfactory', and turns to the papers on his desk, dismissing his son.

This does not, however, end the confrontation – its climax comes as the Colonel finds the letter Mendel had tried so hard to deliver to the Russians, and calls his son back. 'Will you be so good as to glance at this letter?'

The Lieutenant now takes the letter from his father's hands, reads it, and recoils in horror. 'What treachery!', he exclaims. Realising that he now has the instrument which can bring his son back into the fold, the Colonel bids him sit down and speak to him with a gravity and seriousness he had not shown before. 'What you call treachery', he says, 'is really something else. The man who wrote this letter is the very man whose daughter you want to marry. He is not anxious to see you hanged. You mean nothing to him. He wants to keep his daughter, whom he loves just as I love you, whom he fears to lose just as I fear to lose you. This man feels, from his point of view, exactly as I do. He knows' – and here we have the fullest statement yet of the theme around which the whole film has revolved – 'that between you and his daughter there is not only a social difference ... You belong to different worlds.' What is so striking about this is how clearly both Goldscheider and the Colonel see each other's point of view, recognising its justification and correspondence to their own. They both show themselves willing, however, to use any means to save their children from what they both believe to be a step that can only bring them unhappiness in the end. The clockmaker had sent the letter that would have ended the Lieutenant's life; and that very letter now furnishes the ammunition the Colonel has secretly wished for. 'You defend this man?', his son asks. 'No; but I respect his feelings, and I expect my feelings to be treated with like respect. And so I ask you now, as a son who means a great deal to me: are you still determined to marry this girl?' Through clenched teeth the Lieutenant, shaken by what he has just learned, replies that he is. 'I understand', his father replies. 'And you must now understand me. The life of the clockmaker Goldscheider is in your hands.... Unless you now give me your solemn word that you will give up all thoughts of marrying this girl, or ever seeing her again, the clockmaker Goldscheider will be brought before a court martial, condemned, and shot.' 'Father, you wouldn't ...' 'Yes I would. I claim for my attitude the same justification which I concede to my opponent.'

With these words the Colonel ends this thematically so important colloquy, which prepares us for the film's final scene. The setting is once again the clockmaker's workshop, into which the Lieutenant now makes a dramatic entry. Goldscheider looks up from his work as the man he had tried to betray to his enemies confronts him with his newly gained knowledge. 'Mr Goldscheider, you have written a letter. This letter has fallen into my hand.... Once you saved my life. Today I am saving yours. I am saving it by saying goodbye to Esther. We are quits.' With this the Lieutenant turns to leave; but at the door he looks back at the clockmaker, who has buried his face in his hands so that we have once again to guess at the emotions of a silent figure in a film that depends so much on dialogue. 'One other thing', the Lieutenant continues, 'Esther knows nothing about your letter. She must always think that I am a scoundrel, so that she can keep her faith in you, the only person she has now.' As he leaves, without a word from the clockmaker, Esther sees him going out of the front door, realises what is happening, and falls in a swoon. Emerging from his workshop, Goldscheider calls out her name in terror, lifts her unconscious form and carries her towards her room with bitter laughter that ends this uncompromising film. The gulfs remain as deep as ever.

Dupont has shown us fathers wanting to do what is best for their children resort to treachery and blackmail; attempts at protecting a beleaguered community result in the death of an innocent young man; and the injunction, common to Christians and Jews, to love one's neighbour, founder on wartime conditions, ethnic origins, class distinctions and power relationships. Goldscheider, at one point, quotes another biblical injunction better suited to human nature and social conditions, as they are here seen, where only sexual attraction is able to reach across the barriers: 'An eye for an eye ...'. But the Austrian occupiers and the Jews under their temporary authority each have honourable reasons for their behaviour – unlike the Lithuanian pogromists whom we see engaged on pillage, senseless destruction of property, and attempted rape. Few of the original audiences of this film could have guessed how soon such sporadic actions of an unenlightened mob would be surpassed by atrocities planned and sanctioned by a genocidal regime in the cultural heartland of civilised Europe.

Dreyfus

Richard Oswald, like Dupont, carried over into the early sound film the willingness he had first shown in his 'silent' days to deal with the problems encountered by Jews in a largely Christian, and often hostile, environment. His early work included the comedy *Wollen Sie meine Tochter heiraten?* (*Do you want to marry my Daughter?*, 1914), starring Siegfried Berisch, Rosa Valetti and Guido Herzfeld, written by Oswald and directed by Nunek Danuty; *Dämon und Mensch* (*Demon and Man*, 1915), adapted by Oswald from a Yiddish play and starring Rudolf Schildkraut; *Schlemihl: Ein Lebensbild* (*Maladroit: Picture of a Life*, 1916), written and directed by Oswald, again starring Schildkraut along with his son Josef and Guido Herzfeld; and the two parts of *Jettchen Geberts Geschichte* (*The Story of Jettchen Gebert*, 1918), adapted from two novels of German-Jewish life by

Georg Hermann, and directed by Oswald from his own screenplay. In 1920 the journal Film-Kurier carried a notice announcing Oswald's decision to make a film broaching what the journal called '*the* problem of the day and the hour, which urgently calls for a solution': the problem of anti-Semitism. The film, to be called *Antisemiten*, never materialised; but the subject surfaced exactly ten years later in Oswald's *Dreyfus*, adapted from a book in which Bruno Weil had treated this famous judicial scandal in the Second French Republic, written for the screen by Heinz Goldberg and Fritz Wendhausen, with advice on the French background by André Obrecht and on military procedures by André Saint-Germain. Oswald showed greater courage here than other directors – Piel Jutzi, for instance, whose *Berlin Alexanderplatz* of 1931 omitted the episode, so important in Döblin's novel, which shows Biberkopf's adventures in the Jewish quarter into which he drifts immediately after his release from prison. For Fritz Kortner, the actor cast in the title role of Oswald's film, the part represented a kind of coming-out: after his unsympathetic portrayal of an *Ostjude* in Carl Wilhelm's *Landstrasse und Grossstadt* (*Highway and Big City*, 1921) he had rarely been explicitly identified as Jewish in his many films, though audiences will have made such an identification for themselves in such works as *The Woman One Longs For* and even *Pandora's Box*. He had also been, in his day, a famous Shylock on the German stage.

There had been *Dreyfus* films before Oswald's, beginning as early as 1898 with a 'living photograph' of Parisian scenes by the showman Francis Doublier, accompanied by his own spoken commentary; but properly presented, the subject offered peculiar difficulties, described by its British historian:

> The most distinguishing feature of the Dreyfus affair is its complexity. No single man was ever in charge of it, no one person ever dominated all its ramifications, no one understood all its aspects. The mistake that the historian often makes is to assume all the characters drawn together by a common purpose: to establish the innocence, or the guilt, of Dreyfus. But this was not so. A great variety of preoccupations, a multiplicity of side-issues, a series of different initiations and actors ... caused the arguments for or against guilt to become submerged and introduced many new dimensions to the affair ...
> (Johnson 1966: 96)

This meant a great deal of telescoping: important participants like Auguste Scheurer-Kestner, Joseph Reinach, Bernard Lazare and Anatole France on Dreyfus's side, Edouard Drumont and a multitude of representatives of the Catholic Church among his opponents, find no place in the tale told in Oswald's film. That the clerical involvement with the military caste is played down had good diplomatic reasons: concentration on mistaken patriotism and nationalism, personal ambitions, and racial prejudice among the French military was subject enough without the complications of a *Kulturkampf*. Even when telescoped in a way which made protagonists like Commander Picquart and Emile Zola assume some of the tasks history had assigned to others, and playing down the fact that these staunch defenders of Dreyfus had anti-Semitic prejudices of their own, the tale was complicated enough, and so was its cast of characters. Oswald solved this problem by choosing an ensemble of actors with very strong personalities, who gave a high profile even to the tiniest of roles, and then photographing their performances without camera tricks, and with strong reliance on close-ups and semi-close-ups. Cinematic purists may object to the style of staging Oswald adopts, with its close resemblance to theatre-techniques; but for this particular subject, with its climactic trials, public degradation and reinstatement, sudden discoveries, alternations between ministries, boudoirs, places of public resort and entertainment, publishing offices, prisons and penal settlements, and its strongly profiled actors delivering pleas and polemics on one side or the other, such staging proved wholly appropriate.

Since Oswald had been subject to anti-Semitic attacks more often than any other German filmmaker of the time, the Dreyfus case, with its strong anti-Jewish components, held obvious attractions for him. There were, however, additional reasons for this choice of subject. One has already been mentioned: his love of powerful playing, strongly marked personalities enacting individuals that were also representative types; but there were others too. Take the way the opening titles, with their boldly painted white letters on a black background, with the main protagonist's name in larger letters diagonally across the screen, present their subject:

RICHARD OSWALD'S
GREAT ESPIONAGE FILM
"DREYFUS"
THE GREATEST SCANDAL OF MILITARY JUSTICE
AROUND THE TURN OF THE CENTURY

This ties the film to Oswald's previous work (and the scandals some of it provoked). It also enters it into the rubric of a specific genre: the spy film, like Fritz Lang's *Spione*, closely related to the detective genre to which several of Oswald's earlier films belonged, and which was very popular at the time with readers as well as movie-goers. Moreover, judicial abuse of various kinds – *Justizskandale* based on inadequate laws – were much debated in the Weimar Republic, and many *Sittenfilme*, films of contemporary manners and morals, reflected them. The words 'around the turn of the century' make it a historical film, but one which some thirty or forty years on still had repercussions in contemporary society and contemporary debate; and it in fact introduces a trilogy of films in which Oswald deals with recent historical events relevant to problems felt in the Weimar Republic. The others are *1914. Die letzten Tage vor dem Weltbrand* (*1914. The*

Last Days before the World Conflagration), which focuses on the outbreak of the First World War; and *Der Hauptmann von Köpenick* (*The Captain of Köpenick*) which reenacts an event that threw an unexpected light on German worship of military uniforms, and on Prussian habits of automatic obedience to whatever presents itself as *Obrigkeit*, constituted authority.

The short introductory note which appears on the screen after this title elaborates the title's promise:

> In the year 1894 a captain on the General Staff of the French army was accused of high treason *(Landesverrat)*. This resulted in the greatest scandal in the annals of military justice around the turn to the century, throwing agitation into the whole world. The controversy around Captain Dreyfus divided the French nation and the wider world into two hostile camps. Not until many years later did the French public, and the world beyond, learn the true facts...

If we now listen to the dialogue of the short opening scene, in which two emissaries of the French war ministry confront two officers of its security branch (known as the 'Statistical Section'), we hear immediately one of the key words of this and many other Oswald films. Commandant Du Paty de Clam, played by one of the German cinema's favourite villains, Fritz Rasp, and Colonel Henry, played by the thick-set, bull-necked Ferdinand Hardt, are being sternly reminded of recent leakages of confidential military information, and told that 'the public has the right to demand enlightenment (*Aufklärung*) from us'. The sort of 'enlightenment' these intelligence officers, backed by the Chief of their Section and the Minister of War, actually provide in the end turns out to be its very opposite. With a mistaken zeal fuelled by demands for 'äusserste Pflichterfüllung' (strictest adherence to duty), promise of advancement and ingrained prejudice, they initiate proceedings that lead to the arrest of a Jewish officer whom we know, from a scene introducing the activities of the *real* spy, to be innocent.

A notion of 'enlightenment' however, that goes counter to the obfuscations generated by this initial mistake, and to the series of misattributions and downright forgeries that perpetuate it, resounds through the rest of the film, as men and women of good will seek to clear Alfred Dreyfus of the wholly unjustified charge of treason, and to rescind the conviction and degradation that result from it. Dreyfus's wife Lucy, played with dignity and charm by Grete Mosheim, declares that even if she is totally alone in her conviction that her husband is innocent, she will take 'every possible step to bring light into this affair'. Emile Zola, shown proofs of Dreyfus's innocence by Lucy and by Matthieu Dreyfus (the indefatigable *frère admirable*) takes up the challenge: 'I have only one goal: to bring light into this affair (*diese Sache aufzuklären*) in the name of a humanity which has suffered so much and has a right to better days/' Counsel for Zola in his trial for slander and libel accuses the military witnesses, and the panel of judges, of doing everything they can 'not to bring light into this affair' (*kein Licht in die Sache zu bringen*). Zola himself elaborates this in his final plea: 'There is only one way: that of truth and justice. All that obscures light, all that heaps darkness upon darkness, will only deepen the terrible crisis we are passing through. I swear Dreyfus is innocent. I pledge my life and my honour ... It is not Zola alone who is in question here, but the reputation of France throughout the world. We are standing at a turning-point in our country's history.' The imagery of darkness obscuring a light necessary to the life and health of a nation, recurs in Zola's peroration: 'Don't you understand, that the darkness to which you want to confine the nation is fatal to it? That one lie begets the other ?' Enlightenment, as one sympathetic character after another proclaims, means truth and justice, and the triumph of reason over obscurantism. It is not, I think, unreasonable to detect some echoes here of Oswald's own fight for 'enlightenment' through his tellingly named *Aufklärungsfilme*.

Oswald's introduction of the anti-Jewish theme is subtle and gradual. We know from the outset that Dreyfus is innocent, for the film has already introduced Commandant Esterházy, with his cynical humour, womanising habits, gambling bug and constant need of money, and we have been shown Esterházy communication with the German military attaché, sending the list of military secrets (the famous *bandereau*) through an agent who collects 2,000 francs on Esterházy's behalf. 'Nothing new', the attaché says to his aide after perusing his purchase, tears the *bandereau* up and throws the fragments into his waste-paper basket, whence they are retrieved by a cleaning-woman who sells them to Colonel Henry for a mere 100 francs. Henry takes them to his chief, General Boisdeffre, who demands to see a list of officers with access to the sort of information listed in the incriminating *bandereau*. Scrutinising this list in the presence of Henry and Paty de Clam, Boisdeffre is brought up short by the name Dreyfus, which stands out on a page containing names sounding more authentically French. Who is this Captain Dreyfus? Henry volunteers a series of characterisations that set the stage for a 'Jewish' profile. (1) This officer keeps very much to himself; (2) he is very ambitious; (3) his career has taken off remarkably quickly ('they do get on so, don't they!'); (4) he was born in Alsace (with its German connections). It falls to Paty de Clam to add the clincher: (5) 'He is the only Jew on the General Staff.' Later on we also learn (6) that he has extensive private means.

From this preliminary scene, which airs the presumption that Jews are natural traitors because they have loyalties other than those of their fellow-citizens, we pass to one of domestic comfort and contentment. Dreyfus is shown in uniform, playing with his young son, who declares that, like his father, he wants to be a soldier, while Lucy Dreyfus is playing ball with their little daughter. The stand-offish officer has a happy family life – another item in the anti–Jewish catalogue, for is it not known that (7) Jewish families stick together? This is activated after Dreyfus's arrest and wrongful conviction, when his wife and brother move heaven and earth to prove his innocence. A hostile officer describes this as (8) *die Wühlereien de Familie Dreyfus* – the Jewish family's underground burrowing.

Once the verdict is questioned, it seems to be the honour of the French army which is at stake; and this 'justifies' following up earlier illegal manoeuvres with the production of secret documents, and eventually resorting to outright forgery. Colonel Henry concocts a letter attributed to an Italian military attaché in which the name 'Dreyfus' (accompanied by the word 'Jew') appears for the first time in an incriminating context. 'Don't tell anyone', the *faux Henry* has the Italian write to his German counterpart, 'that we have had dealings with this Jew Dreyfus.' Here Dreyfus's opponents have fatally overreached themselves, for after the discovery that the handwriting of the *bordereau* is that of Esterházy, it is the *faux Henry* that leads to Henry's suicide and the reopening of the Dreyfus case. The Esterházy discovery had led to accusations that Dreyfus had cleverly imitated another's handwriting – (9) the Jew as forger! – and accusations of forgery were also made against Colonel Georges Picquart who championed Dreyfus; but now it was shown that it was one of Dreyfus's most persistent accusers who was the real forger. Discovered by Captain Coignet, the forgery is made public by Picquart, who is asked by a fellow-officer why he is willing to risk his career and the reputation of the French army for the sake of a man who, is after all, only a Jew. With all the vehemence of Albert Bassermann's famous voice and manner the film's Picquart replies: 'Ob Jude oder Christ – es gibt nur *eine* Gerechtigkeit' (Jew or Christian – justice is one and indivisible). The film's Zola expands this in his plea on his own behalf when he explains to his judges that by bringing to light what has been wrongfully and illegally done by those who thought they were saving the honour of the army he is in fact the true champion of that honour, and the honour of the nation the army is pledged to defend. There can be no honour without justice.

Oswald's film introduces none of the Jewish champions outside the Dreyfus family that rallied to the side of the falsely accused officer. In fact, the film has no other Jewish characters at all except for the wholly assimilated wife, brother and children of Dreyfus himself. The plausible rogue Esterházy, however, manages to introduce a calculated reference to another famous Jew who figured largely in the anti-Semitic attacks of Drumont and other anti-Dreyfusards. Countering the question of why he made money by various dubious enterprises Esterházy answers, with his usual smiling effrontery: 'Because Rothschild did not offer me a partnership.' This adds a tenth factor to the nine already shown as making up a 'Jewish' profile: ethnic association with a family widely believed to control the financial fate of the world

While Oswald avoided controversy by omitting the anti-Catholic dimension of the Dreyfusard polemics, he skirted danger by following history in numbering Georges Clemenceau among Dreyfus's defenders, assigning the role to Paul Bildt, who had played Napoleon for him in an earlier film, and who gave his new role a Bismarckian look. 'Tiger'

Clemenceau was a hate-figure for many in the Weimar Republic, because he was blamed for using his influence at Versailles to make the terms of the peace treaty far harsher than President Wilson and Lloyd George had envisaged. It is however, one of the difficulties of Oswald's film that while the many performances of generals, lawyers, journalists and minor characters are strongly individualised, spectators who have no detailed knowledge of the Dreyfus case find it hard to assign *names* to all except Dreyfus himself, Zola, and perhaps Picquart. I doubt, therefore, whether all that many realised that the defence counsel who was also editor of the journal in which Zola's *J'accuse* first appeared, is identical with the 'Tiger' of Versailles.

As Zola Heinrich George truly comes into his own. Fighting against tiredness at the end of long-sustained literary effort, silent throughout his first interview with Lucy and Mathieu Dreyfus, he is moved to eloquence after being convinced of Dreyfus's innocence. This can be misdirected, as when he talks in bookish terms to a group of young men he hears cheering Esterházy and the French army, even seizing one of them by the shoulders, and address him as *Jugend* – youth in general. This causes nothing but embarrassment and renewed cheering for the opposite side. What would read well in an article, or sound well as a plaidoyer in formal situations, is ineffective in situations like these. Realising this, George's Zola sinks back into his chair at the restaurant where he has just delivered his appeal to 'Youth' in bookish High German (adapted from one of Zola's printed articles), and subsides into popular speech patterns, recognisably Berlinese: 'Da singense die Marseillaise un verstehn'se nischt' – 'now they're singing the Marseillaise and don't know what it means.' We have, of course, to imagine the French equivalent throughout.

It is this experience which induces Zola to further the cause he has at heart by returning to the medium of print in which he had made his name. He composes his famous address to the President of the French Republic which *L'Aurore* publishes under the heading: *J'Accuse*; and when he is brought to court on a charge of libel he finds a more effective eloquence when addressing his judges than he had shown on the street. George's powerful acting is well matched by that of Bassermann as Picquart, Paul Henckels as Dreyfus's bewildered lawyer Demange, and Fritz Kampers as his more combative colleague Labori who speaks in Zola's defence. Nor does Oswald fall into the tempting error of making all Dreyfus's opponents deep-dyed villains. Esterházy, the real spy, given a marvellously louche performance by Oskar Homolka, is a man of taste in literature and art, as well as very expensive tastes in women and good living. This Esterházy is a rogue who knows what he is and faces this with a cynical humour that gives him a kind of repulsive charm. He gets on well with fellow-officers like Ferdinand Hart's Colonel Henry, who has none of his artistic tastes or self-distancing subtlety, but is out for the main chance too – in Henry's case, however, one cannot wholly discount his plea that he committed his forgery to save the honour of the army and the reputation of the General Staff. Unlike Esterházy, and in a strange way unlike Dreyfus too, he is *not* a survivor, and dies by his own hand once his forgery has been discovered. Fritz Rasp's Paty de Clam, the most unsympathetic character of them all, is a dry stick full of prejudices, devoid of imagination, devoid of empathy, dogged and cruel in his pursuit of a cause in whose justice he believes. General de Pellieux is played by Bernhard Goetzke, Chief Prosecutor Wenk in Lang's *Mabuse* and, more memorably, the personification of Death tired of his function in *Der Müde Tod* (*Destiny*) by the same director. He is a tragic figure, convinced by what he thinks 'proofs' of Dreyfus's guilt, tireless in pursuit of what he believes to be the good of the French army and therefore of the French nation, and then shattered by the revelation of Henry's forgery – 'the deed of a man devoid of honour'. A man of honour himself, he resigns the army commission he values so highly because, as he says, he can no longer claim the respect of his subordinates.

And so to the Dreyfus family, assimilated Jews whose life-style, as Oswald depicts it, has nothing specifically Jewish about it. It may be that Kortner's occasionally rolled *r* ('meine Kinderrrr') is not, as one might suspect, a carry-over from his stage techniques but a suggestion of the slight Alsatian accent Alfred Dreyfus is said to have retained throughout the life. Proud of his status as a French officer, Dreyfus is devastated when the finds a fellow-officer like Clam allowing him to be roughly manhandled by subordinate officials who seek for proofs on his person that he is capable of a treason he abhors as much as much as any. He has, however, a dogged will to live, rejecting the exit through suicide he is offered, keeping himself alive amid the horrors and indignities of Devil's Island, in the hope of clearing his name and reaffirming his honour. It has often been said that showing someone loving is a way to make him lovable – and that seems to be the main purpose of the scene which shows him, before his arrest, in affectionate conference with his wife and children. Here too, however, he wears the uniform which asserts his status and function. His young son is shown in a child's play-version of the same uniform: a subtle reminder that father and son were both to serve in the French army in the First World War, and that the son, Pierre, who entered as a corporal in the ranks, survived Verdun and the Marne, to emerge as a much-decorated officer. That Dreyfus is ordered to appear in the War Ministry (where he will be charged with the treason he never committed) in civilian dress, without his uniform, is a first step in that depersonalisation which carries on when these clothes are invaded by a roughly frisking police official in the presence of his uniformed fellow-officer, and by the degradation ceremony, powerfully staged by Oswald, in which his cap is snatched from his head and trodden underfoot, his officer's epaulettes, froggings, and very buttons are torn from his uniform, and his sword is broken over a guardsman's knee. Kortner's silence and immobility during this dreadful ceremony are counterbalanced by a tautness that suggests what he must be feeling, and by his unceasing cries 'I am innocent' which repeat the same cries he had emitted during his earlier imprisonment. Marched around the grounds of the *École militaire* in which he had just been ceremonially disgraced, with his cries drowned out by drum rolls and the execrations of distant spectators in which the word 'Jude' (or 'Judas') can just be distinguished through the din, Kortner allows himself one demonstrative gesture: an outstretched hand, as he approaches a group of journalists whom he exhorts to proclaim his innocence in their newspapers. We see afterwards how one of these newspapers, Clemenceau's *L'Aurore*, does indeed take up his cause: what we do not see in Oswald's film is the powerful fanning of anti-Dreyfusism and anti-Judaism by men like Edouard Drumont in his book *La France juive* and his widely circulating newspaper *La libre Parole*.

In the Devil's Island scenes, which are effectively intercut with scenes on the French mainland that will ultimately affect Dreyfus's fate, Oswald has toned down the historic facts. We see Dreyfus shackled, guarded by warders who have orders not to talk to him and suppress his letters – though Oswald characteristically introduces one subordinate warder who has the humanity to speak to his prisoner, and whisper news through his barred window, and is reprimanded by a less humane superior. What we are *not* shown is the effect damp heat, malarial fever, noxious bugs and solitary confinement had on the historical Dreyfus, of whom we know that after four years of this he became a desiccated shadow of himself, hardly able to speak, and suffering bouts of mental confusion. Kortner's appearance and demeanour, even in stained clothes, unshaven, and grown grey, hardly alters throughout the film. I suspect that this is meant as an outward sign of the will to live and clear his name, and of the film's contention that what makes him willing, after another rigged trial has refused to exonerate him, to sue for a Presidential pardon, is not simply physical weakness. He does, however, heed his family's argument that another period in prison might make it more difficult for him to pursue his aim of restoring his honour – that he might even die in prison without righting the injustice he has suffered.

After his petition for clemency is approved, we are informed by a voiceover, accompanied by shots of revolving newspaper headlines which are the only instances of trick photography in the whole film, that it took another six years of further effort before rehabilitation came – and that leads over to the film's climactic final scene. Reinstated in the army, and once again in full uniform, Dreyfus marches solemnly onto a parade ground, watched by his family and a cheering group of supporters, to be dubbed a knight of the Legion of Honour. The scene obviously parallels the earlier degradation scene: Dreyfus once again stands stiffly to attention as the central figure amidst serried ranks of his fellow-soldiers, to be, as it were, repersonalised, with his unbroken sword held shoulder high. When, however, he counters a general's ceremonial kiss with a terse 'I cannot thank', we get a glimpse of that haughtily sparing speech which had helped to make the historical Dreyfus (who had a lot in common with his dogged adversary Paty de Clam) personally unpopular even with some of those outside his own family who struggled to obtain justice for him. In the circumstances of this scene, however, his bitterness is understandable; and its effect is immediately dissipated by a handshake with his staunch defender Picquart. The latter's call 'Long live Dreyfus' is countered by Dreyfus's own: 'Es lebe das Vaterland!' 'Long live the Fatherland', called out by a Jew who has suffered grievous wrongs at the hands of those who thought they were defending the country of which they were all citizens, ends Oswald's film. It holds, to be sure, a message for those who wanted to extrude Jews from their community on grounds that had nothing to do with personal guilt – not in nineteenth-century France, but in twentieth-century Germany.

Elaborate sets, Oswald was wont to explain, tend to deflect attention from the players on the screen; and he thought it a worthwhile experiment to have actors exert their fascination in a film before black velvet curtains. He had, as we have seen, done something like that in *Different from the Others*, where Veidt and Schünzel had played crucial scene with brightly lit faces against a totally black screen. *Dreyfus* has no such extreme austerities; but no set is ever allowed to dwarf the actors on whom all attention is focused, with frequent close-ups and semi-close-ups to convey emotions and reactions. When the action requires an elaborate set, like that in which we first see Esterházy in a nightclub that has dancers and musicians on a stage in the background, diners at tables all around and a spectators gallery at the top, Oswald allows the dark figure of the sleazy agent Dubois to loom large at the front and has Esterházy then detach himself from the back to join Dubois in such a way that the two of them block out most of the set. This allows us to gauge the importance of Dubois's offer (of money for information useful to the German government) with a minimum of distraction.

Throughout the film, Oswald and his designers use settings to characterise their occupants, with few, but carefully chosen, paintings, statues and furnishings; and these sets often have a contrasting relation to one another. The domestic comfort of Dreyfus's living room is set against the suspect splendours of the nightclub and gambling scenes, and both against the coldness of offices in the 'Statistical Section' – as well, of course, against the drabness and squalor of Dreyfus's prison cell. Oswald was wont to proclaim that one should not be afraid of long scenes, 200 metres or more, if one had chosen the right quality of actors. He has certainly done that in this film, and put his theory to the test in his staging of the trial of Zola, held in public, unlike the Dreyfus court martials. Tedium is kept well at bay by the inherent tension of the proceedings and the importance of the opposing moral and judicial arguments; and by a camera that moves meaningfully from one group, and one representative character, to another, and often shows the reactions of one person vitally concerned while another is speaking. Such long central scenes are, moreover, framed by, or intercut with, shorter ones that set them off and provide a (sometimes ironic) context.

Seven years after Oswald's *Dreyfus* an actor who had appeared in one of his historical films, *Carlos und Elisabeth*, in 1924, and who had emigrated to Hollywood where he became a respected director – Wilhelm (William) Dieterle – introduced the Dreyfus case into a film called *The Life of Emile Zola*. Paul Muni's performance in the title role is more one-dimensionally sympathetic than George's complex assumption of the same part, and is marred, to my mind, by a plethora of fussy mannerisms that is sometimes mistaken for great acting. Dieterle's staging of the scenes actually involving Dreyfus follows that of Oswald fairly closely; but Josef Schildkraut's Dreyfus is physically nearer to the slight figure of the historic original, who was still relatively young at the time of his arrest, than the stocky, middle-aged Kortner. His physical deterioration on Devil's Island is more clearly marked, and more moving, than Kortner's. Schildkraut's performance is also far less astringent – there is nothing like the curt 'I cannot thank' at the reinstatement ceremony staged by Oswald, and Dieterle even has his Dreyfus tearfully attending Zola's funeral.

Those familiar with Hollywood studio politics and commercial considerations that resulted in directives not to let Jewishness surface in their films will not be surprised to find that in Dieterle's film the theme of anti-Semitism hardly surfaces. Those gifted with rapid vision might catch the entry 'Religion: Jew' against Dreyfus's name in a register of staff-officers with access to the kind of information contained in the incriminating *bordereau*; but the word 'Jew' is never spoken in the whole course of the film, nor is there any reference to the anti-Jewish feelings constantly invoked by Dreyfus's opponents in the whole course of the campaign against him. Dreyfus is not, of course, at the centre of Dieterle's film as he is in Oswald's, or in that of F.W. Kemer and Milton Rosmer, who directed a British film, called *Dreyfus* in England and *The Dreyfus Case* in the USA, in 1931. In that film, based on a play by Wilhelm Herzog and Hans Rehfisch, a non-Jewish actor, Cedric Hardwicke, achieved a good physical likeness to the historic Dreyfus, and played the role with the kind of dignity he was to give to his French bishop in Richard Boleslawski's *Les Misérables* four years later. In Dieterle's film, as Patricia Erens pointed out in her comprehensive study of *The Jew in American Cinema* (1984), the focus at the end is not on Dreyfus at all, but on two Gentile writers who engaged themselves on his side: Emile Zola and Anatole France. 'By concentrating on the writers rather than on Dreyfus', Erens comments, 'the Jew serves as a tool twice over, first as a scapegoat for the French army and secondly as a means of revitalising for the two authors' ibid: 162). That both these authors, like Dreyfus himself, are played by Jewish actors (Paul Muni and Morris Carnovsky) in Dieterle's film, may be savoured as a cinematic *bonne bouche*; but it is clear that Dieterle's account of the Dreyfus affair does not convey anything like the potent warning against the dangers of anti-Semitic prejudice as that contained in Oswald's film, first seen in the final years of the doomed Weimar Republic.

Chapter 9

A NEW FILM MUSICAL

The Challenge of the Sound Track

The 'silent' cinema was rarely enjoyed in actual silence. Early entrepreneurs, and part-time directors like Gustav Schönwald, often stood before their paying public to comment on what went on in the film being shown; but such *conférences* were increasingly shouldered out by musical accompaniments, ranging from the solitary piano and small ensembles of humbler venues to the full orchestras of first-run 'palaces' on the Kurfürstendamm. One of the most famous, and controversial, of Jewish suppliers of music for the 'silent' cinema was Edmund Meisel, a violinist and conductor who wrote music for the theatre productions of Erwin Piscator and was commissioned by Prometheus-Film to write a suitably stirring accompaniment for the German showing of Eisenstein's *Battleship Potemkin* (1926). The avant-garde sounds he produced divided opinion, but earned him the reputation of an exciting and original composer at home and abroad. Other commissions followed, the most important of which was his contrapuntal accompaniment of Walter Ruttmann's *Berlin. Die Sinfonie der Grossstadt* (*Berlin, Symphony of a Big City*, 1927). Here he sought, as he said at the time, to give musical expression to the contemporary city-dweller's daily sensations, and allow the spectators' nerves to swing along with the rhythms of his music. He lived just long enough to provide music for an early English sound-film version of Edgar Wallace's *The Crimson Circle* (British International Picturesm 1928–29) but died tragically early, in November 1930, at the age of 36 – too late to join in the many attempts to formulate principles according to which sound-tracks and visual images should be integrated in the new art of the 'talkies' and film musicals.

Once again many pioneers in this field, as in so many other fields of cinematic theory and practice, were of Jewish origin. One of the earliest of these was Paul Dessau, who had served his apprenticeship as a music director and composer at the Alhambra, one of Berlin's smaller first-run cinemas on the Kurfürstendamm. Dessau published his 'Versuch, etwas über Filmmusik zu sagen' ('Attempt to say something about Film Music') in the journal *Film-Kurier* on 19 January 1929. There he rejected the idea of building up a film-score on the leitmotiv principle, which had served not only Wagner but also providers of scores for the 'silent' cinema to identify personages, situations, themes and emotional tonalities. 'The *Leitmotiv*', he declared, 'is dead. The [Wagnerian] music-drama has been superseded even by composers who, like Richard Strauss, build on Wagner's achievements.' Nor, he continued, should music merely illustrate what we see on the screen. What matters is to find musical forms for the essential atmosphere of cinematic scenes. If, for instance, the screen shows a coffee-house in which a band is playing a waltz, the sound-track may ignore the waltz tune, spinning a musical thread that pervades the whole action over and beyond the visual image. 'This puts music in the happy position of being able to express what is *not* visible. It is reprehensible, on the other hand, to allow mere acoustic illustration to lend excessive weight to the visual aspect of a musical film.' Along with the leitmotiv Dessau rejects 'coffee-house sentimentality and variety dash' ('Caféhaus Schmalz und Varieté-Elan') and asks that serious musicians like Paul Hindemith and Kurt Weill, whom he knew to be keen to compose film music, be commissioned to try their hand at it.

A contrary position was advanced by Friedrich Hollaender after he had been plucked from the cabaret and revue scene to provide not just the songs, but the whole musical structure, of *The Blue Angel*. He had worked throughout in close collaboration with the director, Josef von Sternberg, and knew the vocal range and expressive possibilities of the two actresses, Marlene Dietrich and Rosa Valetti, who were entrusted with the interpretation of his songs. They too had had experience of the cabaret and revue stages which formed so important a feature of the Berlin entertainment scene and which Dessau had sought to keep from dominating the musical film. In the *Reichsfilmblatt* of 10 May 1930 (Vol VIII, No. 19 – Beilage) Hollaender sought to generalise what he learnt from his experience of collaborating on *The Blue Angel*. 'In filmic representation,' he wrote, 'outer as well as inner happenings all tend towards an essential musicality. They can even be significantly advanced and ennobled by the way the music is structured.' Of great significance in this process, Hollaender believed, was a song he composed for Dietrich in the character of Lola-Lola – a song he variously terms a 'Schlager' or a 'Chanson'. In Germany and Austria the French term 'Chanson' had come to be applied to a multi-stanza ditty, often with a witty or satirical point, and with a catchy refrain that could apply to the different stanzas in different ways. 'Schlager', on the other hand was first used to describe the electric effect of operetta tunes that achieved instant popularity. 'Kinder, das hat eingeschlagen' – 'Folks, that's been a real hit' – the singer Alexander Girardi is recorded to have said when, in the 1870s, an air he had performed in an operetta by Friedrich Millöcker was called for again and again. The example from *The Blue Angel* which Hollaender cites is Lola-Lola's song known in German as 'Ich bin von Kopf bis Fuss auf Liebe eingestellt' ('I am geared to love from head to foot') and in English as 'Falling in Love Again'. This, he explains, conveys the essence of Lola's character, creates the right atmosphere, and becomes a leitmotiv in instrumental form from the film's overture onwards. In that overture, and throughout all that follows, it is counterpointed with a contrasting leitmotiv, the chorale-like 'Üb immer Treu und Redlichkeit' ('Be ever faithful, ever honest') chimed by the town-hall clock. What this conveys is the code by which Professor Rath tries to live when first we meet him, before his *amour fou* delivers him to a wandering existence with a group of performers to whose codes and ways of life he finds it impossible to adjust without doing violence to his whole nature.

What was felt to be particularly important in Hollaender's contribution to the debate about music in film is his emphasis on the importance of songs that could become instant Schlager. This obviously fitted a film like *The Blue Angel*, which had a *chanteuse* as its central character; but it became a guiding principle of the new genre of film musical which fed into, and was fed by, a burgeoning media industry. Sheet music, much of it published by Ufa itself, performances by popular bands in cafés and nightclubs, radio and gramophone popularised even further the songs introduced into films whose characters were not professional singers, either on the variety or the operetta stage; and this became an increasingly important economic factor in the life of the German and Austrian peoples.

The new genre, which flourished from the end of 1929 until well into the Third Reich, was often called *Filmoperette*; it had little in common, however, with the *Operetten-Film* which followed the plots and music of popular operettas like *Die Fledermaus* (*The Bat*) or *Im weissen Rössl* (*White Horse Inn*), with their Ruritanian or equally stylised high-life settings, or with the *Sängerfilm*, designed to highlight the art of stars of the opera and operetta stage like Richard Tauber, Jan Kiepura or Martha Eggerth. The chief begetter of the new musical was Erich Pommer, whose production unit within Ufa was responsible for the majority of the best examples. Like Paul Dessau, Friedrich Hollaender and Kurt Weill, Pommer was Jewish; so too was Werner R. Heymann, at least ethnically, though he was baptised into the Protestant faith. Jewish too were the directors Wilhelm Thiele, Ludwig Berger, Hanns Schwarz and Eric Charell, who contributed to the development of the German film musical, along with such writers as Robert Liebmann, Walter Reisch, Franz Schulz and Hans Székely. All of them were soon to be forced out of the German film industry by the advent of the Third Reich.

Josef von Sternberg, the Viennese-born naturalised American director of *The Blue Angel*, shared the same ethnic provenance; and the success of that movie, reinforced by that of the Al Jolson vehicle *The Singing Fool* (whose hit tune 'Sonny Boy' attained phenomenal popularity in Weimar Germany) ensured that it was Hollaender's concept of the role of film music, rather than Dessau's, which became dominant. This meant an emphasis on easily assimilated Schlager, often including folksong reminiscences, but deriving in the main from cabaret and revue rather than recalling the concert-hall or the opera-house. In opposition to composers like Hanns Eisler, who opined in the *Film-Kurier* of 28 July 1931 that film music should consist of 'serious music deriving from the concert-hall', Friedrich Hollaender had formulated a programme of rapid composition that would be unthinkable in concert music designed to outlast the ages:

> Our measure of time has changed. *Tempo commodo* has become *tempo tempesturoso*. We can no longer afford to wait for inspiration. We are trained to discipline our inventive faculties in a kind of *dressage*. ... For the composer it is essential to collaborate, and reach an understanding, with the director, the performer, and the acoustics expert ... The musical collaborator in a film should be constantly present during its shooting. It happens often enough that the director suddenly thinks of an image that needs, just as suddenly, to be complemented by a musical idea. Collaboration at speed means that a suggestion is sketched out on the piano, gets the director's approval, making sure that image and sound harmonise; the instrumentation is sketched out too, then tried out with the orchestra and recorded on the sound-track – all this in half a day. (*Lichtbild-Bühne*, 'Bild und Ton' supplement, 13 December 1930)

'But of course', Hollaender adds, 'not all composition proceeds at such lightning speed. Many melodies are created after studying the film-script, in the course of thorough preparation beside the warm stove at home'.

All this is not to say, however, that the music of Paul Dessau had no place in the Weimar Republic's cinema – only that its home was outside the *Filmoperette* or film musical. He was often called upon to provide sound-complements of silently shot cartoon films, including some early Disneys, Ladislaw Starewitsch's puppet plays, and (especially) the shadow-plays of Lotte Reiniger. He also composed choral and continuity music for three films built around the tenor voice of Richard Tauber, but left Tauber's songs and arias to be provided by others. Dessau earned special praise for his atmospheric compositions tying together the images on the increasingly popular genre of the *Bergfilm* that pitted men and women against the loneliness and danger of mountains. Three of these, *Stürme über dem Montblanc* (*Storms over Montblanc*, 1930), *Der weisse Rausch* (*White Ecstasy*, 1930–31), and *S.O.S. Eisberg* (1932–33) were directed by Arnold Fanck; the two last-named starred Leni Riefenstahl, at the beginning of a career that would soon lead her to her famous – and notorious – career as a director of her own films. For another film, *Abenteuer im Engadin* (*Adventure in Engadin*, 1932) Dessau even wrote a march and a tango. In all this he was able to build on his experiences of providing suitably atmospheric music for accompaniments in the 'silent' days.

Into *Scapa Flow*, a 'silent' film about the German fleet disbanded at the victors' behest in 1918, directed by Leo Lasko in 1929–30, Dessau had introduced patriotic German tunes alongside the socialist-communist 'Internationale' – a provocation which passed off without excessive protest or demonstrations of assent. He earned particular praise for his contribution to E.A. Dupont's *Salto Mortale* of 1931. The critic H. Angel, writing in the journal *Film und Ton* on 22 August 1931, summed up Dessau's achievement in that film by crediting him with 'a rare ability to use the idioms of modern music to convey sense-impressions'. 'Hardly anyone', Angel continues, 'can match his ability to capture in sound the air, colour, and substance of a film'. Beginning with an overture-like exposition, his music comes into the film 'like a curtain whose folds promise the revelation of infinite depths, unknown worlds – and even before the curtain opens fully the audience is stimulated to share the loves and anxieties of the artistes' preparing to exercise the moral and physical "saltos" of which the title speaks.' Musical transitions are managed as lightly as Dupont's visual ones. Dessau also knows when to hold back for greater effect: when the acrobatic *salto mortale* is executed, tension and breathless fear are suggested by just one long sustained note. 'The music is sparing', Angel concludes, 'but it carries on the line that began in *Storms over Montblanc*: divorced from simple imitation of nature, sophisticated in its instrumentation, Dessau's compositions succeed more and more in bringing film-music into consonance with the most modern music performed in concert-halls.'

Dessau's art was shaped by his training in classical German music and admiration for such modern masters as Paul Hindemith. Once, however, he hinted at his Jewish heritage, when, in 1929 he composed a piece to which he gave the Yiddish title *Der Nebbich* (*The Sad Sack*). Produced as an experiment for a *Tobis* sound-film production, it was presented at the prestigious Baden–Baden chamber-music festival.* A filmmaker named Hans Conradi inverted the usual sequence when he fitted a Harold Lloyd-like action to Dessau's preexistent composition – an experiment later matched by Disney when he combined the plot of Goethe's ballad 'The Sorcerer's Apprentice', transposed into music by Paul Dukas, with a Mickey Mouse adventure in his otherwise rather less admirable *Fantasia* of 1940.

The year 1933 did not mean the end of Dessau's distinctive work in films. After working for some years in France he managed to find a niche in Hollywood where he collaborated (sometimes anonymously) on films for Universal, Warner Brothers, Republic and other studios until he remigrated to East Berlin to work for the DEFA studios of the German Democratic Republic and collaborate closely with Bert Brecht.

In the flourishing film musicals or *Filmoperetten* of the early sound era, however, Dessau had no share. These went the way Friedrich Hollaender chose to follow in *The Blue Angel* of 1930 and, with modifications allowing for plots not set in a show-business milieu, in his compositions for Hanns

---

* After discriminatory Nazi laws forcibly reminded many Jews of a heritage they had not always acknowledged, Dessau worked with Helmar Lerski on two films with explicitly Jewish themes marked by Hebrew titles: *Avodah* (*Work*, 1933–34) and *Adamah* (*Soil*, 1947). The Zionist theme of the last-named is underlined by its English subtitle: *Tommorow's a Wonderful Day*.

Schwarz's *Einbrecher* (Burglar[s]) of 1930 and his directorial debut *Ich und die Kaiserin* (*I and the Empress*) of 1932–33. These works, and the rest of the Pommer musicals, appeared in the last phase of the Weimar Republic, which had inauspiciously begun with the hunger, deprivation and street-fighting that followed the First World War and the Versailles Treaty; had then passed through the hell of monetary inflation in the early 1920s; had rallied after the stabilisation of the coinage and the influx of foreign loans between 1925 and 1929, only to have more than its share of world-wide misery, financial ruin and unemployment which followed the New York Stock Exchange crises of October and November 1929. The soil was fertile for what R. Bruce Lockhart described as Hitlerite 'exploitation of hatreds and resentments, nationalist propaganda, racism, flag-waving, and the desire to enforce conformity in the quest for power' (*TLS*, 15 August 2003). It was also well prepared, however, for the kind of holiday from everyday worries offered by film theatres increasingly called 'palaces' (Ufa-Palast, Gloria-Palast, etc.) when they showed films in which attractive men and women sang and danced their way into luxury or simple comforts, and marriages that promised lasting happiness. The most popular example of *that* kind of musical (there were, as I shall show, other kinds) was *Three Men from the Filling Station*, significantly known in its French version as *Le chemin du paradis* – the Paradise Way.

Before turning to this film and its related companions, however, we must cast a final glance at the work of a Jewish composer who envisioned the approach to an earthly paradise very differently, while also following the path of film music indicated by Dessau rather than that advocated and practised by Hollaender. This was Hanns Eisler, who composed the score for the socially conscious and aggressive film *Kuhle Wampe, oder Wem gehört die Welt* (*Kuhle Wampe, or to whom does the World belong?*), directed by Slatan Dudow from a screenplay by Bert Brecht, Dudow and Ernst Ottwald. Eisler not only took on board Dessau's demand that the film composer should keep abreast of modern developments in concert music, but also that of many theorists of the early sound film who maintained that cinematic sound should complement, or counterpoint, rather than merely illustrate, duplicate or reinforce, the image on the screen. He defined this complementarity in a study entitled 'Komposition für Film', written in cooperation with Theodor W. Adorno in 1942:

> Suburban houses in sad decay, a slum-district with all its misery and dirt. The tonality (*Stimmung*) of the image is passive, depressing; it invites melancholy. Against this is set a rapid, incisive music, a polyphonic prelude *marcato* in character. The contrast between the music – strictly formal in its tonal construction – and the images seen on the screen, causes a kind of shock which should provoke resistance rather than sentimental empathy. (Adorno 1976: 35)

Songs in this sharp incisive mode, combative and forward-looking, pervade *Kuhle Wampe*. Their texts are by Brecht, their music is by Eisler. One of these, entitled *Sportlied*, begins by referring to the overcrowded rooms and embattled streets out of which young people stream to engage in sporting competitions – activities that teach them to combine for battle and to strive for victory over the class enemy. Another, the famous *Solidaritätslied*, has remained a favourite anthem of left-wing groups to the present day:

> Vorwärts, und nicht vergessen
> Worin unsre Stärke besteht!
> Bei Hunger und beim Essen
> Vorwärts, nie vergessen
> Die Solidarität!

> Go forwards, and do not forget
> What makes us strong!
> Whether you're hungry, or whether you're eating
> Never forget
> [Our] Solidarity!

This refrain is slightly varied throughout the song, until the last stanza (not quite so often sung nowadays) catches up the conclusion of the Communist Manifesto while also echoing the subtitle of the film:

> Proletarier aller Länder
> Einigt euch und ihr seid frei.
> Eure grossen Regimenter
> Brechen jede Tyrannei!
> > Vorwärts and nie vergessen
> > Und die Frage konkret gestellt
> > Beim Hungern und beim Essen:
> > Wessen ist der Morgen?
> > Wessen ist die Welt?

> Proletarians of all countries
> Unite, and you are free.
> Your great regiments
> Break down every tyranny!
> > Go forward and never forget –
> > And ask concretely
> > (Whether you're hungry, or whether you're eating):
> > Whose is tomorrow?
> > To whom does the World belong?

There is nothing esoteric about Eisler's music here. The song is as easily remembered as any Schlager by Hollaender or Heymann, and has featured on many a march, and at many a socialist sing-song, over the years. I have myself joined in on convivial occasions.

Die Drei von der Tankstelle
(Three Men from the Filling Station)

The creative forces behind this delightful musical, which threw to the winds the Carnegie principles of advancement by hard work and steady application in favour of a modern urban variant of Eichendorff's 'Life of a Ne'er-do-Well', were almost exclusively Jewish. The producer was Erich Pommer; the director was Wilhelm Thiele; the writers were Franz Schulz and Paul Franck; the composer was Werner Richard Heymann; the song texts were by Robert Gilbert. The stars were the distinctly non-Jewish boyman Willy Fritsch, with his eternally attractive smile, and the graceful Lilian Harvey, whose somewhat pinched face was offset by constant dance-like movement that could sashay seamlessly into actual dance; both had pleasant voices, which sounded as natural in conversation as in the Schlager they sang more like members of their audience gifted with a good ear and a good sense of rhythm than like professional singers of the Tauber, Kiepura or Eggerth variety. This 'dream-pair' of the German musical is ably supported by an equally non-Jewish cast of Fritz Kampers, who here subdues the fiery temperament he showed as Zola's defender in *Dreyfus* to play a wealthy Consul and businessman henpecked by his daughter; the stately Olga Tschechowa with her air if wisdom born out of experience, her slight Russian accent and her pearly laughter; and, in an early role, Heinz Rühmann, rapid of speech and movement, eternally talkative, accident-prone (when his two friends fall out and fight each other with boxing-gloves it is *he* who ends up with a black eye) yet resilient and not averse to provoking others through sly verbal thrusts. There is also significant support from The Comedian Harmonists, a singing group made up of three Jews and three Gentiles, which plays variations on the principal love-song by performing it in close harmony after the manner of the American group The Revellers; and by Felix Bressart, who enacts a wonderfully grotesque bailiff superintending the surrealist flight through the air of repossessed furniture. His dance-like advances and rhythmic body movements (as when this black-clad, bowler-hatted figure thrusts his pelvis and chest out in consonance with the two syllables of the word 'Kuckuck') are unforgettable by any who have had the good fortune to see this film.

Bressart is indelibly marked out as Jewish by his appearance; but there is no direct reference to his, or the Comedian Harmonists', ethnic provenance. In two other cases, however, Jewishness is clearly signalled. A lawyer played by Kurt Gerron, charged with conveying bad news to the three friends to whom the film's title alludes, refers to them as 'meshuggene [Yiddish for 'crazy'] Musketiers' as his secretary, Fräulein Mondschein, hands him the telephone; and he announces that what they face is a 'Riesendalles' – another Yiddish term, signifying 'stupendous lack of money'. Hans, the character played by Heinz Rühmann, maliciously suggests that the bad news Gerron's Dr Kalmus is about to announce, is that Kalmus's wife has had a *blonde* baby and that the dark-haired Jew has therefore been cuckolded by a Gentile.

In a similar way the film subtly hints at the Jewishness of Kurt, one of the three friends. He is played by Oskar Karlweis, whose Viennese, slightly self-mocking cabaret-trained charm contrasts with that of the Silesian-born Fritsch and that of Rühmann, who hails from the Ruhr district. Karlweis's unforced grace of movement makes him the most congenial dance-partner Harvey found in any of her pre-1933 musicals. They have a two-step together in and around her character's car which is one of the film's most memorable moments, and allows Karlweis the privilege usually reserved for Fritsch: that of planting a kiss on Lilian's lips. He too is lightly signalled as Jewish by his language. Pretending to conjure, he rhymes the magician's patter 'Abracadabra Kokelores' with the Yiddish 'shvere Tsores' (weighty troubles); and when the first money he receives for his services at the petrol-pump is a mere ten pfennigs, he looks ruefully at the coin and sighs 'Nebbish' – a Yiddish exclamation of pity and regret. The noun 'der Nebbish', which we encountered in its German spelling as the title of one of Dessau's compositions and which I there translated by its American army equivalent of 'Sad Sack', indicates a person who incurs a (usually rather condescending) pity.

Three Men from the Filling Station calls itself an 'operetta', and is organised around a characteristic iambic (xx́xx́) horn signal and three Schlager, two of which achieved instant and lasting popularity. The first of these occurs immediately after an overture which begins with the sound of the motor-horn followed by a brisk variation on it and a slow waltz-like melody whose import we gather when it becomes a hymn to friendship. It is first sung by three once well–to–do young men who return in their car from a long trip, fully expecting to resume their easy life in the home they have shared together with some servants left in charge:

Ein Freund, ein guter Freund,
Das ist das Schönste, was es gibt auf der Welt ...

A friend, a good friend,
Is the best thing the world has to offer ...

In the course of the film, until the prospect of good fortune and sudden wealth removes all obstacles and misunderstandings, the song also signals friendship between a man and a woman when it is reprised by Kampers and Tschechowa, who are 'just friends' before Lilian's objections to her father's re-marriage melt away in face of her own marriage plans.

Heymann and Gilbert provide a second song with Schlager potential, which uses punctuation to paint a love affair that fails to have the expected solution. It begins with a question mark (*ein grosses Fragezeichen*) as the lovers size each other up. This is followed by a dash (*Gedankenstrich*), giving pause for thought before the inevitable kiss; then comes a comma, a kind of coming up for air between kisses; and then inevitably, a full-stop

(*Punkt*) marking a (temporary?) end to the affair as the lover says 'Lass mich in Ruh' ('leave me alone'). In the first instance the letter embodying these sentiments is concocted by Lilian and Edith, but never sent; the second time it is dictated by Willy to Lilian, who pretends to be writing it on a typewriter but composes a promise of marriage instead, which will force Willy into the union that despite all temporary fallings-out they both desire.

That desire finds expression in the third and most popular Schlager of them all, whose refrain is still known to many Germans, and which occupies in the career of Willy Fritsch and Lilian Harvey the same status as 'Falling in Love Again' occupies in that of Marlene Dietrich. It begins with a stanza that proclaims: until now what we feel for each other has been sympathy. When we address each other, we still use the formal 'Sie'. But, the singer continues, in my dreams I already use the familiar 'Du', and I whisper softly:

> Liebling, mein Herz lässt Dich grüssen
> Nur mit Dir allein
> Kann es glücklich sein.
> All meine Träume, die süssen,
> Leg ich in den Gruss mit hinein.
> Lass nicht die Tage verfliessen,
> Bald ist der Frühling dahin!
> Liebling, mein Herz lässt Dich grüssen
> und Dir sagen, wie gut ich Dir bin.

> Darling, my heart sends you greetings,
> Only with you
> Can it find happiness.
> All the sweetness of my dream
> I lay into this greeting.
> Do not let the days go by,
> Springtime will soon be over!
> Darling, my heart sends you greetings,
> And tells you how fond I am of you.
> (Text by Robert Gilbert; music by W.R. Heymann;
> published by Ufaton, Berlin-Munich, 1930)

The song begins with an ascending melody on the kind of text one is likely to find picked out in icing sugar on gingerbread hearts sold at German (and especially Austrian) fairs; yet the 'sweetness' of its dreams – the 'Du'dreams of the opening stanza – is immediately relativised by consciousness of the inevitable passing of this springtime of love. This is one complexity which prevents its heartfelt simplicity from descending into kitsch; another is its avoidance of any excess of sentiment through the reticence of the expression of love towards which the whole song moves: 'wie gut ich dir bin' (how fond I am of you). It fulfils the requirements of the Schlager by being what the German call an 'Ohrwurm', a melody and a set of simple words expressing widely felt emotions, which insinuate themselves into the ear and become memorable after one has heard them several times in the course of the film; yet the musical and literary form is actually quite complex. Lines 1, 4 and 8 are linked by the same melody and by their rhymes; but line 6, bound to them by an echoing, imperfect rhyme, varies the melody, and the rhyming lines 2 and 3 have different melodic and metrical lengths as well as a more rapid rhythm than line 5, to which they are linked by their rhyme. In a similar way the rhyming lines 7 and 9 are rhythmically and melodically distinct – the ninth and final line has the same number of rhythmic peaks, but it is made longer not only by an increased number of words, but also by the reflective pause after the third word, leading up to the muted yet fervent declaration at the end.

For all its complexity this central love song is deliberately folk-like in its vocabulary and ideas: the greeting heart, the sweetness of dreams, the passing of spring, are all familiar elements. Another, very different, musical insert, a mock-address to a bailiff ('Lieber Herr Gerichtsvollzieher') gets its main effect from its punning use of the opening line of a familiar German nursery rhyme, describing the sound of the cuckoo coming from the woods: 'Kuckuck, Kuckuck, ruft's aus dem Wald'. In German usage, Kuckuck is not only the onomatopoeic name of a bird, but also a familiar term for the seal or sticker which a bailiff affixes to items of furniture that are to be repossessed. Around this word and its mocking sound the film spins a musical ballet for Fritsch, Karlweis and Rühmann advancing in waving line towards the grotesquely retreating Bressart, which is one of its most delightful sequences; not least because of surrealist elements which have the singing bailiff literally fly into the house, and the repossessed furniture literally fly out of it.

Another musical motif, as distinctive as the cuckoo tune, is first sounded while the screen is still blank, before the opening credits. Its four notes – ta-tú-ta-tá – later turn out to be the distinctive musical motor-horn signal that heralds the approach of the heroine's car. All three men from the filling station fall in love with her; but since she is played by Lilian Harvey, only her perpetual screen partner Willy Fritsch has any chance of actually winning her hand at the end.

None of the cast are professional singers of the kind German and Austrian audiences would expect to hear on the operetta stage. Yet the opening credits call the film an operetta, and like so many stage works of that kind it opens with an overture which, after the repeated motor-horn signal and a musical variation of it, segues into an instrumental version of its central love song. What happens after that is far removed from what would be expected in an operetta by Franz Lehar, Oscar Strauss or Rudolf Friml; but at the end of a film, when the cast begins to talk in rhyme, and movement becomes stylised, a stage curtain suddenly closes itself behind Fritsch and Harvey (a photographed curtain, of course, not an actual one that would necessitate the principals' physical appearance at every screening). They bend forward and seem to look out at us, the audience, expressing their puzzlement at finding so many strange people out there. 'Whatever do they want?' Lilian finds the answer: the film has called itself an *Operette*, and what would an operetta be without a climactic musical ending? And so the curtain opens again; the Lewis Ruth Band appears, along with a line of high-stepping Tiller Girls and dancers we had already seen in a nightclub sequence earlier on, and the principals and supporting players line up in a modified version of the Tiller Girl routine, with the bulky Gerron kicking up his legs with especial abandon.

The film which ends on this carnivalesque note had begun with a situation all too familiar in the Depression years. Three young men drive up to their home to find that everything they own is to be auctioned off to pay their debts, and all the money they had in their bank accounts has disappeared. They can't think of marketable skills they might have, and contemplate 'stempeln gehn' – queuing for the dole, the degrading horrors of which a contemporary song eloquently expressed:

Keenen Sechser in der Tasche,	Not a penny in your pocket,
bloss 'n Stempelschein.	Only a dole-coupon.
Durch die Löcher der Kledaasche	Through the holes in your clobber
Kiekt die Sonne rein...	The sun peers in ...

That song, popularised by the left-wing singer and actor Ernst Busch, had music by Hanns Eisler; its text, interestingly enough, was written under a pseudonym by Robert Gilbert, who was also responsible for the very different texts Heymann set to music in *Three Men from the Filling Station* and elsewhere. Besides the dreaded 'stempeln', the word that resounds through these opening passage of Thiele's film is *Pleite* – a word derived from the Yiddish, which designates utter bankruptcy. In the ballet already described, Bressart's black-coated and bowler-hatted bailiff even climbs up, mimicking wings with arms held out at right-angles, as the feared *Pleitegeier* – the 'bankruptcy vulture' all too well known to all to many members of the film's early audiences. This too was remembered in a popular song of the 1920s:

Pleite, Pleite sind heut alle Leute!
Ich hab kein Geld, Du has kein Geld
Pleite, Pleite ist die ganze Welt!
Pleite, Pleite sind heut alle Leute!
Ich hab kein Geld, Du hast kein Geld,
Pleite und meschugge ist die ganze Welt!

Everybody is bankrupt today!
I've no money, you've no money –
The whole world is bankrupt today!
Everybody is bankrupt today!
I've no money, you've no money,
The whole world is bankrupt and crazy.
        (Text by Hans Pflanzer, music by Victor Corzilius)

The perspective of world-wide disaster opened up in the third line of this ditty has its parallel in a line from the Gilbert–Heymann 'Friendship Song' of *Three Men from the Filling Station*, which with its internal rhyme, envisages the possibility of the whole world collapsing: '… wenn die ganze Welt zusammenfällt'.

There are other brief gestures in the direction of contemporary fears and realities, when two of the friends have to sleep, turn and turn about, in the same bed, and when they share a breakfast of one cup of milk and one slice of bread-and-jam while remembering the very different meals they enjoyed in their days of affluence. But just as the opening song finds friendship weathering catastrophes, and the cuckoo-ballet and the never-ending cheerfulness of the three bankrupts defuses the Pleitegeier's threat, so reality flies out of the window with the three friends as they leap through that egress into their one remaining possession: their motor car. When it runs out of petrol, they see the need for a petrol station on the road on which they happen to come to a halt; and incredibly, by selling their car they get enough cash to erect and supply such a station and furnish a little house with it too. What troubles they have after that is caused by love-confusions – all three are in love with the same girl without knowing that she *is* the same; their filling station seems to flourish despite the most lackadaisical service; and when they are invited to a swanky nightclub, each suddenly appears in a perfectly tailored 'white-tie-and-tails' outfit, complete with *chapeau claque*, white waistcoat and fresh white gloves, able to drown his love sorrows in expensive-looking drinks. At the end the three young men who in their pre-filling-station days had never worked at anything – one of them confesses that he had only 'seen work from afar, and even then it did not look attractive' – are made directors of a huge enterprise with a multitude of employees in a whole complex of buildings, where they pretend to be busy in a large, well-lit and well furnished office. That office set becomes the venue for the carnivalesque, operetta-like song-and-dance ending of this feel-good film.

Thomas Koebner, to whom we owe the best study of the 'sound-film operetta' (*Tonfilmoperette*) so far, rightly says that the whole story-line of *Three Men from the Filling Station* contradicts how people experienced life in 1930. I would slightly modify that statement by pointing to the passing reminiscences of contemporary fears and realities I analysed earlier. About the whole story-line, however, Koebner is, of course, absolutely right:

> Where fear of the future leaves people breathless, the characters in the film live their daily lives unthinkingly and merrily. Where oppressive want weighs people down, frivolity and lightness prevail here. Where uncompromising fundamentalisms subdue people's spirit, where the liberal-minded citizen is filled with apprehension by rabid street-battles and martial speeches from Nazis on the right and Communists on the left, the film's protagonists relax and idle their time away free of any sense of guilt. These three charming good-for-nothing succeed against all reason and logic … (Koebner et al. 2003)

But all this, Koebner correctly concludes, does not condemn the film. It's part of its virtue, rather; for 'it has a touch of unprovincial urbanity, just because it refuses to duplicate the misery of the period on the screen, or to condemn the protagonists' airy existence with solemnity and hatred' (Koebner et al. 2003: 355). As an example of the film's lighthearted stylisation Koebner cites a night-club scene in which four personable and graceful young women dance on four pianos to a jazzed-up version of the song 'Hallo, du schöne Frau' ('Hello, beautiful woman'). They click their tongues in rhythm with the music, adding a kind of vocal percussion to it; they lie down and let their legs dance in the air; they kiss the pianists while the camera moves slowly upwards – a little revue scene staged with greater simplicity than any Busby Berkeley number, but charming and sensual in a way far removed from the geometric patterning so characteristic of the American Depression musical, to which a film like *Three Men from the Filling Station* forms a German pendant. I would supplement this analysis with the contrast offered by Lilian Harvey, at this stage of her career, and Ruby Keeler. Harvey's dancing seems to arise more naturally from her whole way of moving, so that it is sometimes hardly possible to say where ordinary movement ends and actual dance begins – a transition far more marked in the tightly choreographed passages in which Keeler displays her art in her all too brief heyday.

Ich bei Tag und Du bei Nacht (I by Day and You by Night) – and Others

The critic Willy Haas, writing in 1926, anticipated the spirit in which a film like *Three Men from the Filling Station* was conceived by declaring that he wished he could live in a world in which the complications that normally lead to catastrophes 'resulted in nothing more than comic situations ... and where bankruptcy [der Zustand der Pleite] was nothing but a comic episode' (*Film Kurier*, 12 November 1926). Equally far from tragic realism and biting satire, this charming musical comedy nevertheless hinted, in ways I have tried to describe, at what was actually happening in the lives of many of its original spectators – enough to allow them to measure the distance between this dream world and their waking selves – and thus feel all the more the relief of having the weight lifted off their shoulders for the couple of hours they spent in the warm and comfortable surroundings of the cinema.

While *Three Men from the Filling Station* took its audiences on a dream journey inside their own contemporary German world, other film musicals of the time led them further away – to an imaginary Paris, nineteenth-century Vienna in the age of Johann Strauss, or Metternich's Vienna between the battles of Leipzig and Waterloo. In *Der Kongress tanzt* (*The Congress Dances*), which will be briefly discussed later, the system of class and degree, temporarily disrupted by a love affair is reestablished at the end with the resigned acceptance of a parting seen, from the first, to be ultimately inevitable. This contrasts with the dream of love at the heart of a film in which the Jewish team of Pommer, Thiele, Liebmann, Heymann and Gilbert first introduced themselves to receptive German audiences as makers of *Tonfilmoperetten*, and Harvey and Fritsch first appeared as the German screen's 'dream couple'. The film, which appeared in 1930, a few months before *Three Men from the Filling Station*, bore the title *Liebeswalzer* (*Love Waltz*). It featured a princess from a small state, contracted to marry an Archduke. She falls in love with an American commoner, who estranges her from court ritual to become 'das süsseste Mädel der Welt' ('the sweetest girl in the world') – a phrase from the film's principal song that became a kind of leitmotiv for Harvey. It is actually quoted in *Three Men from the Filling Station*. The American turns out to be heir to a multi-millionaire motor-manufacturer, whose capital is sufficient to salvage the finances of the Princess's bankrupt home state. American millionaires, the film suggests, are the aristocrats of the New World, and a permanent alliance between them and the impoverished aristocracy of the Old is beneficial and desirable for both as a such an alliance between the glove-seller and the Tsar of *The Congress Dances* could never be.

The atmosphere of resignation, lightly hinted at in lines about the inevitable passing of spring in the principal Schlager of *Three Men from the Filling Station* and *The Congress Dances*, also pervades a film written by Walter Reisch (a Jewish author from Vienna) and directed by the Austro-Hungarian Géza von Bolvary. The film's very title, *Das Lied ist aus* (*The Song is Ended*, 1930) suggests that atmosphere, which is made even denser by such songs as 'Wenn das Wörtchen "wenn" nicht wär' ('If the word "if" did not exist'), 'Adieu, mein kleiner Gardeoffizier' ('Farewell, my little officer of the guard'), and – especially – the song later popularised by Marlene Dietrich in her cabaret performances: 'Frag nicht, warum ich gehe / Frag nicht, warum' ('Don't ask why I am leaving, don't ask why'). All these, composed by (the non-Jewish) Robert Stolz, to texts co-written by Walter Reisch, speak of a resignation that relativises the lighthearted atmosphere of the film.

The obvious contrast here is with the song 'Ich bin ja heut so glücklich' ('I am so happy today'), which does *not* give way to melancholy acceptance of ending and loss when sung by Renate Müller in Thiele's *Die Privatsekretärin* (*The Private Secretary*, 1931), made for Greenbaum Film, with music by Paul Abraham. Here the little secretary actually wins her heart's desire, and that of many such secretaries in the film's audiences, and marries the boss. They make a couple more fortunate than that at the centre of one of the greatest works of the Austrian cinema: *Liebelei* (*Playing at Love*), directed by Max Ophüls in 1933, and based on a play by Arthur Schnitzler. Here a Jewish director and a Jewish playwright combine to show how an Austrian officer and a Viennese musician's daughter are destroyed by class-bound codes of honour leading to death in a duel and to suicide.

After his success with *The Blue Angel*, a film to which I shall return along with *The Congress Dances* in the next section, Friedrich Hollaender was given the chance to put his ideas on music in sound films into practice once again in *Einbrecher* (a title which can be read as *Burglar*, in which case it refers to the character played by Fritsch, or *Burglars* which takes in Fritsch's accomplice, played by Oskar Sima). It was directed by Hanns Schwarz, and first seen in 1930. Throughout this work Hollaender plays instrumental and vocal variations on an opening song: 'Lass mich einmal Deine Carmen sein' ('Let me be your Carmen for once'). Despite its dissemination on gramophone records and through the radio, this song never achieved anything like the popularity of other Hollaender Schlager; in *Burglar[s]* it is outshone by a nonsense song performed by Fritsch at the piano, accompanying a dance by Harvey. Here the singer proposes to have his body painted black and go to live a simpler life on the Fiji Islands: 'Ich lass mir meinen Körper schwarz bepinseln ...'

The film's plot has Harvey's character married to an elderly puppet manufacturer, played by Ralph Arthur Roberts, and yearning for greater sexual and emotional satisfaction than her husband is able or willing to offer. Her yearning is answered when she falls for an apparent burglar, played, of course, by Willy Fritsch, who is in reality a writer in search of inspiration for a piece featuring burglary which he is composing. He is aided and abetted by another such writer, played by Oskar Sima, who takes a job as the puppet-maker's servant for similar purposes. The plot, based on a play by Louis Verneuil adapted by Robert Liebmann, calls for a directorial lightness of touch such as Lubitsch possessed and Hanns Schwarz did not. Neither the film, in which Kurt Gerron appears briefly as a police inspector anxious to ingratiate himself with his superiors, nor the songs featured within it, had anything like the success of *Three Men from the Filling Station* and *The Congress Dances* – to say nothing of the international fame of *The Blue Angel*.

In 1932 Pommer entrusted Hollaender with the overall as well as the musical direction of a film. The subject of *Ich und die Kaiserin* (*I and the Empress*) had been suggested by Felix Salten, the Jewish author of *Bambi* and (anonymously) the most popular of pornographic Austrian novels, *Josefine Mutzenbacher*; its screenplay was fashioned by Walter Reisch and, once again, Robert Liebmann. The film is set in Offenbach's Paris, and stars Conrad Veidt as a marquis who is not expected to survive after a hunting accident. On his sickbed he is visited by the French Empress's hairdresser, played by Lilian Harvey, whose only purpose is to retrieve a tell-tale garter she had lost and the marquis had picked up just before his accident. Since his eyes are bandaged, he cannot see her; but she sings him a song that moves him so greatly that after his unexpected recovery he seeks the singer throughout the land. A series of misunderstandings leads him to believe that his mysterious visitor was he Empress herself. All misunderstandings are resolved during a performance of Offenbach's operetta *The Grand Duchess of Gerolstein*, conducted, not by Offenbach himself (who is very sympathetically portrayed by Julius Falkenstein, playing an overtly Jewish part for once) but by his amanuensis, played by Heinz Rühmann. This amanuensis has in fact written the song his fiancée, the Empress's coiffeuse, had sung to the sick marquis. The film has some amusing musical inventions, like the metallic chord struck at intervals by Hubert von Meyerinck, playing the Emperor's aide-de-camp, when he rapidly passes his hand across his bemedalled chest. Conrad Veidt seems ill at ease, however, in these frivolous proceedings, and appears to dampen Lilian Harvey's spirits, while Heinz Rühmann is given little chance to deploy his comedic talents.

Hollaender was anathema to the Nazis and was forced to flee Germany in February 1933. After some weeks in Paris he reached the USA in May 1933, with a three-month contract with Fox Films, succeeded by another three-month contract with RKO Radio Pictures. The last-named studio allowed him to try his hand at directing once again: a modest two-reel comedy Western which starred the singer Ruth Etting and was entitled *Bandits and Ballads*. Released in 1934, it dragged out a short life in supporting programmes; its Western setting ensured that Hollaender was engaged on many later occasions to work on the musical scores of Hopalong Cassidy Pictures, but did not bring further invitations to direct. I do not think we need regret that he concentrated, ever afterwards, on composing and writing, both in Hollywood and, after the collapse of Nazism, in Germany, and left the difficult task of film-directing to others.

Jewish directors, scriptwriters, composers, actors and singers were of crucial importance in the creation of film musicals made in Germany between 1929 and 1933. Inspired mainly by Pommer's eye for international connections, they were usually made in multilingual versions, drawing on the skills of stars like Marlene Dietrich, Lilian Harvey and Käthe von Nagy to perform well in languages other than German. Among these was *Ich bei Tag und Du bei Nacht* (*I by Day and You by Night*), released in 1932 in a French form (*A moi le jour, à toi la nuit*, in which von Nagy reprised her role), and an English one, (*Early to Bed*, in which she was replaced by Heather Angel) as well as in its German original. It is a work for which I have had a long-standing admiration and at which I would now like to cast a closer look.

I by Day and You by Night had a strong Jewish presence behind the camera. Produced by Erich Pommer's unit within Ufa, it was directed by Ludwig Berger, and written by Hans Székely and Robert Liebmann. The songs and incidental music were by W.R. Heymann, who also shared the writing of song texts with his usual collaborator Robert Gilbert; Joe Strassner designed the costumes, Hermann Rosenthal worked on the actors' make-up, and Gerhard Goldbaum controlled the sound recording. Their film revolves around a room in a flat owned by a widowed actress, Cornelia

Seidelbast, whose glory-days were passed as a star of a provincial court theatre in the late nineteenth century. The room has a single bed, which is occupied during the day by Hans, a waiter in an all-night restaurant, played by Willy Fritsch, and during the night by Grete, a manicurist in a busy hairdressing salon, played by Käthe von Nagy. The two have never met each other – the land-lady won't let either of them in until the other is well out of the way. Each is, in fact, angry with the unknown sharer of room and bed, because neither takes sufficient care of the other's clothes – at one stage Grete even drenches Hans's suit with a full jug of water because she has found her best dress crumpled on the floor. When they meet by accident in the street, he mistakes her for the daughter of a company director with a large house, smart car, chauffeur and maid, while she thinks he is a wealthy *flaneur*. They fall in love, go on an outing together, become entangled in other, equally convoluted relationships – there are misunderstandings, quarrels, complications at work, until one night they find themselves in the same room after all, realise each other's identity, and resume their love with clearer sight. 'Isn't it marvellous', Hans says; 'one runs after happiness and finds that one has been sleeping in the same bed with that happiness all along.'

The film uses this plot to bring together five interconnected worlds. The first of these is the world of work in a bustling Berlin. We see the run-down houses and yards from one of which Hans emerges to serve all night in a restaurant significantly called Casanova, and eking out his meagre wages by taking an afternoon job as a supernumerary waiter in a smart café. Grete does her manicuring in the gentlemen's section of Frau Waiser's hairdressing salon, superintends some of the hairdrying and setting in the ladies' section, and manicures selected customers in their own homes. Hans' friend Helmut operates the projection booth of the neighbourhood cinema that overlooks the house which Hans, tired out from his night's work, is not allowed to enter until Grete has left; he therefore spends some of his waiting time in the projection booth from which one can look into the cinema's auditorium. What is remarkable and unusual here is that one actually sees the film's stars doing the work their characters are hired to do, with verisimilitude and efficiency. Hans delivers the waiter's patter listing desirable dishes, negotiates a crowded dance-floor with laden plates, serves food from a side-table onto the diners' plates – until, to forget his anger with Grete, he drinks too much and causes a collision with another waiter. In the same way we see Grete handling the nail files, scissors and other implements of her profession with professional aplomb. The film allows us to follow these characters through a realistically observed Berlin, with poor districts and smart ones, crowded trams, buses, cars, delivery vehicles, passers-by hurrying about their business or trying to get out of the rain, dustmen emptying bins, street singers performing for pennies, women washing clothes or fetching milk, policemen regulating traffic or picking up late-night drunks to see them safely home. It is such a policeman who lets the inebriated Hans into the house at night and thus brings about his presence in the same room in which Grete is sleeping and the meeting that resolves all misunderstandings.

Contrasted with this crowded scene is the world of company director Krüger, played by Julius Falkenstein (the only Jewish actor among the principals), and bank director Meyer, a wealthy *bon vivant* and ladies' man played by Anton Pointner, whom Krüger wants to have as his son-in-law. Krüger's bossy daughter Gertrud, however, a chemistry student played by Elisabeth Lennartz, prefers her diffident fellow-student Wolf, enacted in a very mild and un-wolf-like way by the young Albert Lieven. Falkenstein, a veteran of German 'silent' firm whose talents had been used to great effect by Lubitsch, is not marked out as Jewish either by the name of the character he plays, or by any allusion in the plot; but an early appearance shows him in the same frame with a Jewish *memorah*, similar to that which had appeared in a frame with another Jewish actor, Fritz Kortner, in Pabst's *Pandora's Box*. His is a more spacious, comfortable, luxurious world, with a fine house, elegant chauffeured car, and visits to expensive cafés and restaurants; but it interacts with the world of work because it needs its services. Grete manicures Krüger and massages his head when he pretends to have a headache; Hans waits on Gertrud, Wolf and Meyer in the café and restaurant in which he is employed. But this apparently so affluent world also has its financial worries and uncertainties. Krüger has had an unwelcome visit from the bailiffs, who have affixed the dreaded *Kuckuck*, the sticker that marks goods to be repossessed, to some of his furnishings. He is therefore eager to have his daughter marry the wealthy Meyer, whose bank balance he knows though he has never actually met him. When Meyer calls to press his suit, he sees the *Kuckuck* and abandons plans to marry Gertrud, returning instead to his routine of picking up young women and treating them to fine clothes, perfumes and restaurant meals in expectation of suitable rewards.

What unites both worlds is the stress of life in 1930s Berlin. Most of the characters declare either themselves or another as subject to nervous strain. *Nervös* is a key-note for Hans, Grete, Krüger, Gertrud and Grete's employer Frau Waiser – the latter, played by Ida Wüst, says at one point that it's no wonder people get headaches 'the times being what they are'.

A third world is entered by Hans and Grete during an excursion to Potsdam. The first sight they see when they alight from the taxi Hans can hardly afford is a mill, die Mühle von Sanssouci, around which a famous anecdote about Frederick the Great of Prussia has been spun. They then enter the palace of Sanssouci, where a guide takes them through a series of rooms that speak of Frederick's world in the King's moments of relaxation: rococo paintings and decorations, French books, one of which has a handwritten dedication by Voltaire, a music-room that features the flute Frederick played alongside a music-stand that still has his music-master Quantz's music on it. When they linger in the music-room after the rest of the party has passed on and are accidentally shut in, they find themselves seriously in love, with Grete declaring that life is becoming like the cinema

– only in the cinema there would now be background music. And pat! The music of a flute is suddenly heard. Might that not be the ghost of Frederick the Great? We soon receive a more natural explanation when the screen shows us the palace guide playing the instrument favoured by the great king, whose presence has been made so palpable by this whole excursion sequence. Huge shadows, recalling the silent German cinema, then herald the approach of the guide and some guards who expel Hans and Grete out of Frederick's world into their own: the nocturnal Berlin of buses, trams and *Stadtbahn*, carrying Hans to his job and Grete to her bed in Frau Seidelbast's flat.

It is Frau Seidelbast who brings yet another world into that of Berger's film. Her triumphs as a leading actress in the court theatre of Lippe–Detmold towards the end of the nineteenth century are recalled by lovingly displayed portraits and mementoes. Two of the portraits, she explains, represent her as Princess Eboli in Schiller's *Don Carlos* and as the elfin Rautendelein in Hauptmann's *Die versunkene Glocke* (*The Bell beneath the Water*). Her stage elocution stands out from that of all the other characters, as does her vocabulary and old-fashioned grammar. Moreover, she accompanies what is happening in her life and that of her lodgers with quotations from the classics: Schiller's *Don Carlos*, *Wallenstein* and *Maria Stuart*, Goethe's *Faust* and *Egmont* are prominently represented. The past comes into the present here just as it did in the visit to Frederick the Great's Sanssouci. Amanda Lindner's performance as Cornelia Seidelbast keeps a perfect balance between the comic and the truly dignified, and fits seamlessly into an acting ensemble which hasn't a single weak element.

The fifth and last world we enter is that within the film Helmut projects from the booth in which he receives his friend Hans, and recalled by the radio playing by Grete's bed. The film within the film features a world of palaces brightly lit by crystal chandeliers, with a huge staff of footmen and maids, ministering to a lady in a billowing white dress whom we see descending a huge staircase flanked by her servants. She enters a chauffeur-driven limousine for a tryst with an elegant cavalier singing of his longing for her: 'If you don't come, the roses have bloomed in vain / if you don't come, the larks have vainly trilled their song'. In fact, there is nothing but song in the portions of the 'Bombastik Company's' opus we are allowed to see – no spoken dialogue at all. At the end of this film-within-film, tenor and soprano join in a duet expressing their happiness at being, at last, united.

The opening credits of the film-within-the-film are obviously parodic:

> The Bombastik Film Company
> is privileged to offer
> VERA VERANDA
> and
> TITO DA CAPO
> in
> ALL
> THIS
> IS
> YOURS!

The aptly named Bombastik Company's world of luxury and song is constantly counterpointed with the actual lives of the characters at the centre of our interest. When Helmut counsels Hans to impress the lady who has won his heart by bringing her roses, the film-within-the-film shows hundreds of roses festooning the stairs and balconies of the heroine's palace, and huge bouquets presented to her, while in the world outside the cinema Hans buys a meagre three roses from a flower-seller, counting out a few coins from a small purse. Yet the reach of the Bombastik Company's opus extends beyond the cinema walls, through flowery advertising copy read out by Helmut from a newspaper, and through its principal Schlager which presents the life of luxury depicted by its 'fairy-tale plucked from reality' (*Märchen aus der Wirklichkeit*) as an object of envious admiration by the potential audience: 'When I go to my cinema on Sundays / And see the elegant people in the film / I think: I'd like to be just as happy one day / have champagne and caviar every day …' This Schlager is carried into Grete's room by the radio at her bedside; Hans mocks its promise of happiness by contrasting his life with that of the film's characters; yet at the end we see him happily sitting in the cinema with Grete, turning to kiss her as tenor and soprano sing of their united happiness. They draw shyly apart when house lights go up to signal the end of the film-within-film and the audience's return to their everyday lives.

Frau Seidelbast, remembering her glory-days when there was neither radio nor cinema, holds Schlager, and the films that feature them, responsible for the confusions in her lodgers' life, which resemble *französische Verwechslungsschwänke* – French farces turning on confusions of identity – rather than the classical plays whose heroines she had performed in the Lippe–Detmoid court theatre. Yet despite this outright dismissal, and Hans's bitter mockery of potboiler optimism, the words and music of the Schlager reprised throughout the film speak to Grete of her own modest longings, and bring hope, consolation and pleasure into her troubled life, as they are brought to her bedside by the little radio in her room. When Hans and Grete watch the fantasy life of the "Bombastik" offering in their neighbourhood cinema, happily together after many misunderstandings, they find some of their own happiness reflected by the protagonists on the screen.

In his films with Lilian Harvey, Fritsch is allowed to retain his actual name, 'Willy', just as Harvey retains her 'Lilian'. In *I by Night*, however, in which the tomboyish Harvey is replaced by the more womanly, and sexually attractive, von Nagy, the principal characters are named Hans and Grete. Berger here hints at the fairy-tale quality in his film, true to his often expressed conviction that fairy tales like *Hänsel and Gretel* and *Cinderella* are rooted in reality, and that their fantasy elements are true to human dreams and aspirations. Despite its guying of the Bombastik film, and the clear contrast between its fantasies of luxury and the actual lives of work, worry and nervous strain endured by Hans and Grete in the bustling Berlin of the early 1930s, the divisions of *I by Night* are never as stark and bitter as those between soap opera and actual hospital scenes in Peter Nichols's *The National Health*, directed by Jack Gold in 1973.

'Wenn's schön wird', Grete says, 'when something lovely happens', life resembles the cinema – but such moments are not complete without cinematic background music. No sooner has she said this, as she and Hans kiss in Frederick the Great's music room, than a flute is heard, sweetly playing somewhere beyond. This brings into the film, not just cinematic convention, but a ghost story element. Who but King Frederick, or his music-master Quantz, could be playing the flute in the music room of Sanssouci palace? This playful impression is strengthened by the huge shadows as the menacing guards approach the locked room, recalling not only spectral tales but also the early German cinema's obsession with shadowy apparitions, from *Nosferatu* to *Warning Shadow*. There is, of course, a natural explanations: but the fact remains that reminiscences have been triggered that bring fairy tale, ghost story and Expressionist cinema into the realistic portions of *I by Night*, matching the fantasy element in the impossibly luxurious world of *All This Is Yours*, the film-within-the-film.

Berger and his scriptwriters have placed their characters in carefully delineated linguistic worlds too. These include the Berlinese vernacular of Helmut the projectionist: the carefully learnt pattern delivered with signs of embarrassment by the palace guide, who feels compelled to interject a Berlinese 'jewissermassen' (so to speak) before drawing attention to 'Bacchantische Szenen'; the educated High German of Gertrud Krüger; and the old-fashioned formal vocabulary and grammar of Frau Seidelbast, with its antiquated datives ('im Bette') and its quotations from the German classics. Before we hear Frau Seidelbast herself, there is a (very accurate) parody of her mode of expressing herself from Hans, as he waits impatiently to return to the room and bed he shares, turn and turn about, with Grete. Frau Seidelbast's classical quotations, meanwhile, are ironised by the appearance of similar gobbets in public relations copy handed out to exhibitors by the Bombastik Company and read out admiringly by Helmut the projectionist. This tells the potential audience of *All This is Yours* that Fortune waits on those who seize the right moment, and that the blossom of their dreams will then burst into flower as they do for the protagonists of the film-within-the film. That phrase about the 'blossom of dreams', which Helmut picks up and relates to Hans, has descended from Goethe's poem about Prometheus, who defies the gods by pointing to man's constancy in face of a life in which not all dreams of happiness can find fulfilment: 'weil nicht alle Blütenträume reiften'.

Berger's direction, helped by his excellent (non-Jewish) cameraman Friedl Behn-Grund, merges all these disparate worlds of vision, speech and song into one fluid narrative, with easy transitions from long shot to medium shot and close-up – often alighting on some small detail important for the action, like a hand turning a key, or a card bearing an easily misunderstood message. Point of view and reaction shots constantly vary in consonance with the narrative, never drawing attention to themselves by virtuoso tricks. Scenes are linked to each other by a multitude of visual and verbal hooks and eyes. Berger and his cameraman are particularly good at apt transitions, whether slow fade to black and fading in again or deliberate shock of contrast engineered by a straight cut from one scene to the next. Equally good are their travelling shots conveying important information along the way: as when we share Hans's impatient gaze over the front of a shabby house, looking in at windows where a woman is doing the washing and a man tending a window-box with some pathetic-looking plants, to alight at the window in Frau Seidelbast's flat where the raising of a window blind means that he will soon be allowed to enter the room in which a longed-for bed awaits him after his night's work.

Berger is best known for elegant and imaginative films based on fairy tales, from Cinderella in *Der verlorene Schuh* to the English version of *The Thief of Bagdad* on which he collaborated in 1939–40. I have therefore stressed the fairy-tale and fantasy elements in *I by Day*; but I would like to conclude with a glance at the way in which that film, with its predominantly Jewish provenance, reflects the Depression years within which it was made:

1. The poverty that forces Frau Seidelbast, of the Lippe–Detmold Court Theatre, to let her one spare room, filled with mementoes of her acting past, to two lodgers at once, with all the bed-making and breakfast-serving this entails, and forces Hans to supplement his earnings as an all-night waiter in a busy restaurant by taking an additional afternoon job as waiter in a fashionable café.

2. The appearance of street musicians, singing about keeping cheerful, among the dustbins of a tenement court, dependent on small coins from tenants who are often poor themselves, and on the giving or withholding mood of passers-by.

3. The financial difficulties of the apparently wealthy company director, harried by bailiffs and hoping for a rich son-in-law of dubious character whom his daughter detests.

4. The poverty of the timid student Wolf, who is starving himself with just a single Mark in his pocket, and has to be force-fed by the girl who loves and bullies him with her cry of 'calories, calories calories!'.

5. The catastrophe of losing one's job at a time of high unemployment. This happens to Grete after she is dismissed for striking out at Hans who has come into Frau Waiser's establishment in the guise of a customer and asked for a manicure. It leads her to accept gifts from the philandering banker Meyer, and to be taken by him to the restaurant in which Hans is employed as a waiter. She is there treated to champagne and an expensive meal by her middle-aged escort – a spectacle that leads Hans to some obvious (but, as it happens, wrong) conclusions.

6. The necessity of pleasing a customer able to spend large sums of luxury goods which makes Frau Waiser abandon her avowed principles of not revealing her female employee's addresses to potential wolves.

7. The bitter comments Hans makes on the luxury displayed in the Bombastik film and the consumerist aspirations of the principal Schlager ('caviar every day' – how soon that appeal would fade!), which contrast so starkly with his own harried life. This is reinforced by the contrast between what we see of the lives of Hans and Grete on the one hand, and that of the Krügers and Meyer, whom they serve in varying capacities, on the other.

Yet despite all this, Berger's elegant film is never depressing. Its verbal and visual humour, its gentle but spot-on satire, and the resilience of its characters, keep it light without frivolity. And like King Vidor in *The Crowd*, Berger takes his main protagonists into a cinema at the end, where they can be lovingly together while partaking of communal pleasure in a film remote from their actual lives yet familiar from their dreams.

Viktor und Viktoria – and Some Precursors

The years between 1930 and 1933 produced many musical films in which men of Jewish descent played a crucial part. I would like to look briefly at just two more of them before considering the exceptional role played by the director of *Viktor und Viktoria*, Reinhold Schünzel, whose activities in Germany continued until he too went into exile in 1937.

Der Kongress tanzt (*The Congress Dances*, 1931) was the only film directed by an impresario of lavish stage revues, Erik Charell. The Congress in question is that held in Vienna in 1815, convened by the Austrian Chancellor Metternich to settle the shape of Europe after Napoleon's banishment to Elba. What Charell here offered his public was a Berlinese take on Viennese gaiety, with the Russian Tsar, played by Willy Fritsch, conducting an amorous intrigue with a Viennese salesgirl (Lilian Harvey), while his double, also played by Fritsch, takes his place on ceremonial occasions. The delegates of other states, the comedy asks us to assume, are content to leave a meeting at which crucial decisions are to be made to the wily Metternich, who is thus left to regulate European affairs according to his own wishes while the others are sampling Viennese delights of wine, women and – of course, since this is a musical – song. All plans and intrigues and love affairs are finally thwarted by Napoleon's unexpected return, which sends the delegates scurrying home to prepare for new battles or alliances. This melodious nonsense, which includes the Russian Tsar's offer to sell kisses to an eager queue of Viennese ladies of high society for the benefit of local charities, is acted out by a most accomplished troupe of players (including Conrad Veidt, Lil Dagover, and Adele Sandrock) only one of whom, Paul Hörbiger, can command an authentic Viennese speaking and singing style. Among the Jewish performers we notice the ubiquitous Julius Falkenstein, playing the Austrian finance minister; and especially the great comic actor Otto Wallburg, as the Tsar's portly but swift-moving major-domo Bibikoff, who watches over his sovereign's public and private affairs with alternate deference and spluttering irascibility. The script, by Norbert Falk and Robert Liebmann, allows for a great deal of effective spectacle, with splendid uniforms and Biedermeier costumes, with set pieces that include a central scene in which Lilian Harvey, as the Tsar's temporary favourite, rides in an open carriage towards the luxurious love-nest prepared for her, singing her delight while the townsfolk and country people she passes enthusiastically join in; a grand ball, with Viennese waltzing; and a love tryst in a Viennese *Heurigen* wine-drinkers' garden with a *Schrammel* band accompanying Hörbiger's authentically inflected singing. The all-important songs, by W.R. Heymann with words by Robert Gilbert, were an immediate hit, and have become evergreens still sung by people who have never seen the film. They include the convivial drinking song 'Das muss ein Stück vom Himmel sein / Wien und der Wein' ('That must a piece of heaven come to earth – Vienna and its wine'), and the song sung by Harvey on her coach-ride, and then reprised with new emphasis by Hörbiger at the downbeat ending when the Tsar and his salesgirl have to part: 'Das gibt's nur einmal / Das kommt nicht wieder / Das ist zu schön, um wahr zu sein' ('That happens just once, that won't return, that's too beautiful to be true'). This puts the daydream into its Weimar context, and the inversion of its central line, which circulated at the time and was later used by Curt Bois as the title of one of his autobiographical writings – 'Das ist zu wahr um schön zu sein', that's too true to be beautiful – provides an apt motto for many a film of Lower Depth misery, from Pabst's *Die freudlose Gasse* (*The Joyless Street*) of 1925, set in the Vienna of inflation and profiteering after the First World War, to Phil Jutzi's *Mutter Krausens Fahrt ins Glück* (*Mother Krause's Journey to Happiness*) of 1929. The 'happiness' Mother Krause finds is death by suicide. A film like *The Congress Dances* allows its public to enter a historically distanced dream-world, while still reminding its audiences, through its downbeat ending, that moments of happiness can only be fleeting high-points in ordinary lives.

The girl's resigned acceptance that the affair can only be a short interlude in a life that moves in less exalted regions chimes in with the social conventions of Imperial Vienna. It was tacitly accepted that men from the upper echelons of society would have affairs with girls of the people, *süsse Mädel*, and that they would then go on to contract marriages in their own sphere of life. This could, however, lead to tragedy if one of the parties expected more from the other than a brief liaison – as happens in the film by Max Ophüls mentioned earlier, *Liebelei* (*Playing at Love*), adapted from Schnitzler's play. Ophüls is particularly good at having his actors express social distinctions and varying sentiments in physical action as well as words: one of the officers at the centre of the film waltzes quite differently when dancing with a married mistress from the upper classes than when he holds in his arms the humble musician's daughter, who loves him so deeply that she follows him into death when he is killed in a duel. Ophüls is more overtly critical of social convention here than Schnitzler: in his film the crucial duel fought according to codes of honour is denounced as immoral and unnecessary by another officer, whose affair with a *süsses Mädel* proceeds along less tragic lines.

Ophüls's film is distinguished, not only by superlative performances and smoothly elegant direction, but also by imaginative use of classical music. Its opening mood is set by a passage from Mozart's *Entführung aus dem Serail* (*Abduction from the Seraglio*), which has its relevance to the affair that leads to the fatal duel while it also accompanies the young officer's meeting, at the opera, with the girl who will ultimately feel unable to survive his death. The girl wants to become a professional singer – and at an audition she performs one of Brahms's reworkings of a tragic folksong, which points forward to the tragedy to come. And when that tragedy comes, in the final sequences of the film, we hear fate knocking at the door in the opening movement of Beethoven's Fifth Symphony. Ophüls (Jewish, like Schnitzler) introduces these extended musical quotations into his film with perfect naturalness, because the girl's musician father plays in the orchestra in the Mozart performance at the Vienna opera and at a concert rehearsal of the Beethoven, and the girl herself chooses the Brahms for her audition because its tessitura suits her not very strong or extensive voice. They were selected by Ophüls with his sure sense of period appropriateness and dramatic relevance. None of these musical pieces figure in Schnitzler's play.

The families of many Jewish directors and scriptwriters hailed from the Austro-Hungarian Empire; and though most of them worked in Berlin, the atmosphere of Imperial Vienna fascinated many besides Max Ophüls.

Richard Oswald paid his tribute to it, with *Wir sind vom k. und k. Infanterie-Regiment* (*We belong to the Imperial-Royal Infantry Regiment*, 1926), and his first sound-film, with collaboration on the screen-play by Ernst Neubach, Paul Morgan and Max Ehrlich, and music by Hans May: *Wien, du Stadt der Lieder* (*Vienna, City of Song*, 1930). In the 'silent' period Walter Reisch scripted a tribute to the 'sweet Viennese girl', the *süsses Mädel*, in *Pratermizzi* (*Mizzi from the Prater District*, 1926), and Paul Czinner directed Elisabeth Bergner in an adaptation of Schnitzler's *Fräulein Else* in 1929. The high aspiration of the last mentioned failed, alas – largely because Schnitzler's story (which rivals Joyce's Molly Bloom chapter at the end of *Ulysses* as the finest interior monologue written by a man and attributed to a woman) depends vitally on a flow of verbal and other associations that silent film, even with a stellar cast that included Albert Steinrück, Albert Bassermann, Adele Sandrock and Paul Morgan, simply could not match. Bergner had performed the monologue on stage with great success, in Schnitzler's presence; in her autobiography she condemned the film as the vulgarization (*Verkitschung*) of a great work. It is worth mentioning that while Else, her family, and the man who asks to see her naked as the price of a sum which would rescue her father from disgrace, are clearly marked as Jewish in Schnitzler's story, they are not so in the film. Bergner was Jewish, but her screen father, and the man who drives her into suicide by this outrage to her modesty, are played by non-Jewish actors – though Steinrück, who plays the middle-aged roué who demands his ocular pound of flesh, had famously played Rabbi Loew in *The Golem – How He Came into the World*.

Part of the disappointment felt by many who first saw *Fräulein Else* was that it did not wholly match the appeal Bergner's stage-performances had exerted – an appeal well described, many years later, by her fellow-actor Fritz Kortner:

> Elisabeth Bergner, the little Jewish girl from Vienna, could easily be overlooked off the stage – but on it she had an aura of David whom the public believed to be constantly engaged in battling Goliath. Men and women alike trembled for her safety. They wanted to shield this childlike being from danger and clasp it protectively into yearning arms. Bergner was the incarnation of the child-bride, that object of ancient masculine longings. Add to this that she was half boy, half girl, and so exerted every possible appeal on an excessively love-obsessed Berlinese public. When this melancholy, large-eyed princess with that boyish body became merry and playful, turned somersaults and revealed, in a sudden flash, how perfectly she knew a man's character and used such knowledge to fool and sportively enslave him – then the public's enthusiasm for this precocious, enchanted, childlike creature knew no bounds. The cleverest faun would have to be on guard against this nymph, this self-aware genius of femininity ... She had a pitiless innocence, a fatal magic, and an aura of purity that remained unstained even by its own sinful instincts. (*Aller Tage Abend*, 1969, p. 254)

To feel the full impact of all this cinema-goers had to wait for films in which they could *hear* Bergner as well as see her. This happened in *Ariane*, directed by Czinner in 1930–31, in which Bergner's titular heroine encounters, and eventually captures, a Don Juan figure, played by Rudolf Forster, whose fear of finding love where he only wanted pleasure she has to overcome. Here Bergner's way of speaking is an essential part of the total effect. Sometimes she rushes towards a mid-sentence pause followed by a strong accentual peak: 'Ich freue mich ja – SOO – endlich frei zu werden'. At other times she spits out a sentence very quickly, in childlike anger; she parodies old-fashioned stage diction ('ErHAAbener GrOOSSfürst!'); and at moments of great emotion she finds hushed tones that go with bodily stillness. Her Austro-Hungarian intonation is an additional point of attraction for German audiences – suggesting something slightly exotic, appropriate to the role she plays in *Ariane*: that of a Russian-born girl brought up in Rome and Zurich studying mathematics at Berlin University. All this works, of course, in consonance with her ability to convey emotion through minute changes in facial expression and body language; and to suggest, in the same cinematically effective way, that she is play-acting for her suitor's benefit, and that what she is saying is radically different from what she is feeling.

Paul Czinner, the director she trusted and eventually married, was not one of the world's great film-makers; but he had a sure sense of what Bergner could do, and the ability to wrap this up in an aura of wealth and culture. *Ariane* is full of conspicuous consumption: luxurious hotels, caviar and champagne, buffets overflowing with choice dishes, immaculate evening suits and dresses alternating with discreetly expensive casual wear, the best seats at the opera obtained at a time when the house is ostensibly sold out, servants and waiters at one's private beck and call – all these create artificial gardens in which real toads can play. The film's plot is taken from a once popular French novel, Claude Anet's *Ariane, Jeune fille russe*, first published in 1920. Its much-travelled hero adapts his guiding principle from one of Heine's *Travel Pictures*: 'I wasn't here yesterday; I won't be here tomorrow; but today I am here for …' enjoying myself with a lady that takes my fancy. Its musical ambience is predominantly Mozartian. Ariane and her suitor meet at a performance of *Don Giovanni* (sung in German, though the hero's name is left in Italian on the printed programme). We hear the opera's overture and snatches of the Don's Serenade; and Ariane herself supplements the few lines of Leporello's opening scene we hear in the opera house by singing part of his 'catalogue aria' to her suitor, to drive home her sense of his sexual adventurism. In a later scene we are treated to a performance of Cherubino's '*Voi que sapete*' aria from *The Marriage of Figaro*, appropriate to the androgynous appeal of Bergner herself; Adriane does not appear in this scene, but she is in the principal characters' conversation and thoughts. A Richard Strauss song adds to the erotically charged atmosphere. Czinner's directorial expertise shows itself also in the way he attunes other performances to bring out

Bergner's individuality – her patterns of speech and movement contrast with, and are complemented by, the casual tones and sure, measured, mature body language of her lover. He is an older man, like the other males the film shows us succumbing to Ariana's *gamine* charm – and, no doubt, many other such in the audience, to whose gaze Bergner's performance is particularly well attuned.

Bergner and Czinner were both forced into exile by Nazi racism; and it is surely significant that the only one of Bergner's Shakespearean performances they ever chose to recreate on film was that of Rosalind in *As You Like It*, shot in England in 1936. This is, of course, the play whose hero and heroine are driven from their home by a tyrannous and unjust decree, and find hospitable refuge in a friendly, tolerant and civilised community.

Unlike *Playing with Love*, which was produced for the Elite Tonfilm company, and *Ariane*, credited to Seymour Nebenzahl's Nero-Film, the other early sound films by Jewish Directors so far mentioned in this chapter – *The Congress Dances, Melody of the Heart, Burglar[s], Love Waltz* – were made for the production unit within Ufa headed by Erich Pommer, who specialised in multilingual productions. This unit had its greatest international success, which has kept its place in the repertoire and the history of film classics ever since, with *Der Blaue Engel* (*The Blue Angel*), first shown in 1930.

The Blue Angel was directed, in parallel German and English versions, by Josef von Sternberg, a Jewish native of Vienna, who had made successful films – including a sound film – in Hollywood, and was recruited by Pommer in 1929 to bring Hollywood expertise to what was intended to become a star vehicle for Emil Jannings. Jannings had worked in Hollywood with Sternberg (in a sometimes stormy relationship) and had received the first ever Academy Award for an actor in American films. Jannings's speciality was the fall and degradation of apparently strong men, brought low by their passions, or by social revolutions, or both. In *The Blue Angel* he played a high-school professor seized by *armour fou* for a performer in a low-class variety show. He loses his post when he defies convention to marry her, joins her itinerant troupe, and has to don a clown's make-up as the hapless assistant to a conjurer. He wife deceives him at the very moment in which he is being humiliated as a conjurer's stooge before an audience that had known him as a respected professor; he has a terrifying access of madness that lands him in a strait-jacket. Freed from this, he creeps through familiar streets to his old school, where he drags himself to his former classroom and dies clutching his desk.

Friedrich Hollaender builds up the music of this film, in whose adaptation from Heinrich Mann's novel Robert Liebmann played an important part, around two contrasting musical themes, each associated with the lifestyle of one of the principal protagonists. The professor's theme is that of an old German song enjoining strict probity, played at intervals by the town-hall clock; that of the singer he marries by one of the hit songs composed by Hollaender. That composer was at the time one of the leading lights of the flourishing Berlin cabaret and revue scene, as were two other Jewish participants in the film, Kurt Gerron and Rosa Valetti.

The supreme success of *The Blue Angel*, however, was not Jannings (who was understandably miffed) but Marlene Dietrich, who performs on the stage of the low-class establishment that lends the film its title, a series of songs immediately popularised by radio and gramophone, and repeated, in English translation, in a simultaneously directed Anglophone version of the film. One of these songs, 'Ich bin von Kopf bis Fuss / Auf Liebe eingestellt' ('I'm geared to love from head to foot'), known in English as 'Falling in Love Again', became a staple of Dietrich's later cabaret performances. That might be seen as a vamp's 'come hither' song; but there are others which contain warnings like 'Nimm dich in acht vor blonden Frau'n', bidding men beware of women who were Germanically blonde rather than the exotically dark-haired temptresses featured in other German films; and 'Ich bin die fesche Lola / Der Liebling der Saison' ('I am that smart Lola, the favourite of the season'). This last-named, which speaks ostensibly of a 'pianola' in Lola's possession and warns any of her hearers against trying to 'accompany' her on it, contains sexual double meanings throughout which titillate while ostensibly distancing. Dietrich departed for the USA immediately after the première of *The Blue Angel*, and though she was wholly 'Aryan' by Nazi standards, she refused all blandishments to return to an honoured place in the Nazi film industry.

Between them, Pommer, Sternberg, Hollaender, Franz Wachsmann (who scored the songs), the Weintraubs Syncopators (who performed the instrumental parts, with Hollaender at the piano) and Liebmann (who worked on the script) helped to launch Dietrich into a career of world renown. She was to make six further films under Sternberg's direction, and her association with Hollaender continued in such Hollywood films as *Destry Rides Again, Seven Sinners* and *A Foreign Affair*. Before leaving Germany and making a new career in Hollywood Hollaender appeared as an actor in a German film directed by Robert Siodmak, *Der Mann, der seinen Mörder sucht* (*The Man who Seeks his Murderer*, 1930) to which he also contributed songs to texts by Billie (later Billy) Wilder. He also, as we have seen, directed *I and the Empress*, in which neither his own music nor that of Offenbach could rescue a weak script, only intermittently effective direction, and the lack of sympathetic chemistry between Conrad Veidt and Lilian Harvey.

That films with a strong Jewish presence were not immediately banished from German screens is shown, for example, by Richard Oswald's 'Sängerfilm' *Ein Lied geht um die Welt* (*A Song Goes Round the World*), remade in England as *My Song goes round the World*) in 1934. The German version, produced and directed by Oswald for his company Rio Film of Berlin, in commission for Terra Film, had a screenplay by Jewish scriptwriters (Heinz Goldberg and Ernst Neubach), music by a Jewish songwriter (Hans May, using texts by Ernst Neubach) and starred the Jewish tenor Josef Schmidt. On 30 January 1933 Hitler became German Chancellor; yet *A Song Goes Round the World* received its première in Berlin's most prestigious cinema, the Ufa-Palast am Zoo, in the presence of Josef Goebbels (whom it caused some embarrassment) before being quietly dropped from the German repertoire. Schmidt had achieved great popularity through radio and gramophone performances, but had been denied the opera career he fervently desired because of his small size, which did not exceed that of a normal eleven-year-old boy. Oswald's film allowed him to sing arias from grand opera, *Lieder* by Schubert, and potential Schlager by Hans May, within a plot that in many ways mirrored Schmidt's own life. He plays Ricardo, who becomes a celebrity on radio and gramophone records; but instead of the opera stage he is offered only lucrative appearances as a musical clown. The woman he loves also rejects him, choosing instead his tall and handsome friend, played by Viktor de Kowa. The film leaves open the possibility that the rejection is due, not only to his small size, but also to his markedly Jewish features – which he himself describes as 'ugly', though they would not seem so to an unbiased observer. Schmidt continued his career in Vienna and Brussels, had a successful joint concert at New York's Carnegie Hall with Maria Jeritza; the beginning of the war found him in France, where he sang on the radio and in opera at Avignon. Engagements dried up more and more, however; he took refuge in Switzerland, where he was interned in a transit camp near Zurich, transferred to a hospital where he was treated as a malingerer and sent back to the camp; he died two days later (on 16 November 1942) from a heart attack. He was thirty-eight years old. The sad facts of his end lend a posthumous tragic significance to the rejections his character experiences in *A Song Goes Round the World*.

Despite transition phenomena like *A Song Goes Round the World* it is true to say that the involvement of men and women with Jewish ancestry ended, for the German film industry, in 1933. Even those who had only one Jewish parent, or were baptised into the Christian faith, were affected by the Nazis' racialist decrees. One of these, Fritz Lang, chose to emigrate although the German authorities were willing to disregard the Jewish origins of his mother; he was able to rebuild, in Hollywood, the German career that had culminated in *Metropolis* (1925–26) and *M* (1930–31). Another, however, who had made his name as an actor and screenwriter as well as a director, accepted the offer of a special licence to go on making popular entertainment films in Germany, until Goebbels's increasing hostility made his position untenable in 1936–37. He was Reinhold Schünzel; and the last film he directed, *Land der Liebe* (*Land of Love*, 1937), was truncated by the Nazi censorship and briefly shown before disappearing from German screens.

Schünzel had been acting in German films since 1916, and had soon combined this with writing screenplays, often in collaboration with Jewish authors, who included the young Emmerich Pressburger. He frequently gave himself a major role in the films he directed. As an actor he became especially well known for his embodiment of dubious characters across all classes, from the low blackmailer Bollek in Oswald's *Different from the Others* to the intriguing aristocrat Choiseul in Lubitsch's *Madame Dubarry* (1919) and the corrupt police chief Tiger Brown in Pabst's *Die 3-Groschen-Oper* (*The Threepenny Opera*, 1930–31). His first successful combination of directing and acting was *Das Mädchen aus der Ackerstrasse* (*The Girl from Acker Street*, 1920), a melodrama of seduction and sexual exploitation in proletarian and bourgeois circles, in which Schünzel cast himself in the role of a conscienceless servant. He achieved prominence and popularity as an actor, writer, producer and (for a short time) owner/director of a production firm bearing his name. Schünzel has received much well-deserved attention in recent years by critics who have come to appreciate the wit and originality of such works as the largely improvised situation comedy *Halloh – Casesar!* (1926), whose cast includes Julius Falkenstein and Ilka Grüning. Here Schünzel built on an idea conceived by himself in conjunction with the Hungarian comedian Szöke Szakall, who later continued his career in Hollywood as the much loved 'Cuddles' Sakall.

In the fateful year 1933 Schünzel had his greatest popular success as a film director with *Viktor und Viktoria*. That induced the Nazi authorities to licence him, film by film, to make further directorial contributions to the German cinema, despite the fact that Nazi law sought to exclude what it described as *Halbjuden*, 'half-Jews'. Under such 'Sondererlaubnis' Schünzel directed *Die englische Heirat* (*The English Marriage*, 1934); *Amphitryon. Aus den Wolken kommt das Glück* (*Amphitryon. Good Fortune Descends from the Clouds*, 1935); *Donogoo Tanka. Die geheimnisvolle Stadt* (*The Mysterious City*, 1935–36); *Das Mädchen Irene* (*The Girl called Irene*, 1936), and the ill-fated *Land of Love*. Of *Amphitryon* and *The Mysterious City* Schünzel directed simultaneous French versions. Among the *cognoscenti* much amusement was caused by the news that members of the *SS Leibstandarte Adolf Hitler* appeared in scenes of Amphitryon's homecoming dressed in miniskirts as Greek warriors; and it was difficult not to feel that the film's ironic subtitle (*Good Fortune Descends from the Clouds*) parodied the sequence of Leni Riefenstahl's *Triumph des Willens* (*Triumph of the Will*, 1935–36), which showed Hitler's aeroplane journey towards his massed supporters at the Nuremberg rally while the plane's shadow travels swiftly over the ground below. Goebbels became increasingly irritated by gossip of this kind, and by what he felt to be a 'Jewish' tone of irony and scepticism in Schünzel's films; and after *Land of Love* ran into censorship troubles its director's position became untenable. He emigrated to Hollywood, where he was received with suspicion by many fellow emigrés (had he not 'collaborated' with the Nazis before falling foul of them?), enabled to direct a few only moderately successful films before turning in a handful of memorable performances: in anti-Nazi films made during the war, including Lang's *Hangmen also Die* of 1942 and John Farrow's *The Hitler*

Gang of 1944, and after the war combinations of victim and betrayer in Hitchcock's *Notorious* of 1946 and Jacques Tourneur's *Berlin Express* of 1947–48. He returned to Germany in the 1950s, wrote a screenplay for his erstwhile assistant Kurt Hoffman, and played a sympathetic, uncomplicated minor role in 1953, for which he received a prize as 'best supporting actor'. He died in Munich in 1954, without ever having been able to match his achievements in the cinema of the Weimar Republic and the first years of the Third Reich.

By the time *Viktor und Viktoria*, planned out in 1932, was taken into production in September 1933, Pommer, Hollaender, Heymann and other essential creators of the new German musical no longer had a present or future in the German film industry. The songs were now composed by the 'Aryans' Franz Doelle and Bruno Bolz, and the production group within Ufa was headed by the no less 'acceptable' Alfred Zeisler. Schünzel had special licence to write the script and direct; and only one other participant in the film, the elegant Adolf Wohlbrück, was known by some to have similar 'mixed' ancestry. He, of course, was soon to give his most distinguished performances in the British theatre and British films under his new name Anton Walbrook.

Viktor und Viktoria represents a fresh departure in German film in several important respects. Its plot revolves around the fortunes of the actor Viktor Hempel, played by Hermann Thimig, whose aspirations to be a tragedian in classical plays the film ridicules by showing him chewing the scenery at an audition. To keep himself alive he performs a drag act in sleazy places offering beer and entertainment, where he is paid just ten marks a night. At the agency in which he has one of his disastrous auditions he meets a young girl, Susanne played by Renate Müller, who has unsuccessfully auditioned for a part in musical comedy or operetta. She is a beginner, and he impresses her with photos of himself in various heroic parts (which are, in fact, as hilarious as his earlier declamations) and boasts of successes which she soon realises to be fictitious when she meets him again wolfing a meal in the most modest of eating places. Having pawned his overcoat, he is caught in the rain, catches a cold, loses his voice, and persuades Susanne to take his place for just one night in order to secure the ten marks he needs for his next day's meals. She is reluctantly persuaded to dress as a boy when entering the small theatre (leading to amusing scenes when she has to change into a woman's costume in the dressing-room shared with male entertainers); the mistakes she makes on the stage are taken for deliberate comic touches introduced by a man playing a woman; a visiting agent takes her on; and she becomes an international success with Hempel acting as her manager and amanuensis.

Drag acts, of course, had been a staple of comedy on the stage and in films before – one need think only of the astonishing international success of Brandon Thomas's *Charley's Aunt*; and the spectacle of men playing women belongs to the earliest history of the theatre. What was new in films, however, was the doubling device thought up by Schünzel: a woman dresses up as a man who then has a stage act impersonating a man impersonating a woman, with all the gender confusions, embarrassments, and dubious relationships off-stage, that result. This is quite different, of course, from Shakespeare's theatre, where the audience knew beforehand that female parts would all be played by boys, or all-male productions of *As You Like It* nowadays, where Rosalind dresses as a boy and then has Orlando woo her as though she were a woman; we do not have to stipulate a fictional society 'out there', away from the Globe or the Old Vic or the Royal Shakepeare Company, who have to take the stage deception as 'real', as the fictive audience in Schünzel's film has to do. Robert, the character played by Wohlbrück, grows wise to the double bluff, and teases 'Viktor' by pretending to be taken in and then testing her determination to act 'male' in some traditionally masculine situations in which he involves her.

Schünzel's comedy of gender confusion (of which he also directed a French version, *Georges et Georgette*, in the same year 1933) proved so successful internationally that other stars eagerly followed in Renate Müller's and Meg Lemonnier's footsteps: notably Jessie Matthews in England (*First a Girl*, 1935), Johanna von Koczian in the German Federal Republic (*Viktor und Viktoria*, 1957), and Julie Andrews in the USA (*Victor/Victoria*, 1982). Julie Andrews also starred in a successful adaptation of Schünzel's comedy on the Broadway stage.

The second innovation of Schünzel's original film, which required considerable skill from its excellent cast, was the nature of its dialogue and the way it is integrated with music and movement. Some of the speeches are in rhythmically controlled prose; but this again and again slips into verse, which, in it turn, slides almost imperceptibly into song. Such transitions demanded, and got, perfect timing from its principals, particularly Müller and Thimig, who had to perform a 'Spanish' stage act as well as managing their transitions off-stage; but the other leading actors too, Wohlbrück, Hilde Hildebrand and Aribert Wäscher, succeed fully in fitting themselves into Schünzel's controlled symphony of speech patterns. These range in tempo from Wäscher's machine-gun rapidity of verse-speaking, as an impresario always rushing away to another appointment, to the slow and even drawl of Fritz Odemar's love-lorn and unheroic aristocrat. In addition the timbre of Müller's speaking voice has to veer, at precise moments, from pseudo-masculine to feminine tones, and from the high tessitura in the song she sings, with a charming girlish diffidence, at her unsuccessful audition, to the more confident and deeper-ranging tones she adopts in her masculine disguise and her later stage acts.

Schünzel's third innovation, in German sound film, was his daring insertion of a long passage of mime, without dialogue but with choreographed movements, into the middle of the film. This passage begins with a visit to a sleazy beer-and-dancing cellar in which Wohlbrück's Robert, now aware of the female identity of Müller's Susanne, begins to test the persistence of her male impersonation. It continues with a scene in a barber's shop, where Susanne's beardless face is subjected to the same shaving procedures as Robert's by two barbers who perform, in perfect unison, a veritable ballet of barbering. This is followed by a walk through the streets which culminates in a visit to a flower shop. Here Schünzel achieves a perfect transition from soundless mime back to audible speech: we watch the two principals, who are standing outside the shop, from a vantage-point inside it. They are talking, but the plate-glass window shuts out all sound – until they finally step inside the shop where, once again, we can hear as well as see them.

The flower-shop episode marks an important turning point in the film's plot. Robert is sure, now, of his love for Susanne, whose disguise he has penetrated, and we hear him speak, in more earnest and lyrical tones then any we have heard from him before, of his passionate attachment to the woman to whom he is sending flowers. Susanne, not knowing that he has detected her imposture, thinks the flowers are for Evelyn, a character played by Hilde Hildebrand, and becomes deeply jealous, realising that she desires Robert for herself. What we see on the screen, however, is a mature man in love with the simulacrum of a boyish one. How far Schünzel is here playing on Wohlbrück's widely rumoured homosexuality is not on record; but some might detect the cinematic equivalent of a wink.

Viktor and Viktoria is held together by repetitions, at measured intervals, of the song of hope sung by Viktor Hempel and Susanne at the beginning and taken up by other characters. The most surprising of the latter is a skeletal factotum in a theatrical agency, who intersperses the conventional lyrical idiom of the song with a sudden slang expression, accompanied by a beckoning gesture:

Für jeden kommt's wohl einmal	For everyone there comes a day
Dass ihm die Sonne lacht,	When the sun smiles towards him
Und wo Fortuna endlich	and Fortune, at long last,
Mal 'Winke, winke' macht	Beckons him ...

The lines play on the German expression 'der Wink des Schicksals', the beckoning hand of Fate; 'Winke winke machen', however, is humorous Berlinese, based on the way parents tend to speak to young children. It is characteristic of Schünzel's precise managing of mood that the next passage of the song is sung, sweetly, melodiously, with a yearning sadness, by an aging actress waiting for an audition; and that this should be followed, in its turn, by non-singing prose, spoken by a curmudgeonly old actor whose mantra for the changing times is 'there should be a law against it'.

In addition to the songs and their melodies, repeated in toto or in part, the film is pervaded by internal quotations like the phrase 'ein scheues Reh' ('a timid doe') spoken with various degrees of seriousness and irony. It is held against other zoological comparisons, like the insult 'Dumme Gans' ('stupid goose') flung at a waitress by Viktor at the beginning, and taken up by Douglas in the later part of the film. There Fritz Odemar's

Douglas applies it to a showbusiness girl from Vienna who is a 'timid doe' in Viktor Hempel's eyes. Since Viktor is in love with this 'doe' he issues a drunken challenge to Douglas. Robert, the arch-manipulator, fans the flames assuring each combatant that the other is bent on fighting a duel to the death – a plot finally brought to nought when Viktor and Douglas meet accidentally in the street and discover that neither has a stomach for the fight. The plot device is an old one – we meet it in *Twelfth Night*, for instance; but here it helps to illustrate further Robert's love of manipulating people, signally exemplified in the way he plays on Susanne's assumed masculinity after he has discovered her secret and begun to love her as a woman. This, in its turn, is one of many forms of 'testing' that make up one of the film's dominant themes, beginning with theatrical auditions and culminating in an attempt by the civic licensing authorities to ascertain whether the 'female impersonator' Viktor/Viktoria is a man or a woman – for if he is found to be *really* a woman, his show is based on a deception and should therefore be closed down. When agents arrive to find out the truth by physical examination, Susanne's place has already been taken by Viktor Hempel, who had devised the act in the first place. He is marched to the stage manager's office, where the door closes against actors and theatre staff watching developments with various degree of *Schadenfreude*. It's almost like a scene in one of the Lubitsch films in which our imagination is invited to fill in what may be supposed to be going on behind closed doors. In *Viktor und Viktoria* the door opens at last to allow the examiners to proclaim 'It's a man!', leaving the film to conclude by having Robert and the (now safely female) Susanne, join arms with Odemar's Douglas, Hildebrand's Lilian and Thimig's Viktor who is sure, at last, of success. They all march forward towards the camera until the screen fades to black and the word *Ende* appears in silvery lettering.

Whether the closing and opening door in this final part of the film is a deliberate homage to Lubitsch is now impossible to determine. It is true, however, that Schünzel's film is traversed by various forms of parody. The first and most obvious of these is the witty take-off of declamatory acting in classical plays, exemplified by Viktor's hilarious murdering of speeches from Schiller's *Don Carlos* and the Schlegel–Tieck translation of *Hamlet*. The 'Spanish'-styled stage act of Viktor/Viktoria, is done three times, with various degrees of parody of operettas and 'exotic' settings, twice by Susanne and once by Viktor. And among allusions, part parody, part *homage*, to other styles of filmmaking is a nod in the direction of Hollywood when the camera suddenly moves upwards from a huge stage to watch some two dozen leggy show-girls arrange their bodies in geometric patterns. The camera-work throughout is responsive to such demands, but never draws attention to itself as it passes smoothly from indoors to outdoors, from group to individual, from long-shot to medium shot to occasional close-up. There are no trick shots, and no virtuoso show-pieces like those devised by Karl Freund for Murnau's *Der letzte Mann* (*The Last Laugh*) and Dupont's *Varieté*.

The risky encounters demanded by the plot, in which Robert seems to be declaring love to another man and Susanne tests Lilian's supposed devotion to Robert by seeming to proposition her, with her feminine contours discernible within her masculine get-up, did not fit the image of German men and women the Nazi regime sought to foster. The bulk of the action was therefore removed from Berlin to a London inhabited by elegant idlers and splenetic, slow-witted aristocrats, and by beer-swilling proletarians assembled in subterranean pubs where bouncers eject stroppy patrons, and where fights could break out at any minute, involving every customer in fisticuffs or blows on the head with solid objects.

It is, indeed, striking that three of the few films Schünzel was licensed to make under the new dispensation are set outside Germany – the most successful of them, *Amphitryon*, even in a mythological, pre-Christian era of gods descending on Greek men and women and confusing them as thoroughly as Susanne and Viktor did their own contemporaries. But consideration of the manifold ironies and insinuations of these films would go well beyond the scope of the present book, whose end-point is 1933. They deserve closer analysis in the context of filming under the Nazi regime in which Schünzel cuts an incongruous but fascinating figure.

Epilogue

Many of the films on Jewish themes created in Germany and Austria – like Joseph Delmont's *Die Geächteten* (*The Outlawed*) of 1919, rereleased as *Der Ritualmord* (*Ritual Murder*) in 1921 – are now lost. Our journey through a representative selection has, however, led to encounters with a variety of on-screen characters embodying Jewish experiences in different social, intellectual and psychological situations at specific historical periods and varying stages of integration into surrounding societies. Cooperating with non-Jewish colleagues, and using film-specific means of narration, Jewish scriptwriters, producers, directors, cinematographers and designers exposed to the gaze of their audiences Jews in biblical times (*Das Buch Esther*, 1919); in overcrowded ghettos and voluntary or involuntary religious apartheid; subject to pogroms and anti-Semitic prejudice; under military occupation; at religious ceremonies in the synagogue or the home; on the move from religiously observant families in Eastern Europe to acculturation in the West; making their way in the fashion trade and the world of entertainment; widening traditional Jewish learning through absorption into a metropolitan academy open to all scholars, benefiting themselves and others in equal measure. Jews were seen as Old Testament figures like Mordecai and Esther, as Lessing's wise Nathan at the time of the Crusades, and as more recent rabbis, doctors, lawyers, scholars, army officers, scholars, actors, painters, money-lenders, financiers, shop owners, journalists, marriage-brokers, clockmakers, cobblers, itinerant beggars, young men about town fallen on hard times, *belles Juives*, and playful flappers, in situations ranging from the tragic to the irreverently comic. We saw them faced with charges that ranged from Christ-killing to financial exploitation and high treason, defended, at times, by fair-minded Gentiles; and we watched their dreams of wonder-working but also dangerous *golems*, returns to Zion, acceptance and success in Gentile-dominated societies, along with nightmares of exclusion and expulsion.

The films whose angle of vision and mode of narration were analysed in detail allowed their audiences to observe the aspirations and progress of individual characters facing problems typical of their time and provenance. At one end of the scale audiences shared a filmmaker's vision of a Jewish actor in the nineteenth century, making his way through a series of ambiences from East to West: *shtetl* tradition and orthodoxy, sleazy itinerant troupes in the Austrian provinces, metropolitan aristocracy, and finally a Viennese theatre primarily dedicated to the service of classical Western drama from Shakespeare to Schiller. Though much of this progress was dream-like, it was not without conflict when the demands of family loyalty and an inherited tradition clashed with those of a cherished career and professional imperatives. At the other end of the scale we were able to watch Lubitsch's amused view of a young man on the make in twentieth-century Berlin, shouldering his way from schoolboy prankster to successful head of a fashion emporium and an advantageous exogamous marriage; while another film supplemented this with its presentation of a nervous, fast-talking, small-time entrepreneur trying, unsuccessfully, to con his way into alliance with a socially prestigious Gentile family and having to make do with a more modest marital union in the end. We saw humour used as a weapon of defence, and defiance of authority either dictated by an inner sense of justice, or as compensation for feelings of uncertainty and fear of hostility. Jewish writers and directors made audiences aware that Jewish individuals, like other human beings, had their failings and weaknesses, and that they were capable of intolerance or lack of probity – but that the special form all this took could be understood in the light of their history, precarious social position, and the parallel imperfections of their Gentile contemporaries. Amused or sorrowful contemplation of Jewish failings and imperfections should not be confused with 'self-hatred', and is in any case balanced by the frequent presence, in the films discussed, of Jewish characters capable of engaging an audience's sympathies even when it perceived their human flaws.

The life of Jewish women in predominantly male-dominated societies was exposed to the gaze in many of these films. We met there the all-too-familiar image of the *belle Juive*, always menaced with rape in a way that endowed her image with a secret sexual, sado-masochistic *frisson*. This could merge with that of a girl brought up, with loving protection, in a traditionally observant Jewish enclave of Eastern Europe, who yearned for a kind of learning that could only be obtained outside that sheltering environment, and who was thereby precipitated into a society that allowed her talent to flourish but in which she was also treated as fair game by sexual predators and bigoted authorities that forced a discriminatory 'yellow' passport' on her. A contrary image presented audiences with the spectacle of an emancipated American teenager introduced into the traditional Jewish family in an Eastern province from which her father had emigrated, where she is accepted as a relative in spite of the mischievous disturbance she brought, but where the prospect of married life within its restrictions could only horrify her. We saw a woman who followed her emancipated suitor, from the *shtetl* that had been home to both of them, into a Western capital, and make a new home there without losing her affection for the people left behind; and a woman who runs an affluent, wholly Westernised household in a great capital welcoming a raw young scholar from the East and treating him as though he were her own son. We watched sexual passion strike across religious, social and national boundaries and thwarted by patriarchal authority, entrenched custom and conflicting codes, on both sides of the divide; but we also saw a rising businessman in a Western capital turn away from the boss's Jewish daughter to contract a marriage with a business-wise Gentile woman. Such alliances across ethnic divides remind us of the gamut of attitudes to traditional Judaism exhibited by characters in these films, ranging from unquestioning acceptance of rabbinic precepts and restrictions to as complete a conformity with the surrounding Gentile society as the circumstances allowed.

Though many of these films were set at earlier periods, they all had relevance, as reflection, aspiration, dream, or nightmare, to the times in which they were made and first seen. The figures scrutinised were, of course, fictional constructs – even when, like Dreyfus and his family, they had historic originals. They played their part in works of art of differing aesthetic accomplishment and moral awareness, created within a specific society for specific audiences with varying worries and political, social and sexual attitudes coloured by experiences that included the collapse of empires, a lost war, an over-harsh peace settlement, inflation out of control, unemployment, street battles, and precariously established democratic governments assailed by forces from the extreme right, the extreme left, and resentful military and judicial authorities, as well as capitalists willing to finance any movement that promised greater profit in a resurgent, re-armed Fatherland. It was also a time, however, of artistic experiment and achievement, scientific exploration and advance, and exciting entertainment in which a film industry that sought to address its products to foreign as well as home audiences played an essential part – fuelled, not least, by Jewish artists and entrepreneurs. Even when needed and accepted, these could not be ignorant of anti-Jewish programmes adopted by a growing number of political and social organisations, or fail to feel that removal of legal restrictions and official barriers to integration did not deter enemies from blaming the ills of society on those in their midst who were 'racially' different, and from seeking to bring about their extrusion from an 'Aryan' community.

The films responded to such feelings in a variety of ways. Some reminded their audiences that love of one's neighbour was as central to Jewish ethical teaching as to Christian. There was a shared sense of justice, too, and loyalty to inherited tradition – and these could set up conflicts, across social and religious groupings or within a single human soul, in which both sides might deserve equal respect. Other films showed some of the difficulties and discriminations against which Jews had to battle over centuries of Diasporean existence, and the stratagems both sides evolved to reinforce or to overcome them.

Among the latter was the attempt, by both Gentile and Jewish directors, and by Jewish actors, to perform the task which Lionel Bart and Ron Moody accomplished so well in *Oliver*: that of humanising Jewish characters unsympathetically presented in popular literature. This happened, for instance, when Paul Graetz played Veitel Itzik in Carl Wilhelm's version of

Gustav Freytag's novel *Soll und Haben* (*Debit and Credit*, 1924); or when, nine years before, Ernst Lubitsch took on the role of the parvenu Max Edelstein in Max Mack's version of Gustav Raeder's Biedermeier farce *Robert und Bertram*. Lubitsch's early Jewish comedies take a different way: they show Jews fulfilling the needs and desires of an urban public in various fashion industries and take a humorous view of the stratagems needed to bring success in a competitive world, using mechanisms familiar from Jewish jokes which could be held against them by men of ill will, and misunderstood by those who lacked comedic sense. I also tried to show, however, that such tales of entrepreneurial *chutzpah* could be seen as a compensation phenomenon, as an obverse of feelings of hurt and exclusion, nervousness, and the need to make up for social disadvantages.

My description of the sheer variety of Jewish types, milieu and activities in German and Austrian films, and the implied attitudes and sympathies of their creators, should have done something, I hope, to counter an all too prevalent stereotype of urbanised and culturally assimilated Jews in Central Europe 'indifferent to their Jewish identity and especially indifferent to religious practices' while being 'extremely comfortable with their identity as Germans' (Liberles 2003). However closely they worked with Gentile colleagues, and however remote they themselves were from religious orthodoxy, many of the Jewish writers and directors who have figured in these pages presented Jewish ritual in synagogue and home with evident sympathy, while also showing themselves to be fully aware of problems of hostility, discrimination and exclusion in the history of the Jewish people, and the way many of these reached into their own times.

'On-screen' presences of Jewish figures and themes inevitably occupied a central place in a study such as that attempted in this book; but they constituted only a tiny proportion of the films produced before the catastrophe of 1933. It was therefore necessary to select some typical presences *behind* the screen, beginning with vital contributions to the production, studio management, distribution, exhibition and international exchange. While the achievement of men like Pommer and Davidson was clear for all to see, non-Jewish pioneers in this field, like Oskar Messter in Germany and Count 'Sascha' Kolowrat in Austria, had Jewish collaborators who made important contributions to their work: Maxim Galitzenstein in the former case, Arnold Pressburger in the latter. It is always important to remember that many of the great achievements of the film industry in German-speaking countries was due to the collaboration of Jewish and non-Jewish talent; that Jews never achieved there anything like the power and control exerted by men like Louis B. Mayer, Harry Cohn, or the Warner Brothers in Hollywood's great days, and that many of most creative film workers of the period were born in the Austro-Hungarian dominions but found themselves attracted to what they felt to be greater opportunities in the studios of Berlin and Munich.

One peripheral but none the less important contribution to film culture can only be touched on briefly here: that made by Jewish editors, theoreticians and critics to the knowledge and understanding of the German and Austrian cinema. Kurt Wolffsohn took over the journal *Lichtbild-Bühne* in 1911 and greatly increased its coverage and circulation; he also created a film archive, edited a film industry yearbook, and sponsored authoritative publications like Rudolf Kurtz's *Expressionismus und Film* (1926). A rival journal, founded in 1919, had Alfred Weiner as its long-term managing editor. Among those who combined an interest in individual films with theoretical concerns were Rudolf Arnheim and Béla Balázs; two prominent theatre critics and *feuilletonistes*, Alfred Kerr and Alfred Polgar, did not consider it beneath their dignity to comment on the cinema; and two later historians of the early German film, Siegfried Kracauer (coming from sociology) and Lotte Eisner (coming from art history and cultural studies), first conceived and formulated their concepts in the period of the Weimar Republik. E.A. Dupont wrote on films before he became one of German cinema's most important directors. Among the many Jewish critics whose reviews of current films appeared in a variety of daily and periodical publications and fostered appreciation of this young art form were 'Aros' (Alfred Rosenthal), Hans Feld, Manfred Georg, Kurt Mühsam, Rolf Nürnberg and Hans Sahl. The story of their criteria and influence – reaching well beyond Germany and Austria when Kracauer, Eisner, Georg, Fels and others found themselves in exile outside the German-speaking area – awaits a historian more skilled in reception and media studies than I can claim to be.

The present book selected, for closer scrutiny, three genres in whose creation Jewish artists played a significant part: 'Enlightenment' films or 'films of manners and morals' (*Sittenfilme*); the musicals of the early sound era; and the realism of the 'New Sobriety' (*Neue Sachlichkeit*), tempered by a unique combination of scepticism, human sympathy, feeling for cinematic form, and visual taste. The conspectus of a single important year, 1929, also afforded a glimpse of Jewish pioneering work in thriller, spy and detective films, historical epics, domestic comedy, melodrama, expensive prestige films alongside a great deal of unassuming popular fare produced on limited budgets and released in humbler venues than the picture palaces around the Kurfürstendam. Two contrasting genres must be added to these. The first comprises a group of works, either in portmanteau form or as a sequence of interlinked but separate films, which took their audiences, most of whom were unable to travel far abroad and were conscious of the loss of German colonies and outlying provinces, on exciting adventures in (mostly studio-built) exotic locations. One of these was Joseph Delmont, who directed, and acted in, sensational films whose protagonists had to face wild animals as well as human foes. The best known, however, was Joe May, with his action-star wife Mia May: his *Veritas Vincit* appeared in 1918–19, *Die Herrin der Welt* (*Mistress of the World*) in 1919, and *Das indische Grabmal* (*The Indian Tomb*) in 1921. These differed as widely as anything could from the *Kammerspielfilm* – a genre akin to *Kammerspiele* or 'chamber plays' of the German theatre, in that both had small casts in a few enclosed settings and presented conflicts with often tragic outcome in petty bourgeois or proletarian settings. Films like *Scherben* (*Shattered*, 1921) *Hintertreppe* (*Back Stairs*, also 1921), *Sylvester – Tragödie einer Nacht* (*New Year's Eve – Tragedy of a Night*, 1923) and *Der letzte Mann* (known in England as *The Last Laugh*, 1924) owe their narrative model to their Jewish scriptwriter Carl Mayer – the man who had also, with his co-writer Hans Janowitz, provided the script for *The Cabinet of Dr Caligari*. The expressive distortions of that film brought world-wide attention to the German cinema; but when its director, Jewish like the scriptwriters, sought to repeat the success of that first venture of 1919–20, the results never had the same impact. Nevertheless there is still much to admire in the stylised sets of Robert Wiene's *Raskolnikoff* (1923), based on Dostoevsky's *Crime and Punishment* and featuring a cast of mainly Russian actors, and in his Austrian-made shocker *Orlacs Hände* (*Hands of Orlac*, 1924). Other films that used similar modes of narration were *Das Wachsfigurenkabinett* (*Waxworks*, 1924), directed by Paul Leni, and the (non-Jewish) Karl-Heinz Martin's *Von morgens bis mitternachts* (*From Morn till Midnight*, 1920) which starred Ernst Deutsch. The 'Expressionist' way of making sets and performances nonnaturalistic indications of inner states has been absorbed into world cinema, even though the extreme stylisation of *Caligari* was rarely followed in later works, and its use in such films as *City without Jews* was parodistic.

One genre affected by the 'Expressionist' experiment was the German 'street film' (*Strassenfilm*) that presented the lure and threat of urban streets. Here once again many Jewish artists proved pioneers. The key example is Karl Grune's programmatically entitled film *The Street* of 1923. Its screenplay had been sketched out by Carl Mayer before being elaborated by Grune and Julius Urgiss; the great Jewish painter Ludwig Meidner collaborated on the design of its studio sets, and played stuffy interiors against mysterious streets and exciting but dangerous places of entertainment. The film included such obvious but visually effective symbols as the face of a street-walker suddenly turning into a death's head, or the huge eyes of an advertising sign confronting a frightened and conscience-burdened bourgeois.

Joe May's *Asphalt* of 1929 took a further step towards realism in its story of a young constable enticed way from the path of duty by an attractive jewel-thief, while once again confining its street action to Ufa's impressive studio sets. Other films, however, took their actors and cameramen into the streets and green environs of the city to tell their stories: either with ironic (but not unsympathetic) distancing, like *People on Sunday* in 1929–30, or with more powerful social criticism like *Kuhle Wampe* (1932), whose stirring songs about proletarian solidarity were composed by Hanns Eisler. Since the texts of these songs were by Bert Brecht, they offer yet another instructive example of the fruitful collaboration of Jewish and Gentile artists in the German film industry, before a racist government broke the partnerships up.

From Max Mack's *Wo ist Coletti* (*Where is Coletti*, 1913) to Robert Siodmak's *Der Mann, der seinen Mörder sucht* (*The Man Who Seeks His Murderer*, 1930) and Max Nossek's *Es geht um alles* (*All Is at Stake*, 1932), Jewish directors and scriptwriters showed themselves adept at combining thriller elements with comedy. In sophisticated comedy Lubitsch was king: with his (non-Jewish) star Ossi Oswalda at her mischievous best, he made *Die Puppe* (*The Doll*, 1919) into a cherishable comedy of masculine inhibitions and their conquest, emphasising, through toy-theatre stylisations, the constructed elements of a self-created world that mirrored absurdities and problems of the real one. Many other Jewish directors, like Wilhelm Thiele, contributed to the comedy repertoire; and even rather pedestrian works, like Joe May's first venture into sound film, *Ihre Majestät die Liebe* (*Her Majesty Love*, 1930), could be lifted beyond their script by the talents of the Jewish comic actors Otto Wallburg, Szöke Szakall and Kurt Gerron interacting with non-Jewish stalwarts like Ralph Arthur Roberts and Adele Sandrock.

Not content with his contribution to German comedy, Lubitsch also pioneered a particular form of historical epic which looked to the private lives of monarchs and those who came into touch with them for the causes of historical events. The key works in this genre are *Madame Dubarry* of 1919 and *Anna Boleyn* of 1920, in which Lubitsch also showed a command of large masses of actors, which he had learnt from stage productions by Max Reinhardt. Lubitsch's model was followed internationally by Alexander Korda's *The Private Life of Henry VIII* in 1933 and Michael Curtiz's *The Private Lives of Elizabeth and Essex* in 1939. The Weimar Republic also saw many other attempts by Jewish directors to come to grips with historical events. Oswald's *Dreyfus* is an obvious example; but the same director tried his hand at other periods, too, from *Carlos und Elisabeth* in 1923–24, which reworked an episode in Spanish history that had earlier inspired Schiller to a famous play, to the already mentioned *Last Days before the World Conflagration* of 1930–31, which called on some of the finest acting talents of contemporary German film to portray the principal personalities that shaped events leading up to the outbreak of war in 1914. Hans Behrendt's *Danton* of 1931, with its Büchnerian take on the French Revolution scripted by Heinz Goldberg and Hans Rehfisch, which cast Kortner as Danton, Lucie Mannheim as his lover, and Granach as Marat, alongside Gründgens's mannered assumption of Robespierre, is another memorable example of this trend.

The German Romantic tradition, which had so rich an afterlife in the culture of German-speaking countries, entered German film in its Hoffmannesque form with *Caligari* and later films directed by Henrik Galeen, Richard Oswald and Lupu Pick. Pick made his aptly titled *Grausige Nächte* (*Nights of Terror*) in 1921; Oswald made and remade *Unheimliche Geschichten* (*Uncanny Tales*) in 1919 and 1932, and reworked Galeen's *Alraune* (*Mandrake*) of 1928 into a film of the same title in 1930. The writings on which such films based their plots included popular German authors like Hanns Heinz Ewers, who drew freely on the fictional atmospherics of Hoffmann and Arnim, alongside Robert Louis Stevenson, whose tales of bottle imps, suicide clubs and evil Doppelgänger sorted well with the Black Romanticism of German literature. The more spooky tales of Conan Doyle and Edgar Wallace proved equally congenial. *The Hound of the Baskervilles* was filmed several times, beginning with early versions by Rudolf Meinert in 1914 and Lupu Pick in 1915; *The Crimson Circle* first appeared as *Der rote Kreis* in 1928, under the direction of Friedrich Zelnik. These English authors proved so popular in Germany that a whole series of films whose detective heroes bore approximate English names like Joe Deebs, Harry Higgs and Stuart Webbs were offered to the public by Jewish writers, directors and actors like Joe May, Rudolf Meinert and Ernst Reicher. The ubiquitous Oswald even directed a 'Baskerville Series' for a production firm set up by Jules Greenbaum.

There was, in fact, no field of cinematic endeavour in the period covered by the present book which was not touched by pioneering Jewish talent. One thinks of the meaningful camera distortions of Ernö Metzner's *Überfall* (*Assault*, 1928); the animation and slapstick advertising films of Julius Pinschewer – but also such popular fare as the military farces drawing on the comic talents of Felix Bressart or Siegfried Arno and set in periods well before the First World War. Camera techniques owed much to Jewish cinematographers: notably Eugen Schüfftan, whose 'Schüfftan Process' used an ingenious arrangement of mirrors to combine miniatures and full-size objects in the same frame, and Karl Freund, whose 'liberated camera' ('entfesselte Kamera') was responsible for some of the most impressive 'point of view' sequences in Dupont's *Varieté* of 1925 and Murnau's *Der letzte Mann* (*The Last Laugh*) of 1924. Freund also pioneered the use of hidden cameras in German filmmaking. Some sequences he provided for Walther Ruttmann's great documentary *Berlin, die Sinfonie der Grossstadt* (*Berlin, the Symphony of a Great City*, 1927) were shot with a camera concealed in an appropriately prepared suitcase, using film-stock he had himself sensitised to operate in poor lighting. Neither Murnau nor Ruttmann were Jewish: but their work gained a great deal from their cooperation with Freund, who also (as production chief of Fox Europa) suggested the original idea for Ruttmann's 'symphonic' *Berlin*. Murnau, in even larger measure, came to rely on the scriptwriting talents of Carl Mayer for some of his finest films.

Among others who enriched German filmmaking with original techniques were the cinematographer Helmar Lerski, who brought experiences gained from his work as a still photographer to the motion picture, and Alexander Laszlo, a Hungarian-born musician who experimented with coloured shapes as expressive equivalents and supplementations of musical sounds.

That Jewish directors and screenwriters sought to show inner Jewish conflicts and contrasts as well as problems affecting Jews in historically and geographically specific settings, and to introduce into their films glimpses of picturesque or touching Jewish ritual, does not mean that they felt less committed to the welfare of Germany or Austria than their Gentile colleagues. Whatever their enemies said (with increasing stridency), implied or direct criticism of what they saw to be unjust codes and practices in their German or Austrian homeland was felt to be a patriotic duty: that of demanding fairer treatment for women, young people, homosexuals, the poor and neglected. Of course, Jews as well as non-Jews sometimes climbed aboard the bandwagon of the 'Enlightenment' film to increase profits by promising sexual or sensationalist titillation – though in fact the posters advertising such products usually promised more than the films themselves would or could deliver; but this should not blind us to the humanitarian impulse, and the feeling for social justice, behind many of them. The 'Jewish agenda' designed to subvert or supersede a 'Germanic' or 'Aryan' life-style existed only in the imagination of Jew-baiters; and the widely propagated myth of Jewish world power was proved to be tragically wide of the mark after 1933.

It will have been noticed that both the film *City without Jews*, and the novel on which it was based, subscribed to this same myth, despite their common Jewish authorship. This offers a particularly instructive Austrian example of the involvement by Jewish writers and directors in the confirmation and strengthening of national ideologies that could be turned against them by non-Jewish fellow-countrymen. The Nazis, when they came to power, proved willing to 'forgive' Fritz Lang the Jewish origins of one side of his family because of his exemplary exaltations of Germanic mythology in films based on his 'Aryan' wife's screenplays. *Die Nibelungen* (*The Nibelung Saga*), his two-part epic filmed between 1922 and 1924, based itself on one of the great works of Middle High German literature and delighted audiences with it tales of a noble blonde hero brought down by treachery, its heroic deaths in alien lands, and its spectacle of swarthy dwarves toiling to amass treasure. Patrick McGilligan, in *Fritz Lang: The Nature of the Beast*, quotes Lang himself on his aims:

> By making the Siegfried legend into a film, I wanted to show that Germany was searching for an ideal in her past, even during the horrible time after the First World War in which the picture was made. To counteract the pessimistic spirit of the time, I wanted to film the great legend of Siegfried so that Germany could draw inspiration from her epic past. (1997: 104)

Other nations might well wonder how a work which ends with the death, by fire and sword, of almost all the characters might 'counteract the pessimistic spirit of the time' – but I suppose the thought that Germany had been able to produce so powerful a legend, first embodied in a great work of literature and then in a film that translated its principal characters and incidents to the screen with such ingenuity and visual distinction, might indeed induce pride in the nation's imaginative and inventive genius and its ability to transcend history in myth. The defeated and humbled might identify with characters who reach the tragic heights of the wronged and vengeful Krimhild, and of Hagen, who kills out of a vassal's loyalty and suffers his own fate without flinching – to say nothing of the dragon-slaying, treasure-amassing Siegfried, who conquers the mighty Brunhild until he is slain by – literally – a stab in the back. Like the German armies in 1918? This is the work its makers chose to hand over, in a solemn Dedication that opens the film, to the German people as a permanent possession: 'Dem deutschen Volke zu eigen'.

The Nibelung Saga is not the only instance of the use of German folklore material by Fritz Lang and his wife Thea von Harbou, the scriptwriter who had no Jewish ancestry and who chose to work on in the German film industry when Lang emigrated after the advent of the Nazi government. Their film *Der müde Tod* (*Weary Death*, known as *Destiny* in English-speaking countries and as *Les Trois Lumières* in France), first shown in 1921, drew its main plot from a German folktale, collected and elaborated by the Brothers' Grimm under the title 'Gevatter Tod' ('Godfather Death'). The Grimms' collection also inspired Ludwig Berger's many tributes to the German versions of fairy tales. Having praised them in his writings, he also drew on them in his films: overtly, as a *Der verlorene Schuh* (*The Lost Slipper*, 1923), based on the Grimms' 'Aschenputtel' ('Cinderella'), alongside motifs from Romantic tales by Hoffmann and Brentano; and more obliquely in *I by Day and You by Night*, whose central protagonists bear the names of the Grimms' 'Hänsel and Gretel'.

During the First World War not only did many Jewish filmmakers serve in the German and Austrian armed forces, but they also loyally supported the German High Command's call for positive propaganda to counter the negative impression disseminated by Germany's enemies. In 1916 Julius Pinschewer founded the aptly named 'Vaterländischer Filmvertrieb' ('Patriotic Film Distribution') to make films in support of war loans and to develop strategies for instilling favourable impressions of German character traits and, incidentally, of German manufacturing and craft skills) among British and French prisoners in German camps. In the following year Paul Leni followed the same call by directing a semi-documentary film about a humanitarian German doctor operating in the battle-zone, entitled *Der Feldarzt. Das Tagebuch des Dr Hartl* (*The Army Doctor. Dr Hartl's Diary*). After the war it was left to a Jewish director, Leo Lasko, to make a documentary about its course which was heavily weighted on the German side (*Der Weltkrieg*, 1927).

In *I by Day and You by Night* we had a taste of the veneration inspired by the feats, in peace and war, of Frederick the Great of Prussia. That ruler's heroic image was further built up by Hans Behrend, who collaborated with his non-Jewish colleague Arzen von Cserépy on the four-part epic *Fridericus Rex* (1920–21); by Luise Heilbronn-Körbitz, who composed a screenplay for a film about Frederick's later career and conquests entitled *Der alte Fritz* (*Old King Frederick*, 1927); and especially by Walter Reisch's screenplay for *Das Flötenkonzert von Sanssouci* (*A Flute Concert at Sanssouci*,

1930) – a film in which we are asked to admire the way Frederick initiates a preventive war while playing the flute with an ensemble gathered together in the music-room of his Potsdam palace.

Frederick the Great, usually played by the actor Otto Gebühr, was just one of the popular Prussian heroes celebrated in patriotic films by Jewish directors and scriptwriters. Others so commemorated were men who fought and died in the 'Wars of Liberation' (*Freiheitskriege*) against Napoleon: notably *Die elf Schillschen Offiziere* (*The Eleven Officers of Schill's Regiment*), directed by Rudolf Meinert in 1916, at the height of the First World War; Richard Oswald's *Lützows Wilde verwegene Jagd. Der Heldentod Theodor Körners* (*Lützow's Wild Hunt. The Poet Körner's Heroic Death*, 1927); and most impressively, *Die letzte Kompagnie* (*The Last Company*, 1929–30). The last-named tale of the self-sacrifice of a small Prussian troop, who held a position against overwhelming odds for long enough to ensure the safe withdrawal of their batalion, was directed by Kurt Bernhardt (who later continued his directing career in Hollywood as Curtis Bernhardt) and written by the Jewish team of Heinz Goldberg, Hans J. Rehfisch and Hermann Kosterlitz (renamed Henry Koster in Hollywood). The film starred Conrad Veidt, who was here able to demonstrate, convincingly, that he could play roles far different from the neurasthenic parts to which he was so often confined. A film like *The Last Company* showed Jewish writers and directors, who felt themselves fully part of the German nation and language community, celebrating German heroism and willingness to lay down one's life for one's comrades.

Heroism and self-sacrifice, in face of an implacable nature and inner turmoil, often with a mystical component, were essential components of the *Bergfilm* ('Mountain Film'), a patriotic genre in whose development Jews played a significant part. Béla Balázs and Carl Mayer worked on the script of *Das blaue Licht* (*The Blue Light*, 1931–32), which described itself as 'a mountain legend from the Dolomites', starred the young Leni Riefenstahl, and was produced by a company founded by Riefenstahl's Jewish sponsor, H. R. Sokal. Paul Dessau wrote music for *Stürme über dem Montblanc* (*Storms over Montblanc*) produced by Aafa Film in 1930, and for *Der weisse Rausch. Neue Wunder des Schneeschuhs* (*White Ecstasy. New Miracles of Skiing*, 1930–31), produced jointly by Sokal and Aafa films. Friedrich Wolf, a Jewish doctor and playwright, whose later play about the Nazi persecution of the Jews, *Professor Mamlock*, was made into a powerful Russian film – the first film on this subject which I saw when I came to England in 1939 – worked for a time on another adventure film, *S.O.S. Eisberg*, which featured Leni Riefenstahl in a comparatively small part. He claimed no credit, however, because he disapproved of the resulting film. Kurt Bernhardt, lastly, co-directed *Der Rebell* (*The Rebel*, 1932) with its (non-Jewish) star and scriptwriter, Luis Trenker, who declared that this film about a revolt against Napoleonic occupation in the Tyrolean mountains was designed to mirror, in its tale of 1809, what was happening in Germany after 1918 under the terms of the Versailles Treaty.

The *Heimatfilm*, celebrating the natural beauty of specific regions of Germany and Austria, and sympathetically chronicling the joys and troubles of those who lived there, was another patriotic genre to which Jews contributed enthusiastically. Friedrich Zelnik, for instance, directed *Die Försterchristel* (1925–26) before launching into paeans to Austria in such films as *An der schönen blauen Donau* (*By the Beautiful Blue Danube*, 1926) and *Das tanzende Wien* (*Dancing Vienna*, 1927). In that same year, however, 1927, Zelnik also directed what might be seen as a critical *Heimatfilm*: an adaptation of Gerhart Hauptmann's play *Die Weber* (*The Weavers*), which chronicled the sufferings of Silesian weavers whose livelihood was undermined by the Industrial Revolution and the development of world trade, and their short-lived revolt against employers who depressed their wages to a level at which they could no longer provide for their families. The celebratory *Heimatfilm*, however, which had a predominantly rural setting, found its complement in nostalgic urban films such as those provided by Walter Reisch, whom we have already met as the scenario writer of *Mizzi. The Girl from the Prater District*. He continued his Austrian series with scripts for *Ein Walzer von Strauss* (*A Strauss Waltz*, 1927) and *Donau Walzer* (*Danube Waltz*, 1929), in parallel with German celebrations like *Ein rheinisches Mädchen beim rheinischen Wein* (*Rhenish Girl and Rhenish Wine*, 1927) and the more rural *Schwarzwaldmädel* (*Girl from the Black Forest*, 1929).

Like Balázs and Sokal, who aided Leni Riefenstahl on her way to becoming Hitler's favourite filmmaker, Hanns Schwarz helped to raise Hans Albers, from an earlier film career in which he had played heavies and all sorts of shady characters, to the status of 'der blonde Hans', Germany's most popular action hero. This happened in *Bomben auf Monte Carlo* (*Bombs on Monte Carlo*, 1931), in which Albers, playing a naval captain in command of a crew that included Peter Lorre in an unaccustomedly cheerful role, threatens to shell the Monte Carlo casino (whose understandably worried director is played by Kurt Gerron) unless the part of his losses that belonged to his crew rather than to himself is restored. The enterprising captain wins the love of a Ruritanian princess along with the increased respect of his men in this light-hearted romp with a serious background – that of restoring confidence in masculine German competence and enterprise. Walter Reisch and Kurt Siodmak furthered this enhancement of Albers's image when Reisch adapted Siodmak's novel *F.P.1 antwortet nicht* (*F.P.1 Does Not Answer*) for a film first shown under this title in 1932. Directed by (the non-Jewish) Karl Hartl, this was an expensive multi-language version in which Albers's central role was taken by Conrad Veidt in the English and Charles Boyer in the French version. It told of a crew stranded, by an act of sabotage that endangers them all, on an artificial island created in mid-Atlantic for refuelling aircraft on long-haul flights. The plot of this thrilling and moving film enabled the star German audiences saw to add a touch of melancholy to his heroic image. Continued in later roles, this helped to deepen and humanise Albers's many representations of dashing German masculinity.

German cinema under Nazi control needed actors like Albers, who could portray heroic German types without Teutonic stiffness. It needs to be said, however, that Albers himself was never committed to Nazi ideology. He used his popularity to keep up, undisturbed, his connection with his long-term Jewish companion Hansi Burg, whom he supported while she was living in London during the dark years of Nazi rule, while other prominent colleagues divorced their Jewish spouses to advance their careers. The great Austrian actor Hans Moser (who had played an ultimately repentant anti-Semite in *The City without Jews*) matched Albers's loyalty: his indispensable presence in German and Austrian films ensured that he could shield his Jewish wife from her would-be persecutors and murderers.

The story I have tried to tell, with selected examples that could stand for many more, is a sad one if one considers the fate of those affected by the catastrophe of 1933 and the exile and state-sanctioned murders that followed from it. For me it is also, however, an inspiring one, which shows not only how great a debt German and Austrian film owed to the Jews who worked creatively within it, but also how fruitful cooperation of Jews and non-Jews could be even in the face of hostility, envy and slander. The organisation powers of Pommer and Davidson, the wit and irreverence of Lubitsch, the concern for justice that went with a feel for popular entertainment in Oswald, the musical verve of Hollaender, Heymann, Dessau and Eisler, the film-specific writing talents of Carl Mayer, the visual imagination of Leni and Dupont, the camera ingenuity of Schüfftan and Freund, Berger's ability to combine realism and fantasy in a socially meaningful way, the nostalgic elegance of Max Ophüls, the cool sympathy of Siodmak and his team with urban surfaces, life and pleasure, the acting talents of Kortner, Bergner, Lederer, Karlweis, Valetti, Arno, Bressart, Falkenstein and countless others – all these and more lent interest, meaning and direction to the films in which they had a hand. In every case, however, the result depended on the harmonious working together of Jewish and non-Jewish Germans, Austrian or Hungarians.

What the present book should also have suggested is the crucial role played by Jewish producers and directors in discovering, fostering and inspiring the many talents that sustained the German and Austrian film industries. A masterpiece like *Mädchen in Uniform* (*Girls in Uniform*, 1931), directed by Leontine Sagan (née Schlesinger), developed in a socially and historically meaningful way the critique of unenlightened authoritarianism and sexual attitudes which had been pioneered by the many Jewish writers and directors of 'Enlightenment' and 'Problems of Youth' films. The German careers of Lil Dagover, Pola Negri and many other male and female stars began, and were furthered by, Jewish directors; and the enlightened patronage, casting and employment policies of Erich Pommer and Joe May were responsible for hundreds of successful careers in all the many varieties of cinematic art.

Neither Pommer, however, nor any other Jewish participant in the German and Austrian film industries, ever acquired the kind of control that studio heads in the USA were able to exert. It proved all too easy, in 1933 and 1938, to expel Jews from their work-place by government decree. Some Gentile friends and co-workers tried to help where they could, but there was no effective opposition to such patently unjust wholesale expulsion. Many lesser talents, indeed, profited by it when they stepped into the posts of disbarred Jewish colleagues, who had thought that they were as German or Austrian as the Gentiles with whom they had collaborated, and that they had made important contributions to German and Austrian culture. Even earlier experience of anti-Semitic snipings had not prepared many of them for the shock of finding how easily they could be severed from the civic societies they had considered their own, and from an industry that owed them so much.

Many non-Jewish artists who had worked in harmony with their Jewish colleagues remained in the German and Austrian film industry after its decimation by the brutal ethnic policies of the Nazi government. Some of their talent was misdirected into films that prepared for conquest and genocide; but only a small proportion of films made after 1933 fell into that category. My own early cinema experiences, reinforced by later viewing and reflection, have convinced me, as they have others, that worthwhile films continued to be made even under the censorship restrictions imposed by Goebbels and his henchmen. Many of these films were able to build on what their makers had learnt before the Nazi catastrophe broke over Germany, Austria, and the occupied countries. But essential ingredients went out of the German-speaking cinema with the loss of Jewish experience, imagination, sensibility, musicality, wit, sense of justice, fruitful distancing, international reach, and willingness to experiment in defiance of entrenched authority. The disruption of the fruitful working together that had so enriched the popular medium Jews and non-Jews had created may seem a relatively small matter in face of other disasters brought about by Nazi policies; but it has been painfully felt by gifted filmmakers like Werner Herzog, who has struggled to reconnect to, and build on, what he experienced as a broken tradition. Whether the reengagement of Jewish men and women in the current life and civic affairs of Germany and Austria will eventually lead to anything like the degree of artistic collaboration the present book has tried to describe, only the future can tell.

Appendix

JEWISH ARTISTS AND ADMINISTRATORS WORKING IN THE GERMAN AND AUSTRIAN FILM INDUSTRY IN 1929

Production Firms

Aafa Film AG
Bloch-Rabinowitsch-Produktion
Filmproduktion Löw & Co.
Greenbaum Film GmbH
Karl Grune-Film GmbH
Nero Film AG
H.R. Sokal-Film GmbH
Stein-Film GmbH
Strauss-Film Fabrikation und Verleih, GmbH and others

Production Managers, Executive Producers (Produktionsleiter)

Erich Cohn
Hans Davidson
Wolfgang Hoffmann-Harnisch
Georg M. Jacoby
Wilhelm von Kauffmann
Paul Kohner
Jacob Lorsch
Leo Meyer
Herman Millakowsky
Joe Pasternak
Erich Pommer

Arnold Pressburger
Gregor Rabinowitsch
Max Schach
Herbert Silbermann
Viktor Skutezky
H.R. Sokal
Josef Somlo
Josef Stein
Julius Sternheim
Friedrich Zelnik

Directors

Ernst Angel
Felix Basch
James Bauer
Hans Behrend
Ludwig Berger
Kurt Bernhardt
Paul Czinner
Constantin David

E.A. Dupont
Friedrich Feher
[Jakob and Luise Fleck]
Karl Grune
Robert Land
[Fritz Lang]
Max Mack
Joe May

Rudolf Meinert
Ernö Metzner
Leo Mittler
Manfred Noa
Richard Oswald
Lupu Pick
[Reinhold Schünzel]
Hanns Schwarz
Robert Siodmak

Josef von Sternberg
Paul (Pal) Sugar
Wilhelm Thiele
Victor Trivas
Adolf Trotz
Conrad Wiene
Carl Wilhelm
Willi Wolff

Writers

Emanuel Alfieri
Jacques Bachrach
Béla Balázs
Vicki Baum
Siegfried Bernfeld
Julius Brandt
Max Ehrlich
Paul Frank
Henrik Galeen
Fritz Grünbaum
Willy Haas
Carl Heinz Jarosy
Max Jungk
Hans Kahan
Rudolf Katscher
Hermann Kosterlitz
Leo Lania
Adolf Lantz
Elizza La Porta
Lajos Lázár

Robert Liebmann
Hans Marschall
Carl Mayer
Jacques Natanson
Ludwig Nerz
Alfred Polgar
Hans J. Rehfisch
Walter Reisch
Herbert Rosenfeld
Alfred Schirokauer
Walter Schlee
Franz Schulz
Berthold Seidenstein
Kurt Siodmak
Hans Szekely
Julius Urgiss
Ladislaus Vajda
Walter Wassermann
Billie Wilder
Hans Wilhelm

Cinematographers

Werner Brandes
Fritz Brunn
Curt Courant
Hans Davidson
Siegfried Dessauer
Karl Ehrlich
Akos Farkas
Willi Goldberger
Mutz Greenbaum

Ferdinand Hart
Otto Heller
Otto Kanturek
Helmar Lerski
Harry Meerson
László Schäffer
Hans Scheib
Adolf Schlasy

Set Designers, Set Builders

Rudolf Bamberger
Artur Berger
Hans Jacoby
Alfred Junge
Osio Koffler
Herbert Lippschitz
Lazare Meerson

Ernö Metzner
Robert Neppach
August Rinaldi
Jack Rotmil
Emil Stepanek
Ernst Stern

Composers for the Early German Sound Film (1929)

Paul Abraham
Paul Dessau
Werner Richard Heymann
Friedrich Hollaender

Hans May
Franz Wachsmann
Artur Guttmann (arranger and conductor)
Alexander Schirmann (ditto)

Actors

Josel Almas
Lutz Altschul
Betty Amann
Bruno Arno
Siegfried Arno
Paul Askonas
Hans Behal
Oskar Beregi
Elisabeth Bergner
Siegfried Berisch
Trude Berliner
Paul Biensfeld
Curt Bois
Eugen Burg
Hans Casparius
Dolly Davis
Hugo Döblin
Karl Falkenberg
Julius Falkenstein
Robert Garrison
Valeska Gert
Kurt Gerron
Carl Goetz
Paul Graetz
Alexander Granach
Albert Heine
Else Heller
Martin Herzberg
Evelyn Holt
Oskar Homolka
Karl Huszar-Puffy
Erwin Kalser
Kurt Katsch
Robert Klein-Lörck
Heinz Kleinmann
Walter A. Klinger
Arnold Korff
Martin Kosleck
Iwan Kowal-Samborski
Hermann Krehan
Franz Lederer
A.E. Licho
Trude Lieske
Fee Malten
Lucie Mannheim

Paul Morgan
Grete Mosheim
Anita Mutsam
Jack Mylong-Münz
Lizzi Natzler
Eugen Neufeld
Max Nosseck
Ressel Orla
Paul Otto
Sophie Pagay
Dita Parlo
Ida Perry
Hermann Picha
Eddie Polo
Ernst Reicher
Ellen Richter
Walter Rilla
Elfe Rosen
Willy Rosen
Josef Rovensky
Margarete Schlegel
Alfred Schlesinger
Rosa Schlesingerova
[Reinhold Schünzel]
Wladimir Sokoloff
Maria Solveg (Matray)
Camilla Spira
Fritz Spira
Leonard Steckel
Lotte Stein
Hans Sternberg
Ludwig Stössel
A. Svarc
Szöke Szakall
Eugen Thiele
H. H. von Twardowski
Rosa Valetti
Hermann Vallentin
Ernst (Ernö) Verebes
Hanna Waag
Otto Wallburg
Géza Weisz
Max Wogritsch
Max Zilzer
Wolfgang Zilzer

Ancillary Services

(a) *Sound System Supervision*
 Producer Hermann Millakowsky
 Michael Safra
 Rudolf Schwarzkopf

(b) *Still Photography*
 Hans Casparius
 Walter Lichtenstein

(c) *Title Design*
 Joe Steiner

(d) *Publicity Design*
 Rudi Feld

(e) *Furnishings*
 Beermann & Co.

(f) *Costumes*
 Theaterkunst Hermann J. Kaufmann
 Joe Strassner

(g) *Medical Consultants*
 Dr Magnus Hirschfeld
 Dr S. Levy-Lenz

(h) *Legal Consultant*
 Dr H. Wertheimer

Film Critics

Rudolf Arnheim
'Aros' (Alfred Rosenthal)
Hans Feld
Manfred Georg
Leo Hirsch
Hanns Horkheimer
Walter Kaul

Siegfried Kracauer
Paul Lenz-Levy
Hans G. Lustig
Paul E. Marcus (PEM)
Rolf Nürnberg
Hans Sahl
and others

Publishers of Film Journals and Commissioning Editors

Emil Perlmann (*Der Kinematograph*)
Alfred Weiner (*Film-Kurier*)
Karl Wolffsohn (*Lichtbild-Bühne*)

A valuable descriptive list of artists working in the German and Austrian film industry in preceding and subsequent years may be found in the long essay by Hans Feld listed in my Bibliography. The Bibliography also contains the titles of works by Ronny Loewy, Jan-Christopher Horak and Kevin Gough-Yates which list Jewish emigrés and expellees who tried, with varying success, to continue their careers in the American and English cinema, often with an intermediate stage in pre-*Anschluss* Austria, France, Holland, Czechoslovakia or Hungary.

BIBLIOGRAPHY

Achenbach, Michael, *Projektionen der Sehnsucht: die erotischen Anfänge der Österreichischen Kinematographie* (Vienna: Film Archiv Austria, 1999).
Adorno, T. W., *Gesammelte Schriften* Vol. 15, Frankfurt-on-Main, 1976.
Aurich, Rolf, and W. Jacobsen (eds.), *Werkstatt Film. Selbstverständnis und Visionen von Filmleuten der zwanziger Jahre* (Munich: text+kritik, 1998).
Bandmann, Christa, and J. Hembus, *Klassiker des deutschen Tonfilms, 1930–1960* (Munich: Goldmann, 1980).
Barlow, J.D., *German Expressionist Film* (Boston: Twayne, 1982).
Barsacq, L., *Caligari's Cabinet and other Grand Illusions*, (New York Graphic Society, 1976).
Beckermann, Ruch, and C. Blümlinger (eds.), *Ohne Untertitel. Fragmente zu einer Geschichte des Österreichischen Kinos* (Vienna: Sonderzahl, 1996).
Belach, Helga, *Henny Porten. Der erste deutsche Filmstar 1890–1960* (Berlin: Haude und Spener, 1986).
———, and W. Jacobsen (eds.), *Richard Oswald. Regisseur und Produzent* (Munich: text+kritik, 1990).
Bergfelder, Tim, E. Carter and D. Göktürk (eds.), *The German Cinema Book* (London: British Film Institute, 2002).
Bergman, Andrew, *We're in the Money. Depression America and Its Films* (New York University Press, 1971).
Bergner, Elisabeth, *Bewundert viel und viel gescholten. Unordentliche Erinnerungen* (Munich: Bertelsmann, 1978).
Bock, Hans-Michael (ed.), *CineGraph: Lexikon zum deutschsprachigen Film* (Munich: text+kritik, 1984– [ongoing].
———, and M. Töteberg (eds.), *Das Ufa-Buch. Kunst und Krise, Stars und Regisseure, Wirtschaft und Politik* (Frankfurt-on-Main: Zweitausenins, 1992).
——— (ed.), *Film Materialien: Siegfried Arno* (Hamburg and Berlin: CineGraph, 1992).
——— (ed.), *Paul Leni* (Frankfurt-on-Main: Deutsches Film-Museum, 1982).
———, and W. Jacobsen (eds.), *Film Materialien: Henrik Galeen* (Hamburg and Berlin: CineGraph, 1992).
——— (eds.), *Film Materialien: Ludwig Berger* (Hamburg and Berlin: CineGraph, 1992).
Bois, Curt, *Zu wahr, um schön zu sein* (Berlin: Henschel, 1982).
Brennicke, Ilona, and J. Hembus, *Klassiker des deutschen Stummfilms*, (Munich: Goldmann, 1983).
Bretschneider, Jürgen (ed.), *Ewald André Dupont. Autor und Regisseur*. (Munich: text+kritik, 1992).
Brownlow, Kevin, *Behind the Mask of Innocence* (New York: Knopf, 1990).
Budd, M. (ed.), *The Cabinet of Dr Caligari* (New Brunswick: Rutgers University Press, 1990).
Büttner, Elisabeth, and C. Dewald, *Das tägliche Brennen. Eine Geschichte des österreichischen Films von den Anfängen bis 1945* (Salzburg and Vienna: Residenzverlag, 2002).
Carney, Raymond, *Speaking the Language of Desire. The Films of Carl Dreyer* (Cambridge University Press, 1989).
Coates, P., *The Gorgon's Gaze. German Cinema, Expressionism, and the Image of Horror* (Cambridge University Press, 1991).
Dagover, Lil, *Ich war die Dame* (Munich: Schneekluth, 1979).
Distelmeyer, Jan (ed.), *Tonfilmfrieden/Tonfilmkrieg. Die Geschichte der Tobis vom Techniksyndikat zum Staatskonzern* (Hamburg: CineGraph, 2002).

—— (ed.) and E. Wottrich, *Alliierte für den Film. Arnold Pressburger, Gregor Rabinowitsch und die Cine-Allianz* (Hamburg: CineGraph, 2003).
Doaene, M.A., *Femmes Fatales. Feminism, Film Theory, Psychoanalysis* (New York and London: Routledge, 1992).
Eisner, Lotte, *The Haunted Screen*, translated by Roger Greaves (London: Secker and Warburg, 1973).
Elsaesser, Thomas, *Weimar Cinema and After. Germany's Historical Imaginary* (London and New York: Routledge, 2000).
——, *Filmgeschichte und frühes Kino. Archäeologie eines Medienwandels* (Munich: text+kritik, 2002).
—— (ed.), *Early Cinema: Space, Form, Narrative* (London: British Film Institute, 1990).
——, *A Second Life. German Cinema's First Decade* (Amsterdam: Amsterdam University Press, 1996).
—— and M. Wedel (eds.), *The BFI Companion to German Cinema* (London: British Film Institute, 1999).
—— and M. Wedel (eds.), *Kino der Kaiserzeit. Zwischen Tradition und Moderne* (Munich: text+kritik 2002).
Erens, Patricia, *The Jew in American Cinema* (Bloomington: Indiana University Press, 1984).
Feld, Hans, 'Jews in the Development of the German Film Industry. Notes from the Recollections of a Berlin Film Critic' (London: Leo Baeck Institute Year Book XXVII, 1982).
Felsmann, Barbara, and K. Prümm, *Kurt Gerron – Gefeiert und gejagt, 1897–1944. Das Schicksal eines deutschen Unterhaltungskünstlers* (Berlin: Henrich, 1992).
Fritz, Walter, *Kino in Österreich 1896–1930: Der Stummfilm* (Vienna: Bundesverlag, 1981).
——, *Kino in Österreich 1929–1945: Der Tonfilm* (Vienna: Bundesverlag, 1991).
Gabler, Neal, *An Empire of their Own. How the Jews invented Hollywood* (London: W.H. Allen, 1989).
Gandert, Gero, *Der Film der Weimarer Republik: 1929. Ein Handbuch der zeitgenössischen Kritik* (Berlin: De Gruyter, 1993).
Gay, Peter, *Weimar Culture. The Outsider as Insider* (London: Secker and Warburg, 1969).
Gesek, Ludwig, and O. Wladika (eds.), *Kleines Lexikon des österreichischen Films* (Vienna: Bundesverlag, 1959).
Geser, Guntram, and A Loacker (eds.), *Die Stadt ohne Juden* (Vienna: Filmarchiv Austria, 2000).
Gough-Yates, Kevin, 'Jews and Exiles in British Cinema', (London: Leo Baeck Institute Yearbook XXXVII, 1992).
Granach, Alexander, *There Goes an Actor* (New York: Doubleday, 1945).
Grange, William, *Comedy in the Weimar Republic. A Chronicle of Incongruous Laughter*, (Westport and London: Greenwood Press, 1996).
Gregor, Erika, U. Gregor and others (eds.), *Jüdische Lebenswelten im Film* (Berlin: Freunde der deutschen Kinemathek, 1992).
Gregor, Joseph, *Das Zeitalter des Films* (Vienna: Reinhold, 1932).
Greul, Heinz, *Bretter, die die Zeit bedeuten. Die Kulturgeschichte des Kabaretts*, Vol. I (revised edition, Munich: dtv, 1971).
Greve, Ludwig, M. Pehle and H. Westhoff (eds.), *Hätte ich das Kino. Die Schriftsteller und der Stummfilm* (Munich: Kösel, 1976).
Güttinger, Fritz, *Kein Tag ohne Kino. Schriftsteller über den Stummfilm* (Frankfurt-on-Main Deutsches Filmmuseum, 1984).
Hagener, Malte, *Geschlecht in Fesseln. Sexualität zwischen Aufklärung und Ausbeutung im Weimarer Kino, 1918–1933* (Munich: text+kritik, 2000).
——, *Als die Bilder singen lernten. Krise und goldenes Zeitalter des internationalen Musikfilms 1925–38* (Hamburg: CineGraph, 1998).
—— (and J. Hans), *Als die Filme singen lernten. Innovation und Tradition des internationalen Musikfilms* (Munich: text+kritik, 1999).
Hake, Sabine, *Passions and Deceptions. The Early Films of Ernst Lubitsch* (Princeton University Press, 1992).
——, *German National Cinema* (London: Routledge, 2002).

Hardt, Ursula, *From Caligari to California. Erich Pommer's Life in the International Film World* (Providence and Oxford: Berghahn, 1996).
Hobermann, J., *Bridge of Light. Yiddish Film between Two Worlds* (New York: Schocken, 1991).
—— and J. Shandler, *Entertaining America. Jews, Movies and Broadcasting* (Princeton and Oxford: Princeton University Press, 2003).
Hofmann, Felix, and S.D. Youngkin, *Peter Lorre* (Munich: Belleville, 1998).
Horak, Jan-Christopher (with Elisabeth Tape), *Fluchtpunkt Hollywood* (revised edition, Münster: MAkS, 1986).
Jacobsen, Wolfgang, A. Kaes and H.H. Prinzler (eds.), *Geschichte des deutschen Films* (Stuttgart: Metzler, 1933).
Johnson, Douglas, *France and the Dreyfus Affair* (London: Blandford Press, 1966).
Jung, Uli, and W. Schatzberg (eds.), *Filmkultur zur Zeit der Weimarer Republik* (Munich: K.G. Saur, 1992).
—— (eds.) *Der deutsche Film. Aspekte seiner Geschichte von den Anfängen bis zur Gegenwart* (Trier: Wissenschaftlicher Verlag, 1993).
Kaes, Anton, *Kino-Debatte. Texte zum Verhältnis von Literatur und Film, 1909–1929* (Tübingen: Niemeyer 1978).
——, M. Jay and E. Dimendberg (eds.), *The Weimar Republic Sourcebook* (Berkeley: University of California Press, 1994).
Kaul, Walter, and R.G. Scheuer (eds.), *Richard Oswald* (Berlin: Deutsche Kinemathek, 1970).
Klein, Albert, and R. Kruk, *Alexander Granach. Fast verwehte Spuren* (Berlin: Edition Hentrich, 1994).
Klöckner-Draga, Uwe, *Wirf weg, damit du nicht verlierst. Lilian Harvey – Biographie eines Filmstars* (Berlin: Quintessenz Verlag, 1999).
Koebner, Thomas, N. Grob and B. Kiefer (eds.), *Diesseits der dämonischen Leinwand. Neue Perspektiven auf das späte Weimarer Kino* (Munich: text+kritik, 2003).
Kortner, Fritz, *Aller Tage Abend* (Munich: Kindler, 1959).
Kracauer, Siegfried, *From Caligari to Hitler. A Psychological History of the German Film* (London: Dennis Dobson, 1947).
Kreimeier, Klaus, *Die Ufa Story. Geschichte eines Filmkonzerns* (Munich: Hanser, 1992). Its English version appeared in 1999 as *The Ufa Story: A History of Germany's Greatest Film Company, 1918–1945* (Berkeley: University of California Press).
Kurtz, Rudolf, *Expressionismus und Film* (Berlin: Lichtbildbühne, 1926).
Laube, Heinrich, *Gesammelte Schriften*, Vol. 16 (Vienna: Braumüller, 1882).
Ledig, Elfriede, *Der Stummfilm. Konstruktion und Rekonstruktion* (Munich: Schaudig, 1988).
Liberles, Robert, *Persistent Myths and Stereotypes in the Image of German Jews: A Social Perspective* (New York and Berlin: Leo Baeck Institute, 2003).
Loewy, Ronny (ed.), *Von Babelsberg nach Hollywood. Filmemigranten aus Nazideutschland* (Frankfurt-am-Main: Deutsches Filmmuseum, 1987).
Manvell, R. (ed.), *Masterworks of the German Cinema* (London: Lorrimer, 1973).
Martersteig, Max, *Das deutsche Theater des 19. Jahrhunderts. Eine kulturgeschichtliche Darstellung* (Leipzig: Breitkopf und Härtel, 1904).
McGilligan, Patrick, *Fritz Lang. The Nature of the Beast* (London: Faber and Faber, 1997).
Meyer, Mark Paul and P. Read (eds.), *The Restoration of Motion Picture Film* (Oxford: Ingram, 2000).
Milne, Tom, *The Cinema of Carl Dreyer* (London: Zwemmer, 1971).
Minden, Michael and H. Bachmann (eds.), *Fritz Lang's 'Metropolis'. Cinematic Visions of Technology and Fear* (Rochester: Camden House, 2000).
Monaco, Paul, *Cinema and Society. France and Germany during the Twenties* (New York, Oxford, Amsterdam, 1976).
Mulvey, Laura, 'Visual Pleasure and Narrative Cinema', *Screen*, Vol. I, No. 3, 1975).
Nichlin, Linda, and T. Grab, *The Jew in the Text. Modernity and the Construction of Identity* (London: Thames and Hudson, 1995).
Nowell-Smith, Geoffrey (ed.), *The Oxford History of World Cinema* (Oxford: Oxford University Press, 1997).
Ophüls, Max, *Spiel im Dasein. Eine Rückblende* (Stuttgart: Goverts 1959).

Passek, Jean-Loup, and J. Brisbois (eds.), *Vingt ans du cinéma allemand* (Paris: Centre Georges Pompidou, 1978).
Pertsch, Dietmar, *Jüdische Lebenswelten in Spielfilm und Fernsehspielen. Filme zur Geschichte der Juden von ihren Anfängen bis zur Emanzipation 1871* (Tübingen: Niemeyer, 1992).
Peter, Frank Manuel, *Valeska Gert. Tänzerin, Schauspielerin, Kabarettistin* (Berlin: Fröhlich und Kaufmann, 1985).
Petro, Patrice, *Joyless Streets. Women and Melodramatic Representations in Weimar Germany* (Princeton: Princeton University Press, 1989).
Prawer, S.S., *Caligari's Children: the Film as Tale of Terror* (Oxford: Oxford University Press, 1980).
———, Introduction to *Das Cabinet des Dr Caligari. Drehbuch von Carl Mayer and Hans Janowitz* (Munich: text+kritik, 1995).
———, *The Blue Angel* (London: British Film Institute, 2002).
Rainer, Otto, and W. Rösler, *Kabarettgeschichte* (Berlin: Henschel, 1977).
Rentschler, Eric, (ed.), *German Film and Literature. Adaptations and Transformations* (New York and London: Methuen, 1986).
——— (ed.), *The Films of G.W. Pabst. An Exterritorial Cinema* (New Brunswick: Rutgers University Press, 1990).
Salt, Barry, 'From Caligari to who?', in: *Sight and Sound*, Spring 1979.
———, *Film Style and Technology. History and Analysis* (London: Starword 1992).
Saunders, T.J., *Hollywood in Berlin. American Cinema and Weimar Germany* (Berkeley: University of California Press, 1992).
Schier, A., (ed.) *Arnims Werke*, Vol. II (Leipzig and Vienna: Bibliographisches Institut, n.d.).
Schlüpmann, Heide, *Unheimlichkeit des Blicks: Das Drama des frühen deutschen Kinos* (Frankfurt-am-Main: Stroemfeld, 1990).
Schöning, Jörg (ed.), *Reinhold Schünzel. Schauspieler und Regisseur* (Munich: text+kritik, 1989).
——— (ed.), *London Calling. Deutsche im britischen Film der dreissiger Jahre* (Munich: text+kritik, 1993).
Shandler, Jeffrey, '"Ost und West". Old World and New, Nostalgia and Anti-Nostalgia on the Silver Screen', in: *When Joseph met Molly. A Reader on Yiddish Film*, ed. Sylvia Paskin (Nottingham: Five Leaves Publications, 1992).
Spaich, Herbert, *Ernst Lubitsch und seine Filme* (Munich: Heyne 1992).
Spies, Eberhard, *Carl Mayer. Ein Autor zwischen Expressionismus und Idylle* (Frankfurt-on-Main: Dif, 1979).
Steiner, Gertraud, *Film Book Austria. The History of the Austrian Film from its Beginnings to the Present Day*, second edition (Vienna: Federal Chancery Press Service, 1997).
Stratenwerth, Irene, and H. Simon, *Picniere in Celluloid. Juden in der frühen Filmwelt* (Berlin: Henschel Verlag, 2004).
Taylor, J.R. *Strangers in Paradise: The Hollywood Emigrés 1933–1950* (London: Faber and Faber, 1983).
Uhlenbrock, Katja, *MusikSpektakelFilm: Musiktheater und Tanzkultur im deutschen Film* (Munich: text+kritik, 1998).
———, and R. Wohlleben, *... aus dem Geist der Operette*, Hamburg: CineGraph, 1997).
Ward, Janet, *Weimar Surfaces. Urban Visual Culture in 1920s Germany* (Berkeley: University of California Press, 2001).
Wedel, Michael, *Max Mack. Ein Showman im Glashaus* (Berlin: Freunde der deutschen Kinemathek, 1997).
Willett, John, *The New Sobriety* (London: Thames and Hudson, 1978).
Witte, Karsten, *Lachende Erben. Toller Tag* (Berlin: Vorwerk 8, 1995).
Woods, Paul A., 'The Silver Screen Shadows of Weimar', in: *Monsters of Weimar* (London: Nemesis Books, 1993).
Wottrich, Erika (ed.) *M wie Nebenzahl. Nero–Filmproduktion Zwischen Europa und Hollywood* (Munich: text+kritik 2002).
———, (ed.), *3 O x Nebenzahl. Eine deutschamerikanische Produzentenfamilie zwischen Europa und Hollywood* (Hamburg: CineGraph 2001).
Zif, Avner, and A. Zajdman, *Semites and Stereotypes. Characteristics of Jewish Humour* (Westport, Conn.: Greenwood Press, 1993).

Index

A
Aafa Film 207
Abenteuer im Engadin 163
Abraham, Paul 85, 174
Achtung! Kriminalpolizei! 87, 93
Achtung! Liebe! Lebensgefahr! 83
Adalbert, Max 131
Adieu, Mascotte 89
Adlersfeld-Ballestrem, Eufemia von 88
Adorno, Theodor W. 165
Adventure in Engadin 163
Albers, Hans 93, 208, 209
Alkohol 74
All is at Stake 203
All This Is Yours 181–82
Allen, Woody 51
Alles für Geld 5
The Alley Cat 83
Allgemeine Kinematographische Theatergesellschaft 2
Allianz Tonfilm GmbH 130
Alone at last 51
Der Alpenkönig und der Menschenfeind 130
Alraune 203
Der Alte Fritz 206
Das Alte Gesetz Fig. 14, 21–28
Alte Kleider 82
Althoff, Gustav 125, 129
Amerikaner Shadchen (American Matchmaker) 128
Amann, Betty Fig. 19, 93
Amphitryon 191, 196
An der schönen blauen Domau 208
The Ancient Law Fig. 14, 21–28, 41, 83, 141
Anders als die Andern Fig. 11, 72–75, 75, 76–81
Ander, Charlotte Fig. 29
Andrews, Julie 193
Anet, Claude 187
Angel, H. 164
Anna Boleyn 3, 5, 203
Ariane 187, 188
The Army Doctor 206
Arnheim, Rudolf 201
Arnim, Achim von 33, 204
Arno, Siegfried Fig. 30, Fig. 31, 82, 83, 84, 91, 123, 124, 126, 127, 128, 129, 204, 209
'Aros' *See* Rosenthal, Alfred
Arzner, Dorothy 13
As You Like It 188, 193
Asphalt Fig. 19, 85, 89, 91, 92–98, 202
Assault Fig. 20, 204
Associated Film Industries 130
Atlantic 28, 82, 84, 85
Die Augen der Mumie Ma 3, 21
Aus den Erinnerungen eines Frauenarztes 74
Die Austernprinzessin 82
Austrian Alliance of Cinema Industrialists 130
Ayrton, Randle 145

B
Back Stairs 202
Balázs, Béla 201, 207, 208
Balkan-Orient-Film/Soarele 8
Bandits and Ballads 176
Bart, Lionel 199
Basch, Felix 97
Bassermann, Albert 155, 186
The Bat 162
Battleship Potemkin 160
Bauer, James 97
Becce, Giuseppe 90
Beerman & Co 90
Behn-Grund, Friedl 182
Behrend, Hans 83, 206
Behrendt, Hans 130, 203
The Bell beneath the Water 179
La Belle Hélène 130
Bennett, Arnold 28
Berber, Anita 75, 77
Beregi, Oskar 63
Berg, Armin x, 54
Berger, Ludwig 10, 11, 162, 176, 181, 182, 183, 206, 209
Die Bergkatze 5
Bergner, Elisabeth ix, Fig. 8, 84, 85, 86, 186–88
Berisch, Siegfried 83, 126, 149
Berlin: Die Sinfonie der Grossstadt (Berlin: Symphony of a Big City) 160, 204
Berlin Express 192
Bernhardt, Kurt (later Curtis) 74, 84, 86, 89, 207
Bettauer, Hugo 53, 54, 62
Between Two Fires 6
Beyond the Street 89, 92, 115
Bild und Film Amt (BUFA) 4, 8
BIP *See* British International Pictures
The Black Cat 90
Blackwell, Carlyle 86
Blade af Satans Bog 29
Der Blaue Engel Fig. 22, 12, 78, 84, 88, 138, 139, 161, 162, 164, 175, 188–89
Das blaue Licht 207
Bloch, Chajim 34
Bloch, Iwan 73, 74
Bloch, Noé 98
The Blouse King 49, 50
The Blue Angel Fig. 22, 12, 78, 84, 88, 138, 139, 161, 162, 164, 175, 188–89

The Blue Light 207
Blumenthal, Ben 5–6
Der Blusenkönig 49
Boese, Carl 35, 36, 47, 123, 125, 127, 128
Bogarde, Dirk 76
Bois, Curt 122, 184
Boleslawski, Richard 29, 159
Bolvary, Géza von 174
Bolz, Bruno 192
Bomben auf Monte Carlo (Bombs on Monte Carlo) 208
Borchert, Brigitte *Fig. 21*
Borsody, Julius von 58
Boyer, Charles 208
Braun, Curt J. 123
Der brave Sünder x, *Fig. 26*, 123, 130–40
Brecht, Bert 164, 165, 202
Das brennende Herz 86
Brennert, Hans 16
Brentano, Clemens 16, 206
Breslauer, Hans Karl ix, 54, 57
Bressart, Felix *Fig. 25*, 52, 82, 124, 128, 131, 167, 170, 171, 204, 209
Bridal Night in the Forest 72
British International Pictures (BIP) 28, 141
Brodskey, Nikolaus 139
Brooks, Louise *Fig. 18*, 86, 91
Brunner, Karl 74, 75
Buber, Martin 69
Das Buch Esther 197
Die Büchse der Pandora Fig 18, 7, 84, 91, 123, 150, 178
BUFA *See* Bild und Film Amt
Burg, Hansi 209
Burglars 165, 175, 188
Busch, Ernst 171
By the Beautiful Blue Danube 208

C
Das Cabinet des Dr Caligari (The Cabinet of Dr Caligari) viii–ix, *Fig. 12*, 9, 10, 12, 58, 77, 92, 202, 203
Cagliostro 86
Caligari see *Das Cabinet des Dr Caligari*
Calthrop, Donald 146
Cancy, Ralph 88
The Captain of Köpenick 95, 152
Carlos und Elisabeth 159, 203
Carmen 5
Carney, Raymond 32
Carnovsky, Morris 159
Cartier, Rudolph (born Katscher) 97
The Caviar Princess 123
Chalupec, Barbara Apolonia *See* Negri, Pola
Chaplin, Charlie 122
Charell, Erik ix, 162, 183–84
Charley's Aunt 122, 192
Le Chemin du paradis 12, 165
Children, Mother, and a General 14
Christians, Mady 86
Cinderella 11, 181
City of Song 130
The City without Jews ix, x, 53–62, 63, 68, 202, 205, 206, 209
Clair, René 139
Cohn, Harry 90, 200
Column X 89
Comedia Films 22
Comedian Harmonists 167
Comradeship 7
The Congress Dances ix, 12, 173, 174, 175, 183–85, 188

Connard, Leo 77
The Convict from Istanbul 84
Corzilius, Victor 171
Courts-Mahler, Hedwig 88
Creatures of the Night 83
Crime and Punishment 202
The Crimson Circle 160, 204
Crosland, Alan 27
The Crowd 183
Crucified Girls 85
Crying out for Women 72
Cserépy, Arzen von 206
The Curse 21
Curtis, Michael *See* Curtiz
Curtiz, Michael (later Curtis) ix, 203
Cyankali 74
Czinner, Paul ix, 85, 86, 186, 187, 188

D
Daghofer, Martha *See* Dagover, Lil
Dagover, Lil 9, 184, 209
Dämon und Mensch 149
Dancing Vienna 208
Danton 130, 203
Danube Waltz 208
Danuty, Nunek 149
Dare we keep Silent 75
Davidson, Paul *Fig. 1*, 1–7, 9, 10, 16, 21, 34, 35, 42, 46, 200, 209
Dawison, Bogumil 22–23, 25, 26, 33
Day of Wrath 32
Dear Homeland 87
Dearden, Basil 76
Debit and Credit 200
Deception 3, 5
Decla (Deutsche Eclair) 8–10
Decla-Bioscop 10
DEFA 164
Die Defraudanten 131
Delmont, Joseph 197, 201
Delschaft, Maly 86, 125
Demimonde 73
Demon and Man 149
Der Stolz der Firma 49
Dessau, Paul 160, 161, 162, 163, 164, 165, 207, 209
Destiny 11, 156, 206
Destry Rides Again 189
Detour 90
Deulig 4, 11
Deutsch, Ernst *Fig. 13*, *Fig. 14*, 23, 25, 26, 27–28, 35, 37, 41, 202
Deutsch, Sigmund 7
Deutsche Bioscop 10
Deutsche Eclair *See* Decla
Das deutsche Mutterherz 140
Deutsche Universal 90
Les Deux mondes 141
Diary of a Lost Girl 86, 91
Dida Ibsens Geschichte (Dida Ibsen's Story) 75
Diegelmann, Wilhelm 77
Dieterle, Wilhelm (William) 159
Dietrich, Marlene *Fig. 22*, 12, 84, 161, 169, 174, 176, 189
Different from the Others 72–75, 75, 76–81, 158, 191
Disney, Walt 163, 164
Do you want to marry my Daughter? 149
Döblin, Hugo 29, 82, 89
Doelle, Franz 192

The Doll 53, 203
Don Carlos 195
Donau Waltzer 208
Donogoo Tanka 191
Dora, Josefine 137
Dostoevsky, Fyodor Mikhaylovich 202
Doublier, Francis 150
Doyle, Conan 204
Dr Hart's Diary 4
Drei Tage Mittelarrest 124, 135
Die Drei von der Tankstelle Fig. 24, 12, 124, 135, 165, 167–75
Dreyer, Carl Theodor 29–33
Dreyfus Fig. 23, 149–59, 203
The Dreyfus Case 159
Die 3-Groschen-Oper 7, 191
Drumont, Edouard 150
Dubson, Michael 84
Dudow, Slatan 165
Dukas, Paul 164
Dupont, Ewald André Fig. 3, 21–28, 74, 84, 85, 141, 142, 143, 144, 146, 149, 163, 195, 201, 204, 209
Dürfen wir schweigen 75
Duvivier, Julien 85
Duwan-Torzow, Iwan 29

E
East and West 63–71
Eclair 8
EFA *See* European Film Alliance
Effenberger, Hans 59
Eggerth, Martha ix, 162
Egmont 179
Die Ehe der Maria Lavalle 97
Ehe in Not 86
Ehrlich, Max 90, 186
Eichberg, Richard 122
Einbrecher 165, 175, 188
Eisenstein, Sergei 160
Eisler, Hanns 163, 165, 166, 171, 202, 209
Eisner, Lotte 26, 201
Ekkehard, Arendt 137
El Dura 86
Die elf Schillschen Offiziere (The Eleven Officers of Schill's Regiment) 207
The Elfin King of the Alps and the Misanthropist 130
Elite Tonfilm 188
Elsaesser, Thomas 15
Elstree Studios 141
The Embezzlers 131
Emelka 20
Emil-Jannings-Film GmbH 5
Endlich Allein 51
Englisch, Lucie 125, 131
Die englische Heirat (The English Marriage) 191
Erens, Patricia 159
Erich Pommer Produktion der Ufa 11
Ernst Lubitsch Film GmbH 6
Eros in Ketten (Eros Enchained) 86
Der Erzieher meiner Tochter 82
Es geht um alles 203
Es werde Licht! 73
The Eternal Jew 69
Etting, Ruth 176
European Film Alliance (EFA) 5, 6
Everything for Money 5
Ewers, Hanns Heinz 204
Der Ewige Jude 69

The Eyes of the Mummy 3, 5, 21
Eywo, Hugo 58

F
Falk, Norbert 184
Falkenstein, Fritz 123
Falkenstein, Julius 89, 176, 178, 184, 191
Famous Players 5
Fanck, Arnold 163
Fantasia 164
Farrow, John 191–92
Fassbender, Max 80
Father and Son 83
Faust 11, 38, 130, 179
Feld, Hans 201
Feld, Rudi 46, 90
Der Feldarzt 206
Fels, Hans 201
Fenneker, Josef 74
Ferdinand Lassalle 141
Filmstudio 1929/Moriz Seeler 115
First a Girl 193
Fleck, Jakob 85
Fleck, Luise 85
Die Fledermaus 162
Das Flötenkonzert von Sanssouci 206
Der Fluch 21
A Flute Concert at Sanssouci 206
For Daily Bread 97
A Foreign Affair 189
Forst, Willi ix
Forster, Rudolf 187
Die Försterchristel 208
Fortune's Fool 5
Fox Europe 13, 204
Fox Films 176
F.P.1 antwortet nicht (F.P.1 Does Not Answer) 208
France, Anatole 150, 159
Franck, Paul 167
Frankenstein 39
Franz Josef, *Emperor* ix
Franzos, Karl Emil 63
Die Frau, nach der man sich sehnt 84
Die Frau in Talar 84, 88
Frauen am Abgrund 83
Fräulein Else ix, 85, 186
Fräulein Lausbub 83
Freie Liebe – ein psychologischer Film (Free Love – a Psychological Film) 74
Frenkel, Hermann 4
Freud, Sigmund 73
Die freudlose Gasse ix, 62, 184
Freund, Karl 3, 8, 35, 85, 90, 195, 204, 209
Freytag, Gustav 57, 200
Fridericus Rex 206
Fritsch, Willy Fig. 27, 12, 18, 85, 86, 167, 168, 169, 170, 174, 175, 177, 184
Fröhlich, Gustav Fig. 19, 86
From Morn till Midnight 202
Frühlings Erwachen 75, 78, 86
Frye, Dwight 38
Fuchs, Leo 129
Der Fürst von Pappenheim 122
Fürth, Jaro 89

G

Gad, Urban 2–3
Gajdarow, Wladimir 29
Galeen, Hendrik 34, 35, 63, 203
Galitzenstein, Maxim 2, 200
Galla, Dina 125
Gallone, Carmine 130
Garat, Henri 12
Garrison, Robert 23, 24, 26, 82–83
Gaumont 8
Die Geächteten 197
Gebühr, Otto 35, 207
Geheimnisse einer Seele 96, 139
Das gelbe Haus 75
Der gelbe Schein 5, 16–21
Gentleman's Agreement 20
Georg, Manfred 201
George, Heinrich 155, 159
Georges et Georgette 193
Gerron, Kurt *Fig. 7*, 83, 91, 120, 167, 171, 175, 203, 208
Gert, Valeska 86, 91, 119
Gertrud 32
Gesetze der Liebe 76, 77, 78
Die Gezeichneten 29–33
Giehse, Therese 14
Giese, Kurt 78
Giftgas 84
Gilbert, Robert 167, 168, 169, 171, 172, 174, 176, 184
Girardi, Alexander 161
The Girl called Irene 191
The Girl from Acker Street 191
Girl from the Black Forest 208
The Girl with the Whip 123
Girls Ripe for Marriage x
Girls in Uniform 209
Gliese, Rochus 35
Glucksmann, Laura 68
Goebbels, Josef 13, 91, 190, 210
Goethe, Johann Wolfgang von 130, 136, 164, 179
Goetz, Carl 84
Goetzke, Bernhard 156
Goldbaum, Gerhard 176
Goldberg, Heinz 150, 189, 203, 207
Goldin, Sidney 63, 68, 69, 70
Der Golem – wie er in die Welt kam (The Golem – How He Came into the World) Fig. 13, 33–41, 123, 145, 186
Der Golem und die Tänzerin (The Golem and the Dancer) 34
Gotho, Heinrich *Fig. 20*
Gottowt, John 130
Gottschalk, Ludwig 7
Graatkjaer, Axel 3
Graetz, Paul 123, 146, 199
Granach, Alexander 130, 203
The Grand Duchess of Gerolstein 175–76
Grasset, Georges 8
Grausige Nächte 203
The Green Monocle 88
Greenbaum Film GmbH 90, 97, 174
Greenbaum, Jules (born Julius Grünbaum) ix, 7, 204
Greenbaum, Mutz *See* Greene, Max
Greenbaum-Film GmbH 141
Greene, Max (formerly Max Grünbaum *and* Mutz Greenbaum) 7, 90, 142, 143
Griffith, D.W. 32, 142
Grimm, (Brothers) 206

Grimm, Jakob 33
Grünbaum, Fritz x, 87, 130, 131, 133, 137, 138
Grünbaum, Julius *See* Greenbaum, Jules
Grünbaum, Mutz *See* Greene, Max
Gründgens, Gustaf 130, 203
Grune, Karl ix, 87, 92, 115, 202
Das grüne Monokel 88
Grüning, Ilka 191
Guiltlessly Outlawed 76
Guiness, Alex 141
Günther-Geffers, Elsbeth 89
Guter, Johannes 82
Guttmann, Artur 90, 129, 139
The Gypsy Chief 83

H

Haas, Dolly 137
Haas, Willy 87, 90, 173
Hake, Sabine 49
Halbe Kinder 86
Halbseide 75
Halbwelt 73
Half a Child Still 86
The Hall of the Seven Sins 72
Halloh – Casesar! 191
Hameister, Willy vii
Hamilton Theatrical Corporation 5
Hamlet 195
Hands of Orlac ix, 202
Hangmen also Die 191
Hänsel and Gretel 181
Harbou, Thea von 11, 91, 206
Hardt, Ferdinand 152
Hardwicke, Cedrick 159
Harlan, Veit 83
Hartl, Karl 208
Harvey, Lilian *Fig. 24*, 12, 21, 89, 167, 168, 169, 170, 173, 174, 175, 176, 181, 184, 189
Hasselquist, Jenny 52
Hasler, Emil 12
Hauptmann, Gerhart 4, 179
Der Hauptmann von Köpenick 152
Heart Aflame 86
The Heart of a German Mother 140
Hegesa, Grit 141
Heilbronn-Körbitz, Luise 206
Der Held aller Mädchenträume 86
Hempel, Viktor 194
Henckels, Paul 155
Her Majesty Love 203
Herlth, Robert 93
Hermann, Georg 150
The Hero of Every [German] Maiden's Dream 86
Der Herr Bürovorsteher Fig. 25
Herrenfeld Brothers 51
Die Herrin der Welt 201
Herzfeld, Guido *Fig. 10*, 16, 43, 50, 141, 149
Herzfeld, Josef 149
Herzl, Theodor 63
Herzog, Wilhelm 159, 210
Heymann, Werner Richard 12, 21, 85, 140, 162, 166, 167, 168, 169, 171, 172, 174, 176, 184, 192, 209
Highway and Big City 150
Hildebrand, Hilde 193, 194, 195
Hindemith, Paul 161, 164
Hinkemann 85
Hintertreppe 202
Hirschfeld, Magnus 73, 74, 75, 76, 77, 78, 80, 90

His Majesty's Lieutenant 85
Hitchcock, Alfred 28, 192
Hitler, Adolf viii, 189
The Hitler Gang 192
Hoberman, J. 69
Hoffman, Kurt 192
Hoffmann, E.T.A. vii, 204, 206
Hoffmann, Carl 9
Hollaender, Friedrich ix, *Fig. 31*, 12, 21, 140, 144, 161, 162, 163, 164, 165, 166, 175, 176, 188, 189, 192, 209
Homolka, Oskar 155
Hopalong Cassidy Pictures 176
Hörbiger, Paul 83, 184
Die Hose 83
The Hound of the Baskervilles 86, 204
Hugenberg, Alfred 4, 11, 13, 91, 98
Human Hyenas 72
Hunte, Otto 12
Huszar-Puffy, Karl 82, 83, 86

I
I by Day and You by Night Fig. 27, 176–83, 206
I and the Empress ix, 165, 175, 189
I Kiss your Hand, Madam 86
Ich bei Tag und du bei Nacht Fig. 27, 176–83
Ich küsse Ihre Hand, Madam 86
Ich und die Kaiserin ix, 165, 175
Ideal Film Gesellschaft 58
Ihre Majestät die Liebe 203
Illés, Eugen 16
Im Sumpfe der Grosstadt 75
Im weissen Rössl 162
In the Claws of Sin 72
In the Morass of Big Cities 75
The Indian Sepulchre /Tomb 91, 201
Das indische Grabmal 91, 201
Die Insel der Seligen 4
Intercontinental Film GmbH 14
International Film Sales 2
Internationale Vertriebs-Gesellschaft 2, 3
Intolerance 32
Isersohn, Wilhelm *See* Thiele, Wilhelm
The Isle of the Blest 4
IVG *See* Internationale Vertriebs-Gesellschaft

J
Jacoby, Georg 83, 84–85
Jannings, Emil 3, 5, 6, 12, 21, 45, 188
Janowitz, Hans vii, 9, 202
Janson, Victor 5, 16, 17
Jazz Singer 25, 26, 27, 98
Jenbach, Ida 54
Jenseits der Strasse 89
Jeritza, Maria 190
Jettchen Geberts Geschichte 149
Jeune fille russe 187
Jiskor (Gedenket) 63
Joinville Studios 90
Jolson, Al 27, 135, 162
Jonass & Co 90
Journal for Hermits 33
The Joyless Street ix, 62, 89, 184
Der Judenstaat (The Jewish State) 63
Die Jüdin von Toledo (The Jewess of Toledo) 63
Judith Trachtenberg 63
Jugendtradödie 88
Junge, Alfred 90, 144
Der Jüngling aus der Konfektion 122

Jutzi, Phil 97, 185
Jutzi, Piel 150

K
The Kaiser, Beast of Berlin 97
Kalich, Jacob 66, 69, 70
Kalman, Emmerich 87
Kameradschaft 7
Kampers, Fritz 155, 167
Karloff, Boris 38
Karlweis, Oskar *Fig. 24*, 168, 170, 209
Kataev, Valentin 131
Katharina Knie 87
Katscher, Rudolph *See* Cartier, Rudolph
Kauffmann, Wilhelm von 90
Die Kaviarprinzessin 123
Keeler, Ruby 173
Keine Feier ohne Meyer 47, 122–30
Kellner, Sandor *See* Korda, Alexander
Kerr, Alfred 201
Kettelhut, Erich 93
Kiba 130
Kiepura, Jan ix, 130, 162
Kinder, Mütter, und eine General 14
Kinderseelen klagen euch an 74
Kinski, Klaus 14
Klitzsch, Ludwig 11, 13, 91
Koczian, Johanna von 193
Koebner, Thomas 173–74
Kohner, Paul 90
Kolonne X 89
Kolowrat-Krokowski, *Count* Alexander ix, 130, 200
Der Kongress tanzt ix, 12, 173, 174, 175, 183–85, 188
Korda, Alexander (born Sandor Kellner) ix, 13, 203
Kortner, Fritz ix, x–xi, *Fig. 6*, *Fig. 23*, 84, 86, 89, 96, 130, 131, 138, 150, 156, 157, 159, 178, 186, 209
Koster, Henry (born Hermann Kosterlitz) 90, 207
Kosterlitz, Hermann *See* Koster, Henry
Kowa, Viktor de 190
Kracauer, Siegfried 201
Kraemer, F.W. 159
Krafft-Ebing, Richard 81
Kräly, Hanns 3, 5, 16, 42
Krampf, Günther 138
Krauss, Werner vii, *Fig. 12*, 9, 75, 87
Kreisler, Otto 63
Kuhle Wampe 165, 202
Kühne, Friedrich 29
Kupfer, Margarete 17
Kurtz, Rudolf 201

L
Lady in the Spa 82
Laemmle, Carl 97
Laemmle family 90
Lähn, Peter 2
Lamac, Carl 123
Lambert-Paulsen, Harry 9
Land der Liebe (Land of Love) 190, 191
Land, Robert 21, 86
Landa, Max 88
Landstrasse und Grosstadt 150
Lang, Fritz 7, 9, 10, 11, 13, 55, 87, 91, 122, 138, 150, 156, 190, 191, 205
Lania, Leo 90, 97
Lardner, Ring Jr. 20
Lasko, Leo 163, 206
The Last Company 207

Last Days before the World Conflagration 203
The Last Laugh 11, 95, 195, 202, 204
Laszlo, Alexander 204
Laube, Heinrich 22
Laughton, Charles 13
Laws of Love 76, 77, 78
Lazar, Lajos 87
Lazare, Bernard 150
Leaves from Satan's Book 29
Lederer, Franz *Fig. 18*, 84–85, 98, 209
Leipziger, Leo 1
Lemmonier, Meg 193
Leni, Paul 4, 202, 206, 209
Lennartz, Elisabeth 178
Lerski, Helmar 119, 204
Lessing, Gotthold Ephraim 20
Let There be Light! 73, 74, 75
Die letzte Kompagnie 207
Der letzte Mann 11, 95, 195, 202, 204
Der Leutnant seiner Majestät 85
Levy-Lenz, Ludwig 90
Lewis Ruth Band 171
Leyvick, H. 41
Licho, Adolf Edgar 18, 82
Liebelei 174, 185
Liebeswalzer 174, 188
Liebmann, Robert 12, 21, 83, 90, 97, 162, 174, 175, 176, 184, 188, 189
Ein Lied geht un die Welt Fig. 29, 189, 190
Das Lied ist aus 174
Liedtke, Harry 5, 18, 52, 86
Lieven, Albert 178
The Life of Emile Zola 159
Lind, Jens 29
Lind, Marga 17
Lindau, Paul 55
Lindner, Amanda 179
Linke, Emil 79
Lobenstein, Albert 1
Lockhart, Bruce 165
Loew ben Bezalel, Jehuda (Rabbi) 34, 38
Loewenbein, Richard 86, 122
Lombard, Carole 13
Look out! Plain Clothes Police! 87, 93
Lorre, Peter ix, 122, 208
The Lost Slipper 206
Louis Ferdinand, Prince 97
Love One Another 29, 31
Love Waltz 174, 188
The Loves of Pharaoh 6
Lubitsch, Ernst xi, *Fig. 4, Fig. 9*, 3, 5, 6, 16, 21, 42, 45–52, 82, 83, 89, 122, 128, 129, 175, 178, 191, 195, 200, 203, 209
Ludendorff, Erich 4
Ludwig der Zweite, König von Bayern (Ludwig II, King of Bavaria) 97
Lueger, Karl 53
Lützows wilde verwegene Jagd (Lützow's Wild Hunt) 123, 207

M
M 7, 122, 190
Mabuse 11, 156
McGilligan, Patrick 205
Mack, Max 74, 200, 203
Madame Dubarry 3, 5, 9, 21, 191, 203
Madame im Strandbad 82
Mädchen am Kreuz 85

Das Mädchen aus der Ackerstrasse 191
Das Mädchen Irene 191
Mädchen in Uniform 209
Mädchen zum Heiraten x
Das Mädel mit der Peitsche 123
Madelung, Aage 29
Maladroit: Picture of a Life 149
Malleson, Miles 141
Maman Colibri 85
Mamroth, Paul 4
Mandrake 203
Der Mann, der seinen Mörder sucht (The Man who Seeks his Murderer) 189, 203
Mann, Heinrich 188
Mannheim, Lucie 130, 203
Manon Lescaut 123
Marcuse, Max 73
Maria Stuart 179
Marked Out 29–33, 36, 41
Marr, Wilhelm 53
The Marriage of Maria Lavalle 97
Marriage in Trouble 86
Martersteig, Max 26
Martin, Karl-Heinz 202
Marx, Salomon 4
Mascottchen 97
Masken (Masks) 88
Matthews, Jessie 193
May, Hans 186, 189, 190
May, Joe ix, 11, 85, 91, 92, 95, 96, 201, 202, 203, 204, 210
May, Mia 201
Mayer, Carl vii, ix, 9, 202, 204, 207, 209
Mayer, Louis B. 90, 200
Mayflower Picture Corporation 13
Mazl Tov 65
Mehring, Walter 123
Meidner, Ludwig 92, 202
Meineid 85
Meinert, Rudolf 9, 88, 204, 207
Meisel, Edmund 60
Méliès, Georges viii
Melodie des Herzens (Melody of the Heart) 82, 85, 188
Menschen am Sonntag Fig. 21, 115–21, 202
Messter Company 1–2
Messter, Oskar 1–2, 200
Metro-Film GmbH 7
Metropolis 11, 12, 138, 190
Metzner, Ernö 204
Meyer aus Berlin 16, 50
Meyer, Johannes 29, 30
Meyrinck, Hubert von 176
Meyrink, Gustav 34, 41
MGM 11
Michael 32
Milety, Anny 57
Millöcker, Friedrich 161
Milne, Tom 31, 32
Mischievous Miss 83
Les Misérables 29, 159
Mistress of the World 201
Die Mitternachtstaxe 83
Mittler, Leo 89–90, 92, 115
Mizzi from the Pater District 186, 208
Moody, Ron 199
Morawsky, Erich 7, 8
Morena, Erna 5
Morewski, Avrom 23, 26

Morgan, Paul 82, 130, 186
Moritz macht sein Glück (Moritz makes his Fortune) 123
Moser, Hans *Fig. 17*, 54, 209
Mosheim, Grete 152
Mosse, Rudolf 1
Mother Krause's Journey to Happiness 185
Moulin Rouge 144
The Mountain Cat 5
Mozart, Wolfgang Amadeus 187
Der müde Tod 11, 156, 206
Mühsam, Kurt 201
Müller, Renate *Fig. 28*, 87, 174, 192, 193
Muni, Paul 159
Murnau, F.W. 10, 11, 38, 195, 204
Müthel, Lothar 36
Mutter Krausens Fahrt ins Glück 185
My Daughter's Tutor 82
My Song goes round the World Fig. 29, 189, 190
Mystery of the Air 8

N
Eine Nacht in Venedig 4
Nachtgestalten 83
Nagy, Käthe von *Fig. 27*, 177, 181
Napoleon auf Sankt Helena 87
Nathan, Saul 68
Nathan der Weise (Nathan the Wise) 20
The National Health 181
Natur-Film Friedrich Müller 7
Nebenzahl family x, 7
Nebenzahl, Harold 7
Nebenzahl, Heinrich 7, 115
Nebenzahl, Seymour 7, 188
Negri, Pola *Fig. 10*, 3, 5, 6, 11, 16–21, 52, 86, 209
Nero Film 7, 90, 188
Nest, Loni 35
Nestroy, J. 130
Neubach, Ernst 186, 189
Neufeld, Eugen 68
1914: Die letzen Tage vor dem Weltbrand 151–52
Neuss, Alwin 9
New Year's Eve – Tragedy of a Night 202
Die Nibelungen 11, 12, 87, 205, 206
Nichols, Peter 181
Nielsen, Asta 2–3, 5, 37
A Night in Venice 4
Nights of Terror 203
1914: The Last Days before the World Conflagration 151–52
Ninochka 52
Nissen, Aud Egede 52
Noa, Manfred 20, 73, 74
Nosferatu 181
Nossek, Max 122, 203
Not Quite Silk 75
Notorious 192
Nürnberg, Rolf 201

O
Oberländer, Karl 51
Obrecht, André 150
Odemar, Fritz 193, 194, 195
Off the Straight and Narrow 8
Offenbach, Jacques 130, 175, 189
Old Clothes 82
Old King Frederick 206
Oliver 199
Oliver, David 4

Oliver, Paul 7
Olivier, Laurence 12
Ondra, Anny 123
Ophüls, Max 13, 174, 185, 209
Opium 72
Ordet 32
Orla, Ressel 9
Orlacs Hände ix, 202
Orphans of the Storm 32
Orphée aux Enfers 130
Ost und West/Mizreh un Mayrev Fig. 15, 63–71
Oswald, Richard (born Ornstein) ix, *Fig. 5*, 7, 73, 74, 75, 76, 78, 80, 81, 86, 123, 149–59, 186, 189, 190, 191, 203, 204, 207, 209
Oswalda, Ossie 3, 5, 43, 203
Ottwald, Ernst 165
The Outlawed 197
The Oyster Princess 82, 89, 122

P
Pabst, G.W. ix, 7, 27, 62, 84, 89, 91, 96, 139, 178, 184, 191
PAGU *See* Projektions Aktien-Gesellschaft 'Union'
Pallenberg, Max x, *Fig. 26*, 122, 123, 130, 131, 135, 136, 137, 138, 140
Pampulik als Affe (Pampulik as a monkey) 123
Pampulik hat Hunger (Pampulik is Hungry) 123
Pampulik kriegt ein Kind (Pampulik gets a child) 123
Pandora's Box Fig. 18, 7, 84, 91, 123, 150, 178
Panties 83
Paradies der Dirnen (Paradise of Prostitutes) 74
Paramount 90
Parlo, Dita 85
The Parson's Wife 32
Passion 3, 5, 21
The Passion of Jeanne d'Arc 32
Pasternak, Joe 90, 97
Pathè Frères 72
Patriotic Film Distribution 206
Paul Davidson Aktiengesellschaft 6
Peck, Gregory 20
People on Sunday Fig. 21, 115–21, 202
Perjury 85
Peter der Matrose (Peter the Mariner) 89
Pflanzer, Hans 171
Phantome des Glücks (Phantoms of Happiness) 89
Phoenix 130
Photo and Film Agency 4, 8
Piccadilly 144
Pichler, Banquier 131
Pick, Lupu 9, 73, 74, 87, 203, 204
Picon, Molly *Fig. 15*, 65, 66, 69, 70, 71
Picquart, Georges 150
Piekowska, Polina 29
Piel, Harry 7, 83
Pinajeff, Elisabeth 87
Pinschewer, Julius 7, 204, 206
Piscator, Erwin 160
Playing at Love 174, 185
Playing with Love 188
Plessner, Clementine 77
Poelzig, Hans 35
Pointexter, Rose 137
Pointner, Anton 178
Poison Gas 84
Polgar, Alfred 131, 135, 201
Pommer, Albert 8

Pommer, Erich (later Eric) vii, *Fig. 2*, 7–15, 21, 28, 85, 90, 91, 98, 162, 167, 174, 175, 176, 188, 189, 192, 200, 209, 210
Pommer, Gustav 7
Porten, Henny *Fig. 14*, 25, 27, 90
Powell, Michael 90
Pratermizzi 186
Preiss, Eugen 69
Preiss, Leo 1
Preminger, Otto ix
Pressburger, Arnold 90, 130, 131, 200
The Pride of the Firm 49, 50
Primus Film 29
Der Prinz von Pappenheim (The Prince of Pappenheim 122
The Private Life of Henry VIII 203
The Private Lives of Elizabeth and Essex 203
Die Privatsekretärin (The Private Secretary) 174
Professor Mamlock 207
Projektions Aktien-Gesellschaft 'Union' (PAGU) 2–6, 9, 10, 16, 19, 34, 35, 42, 46
Prometheus-Film 160
Prostitution 75
Der Prozess 27
Prümm, Karl 27
Die Puppe 53, 203
Putti, Lya de 21

R
Rabinowitsch, Gregor 90, 98
Rachman, Samuel 5–6
Raeder, Gustav 200
Ralph, Louis 137
Raphaelson, Samson 27
Rappaport, Romuel 7
Raskolnikoff 202
Rasp, Fritz 86, 152, 156
Rastratchiky 131
Der Rebell (The Rebel) 207
Das Recht auf Liebe 85–86
Das Recht der Ungeborenen 88
Rehfisch, Hans 159, 203, 207
Reicher, Ernst 88, 204
Reichsfilmkammer x
Reimann, Walter vii
Reinach, Joseph 150
Reinert, Robert 72
Reinhardt, Max 4, 25, 42, 52, 54, 130, 136, 203
Reininger, Lotte 163
Reisch, Walter 21, 87, 90, 162, 174, 175, 186, 206, 208
Remembrance 63
Reminiscences of a Gynaecologist 74
Reno, Paul 22
Reuter-Eichberg, Adele 29
Ein rheinisches Mädchen beim rheinischen Wein (Rhenish Girl and Rhenish Wine) 208
Richter, Kurt 3, 35
Riefenstahl, Leni 7, 163, 191, 207, 208
Riemann, Johannes 59
The Right to Love 86
The Right of the Unborn 88
Rilla, Walter 97
Rio Film 189
Rippert, Otto 9
Rittau, Günther 12, 93
Der Ritualmord (Ritual Murder) 197
RKO Radio Pictures 176
Robert und Bertram 200

Roberts, Ralph Arthur 125, 175, 203
Robison, Arthur 123
Der Rodelkavier 16
Röhrig, Walter vii, 93
Rooms to Let in a Quiet Home, with Use of Kitchen 87
Rosenthal, Alfred ('Aros') 201
Rosenthal, Hermann 176
Rosher, Charles 142
Rosmer, Milton 159
Der rote Kreis 160, 204
Rotter, Fritz 139
Rudensky, Dyk 97
Rudolf-Meinert-Film-Gesellschaft 9
Rudolph, Emperor 34
Ruhiges Heim mit Küchenbenutzung 87
Rühmann, Heinz 131, 137, 140, 167, 168, 170, 176
Ruttmann, Walter 160, 204

S
Sachs, Ludwig 83
Sagan, Leontine 209
Sahl, Hans 201
Saint-Germain, André 150
Sakall, S.K. 'Cuddles' *See* Szakall, Szöke
Salmonova, Lyda 34, 35, 37
Salten, Felix 175
Salto Mortale 164
Sandrock, Adele 125, 184, 186, 203
Sarony, Leslie 120, 121
Sascha ix, 130, 200
Saturn-Film 72
Scapa Flow 163
Schell, Maximilian 14
Scherben 202
Scheurer-Kestner, Auguste 150
Das Schiff der verlorenen Menschen 84
Schildkraut, Josef 159
Schildkraut, Rudolf 63, 149
Schiller, Johann Christoph Friedrich von 131, 179, 195, 203
Schleicher, Joseph 62
Der Schlemihl 122
Schlemihl: Ein Lebensbild 149
Schlesinger, Leontine *See* Segan, Leontine
Schlettow, Hans Adalbert 87, 93
Schmidt, Josef (Joseph) *Fig. 29*, 189–90
Schmitz, Sybille *Fig. 20*
Schnitzler, Arthur 4, 55, 85, 174, 185, 186
Schoenerer, Georg von 53
Schönfelder, Erich 42, 46, 49
Schönwald, Gustav 160
Schroeder, Greta 39
Schuberts Frühlingstraum (Schubert's Dream of Spring) ix
Schüfftan, Eugen 117, 121, 204, 209
Schuhpalast Pinkus 42–53
Schuldlos Geächtet 76
Schulz, Franz 21, 141, 162, 167
Schulz, Fritz 77, 78, 131, 141
Schünzel, Reinhold *Fig. 11*, 5, 77, 78, 89, 158, 183, 190–96
Schwartz, Maurice 63
Schwarz, Hanns 11, 89, 162, 164–65, 175, 208
Schwarzschild, Leopold 5
Schwarzwaldmädel 208
Secrets of a Soul 96, 139
Seeber, Guido 3
Seeler, Moriz 115

Segal, Jakow 31
Seidenstein, Berthold L. 97
Servaes, Dagny 63
Seven Sinners 189
Sexualnot der Jugend (Sexual Distresses of the Young) 86
Shadow of a Mine 97
Shakespeare, William 188, 193
Shandler, Jeffrey 64, 66, 69–70
Shattered 202
The Ship of Lost Men 84
Shoe Salon Pinkus 42–53
The Shop around the Corner 128
Sima, Oskar 175
Sinful Mothers 75
Die singende Stadt 130
Singer, Bashevis 65
The Singing Fool 135, 162
Siodmak family 121
Siodmak, Kurt (Curt) 7, 90, 97, 115, 208, 209
Siodmak, Robert 7, 90, 115, 189, 203
H.R. Sokal Film 90, 207
Sokal, H.R. 7, 207, 208
Soll und Haben 200
Somnambul 84, 88–89
A Song Goes Round the World Fig. 29, 189, 190
The Song is Ended 174
S.O.S. Eisberg 163, 207
The Souls of Children Accuse You 74
Sparkuhl, Theordor 3, 26, 27
Die Spinnen (Spiders) 9
SPIO 10
Spione 151
Spoliansky, Mischa 140
Spring's Awakening 75, 78, 86
Srzednicki, Boleslaw Riszart *See* Boleslawski, Richard
Die Stadt ohne Juden ix, x, Fig. 16, Fig. 17, 53–62, 63, 68, 202, 205, 206, 209
Starewitsch, Ladislaw 163
Stauss, Emil Georg von 4
Stein Film 90
Steinhoff, Hans 83
Steinrück, Albert Fig. 13, 35, 36, 41, 92, 186
Stern, Ernst 90
Sternberg, Josef von ix, Fig. 22, 12, 86, 138, 139, 161, 162, 188, 189
Stevenson, Robert Louis 204
Stiller, Maurice 11
Stolz, Robert 85, 174
Storms over Montblanc 163, 164, 207
The Story of Jettchen Gebert 149
Der Sträfling aus Stambul 84
Stransky, Otto 144
Die Strasse 92, 115, 202
Die Strasse der verlorenen Seelen 86
Strassner, Joe 176
Strauss, Richard 161, 187
A Strauss Waltz 208
The Street 92, 115, 202
Streisand, Barbra 65
Struwwelpeter 139
Sturm, Hans 36
Stürme über dem Montblanc 163, 164, 207
Stüwe, Hans 86
Sugar, Paul 87
Sumurun 52
Sündige Mutter 75

Sylvester – Tragödie einer Nacht 202
Szakall, Szöke (later S.K. ['Cuddles Sakall] 191, 203
Szekely, Hans 92, 162, 176

T
Das Tagebuch des Dr Hart 4
Tagebuch einer Verlorenen 86, 91
Take care! Love! Danger to Life! 83
Das tanzende Wien 208
Tasso-Lind, Ilse von 77
Tauber, Richard ix, 86, 162, 163
Taxi at Midnight 83
Tempelhof studios 2, 17
Terra Film 189
Das Testament des Dr Mabuse (The Testament of Dr Mabuse) 7
Teure Heimat 87
The Shop Around the Corner 52
'Theaterkunst Hermann J. Kaufmann' 90
Theodor Herzl, Bannerträger des jüdischen Volkes (Theodor Herzl, Champion of the Jewish People) 63
The Thief of Bagdad 182
Thiele, Wilhelm (born Wilhem Isersohn) 21, 162, 167, 171, 174, 203
Thiery, Fritz 12
Thimig, Hermann 192, 193, 195
Thomas, Brandon 192
Thomas, Jameson 28
Three Days Confined to Barracks 124, 130–31, 135
Three Men from the Filling Station Fig. 24, 12, 124, 135, 165, 167–75
The Threepenny Opera 7, 191
Tiedtke, Jakob 24, 26
Tiller Girls 171
To Be or Not to Be 52
The Tobogganing Cavalier 16
Tonbilder 1
Tourneur, Jacques 192
Tourneur, Maurice 84
Tragedy of Youth 88
Trenker, Luis 207
The Trial 27
Triumph des Willens (Triumph of the Will) 191
Les Trois Lumières 206
Trotz, Adolf 84, 88–89
Truffaut, François 119
Tschechowa, Olga 167
Twelfth Night 195
Two Worlds 21–22, 28, 141–49

U
Überfall Fig. 20, 204
Ucicky, Gustav 84
Ufa *See* Universum Film Aktiengesellschaft
Ufa-Union studios 16
Ulmer, Edgar G. 15, 90, 128
Ums tägliche Brot 97
Uncanny Tales 203
Unheimliche Geschichten 203
'Union' *See* Projektions Aktien-Gesellschaft 'Union'
Union-Theater 2
Universal Corporation 97, 164
Universum Film Aktiengesellschaft (Ufa) 3, 4–6, 10–14, 16, 19, 35, 46, 82, 85, 90, 91, 93, 98, 130, 131, 162, 188, 192, 202
Urgiss, Julius 202
U.T. am Kurfürstendamm 4

V

Valetti, Rosa 94, 149, 161, 209
Vallentin, Hermann 25, 26, 145
Vanloo, Rolf E. 92
Varieté 21, 144, 195, 204
Varno, Rolant 88
Vater und Sohn 83
Vaterländischer Filmvertrieb 206
Veidt, Conrad vii, *Fig. 11*, *Fig. 12*, 12, 77, 79, 158, 175, 176, 185, 189, 207, 208
Verband deutscher Bühnenschriftsteller 4
Verebes, Ernst 87
Verirrte Jugend 86
Veritas Vincit 201
Der verlorene Schuh 11, 182, 206
Verneuil, Louis 175
Die versunkene Glocke 179
Victim 76
Vienna, City of Song ix, 186
Viktor und Viktoria Fig. 28, 183, 191–95
Vindobono Film ix
The Virtuous Sinner x, *Fig. 26*, 123, 130–40
Vita Film ix
Vitascope 4
Von morgens bis mitternachts 202

W

Das Wachsfigurenkabinett 202
Wachsmann, Franz 189
Wagner, Wilhelm Richard 161
Wakowski, Erich 20
Walbrook, Anton (born Adolf Wohlbrück) *Fig. 28*, 192, 193
Wallace, Edgar 204
Wallburg, Otto 184, 203
Wallenstein 179
Waltershausen, Wolfgang von *Fig. 21*
Ein Walzer von Strauss 208
Ward, Warwick 21
Warm, Hermann vii
Warner Brothers 164, 200
Warning Shadow 181
Was eine Frau im Frühling träumt 83
Wäscher, Aribert 193
Waschneck, Erich 96
Wassermann, Max von 4
Waxworks 202
We belong to the Imperial-Royal Infantry Regiment 186
We Stick Together through Thick and Thin 84
Weary death 206
Die Weber (The Weavers) 208
Wedekind, Frank 78, 86
Wegener, Paul *Fig. 13*, 34, 35, 36, 38, 41, 52
Das Weib des Pharao 6
Weil, Bruno 150
Weill, Kurt 161, 162
Weiner, Alfred 201
Weininger, Otto xi
Weinmann, Friedrich 29
Weintraubs Syncopators 189
Weiss, Bernhard 97
Der weisse Pfau 144
Der weisse Rausch 163, 207
Die weissen Rosen von Ravensberg 88
Weizmann, Ernst 21
Der Weltkrieg 206
Wendhausen, Fritz 150
Werbezirk, Gisela x, 54
Westfront 7
Whale, James 38–39, 41
What a Woman Dreams of in Springtime 83
Where is Coletti 203
White Ecstasy 163, 207
White Horse Inn 162
The White Peacock 144
The White Roses of Ravensberg 88
Whitechapel 141
Wien, du Stadt der Lieder ix, 186
Wiene, Conrad 86
Wiene, Robert vii, ix, 9, 202
Wiener Kunstfilm ix
Wiener-Autoren-Film 8
Wienfilme ix
Wilczynski, Karl 129
Wilder, Billie (later Billy) ix, 90, 115, 121, 189
Wilhelm II, *Emperor* ix, 97
Wilhelm, Carl 87, 150, 199
Wilhelm, Julius 87
Wir halten fest und treu zusammen 84
Wir sind vom k. und k. Infanterie-Regiment 186
Without Meyer, No Celebration is Complete 47, 122–30
Wo ist Coletti 203
Wohlbrück, Adolf *See* Walbrook, Anton
Wolf, Friedrich 74, 207
Wolff, Peter 137
Wolffsohn, Kurt 201
Wollen Sie meine Tochter heiraten? 149
A Woman 122
The Woman in the Attorney's Gown 84, 88
The Woman One Longs For 84, 86, 150
The Woman on Trial 11
Woman in the Window 55, 58–59
Women on the Edge of an Abyss 83
The Wonderful Lie of Nina Petrowna 84–85, 98
Wong, Anna May 28
Die wunderbare Lüge der Nina Petrowna 84–85
Wüst, Ida 178

Y

The Yellow House 75
The Yellow Passport 5, 6–21, 30, 33, 36, 41, 42
The Young Man from the Ragtrade 122
Youth Gone Astray 86

Z

Zeitung für Einsiedler 33
Zelnik, Friedrich 74, 204, 207, 208
Zéro de Conduite 31
Ziener, Bruno 83
Der Zigeunerprimas 83
Zinnemann, Fred 121
Zola, Emile 150, 152–53, 159
Zuckmayer, Carl 87
Zukor, Adolph 5
Zwei Welten 21–22, 28, 141–49

www.ingramcontent.com/pod-product-compliance
Lightning Source LLC
Chambersburg PA
CBHW071230080526
44587CB00013BA/1559